Kings and Kingship
in the
Hellenistic World
350–30 BC

Kings and Kingship in the Hellenistic World 350–30 BC

John D. Grainger

Pen & Sword
MILITARY

First published in Great Britain in 2017 by
PEN & SWORD MILITARY
An imprint of
Pen & Sword Books Ltd
47 Church Street
Barnsley
South Yorkshire
S70 2AS

ISBN 978-1-47386-375-0

Typeset by Concept, Huddersfield HD4 5JL.
Printed and bound in England by TJ International Ltd, Padstow, PL28 8RW.

Pen & Sword Books Ltd incorporates the imprints of Pen & Sword Archaeology,
Atlas, Aviation, Battleground, Discovery, Family History, History, Maritime,
Military, Naval, Politics, Railways, Select, Social History, Transport, True Crime,
and Claymore Press, Frontline Books, Leo Cooper, Praetorian Press,
Remember When, Seaforth Publishing and Wharncliffe.

For a complete list of Pen & Sword titles please contact
PEN & SWORD BOOKS LIMITED
47 Church Street, Barnsley, South Yorkshire, S70 2AS, England
E-mail: enquiries@pen-and-sword.co.uk
Website: www.pen-and-sword.co.uk

Contents

Introduction

Kings, Kingdoms, Kingship

Between *c*.350 BC and 30 BC the Mediterranean world was one in which kings ruled. The exceptions were some of the Greek cities and all Roman Italy and Carthaginian Africa. But for most of that period these republican areas were not central to the events in the eastern Mediterranean. For the crucial centuries between Alexander the Great and the Roman conquest of Macedon in 167, the political running was made by kings, and it is their work and lives and loves and experiences which is the subject here. Rome's expansion successively extinguished a series of monarchies, and this pushed back the areas which were ruled by kings for a time, but the process of building a republican empire eventually rebounded on the city, and the Roman Empire became ruled by an emperor who was in fact a good facsimile of a Hellenistic king, right down to the personal irresponsibility and the liability to be assassinated. The Roman emperors are increasingly seen as providing the template for the kings of the Middle Ages and later, and so it was the Hellenistic kings who provided the original pattern.

In 350 BC, a date which is only partly chosen at random, there were half a dozen monarchies already in the Greek world, though most are only peripheral, both geographically and in terms of power. The greatest of course was that of the Persian Empire, where various members of the Akhaimenid dynasty had ruled as Great Kings, as the Greeks called them, for two centuries. This was a gigantic empire, but one which was curiously passive in its internal affairs, economically inert, culturally of little account; the Great Kings were content simply to hold on, and not to use their great power and wealth for any obvious purpose, certainly not for the betterment of their subjects. By 350 the empire was clearly failing, though still a major power and dangerous to its enemies. Its effect on the subsequent Hellenistic period is extremely difficult to gauge, though investigations are now tending to emphasise some influences. It remains a fact, however, that the Hellenistic kings were Greco-Macedonian in almost all respects, descent, behaviour and activity.

Three other monarchies in about 350 were small and Greek. Sparta's monarchy required the simultaneous rule of two kings from different families, though in practice one of the kings usually dominated. This was not the only matter in which Sparta was different; it had recently lost half of its territory to vengeful neighbours and enemies, and it would not stop trying to get it back until well into the Roman imperial times. Macedon was a monarchy, one of a group of similar polities in the southern Balkans, reckoned by outsiders as only partly Greek; in 350 it was under the kingship of Philip II, who was turning out to be the master statesman of the age, though he had no real hereditary right to the kingship – his hold on power depended on continuing success in his policies and wars, and in 350 he had made only minor progress towards his future domination of Greece, and none towards his later goal of conquering territory from the Persians. In Sicily the monarchy of Dionysios I, based at Syracuse, was visibly failing under the rule of his son, who was beset by rivals and rebels and would last only a few more years. That monarchy – called by the Greeks a tyranny – was a revival of an earlier monarchic version of the fifth century BC; it would collapse in the next decade, but would be reconstituted twice in the next century and a half before being taken over by Rome (more or less as a going concern). It is often taken as a model for Hellenistic monarchy, but because of the peculiar circumstances in Sicily it was much more a home-grown thing, as individual in its way as that of Sparta. In the event it took its place comfortably enough into the system of Hellenistic monarchies, but it was also the first to fall to Rome. It therefore had little influence on the development of monarchies in the rest of the Mediterranean area.

A fourth, rather odd, monarchy was a neighbour of Macedon to the west. In 300 BC it adopted the name Epeiros, but at base it was the Molossian tribe to which neighbouring tribes had become attached, either by conquest or voluntarily, and the kings were kings of the Molossi. The polity was somewhat unstable, and the royal family tended to division and dispute, just as the kingdom was more a federation with a king on top than a typical monarchy. The king's powers were distinctly limited. In many ways it was similar to the Macedonian kingdom, but weaker, more distant and even less Hellenised. Its kings were intermarried with the Macedonian royal family, and Alexander the Great as the son of the Epeirote princess Olympias; his sister was married to Olympias' brother, another Alexander. These two states provided much of the pattern for those which came after; they might be reckoned the first of the Hellenistic kingdoms.

Three more monarchies were ranged around the fringes of the Persian Empire. In the north was the Bosporan kingdom, half-Greek, half-Scythian, which was based in the eastern half of the Crimea, straddling the Kertch Straits. The dynasty which ruled there from 438, the Spartokids, was mainly

Thracian in origin, though subject to much Greek cultural influence, and the kings had successfully integrated locals and Greeks into a single society. They and their kingdom had become wealthy as a trading intermediary, funnelling Scythian grain to the hungry Greek cities. The other two monarchies were fragments of the Akhaimenid Empire which had more or less broken away. In Karia, in southwest Asia Minor, was the satrapy of Mausollos, who had largely detached his province from Persian control, but had done so without angering his suzerain too much, and was able to pass on his power to his successors. His new quasi-independence was one of the strongest indications of the declining power of the Persian Empire. The other kingdom was Egypt, a perennially rebellious province of any empire ventured to conquer it. It had been independent of the Persian Empire for half a century, since 404, but would soon be reconquered, a powerful indication that the decline of the Akhaimenid monarchy was perhaps not irreversible. Egypt did not therefore seem strong enough to stand alone, despite its extremely favourable geographical situation, but it was a wealthy land and it was partly for this reason that it was attacked. The paradox was clearly a matter of internal organisation, for the country, behind its desert frontiers, was eminently defensible.

These kingdoms and dynasties exhibit many of the characteristics to be seen in the Hellenistic period. Among the Spartokids there were episodes of shared rule between brothers, and civil wars between brothers, and eventually the menace of barbarian attack which was followed by a near friendly takeover by a foreign monarchy – and finally protection by a Roman garrison. Internal disputes and foreign menaces were the stuff of Hellenistic monarchies. And the Spartokids equally exhibit one other Hellenistic characteristic, a strict hereditary succession over several generations but which was at last disrupted by one of those family disputes; but this succession was also the best safeguard against trouble while the hereditary system operated.

This catalogue of the pre-Hellenistic kingdoms, all of which (except the Persian) continued into the Hellenistic period, is made simply to point out that monarchies of various sorts were by no means unfamiliar to the Greeks, and so when the Hellenistic monarchies emerged they could be fitted into their political system without too much difficulty. But it is worth noting the variety of monarchies involved: the Persian Great King was the ruler of a huge empire, in which every time a Great King died there was a fight, murders and coups to find a successor: the Macedonian monarchy was only marginally less unstable, and Philip II was technically an usurper; Sparta's irredentist ambitions continually disturbed Greece; the Epeirote kingship was precarious and was destined to vanish in eventual collapse; the Egyptian pharaohs were about to be defeated and eliminated by their Persian enemies;

the Sicilian kingdom – the rulers did not use the title, but it was a monarchy nonetheless, and its rulers succeeded by hereditary succession – was about to disappear in civil war and foreign invasion from both Carthage and Greece; Mausollos was in the most precarious position of all, with no title to his independence; only the Spartokids of the Crimea had a stable hereditary monarchy, for a time, but this tended to break down into dynastic civil war later. And these monarchies, though generally controlling larger geographical areas than most other contemporary states, varied in size from a few cities to a huge empire. If one is looking for precedents for the monarchies of the Hellenistic world, the one common factor in all these kingships is their ultimate instability, though this is something several Hellenistic kingdoms successfully avoided for quite some time; the variety of these early kingdoms could provide precedents for almost anything which might later occur.

The campaign of conquest by Alexander the Great between 334 and 323 BC resulted in the break-up of the Persian Empire. The steadily increasing weakness of the resulting kingdoms led to ever more and smaller kingdoms appearing as fragments broke away from the parent state. The four Hellenistic kingdoms which existed in 300 BC – two of whose dynasties disappeared within 20 years – had more than doubled in number by 200, and still more appeared in the next century. Rome's advance eastward encountered and swallowed up at least twenty. The stability of each of the states depended almost entirely on the kings' abilities, and despite this progressive fragmentation, to a large extent they did succeed in creating a political space in which ordinary people could flourish, at least for a century and a half. In large areas of the Middle East life was infinitely better after 300 BC than it had been under the previous Akhaimenid imperial regime or that of violent and erratic Alexander.

Each of the kingdoms was ruled by a succession of kings. The basis for their kingship was essentially, at least at first, conquest, and therefore and thereafter their control of armed power. Macedon was as close to a national monarchy as perhaps anything in the ancient world, and the kings there were referred to as 'kings of the Macedonians'; most of the other kings simply have the title with no geographical element to it. Eventually, of course, royal authority came to rest on heredity and so the process of succession became the crucial event in all the kingdoms. It did become much better managed than it had been in the past, either in the Akhaimenid Empire or in the Macedonian kingdom, or above all among the Sicilians. But this success did not last, and the whole region eventually descended into internecine warfare and conquest. But the period of stability, perhaps from 315 to about 170 BC, was sufficient to imprint a clear pattern of monarchy and its requirements in the whole region from Sicily to India. This was the work of the Hellenistic kings. It is the life, behaviour, and activities of these men (and a few women) which is the subject of this book.

*   *   *

The approach here is to subdivide what the kings were and did into their relationships with others and their various activities. As a result, a certain degree of repetition occurs. This note therefore is in the nature of a warning and an apology for this, but several episodes and events really are so significant that they merit consideration from different points of view, hence the repetition, hopefully expressed in each case in somewhat different ways.

Chapter 1

Becoming a King

The true progenitor of Hellenistic kingship, despite the varied models available from Sicily to Persepolis, was Philip II of Macedon (359–336). He was a usurper, and his successor, Alexander the Great, seized the throne of Macedon in a *coup d'état* in which the rightful king, Amyntas, who had been displaced by Philip but left alive, was murdered, as were a whole series of other likely competitors then and in the following years. When Alexander died in 323 his halfwit half-brother Philip III Arrhidaios and his unborn son (who became Alexander IV when born) were made kings by acclamation of the army in spite of the recommendations of the senior commanders. Both of these kings were murdered, as was Alexander's sister Kleopatra who, by marrying, might have awarded the kingship to a husband, and so was his illegitimate son Herakles. Their deaths all-but extinguished the dynasty. Some time after the secret murder of Alexander IV in about 310 BC, the man who claimed to be his political heir, Antigonos Monophthalamos, proclaimed himself, and his son Demetrios Poliorketes at the same time, as the successors to Philip and Alexander. Antigonos was, however, neither king in Macedon nor did he have control over several other regions which Alexander had ruled.

In quick succession those who did control the areas free of Antigonos' rule, Ptolemy in Egypt, Seleukos in the east, Kassandros in Macedon and Lysimachos in Thrace, also proclaimed themselves kings, and they were soon joined by the new tyrant Agathokles as king in Sicily. Each of these men based his authority on control of an army. Suddenly, within about a year, the Hellenistic world went from having no visible king (though documents were dated by the years of Alexander IV until 306, as though he was still alive) to having no less than seven kings – plus three more who had survived from the pre-Philip times.

The pattern was thus set for the next two centuries: kings were made by self-proclamation, by *coups d'état*, by usurpation, or by hereditary right, and to maintain their claims they needed clear military support. In that sense they were 'military monarchies', though they soon shed that image, if not the reality. One of the aims of these kings was to cultivate their legitimacy as royal rulers, which required presenting themselves as kings by right, rather than to obviously relying on force. Therefore, by a variety of means it became expected that the eldest son of a king had the greatest right to succeed him, though it was also necessary that he be nominated by his predecessor – unless, like Philip and Alexander and the new kings, he could carry out a coup. Inheritance from father to son in such a way was normal in Greek society, and these jumped-up kings therefore simply went along the groove of the society in which they had grown up. This did not mean, however, that the sons had necessarily to wait until their fathers died to inherit the kingship. One of the reasons for the disintegration of the Hellenistic world of the kings, and its conquest by Republican Rome was that usurpation became steadily more common, even acceptable, as a means of becoming king. The royal families thus undermined their own system.

For a time, nevertheless, heredity and direct inheritance worked best. The early greater dynasties established the pattern of the eldest surviving sons succeeding their fathers, and in three cases this system lasted for a century and more, but their histories also demonstrate the difficulties involved. The most stable dynasty for some time was that founded by Ptolemy son of Lagos, called Soter ('saviour'), in which son succeeded father from 306 BC to 145 BC, a line of six kings. In only one case did the eldest son not succeed, when the son of Ptolemy II (Ptolemy 'Epigonos', 'the Son') was murdered while acting for his father as viceroy in Ephesos; but, not to worry, Ptolemy II had a spare son who became Ptolemy III.[1] However, on a more detailed view this dynasty was less stable than it seemed. The first succession, from Ptolemy I to Ptolemy II, was disputed, and only secured by a series of murders; the fifth king was murdered; the sixth disputed the kingship for almost half a century with his brother. Direct hereditary succession was not necessarily therefore a guarantee of peace and dynastic tranquillity. There was a dispute, that is, more or less every time a king died.

The least successful of the early dynasties in establishing hereditary succession – apart from the Argaiad dynasty of Philip and Alexander – was that of Antipater, who had been regent for Alexander the Great and his successors while Alexander was away conquering in the east. Antipater never made himself king (he died in 319 loyal to Philip III and Alexander IV), but his son Kassandros did take the royal title (and was the instrument of the death of Alexander IV).[2] He could claim a certain hereditary right in that he had married one of Philip II's daughters, Thessalonike – who was thus the aunt of the murdered child. Their son succeeded as Philip IV when Kassandros died, but he died soon after his father, apparently from illness; the next two sons, Antipater and Alexander V, succeeded jointly, but quarrelled, one killed the other (and his mother), and the survivor was killed by a rival.[3] The dynasty thus failed within three years of Kassandros' death. (Thessalonike had been murdered by her son even before this final debacle.) And yet Antipater's progeny was widely spread through the other dynasties by the marriages of his many daughters, who married contemporary kings – Demetrios, Lysimachos, and Ptolemy among them – so that Antipater's succession, while it failed in the direct male line, lived on through the other dynasties.

Kassandros' dynasty, however, failed as kings of Macedon, and two other kings of those who also proclaimed themselves in 306–305 failed to establish any sort of a dynasty. Agathokles of Sicily had, like the others, forced himself to territorial rule first, then proclaimed himself king. He had a turbulent time facing rebellions and invasions, but generally succeeded in holding on. He was brought into the society of Hellenistic kings by marriage with Theoxene, one of Ptolemy I's daughters. But he had older children, and reserved the succession to them. Or so he intended, and he sent Theoxene and her children back to her father to clear the way. But in a lurid episode of violence and betrayal his son and grandson both died as he himself was dying. The intended dynasty thus lasted only one lifetime, though the monarchy he established was soon revived by one of his commanders, Hiero.[4]

The other failed dynast was Lysimachos, who began his royal career as ruler of Thrace, for which he had had to fight hard and long, and he acquired perhaps the most potentially powerful of the successor kingdoms, Asia Minor, to add to his territories in Thrace, when he and his allies defeated Antigonos Monophthalomos, and to these territories he later added Macedon. This great realm, stretching from the Pindus Mountains to the Taurus, gave him access to a greater armed power, military and naval, and to greater economic power, than any of the other kings, and he had long shown that he was expansionist-minded.[5] He was, therefore, an obvious threat to the other kings. Yet simply by quarrelling with his eldest son, the very capable Agathokles, and then ordering his execution, Lysimachos forfeited whatever acceptability he had gained among his subjects. (He was not particularly well-liked, being harsh and unforgiving, but was latterly accepted in part because Agathokles was popular and expected to succeed – which may well be one of the reasons why Lysimachos came to dislike him so much that he had him executed.) His unpopularity therefore made him vulnerable, and when his kingdom was invaded by Seleukos, he received less than full support from his family and his subjects, and none from the international enemies he had made; he died in the final battle.[6] Like both Agathokles and Antipater, he lived on through the marriages of his daughters, for a time.

Lysimachos' nemesis was Seleukos, who succeeded in founding a dynasty which, while not so successful in contriving a direct hereditary succession as was that of Ptolemy, was certainly successful in keeping the kingship within the family for more than a couple of centuries. There were several near disasters in the process, however, and the dynasty more than once was on the verge of destruction or extinction. The second king, Antiochos I, felt compelled to execute his own eldest son, Seleukos, presumably for displaying a too-obvious ambition and eagerness to succeed his father.[7] The death of Antiochos II (who became king because Seleukos the prince was dead) led to a disputed succession between his two wives and three of his sons, and twenty years of civil war.[8] Twenty years later the dynasty was reduced to a single unmarried male representative, Antiochos III, who faced two rebels, both seeking to remove him, an intriguing minister who may have had greater ambitions, and a war with the current Ptolemy.[9] Forty years later again the interference of Rome interrupted the direct succession. Demetrios, the eldest son of Seleukos IV, was held hostage in Italy, which let his uncle Antiochos IV seize the throne, who then murdered his nephew Antiochos, who was technically king, but under age.[10] After that the condition of the dynasty only deteriorated to a long series of murders and usurpations. The dynasty was obviously vulnerable, and during the next century the members of the family disputed the succession in every generation.

Even more hair-raising was the zigzag progress – if progress is a suitable term in the context – of the dynasty founded by the first man to make himself a Hellenistic king, Antigonos I. He had made his eldest son Demetrios king along with him, but the two of them tended to operate separately. Antigonos after all was 76 years old when he made himself king in 306, and so he left active campaigning to Demetrios.[11] But Antigonos' ambition never waned, and he was finally brought down, still actively fighting, in battle at Ipsos at the age of over 80, by a coalition of his enemies, who had finally combined with the intention of doing just that. Demetrios survived and escaped from the final battlefield, then roamed the seas with his fleet for several years before seizing Macedon (he was the one who killed off the last of Antipater's grandsons). But he was as arrogant and ambitious as his father, and when the Macedonians finally realised his ambition they threw him out. He campaigned into Asia Minor, but was shepherded out by Lysimachos' son Agathokles (whose success only fuelled his father's antagonism). Demetrios was finally captured by Seleukos, kept in gilded confinement, and died of drink; he had made as comprehensive a set of enemies as his father.[12]

Between the death of Antigonos I in 301 and that of Lysimachos in 281, seven kings died, only three of them by 'natural causes', and three potential dynasties were extinguished. This was followed by the invasion of Macedon and Greece by the Galatians, in the course of which members of the Ptolemaic, Antpatrid, and Lysimachid families all died. It was, that is to say, a dangerous profession, being king.

The death of Demetrios might have been the end of this brief dynasty, but Demetrios had an able son, Antigonos II Gonatas, much less mercurial, more cautious, and eventually more successful. He inherited his father's fleet and his ambition to rule in Macedon. This took some doing, but in the end, by taking advantage of the kingdom's destruction by the invasion of the Galatian barbarians, Antigonos succeeded in making himself king. (His most masterly ploy was to recruit an army of Galatians, and use it to drive out the other Galatian invaders; this is the sort of achievement, cunning and anti-barbarian, that appealed to the Hellenistic public.) He was the true founder, or re-founder, of the dynasty, which lasted another century in Macedon until the final king, Perseus, was destroyed by Rome – a result which the locals no doubt considered to be another barbarian invasion.

These dynasties therefore exhibit in their beginnings the characteristic methods of becoming king, methods which became normal, if that is the right word, for the next two centuries and more. The requirements were ambition, control of an army, above all one of Macedonian soldiers, victory, and dominance of an extensive territory. These became the necessary basic requirements for later kings, though a king who inherited a throne was under less pressure to exhibit ability and ambition than a man who set out to found his own dynasty anew.

Once in control of the kingdom a king was thereafter preoccupied with two things, first holding onto the territory he had gained and increasing it if possible, and second, retaining his royal position and passing it on to his son. Kings faced competition from opponents, notably in the two-century-long rivalry between the Ptolemies and Seleukids for control of Palestine and Phoenicia (Koile Syria), but there was also the problem of maintaining control of relatively distant parts of the kingdoms, some of which were very large. This latter issue particularly affected the Seleukid kingdom, which sprawled from the Gallipoli Peninsula to the Hindu Kush when its founder died. Over the next two centuries sections of the kingdom broke away and were formed into independent kingdoms – notably in Baktria in the Far East, in southern Iran, and in Asia Minor – and in each of these regions the new kings had to exhibit the requirements of the founders of the original dynasties, usually by defeating an attempt by the parent kingdom to recover control. Egypt suffered similar secessions, notably when Cyrenaica broke away (more than once), but also in a huge rebellion by native Egyptians during which the rebels founded a new pharaonic regime in the south of the country which lasted for two decades.

All of the original founders of the greater dynasties had been military commanders, learning their military trade as participants in the wars of Philip II and Alexander the Great. Their original power rested unequivocally on command of their soldiers. This became the crucial element in the exercise of royal authority, and every new king, however he achieved that position, was required to demonstrate military success, if not necessarily military prowess (on which see Chapter 9). But there was a difference between the upstart kings and the kings by inheritance. The upstarts had to begin by demonstrating their military ability, while for those who inherited the reverse was the case: they started as kings and then showed military capability.

It was even necessary to achieve successes against the same enemies as their rivals and competitors. So Antigonos II defeated the Galatian invaders of Macedon in the early 270s, and Antiochos I defeated the Galatian invaders of Asia Minor later in that decade; therefore it followed that their competitor Ptolemy II was under the necessity of achieving a Galatian victory as well, which he did when a regiment of Galatian mercenaries he had recruited went on strike, and he used the rest of his army to besiege and destroy them, thereupon proclaiming himself the victor in a Galatian war.[13] His contemporaries and rivals no doubt regarded this achievement with sardonic amusement, but it also suggests a powerful awareness of the uses of political propaganda for the royal reputation.

These new kingdoms were not always successful – the rebel Egyptian kingdom was extinguished after only twenty years, and that of Antiochos III's cousin Akhaios in Asia Minor after less than ten – but their founder kings used the same self-proclamation methods as the original founders of the greater dynasties.

The process of forming a new kingdom out of a fragment of another largely depended on securing the support, paradoxically, of an existing king. The early kings were so overwhelmingly powerful that an ambitious would-be king had to tread very lightly and carefully, a mouse among the clumping feet of the great elephants. It could take a generation or more to go from the original founder of the dynasty who proclaimed himself king to achieve recognised royal status, the intervening period being occupied with supporting the greater dynasty, as an ally or a client, or simply keeping quiet in the hopes that one of the kings would not turn on the aspirant. Two detaching fragments of the Seleukid kingdom may be taken as examples. In Asia Minor a man called Philetairos, probably originally a Paphlagonian, but from his name a Greek-speaker, and who certainly acted as a Greek throughout his life, had been appointed by Lysimachos as custodian of a royal treasure held in the fort at Pergamon. When Seleukos attacked Lysimachos in 282, Philetairos chose to support Seleukos. It is presumed that this decision was based on Philetairos' calculation of political advantage to himself, but it may also be that he did not like Lysimachos or his policies, even though he had been trusted by the king. Philetairos was able to demonstrate his loyalty towards the Seleukid family only a year later. Seleukos had been murdered as he visited an isolated altar on the Gallipoli Peninsula, and his body left lying where it fell; Philetairos recovered the body, cremated it ceremonially, and handed the ashes over to Seleukos' son and successor, Antiochos I, when he arrived in Asia Minor, perhaps a year later.[14]

Philetairos' custodianship of Lysimachos' former treasure appears to have continued under his conqueror, and by putting Antiochos under an obligation Philetairos was safe in his local eyrie until he or Antiochos died. He developed and fortified the castle of Pergamon, presumably using part of the treasure entrusted to him, and the castle became the basis of a new city; the treasure does not ever seem to have been claimed by either Seleukos or Antiochos. Philetairos had no children of his own – and was later rumoured to be a eunuch – but he had nephews and it was one of these who succeeded him in control of Pergamon when Philetairos died. This was Eumenes I, and for the representative of the family which originated with a man who was probably no more than a glorified clerk, it was necessary for Eumenes to demonstrate military ability if he was to retain any real authority. He did so by defeating a force supposedly commanded by Antiochos I, in about 263.[15] This was ignored by Antiochos, and it was scarcely serious enough to do more than cement Eumenes' local authority in Pergamon and its surrounding country-side, but that is what it did. (It seems unlikely that Antiochos was the victim, and we probably have here another example of royal propaganda manip-ulating the truth; it may be significant that despite such a victory, Eumenes never claimed the royal title.) Eumenes was successful enough to be able to hand on his power in his small principality to his son Attalos in 241, and Attalos lost no time in describing himself as a king. He succeeded at a time when the Seleukid family was involved in a civil war, and he gained a useful military reputation by defeating an army of Galatians, who terrified the cities of Asia Minor unless they were restrained by just such a defeat as Attalos administered. This victory further entrenched his and his family's local power, and he was able to extend his grip from Pergamon towards the sea, where he developed the small port of Elaia into a naval base.[16]

It may be, in fact, that Antiochos ignored his defeat by Eumenes because he scored his victory over one of Antiochos' generals. This sort of thing had been something of a local specialty. In 281, Mithradates, a Persian nobleman in north Asia Minor who was descended from an Akhaimenid satrap of the region, defeated a general of Seleukos I, and then established himself as king of Pontos, a kingdom stretching along the coastal plain east of the Greek city of Sinope. In the same way, a few years later, Zipoetes, a chieftain in Bithynia, in northwest Asia Minor, resisted both Lysimachos and Antiochos I, and took the royal title. To defend himself later, however, his son Nikomedes allied with the Galatians and let them into Asia Minor. This, from his point of view, was a most successful ploy, since his enemies were thereafter fully occupied against the invaders.[17] Attalos, therefore, was following in the local fashion rather tardily; the forty-year delay in promoting the family to royal status is perhaps best explained geographically. Pontos and Bithynia were kingdoms on the periphery, and as such the Seleukids could ignore them; Pontos in fact was protected by the Galatians who had settled between it and Seleukid territory; Bithynia was protected in much the same way by its long-standing alliance with the Galatians. Pergamon, however, was much more centrally placed in Asia Minor, not very far north of the main administrative centre for Seleukid Asia Minor at Sardis, and at the same time made a virtue of its enmity to the Galatians. It behoved the family of Philetairos to tread very carefully, therefore, to avoid being squashed. That they succeeded in doing so is a testimony to their political skills, and above all to the loyalty which the members of the family always displayed towards each other; there were never any civil wars in the Attalid family – but it was also for a long time a testimony to their unimportance. Even so, the duration of the dynasty was only a century and a half, somewhat shorter that most of the greater dynasties.

At the eastern end of the Seleukid kingdom, the region of Baktria experienced a rather similar development to that of the Attalids, but suffered more in the process. Superficially the differences between the two are very great: Philetairos controlled no more than a single castle at the start, Baktria was always a major province. But the way in which the rulers edged their way into independence and royalty is very similar.

Baktria had something of a tradition of independence. It may well have been a kingdom of its own before being annexed to the Akhaimenid Empire back in the sixth century BC. It had been conquered by Alexander the Great with great brutality, but did not settle down comfortably as part of his empire. Seleukos in turn had conquered it, and had placed his son Antiochos there as his viceroy, though he also had the title of king and so he was virtually independent. One of the reasons for appointing Antiochos is presumed to have been that Seleukos had married a princess from the province to the north of Baktria, Sogdiana, and so Antiochos therefore was half-Baktrian by descent. He spent ten years or more governing the territory, having the full backing of his father, and presumably with a substantial fraction of the Seleukid army at his command. This appears to have settled the region down as a more or less contented part of the empire, and when Antiochos inherited the rest of the kingdom a governor was left to continue the Seleukid rule.

The name of the first governor is not known, but by the 250s a man called Diodotos was in place, and he remained there for at least twenty years. This was a disturbed time in the rest of the Seleukid kingdom, with a war with Ptolemy in the 240s followed by rebellions and civil wars and invasions. One of the invasions came into the province of Parthia, just to the west of Baktria, and seems to have been successful enough to sever the land links between Baktria and the main part of the kingdom in the west. This must be one of the chief reasons for Diodotos staying in post for such a long time – added to which he was presumably successful. He appears to have died in about 235, which is exactly the year in which King Seleukos II made an unsuccessful attempt to suppress the Parthian invaders. Diodotos was succeeded as governor by his son, also Diodotos. It is not known if either of these men assisted Seleukos II in his Parthian war, but it is probable that they did not.

Being in power in a large and rich province for twenty years, during most of which he had only the most tenuous communications with headquarters in Syria, it would not be in the least surprising to find that Diodotos I had harboured ideas of independence. We have, however, no evidence whatsoever for his thoughts or plans. The only hint comes in the coins he had minted, which by the end of his time as governor were showing his own head in place of or sometimes together with that of the Seleukid king. This would certainly suggest a certain ambition and arrogance in the man. His son, however, Diodotos II, did not have the doubts which may be imputed to the more hesitant – or loyal – father. From soon after succeeding to the governorship he began to call himself king. The territory therefore, like Pergamon under Philetairos and Eumenes I, had become habituated to rule by a governor (or bureaucrat) for a generation so that when the first governor's successor chose to call himself king, it may be that only the title changed.[18]

Information about Baktria is poor, and much has to be assumed from a study of the coinage. It may be surmised that both Diodotoi were accomplished warriors, since Baktria was a frontier region liable to be raided by enemies from outside. In proclaiming himself king, therefore, Diodotos II may well have, as a preliminary, won some sort of victory. A further similarity with Attalid history may well be that the two Diodotoi worked well together, just as the successors of Philetairos were famous for their familial affections. But at that point the histories of the dynasties diverged. Diodotos II was removed from power, presumably killed, by a man called Euthydemos of Magnesia, who founded another brief dynasty, lasting perhaps two or three generations, which was then also overthrown by a rebel. Sections of Baktria were erected into independent kingdoms, thus doing to the Baktrian kings what the Diodotids had done to the Seleukids. The coinages of the kings, often superb specimens of numismatic art, are regularly called on to provide evidence for the relationships between the several kings, not always very convincingly.[19] No dynasty of this area can be said to have been successful, though it has been argued that there were family connections between several of them.

Two particular methods of becoming king, therefore, have now been isolated – setting aside the original kings of the time of Antigonos I. The establishment of hereditary authority over a particular province, as with the Attalids and the Diodotids, could well lead to the governing family making itself royal by the usual method of self-proclamation; the population will have become habituated to their rule, but it also required that their overlords, the Seleukid kings, were preoccupied with much more dangerous affairs if their proclamations of royalty were to stick. It also argues that loyalty to the Seleukids was not a major factor – but at the same time loyalty to the new insurgent dynasty was probably no stronger. In both Pergamon and Baktria these proclamations of new kings took place while the parent kingdom was embroiled in a dynastic civil war. By the time that civil war was over, the new kings had been royal for ten or twenty years and the Seleukid kings permitted – it is not too strong a term – them to continue in their dynastic independence.

The second method of reaching royal independence was not really that different. Zipoetes of Bithynia and Mithradates of Pontos both had local authority in their territories, just as Philetairos and Dodotos had, though they were not governors of their territories, but local chieftains whose authority rested on local acceptance. When they came under attack from a Seleukid army and defeated that army, they used their victory to proclaim their royalty, but this probably did little to enhance their local power. A certain loyalty to the ruling family may therefore be presumed – Pontus and Bithynia may be considered as quasi-nation states. In the case of the Attalids, the sequence is much the same, though the military victory over a Seleukid force did not immediately lead to kingship; that came with a much more significant victory over the Galatians, who were much more a universal enemy to the rest of Asia Minor.

It is, therefore, clear that new kings required above all to have discernible and undisputed local authority over a distinct territory before attempting to make themselves royal. There are several cases where ambitious men failed in this preliminary requirement. In the province of Parthia, probably in 246, the governor Andragoras began producing coins in which he named himself as king. The moment was well chosen, with the Ptolemaic invasion of Syria, a collapse of royal Seleukid authority, and a dynastic civil war beginning, so it would seem that Andragoras had a good chance. He did not last very long, however, because he was destroyed by the invasion of the nomads from the north of his territory who later became referred to as the Parthians. Whatever authority Andragoras had within his province, it was not enough to survive such an invasion; the very fact of the invasion would probably lead to his forfeiting all local authority, for the obvious conclusion was that the invaders arrived because he had made himself independent, and had therefore lost all hope of support from the rest of the Seleukid kingdom.[20]

In Asia Minor a man connected with the Seleukid family who also had strong local connections, Akhaios, was sent on behalf of Antiochos III to re-impose Seleukid authority over the distracted, confused, and rebellious region. This he succeeded in doing, but then chose to make himself king. Again, the moment was well chosen, since Antiochos III was beset by a rebellion in Iran and by an unsuccessful war against Ptolemy IV, while Akhaios was victorious in fighting in Asia Minor. Akhaios' local connections were strong, for his grandfather (also Akhaios) was a major landowner, and was perhaps a younger son of Seleukos I, while Akhaios himself was married to the daughter of another major local landowner. Having made himself king, he collected his army, and set off marching eastwards. His army consisted of men of Asia Minor, and his intention was to invade Syria and remove Antiochos III, thereby making himself Seleukid king. However, he failed to communicate this intention to his army, and when he did so (by which time it was clear that he was intent on more than just simply establishing his local authority) the men refused to march further east. It is reported that they refused to fight 'the king', meaning Antiochos III; it is more likely that they were refusing to fight the much larger Seleukid army. They were, however, fully prepared to accept Akhaios as king in Asia Minor. He turned back and launched his forces against other enemies. When Antiochos III invaded Asia Minor a few years later the same men fought for him to the end.[21]

Akhaios could be said therefore to have successfully established his independent authority in a large part of Asia Minor, but unlike Diodotos or the Attalids, he had left himself open to suppression by the parent kingdom. He clearly had substantial local support, but his greater ambition led to a divergence from the wishes of his supporters. The reaction of his supporters when Antiochos III invaded indicates that there was a strong sentiment in Asia Minor for that territory to become independent of the Seleukid kingdom. Had Akhaios contented himself with being king there, he may well have been able to maintain himself against Seleukid hostility. His situation in that circumstance would have been little different from that of the Baktrians or the Attalids and Antiochos III later showed that he was quite willing to accept the independence of those rebellious dynasties. Akhaios' mistake was in attempting too much.

Pontos and Bithynia were kingdoms in which the non-Greek local populations could shelter in the face of the overwhelming power of the Seleukid kings under the authority of native chieftains. Other kingdoms with essentially the same purpose and origin emerged all along the northern Seleukid boundary. In northern Iran, even in the time of Seleukos I, part of Media had been organised as a local kingdom by Atropates, an Akhaimenid governor who had skilfully detached himself from both the Akhaimenids and Alexander. His kingdom was sheltered by major mountain ranges, and the kings repeatedly deflected any Seleukid hostility by timely submissions. The sequence of kings is not known, but can be assumed to be dynastic; the kingdom took its name, Atropatene, from its founder.[22] In a way the kingdom to the east, Parthia, was a similarly native state, but much more welcoming of Hellenisation than Atropatene or other of the Iranian minor states; its founder was Arsakes, and each succeeding king used that name as his throne name; it was obviously a factor both of homage to the founder and of dynastic continuity. And to the west of Atropatene the formidable mountains of eastern Anatolia formed the basis for an Armenian state, in which the ruling family was descended from the governor of the time of the last Akhaimenids. This state was inevitably dominated from the south by the Seleukids, whose armies could penetrate along the river valleys, and it was partially suppressed by Antiochos III. He defeated, but then confirmed in office, the Armenian king, Xerxes, who was supposed to be controlled by being married to a female relative of Antiochos, but she killed him, presumably because he was not working to the script, and she returned to Antiochos. Two governors, also Armenians, Artaxias and Zariadres, were then installed by Antiochos, so replacing the original kingdom with two subordinate provinces; they quietly detached themselves when he was defeated by Rome in 188; the two men then made themselves kings, successfully founding two Armenian dynasties which lasted for several centuries, a more successful version of the work of the Diodotids in Baktria.[23]

The Seleukids in particular were never averse, after learning their lesson from the minor defeats by such upstarts as Eumenes I, Mithridates I, and Zipoetes, to recognising the existence of kingdoms where their own control was poor or exceedingly difficult – Atropatene and Armenia are examples. The arrival of the Galatians into central Asia Minor had caused great trouble to the inhabitants all around them. Antiochos I fought a great war to limit their ravages, which were largely concentrated on looting the wealthy Greek cities,[24] but it seems probable that not only their ally Bithynia but also Pontos had been happy to see them continue in existence as a barrier separating them from any Seleukid revival in the north. There was also the region of Kappadokia south of the centres of Galatian power but north of the Taurus Mountains, where the Seleukids had little control, perhaps because the region was thinly populated, and was very vulnerable to Galatian raids. The precise situation in the area is wholly unclear for quite some time, and regular raids by the Galatians may be assumed. Then in 255 a local chieftain called Ariarathes was given a Seleukid princess, Stratonike, the daughter of Antiochos I, as his wife. This marked, in effect, his diplomatic recognition as king, but also his subordination to the Seleukid kingdom. He had evidently succeeded in establishing his control over the region, and by supporting him the Seleukids benefited from his protection just as he benefited from their assistance.[25]

It was therefore possible, as Antiochos II at Kappadokia showed, to use these local loyalties for the good of the Seleukid kingdom. Another version of this came with the recognition of the independence of Cyrenaica. This land had been seized by Ptolemy I, rather against the wishes of the local people. He had evaded the problem of establishing his direct control in the face of local hostility by installing as his governor his stepson Magas, who remained as governor for a quarter of a century and more. Then in 275 or 274 Magas was awarded a Seleukid princess, Apama, as his wife. She was the daughter of Antiochos I, and the marriage was in effect Antiochos' recognition of Magas as an independent king, which is what he immediately began to call himself. At more or less the same time Antiochos launched a war against Ptolemy in Syria. By the time that war was finished Magas had succeeded in establishing his independence. This suited the Cyrenaicans, of course, who still hankered for independence, it suited Magas, who became a king, and it suited Antiochos who gained an ally in Ptolemy's rear; it did not suit Ptolemy II, but he put up with it, and appears to have recognised Magas in an oath-bound treaty in order to concentrate on the war against Antiochos. After all, the essential situation had not changed, for Magas as king had no more real power than Magas as governor; Ptolemy finally turned the tables when his son, who became Ptolemy III, married Berenike, the daughter of Magas and Apama, after the former's death. Egypt was thereby reunited with Cyrenaica.[26]

In its way, the Cyrenaican kingdom was as much a local project to deflect control by one of the Great Powers as was the self-promotion of Bithynia and Pontos. This, however, was much more the sort of project fostered by non-Greek speakers than by Greeks. The northern tier of kingdoms in Anatolia and Iran were all in some ways anti-Greek, or perhaps it would be better to say anti-Macedon. Atropatene, for example, was self-consciously Zoroastrian, and its main city was centred on a great fire temple; Kappadokia was centred similarly on the temple of Ma at Komana – religion was long the primary force of loyalty for most of the local communities in the Middle East. Bithynia was a kingdom of Thracians who had migrated to Asia centuries before, Pontus and Media Atropatene were both ruled by descendants of Iranian aristocrats whose ancestors had served the Akhaimenids. In the south of Iran kingdoms emerged, though not very clearly, and not decisively until the second century BC. In Persis, the original metropolitan centre of the Akhaimenid Empire – another kingdom emphasising its fire temples, even on its coins – and intermittently in Susiana under the rule of local, anti-Greek,

Iranian warriors, or perhaps they were priests. They certainly emphasised their Iranian-ness on their coins, by showing images of their fire temples in place of the Greek gods which were usual with the Macedonian kingdoms.[27]

The peripheral location of all these places, Cyrenaica included, was their essential salvation; it was not worth a major effort by any of the Great Powers to reconquer them. In one particular case, however, that of Judaea, a movement into independence took place as a result of a complex religious dispute which emerged into a civil war. The leaders of the Judaean forces, the sons of the priest Mattathias, who became called either Hasmoneans (from Mattathias' father) or Maccabees (from the nickname of the first of the leaders), emerged as political and religious leaders as well as military commanders. They began as the latter, led by the elder brother, Judah, in which role he failed, their territory being conquered by the Seleukids after several years of fighting. From the Seleukid point of view they were a nuisance; the territory they were controlling, the upland area of Judaea, was of little economic value, but it was inconveniently close to the main route connecting northern Syria with the frontier against Ptolemaic Egypt, and one of the reasons why the fighting had originally begun was that King Antiochos IV believed that the Judeans had rebelled during the Sixth Syrian War. One of the Maccabean political aims was to establish a connection with the sea, so as to tap into the riches of maritime commerce; this would involve them securing control over part of that international route, which was not something the Seleukids could accept. The Maccabean family gradually emerged as the new ruling dynasty. The movement for independence revived after several years, led by a second brother, Jonathan Maccabee, who took advantage of a Seleukid civil war to secure for himself the title of high priest. This was a traditional position, recognised by the Seleukid kings as being the local civil as well as religious authority, and was traditionally in the gift of the king, which the Seleukids had inherited from the Akhaimenids. He, and then his brother Simon, successfully defended their principality against further attacks until they secured recognition for their partial independence from Antiochos VII in 134 BC. Five years later, once Antiochos had died in battle in Iran, the next Maccabean high priest, John Hyrkanos, succeeded in fully establishing Judaea's independence. He was the fourth of the family to hold the title, and his son, Aristoboulos, took the title of king, thereby finally establishing the family as the dynastic rulers; the dynasty lasted for another two centuries, though eventually, in the family of Herod, only as clients of Rome. (It will be noticed that, although the original rebellion was directed against the Seleukids as Greek speakers, and against the imposition of the worship of Greek gods, Hellenisation of the kingdom and particularly of the dynasty continued apace; from Hyrkanos onwards all the kings had Greek names, except the greatest and most unpopular of them, Herod.) The Seleukid tolerance of local gods, as in Persis and Kappadokia and Atropatene, had extended to Judaea before the revolt; it was when the Jews were perceived as being in rebellion that the war began – the Maccabees therefore brought the war on themselves. The result was intermittent fighting for a long generation.[28]

The Judaean kingdom was unpleasantly aggressive. Hyrkanos oversaw the destruction of more than one Greek city, and his son Alexander Yannai gained control of almost all Palestine. But their aggressiveness was not directed solely against Greeks and Macedonians. One of the results of their campaigns was to push the Aramaic-speaking peoples east of the River Jordan into developing their own Nabataean kingdom in self-defence. The Judaean rebellion, from being explicitly anti-Macedonian, or perhaps only anti-Seleukid, had become a kingdom which metamorphosed into an imperialistic state which threatened all its neighbours, Greek, Macedonian, or native-Syrian. The Nabataean dynasty, which had relied on its desert location to defend it earlier, necessarily developed a substantial military capability, to the extent that conflict with it was avoided even by the Romans, and it outlasted all the rest of the Syrian kingdoms.

The pattern of a high priest developing into a local king was made explicit in Judaea. It had been in the background earlier in Atropatene and Persis, and perhaps in Kappadokia. In Syria it was copied by several of the kingdoms which emerged at the end of the second century BC – in Emesa, the Ituraeans, the Nabataeans, and others. The worship of local gods had been the basis of resistance to foreign rule since the time of the Assyrian conquest – that of Yahweh of Jerusalem is only the best-known – and with the weakening of royal Seleukid authority, these local entities emerged as kingdoms.[29]

Much less successful, but of rather greater importance in the wider scheme of things, was the rebellion of Egyptians which began in 207 BC in the south of Egypt. This began with the usual advantage of being on the periphery, on the southern fringe of the Ptolemaic state, and had a certain amount of success for a number of years (based, of course, around control of the great temple at Thebes – it was as much a religious revolt as a nationalistic). But it was far too close to the centre of Ptolemaic power in the north for safety, and posed a far more serious threat to the Ptolemaic kingdom as an entity than almost any other rebellion or secession in the Hellenistic world. The Judaean rebels, for example, never threatened the existence of the Seleukid kingdom. Nor did the Egyptians apparently succeed in establishing a dynasty. We know of the names of two of the rebel pharaohs, but there is no indication that they were related, or of the mechanism by which the second succeeded the first. The existential threat the rebels posed to the Ptolemaic dynasty and regime compelled a strong and determined reaction, and its temporary success was largely due to the combination of a royal minority, the accompanying government paralysis and incapacity, and external wars. Once these were overcome, the Ptolemaic forces suppressed the rebellion militarily, though they had to make certain political or religious concessions towards the native Egyptian priesthood in order to succeed.[30]

Among the Seleukids two major rebellions took place which did threaten rule by the Seleukid dynasty, but not, possibly, the Seleukid state. Akhaios has already been mentioned, but when his army went on strike rather than invade Syria, he ceased to be a threat to Antiochos III; his contemporary Molon, however, not only proclaimed himself king but threatened to overthrow and replace the Seleukid regime and family; sixty years later another rebel emerged from Iran, Timarchos, with the same aim and threat and claim. Both of these were defeated when the Seleukid regime mustered all its forces.

As the Hellenistic political system disintegrated in the face of Roman and Parthian attacks from the west and east, more and more minor kingdoms emerged in the wreckage. Kommagene, Osrhoene/Edessa, Adiabene, Charakene were fragments of the Seleukid kingdom whose governors seized the opportunity of the collapse of that kingdom to make themselves kings, though it was usual for the founders to avoid taking the royal title; only after the independence of the new state had lasted for a generation could a successor assume the title of king – just as much earlier with the Baktrians and the Attalids. Some of these minor dynasties lasted for centuries, though never wielding any great power nor ruling any great extent of territory beyond what they started with. Some of them lasted largely because they came under the protection or sponsorship of Rome or Parthia, but the original basis for their emergence as independent regimes, and later kingdoms, was a repudiation of Greco-Macedonian culture and royalty.

The irony is that in order to maintain their independence, it was necessary for the new states to adopt the type of government, and even the culture, which they were rejecting. The kings of the Parthians regularly adopted the epithet 'Philhellene' even as they fought against the most Hellenic of kings. The violent Maccabean attacks on anything Greek, up to and including the destruction of the Macedonian colony of Samaria, had within a generation shifted to the acceptance of Greek names for the kings who were descended from the original rebels, and the establishment of a peaceable suzerainty over the Greek cities of Palestine. The populations of these new states were also profoundly affected by the attractions of Greek culture and the pleasures and opportunities of living in Greek cities.

The act of making oneself a king, therefore, began as a replacement for the extinct dynasty of Alexander the Great, and continued as a set of insurrections against that first king (Antigonos), but the example proved to be infectious to others, both ambitious men and resentful peoples, particularly when the powers of the new dynasties proved to be rather less than they pretended. Attempts to establish a clear hereditary succession were often unsuccessful because of the essential weakness of such a method of succession, which tended to produce irresponsible and incompetent heirs, or infants – the two kings who succeeded Alexander the Great, a halfwit and a new-born baby, should have been a clear warning of this. It seems altogether clear that many of the new smaller states were founded on particular local loyalties, which had been articulated over previous centuries in the form of the worship of local gods around local shrines. This is something both the Akhaimenids and Alexander had overridden, though with gestures towards local susceptibilities. The Ptolemies and the Seleukids clearly recognised the problem, which was essentially a lack of loyalty among the Egyptian and Asian populations towards them, and did their best to conciliate that feeling by honouring the local gods and temples, or favouring them in other ways. In the end this was unsuccessful, and the kingdom most vulnerable to such insurrection, the Seleukid, disintegrated into a large number of independent cities and minor kingdoms. By contrast the Antigonid kingdom in Macedon was actually based on the loyalty of the Macedonian population, but only when Antigonos II Gonatas had proved himself capable of defending the kingdom, and made it clear that he had no intention of launching into another great campaign of conquest such as had brought his grandfather and father to destruction, was he fully accepted as king.

Macedon, therefore, can be seen as the first of those insurrectionary kingdoms whose emergence over the next three centuries brought the greater empires to their ends. It was at one in this with Bithynia, the Egyptian rebels, Judaea, Persis, Armenia, and so on, though they perhaps did not recognise their kinship at the time (or later). The failure of the kings of all these places to make any attempt to found new imperial states may perhaps be seen as a recognition that empires were an unsuccessful political form – or more likely that they did not have the power.

Becoming a king, therefore, required above all a powerful ambition, together with the command of an effective armed force – or the possession of a father who was already a king. It was a highly dangerous thing to be, and very large numbers of those who reached such a position, and still more of those who aspired to it, died violently. And yet, despite this, men continued to aim to become kings.

Chapter 2

Kings and the Gods

The relationship between kings and gods in the Hellenistic period was one of the crucial elements in maintaining royal power. All dynasties of which we have some knowledge of their claimed origins located a divine ancestor. For the Seleukids it was Apollo, and stories were told that the oracle at Didyma already recognised Seleukos as monarchic material as he passed by during Alexander's campaign in western Asia Minor in 333.[1] Apollo appeared repeatedly on Seleukid coins, and the temples of Apollo at Delos and Delphi profited considerably from this identification.[2] The local shrine at Daphne near Antioch, with laurels around the spring, was identified as that of Apollo, and it was even said that the spring there was fed from the Castalian spring at Delphi through an underground channel.[3] A great deal of inventive work was evidently done to plant this divine-dynastic connection in the public mind.

The Ptolemies leaned towards an identification with Dionysos – Ptolemy II Philadelphos was portrayed with small bulls' horns in an identification with that god – but also included Herakles in their ancestry, and their great processions were in part glorifications of those particular gods.[4] The Attalids, perhaps because of their very civilian, even non-Greek, origins, also associated themselves strongly with Dionysos, and went to considerable lengths to emphasise their victories against the Galatians of central Asia Minor, which they claimed to be the means of saving civilisation against barbarism.[5] Identifications of divine origins could change, depending on the wishes of a particular king. Pyrrhos of Epeiros, for example, changed his dynasty's origin from Herakles to Achilles, or perhaps added Achilles to his ancestry.[6]

The prevalence of gods who had begun as mortals, Dionysos, Herakles, Achilles – is suggestive, for one of the elements of royal power was that it was similar to that attributed to the gods, in particular that it could be – and should be – exercised in protection of their subjects. Having such godlike powers in their mortal existence, it was no stretch to assume that when they died their power would continue as actual gods.

None of this prevented other gods from being honoured. Dionysos for the Ptolemies signified celebration, being the god of wine, among other things, and was a favourite deity of Alexander, being identified as a precursor in the campaign in Afghanistan and India; co-opting him as an ancestor provided a helpful link back to the conqueror; it was this god who presided over their great processions.

The Attalid palace at Pergamon was established on a hill on which there was already a shrine of a local Mysian goddess whom the Greeks identified with Athena, and even after all the constructional development of the rock, this small temple remained the physical centre of the site, inside a precinct 50m wide and more than 60m long. The Attalid kings greatly expanded this shrine, though they kept and decorated the original fairly small temple. Another Athena shrine outside the site became Athena Nikephoros, to help with their identification with victory; its existence outside the palace area made it more visible to the general population, and the victories therefore the more obvious. The Epeirote kings had the temple of Apollo at Dodona in their territory. The adoption by the kings of such an established shrine became one of the patterns for other dynasties; or if one did not already exist, it was invented – Apollo at Daphne is a prime example, but the development of the cult of Serapis in Egypt was a similar production.[7] All the Olympian gods were honoured, though some more than others, by all the dynasties, in particular by gifts, often extravagant, to the old Greek shrines, of which Delos, Delphi, and Didyma were particularly honoured.

This was fine for those dynasties which ruled in Greek territory. The Antigonids could continue the ancestral honouring of their predecessor Herakles, as could the Epirotes. Herakles was particularly popular in this regard because he was portrayed as a warrior, as the saviour of civilisation over against barbarism, and as a mortal hero whose achievements graduated him to Olympos – hence his identification as the ancestor of Ptolemies, Antigonids, Attalids, and even the Pontic and Numidian dynasties, for promotion to divine status was part of being a king. For those dynasties domesticated in Asia, on the other hand, there was a whole series of other, non-Greek gods, who had to be honoured as well.

Ptolemy I inherited a certain Greek sympathy for Egypt, which had already been displayed by Alexander to the extent that it was said he had asked to be buried at the Ammon temple at Siwa, where he had received some sort of revelation on his visit there in 331. In Egyptian temples Alexander is displayed as a pharaoh, whether or not he actually claimed that position.[8] He is shown as being presented by the usual pair of Egyptian goddesses Nekhmet and Wadjet, and in one case as conducting sexual intercourse with one of them, as depicted on the wall of a temple at Luxor. This was merely the traditional Egyptian depiction of a new king, and perhaps was no more than the involuntary reaction of the temple priests on being relieved by Alexander's conquest of the burden of Persian rule. On the other hand, the assertion of pharaonic authority was repeated for later Ptolemies. Ptolemy I, when he took over in

Egypt in 323, established himself first at Memphis, which was, if any place was, the traditional 'capital' of Egypt, the city founded three millennia earlier as the symbol of the unification of North and South, Upper and Lower Egypt, the Nile Valley and the Delta, and referred to as the 'Balance of the Two Lands' in Egyptian sources.[9] By doing so, of course, Ptolemy was establishing himself as the successor of the more recent pharaohs, and of Alexander, and as a ruler who rejected the Persian domination which had existed intermittently since the sixth century. Also the sarcophagus containing Alexander's body remained at Memphis until Alexandria had been built.[10] Rejection of Persian rule was absolutely essential in Egypt at this time; the memory of Persian oppression was seared into Egyptian tradition; in addition, Ptolemy I had rescued Egypt from the rapaciousness of Kleomenes, but he then instituted his own tax-extraction system, made even more 'efficient' by his son.[11]

In this consideration, established at the traditional Egyptian administrative centre, and inheriting a good deal of Egyptian goodwill by way of Alexander, Ptolemy inevitably had to honour the Egyptian gods, notably Zeus of Ammon and the newly developed Serapis.[12] He was perhaps not very enthusiastic about this, though he did collect monuments from pharaonic Egyptian sites to adorn Alexandria.[13] This was to imply a continuity with the past which the foundation of Alexandria emphatically denied, as did the city's description as 'Alexandria-by-Egypt' (not 'in'). The Ptolemaic kings for a long time paid little attention to the Egyptians, as individuals or communities, other than to extract taxes from them – which earned them repeated rebellions. But Ptolemy II Philadelphos put a statue of his sister-wife Arsinoe II, after her death, in the main Memphis temple of Ptah, and there she was worshipped as Ptah's wife – thus associating Ptolemy himself with Ptah and the other Egyptian temples.[14] That is, she was made divine. For the next quarter-century Ptolemy II was able to oversee the cult of his god-wife, even to the extent of a joint temple of the two in Alexandria in his own lifetime. This in fact was as much a political gesture as a religious one and was significantly situated in the Greek city.

It was thus some time before serious and detailed Ptolemaic attention was devoted to the Egyptian gods. Of course, devotion to these gods had been part of the necessity of rule, but it seems to have been formal rather than enthusiastic. But the great rebellion which began in 207 and lasted twenty years required a political alliance with the priests of the Egyptian temples, since they clearly had considerable influence with the population, and they probably felt threatened by the revolt as well. During the second century, therefore, the Ptolemaic kings turned to honouring the old Egyptian gods more than before, and, in the same way that they honoured the Greek gods, land and wealth flowed to the Egyptian temples. In crude terms, the priests were bought off; in political terms, it was an alliance between the dynasty and the temple priesthoods.[15] But it also meant that the priests understood their own potential power, and so required to be paid full attention by the kings from then on.

The Attalids, as noted with the shrine of Athena at the palace at Pergamon, took care from the start to honour the local deities in their territory. As their kingdom expanded they found themselves neighbours of the great temple at Pessinos in the interior, and close to the shrine of the mother goddess on Mount Ida in the Troad. Attalos II conducted a well-recorded correspondence with the priest of Men at Pessinos;[16] it was his permission also which the Romans sought in carrying off the symbol of the mother goddess from Mount Ida to Rome for her to provide assistance in defeating the Carthaginians. The goddess on Mount Ida was already more or less Hellenised, but the shrine at Pessinos was very much that of an Anatolian god inherited from the Hittite past. It was clearly politic – and all this religious policy by all the dynasties was essentially political – for the dynasty to conciliate the local deities, which was also a means of conciliating the local populations as well.

It was the Seleukids who had the really major religious problem. The Ptolemies, who dominated Egypt by way of the traditional Egyptian administrative system, were able to control the temple priesthood, and could afford for a while to pay lip service to the honouring of the Egyptian gods; the Attalids could pursue their own version of an inclusive religious policy, based on the existing temples and shrines in Asia Minor; but the Seleukids had to cope with a huge variety of more or less 'national', and even local, deities. At one point they had to manage the temple at Pessinos, with establishing the Apollo shrine at Daphne, with the demands of the priesthood in Babylonia, with the resentful surviving population of Persians with their fire temples in Persis and Atropatene, with the local gods and goddesses in Syria, and deal with gods in Media and in Baktria – and this was before they had to cope with Yahweh in Jerusalem. It was during that time also Zoroastrianism became prevalent in Iran.

The priests of the Esagila temple at Babylon provided a particular example of the problems the kings would encounter. The preceding Akhaimenid kings, and Alexander, had subsidised the maintenance of the great temple of Esagila in the city, which evidently needed to be constantly rebuilt, or so the priests claimed. In 310 or so Seleukos, not yet formally king, but accepted as exercising royal authority by the Babylonians, began the process of establishing a new city, to be called Seleukeia, on the Tigris, perhaps 50 miles from the city of Babylon. This clearly posed a threat to the prosperity of Babylon, and hence to the temple of Esagila and its priests, since the new city, a likely source of prosperity, for it would include the royal palace, would attract to itself many of the people of Babylon. The priests used their astrological powers of prediction to attempt to thwart the foundation of the city. They were asked to find the most propitious date for beginning of the work of construction, but, having done so, they announced an unlucky date. Seleukos, perhaps the most politically inventive, not to say cunning, of the successors of Alexander, clearly discovered this subterfuge. On the 'right' day, so it was later explained, the army spontaneously began the work. Of course, no army would 'spontaneously' begin labouring work, digging foundations, making bricks, and so on. It was clearly by Seleukos' order, designed to bypass the priests' obstructions, but without doing so in such a way that they were compelled to lose face. No doubt their later researches 'discovered' their earlier 'error'. Meanwhile, Seleukos was seen to be favoured by the gods, the priests had lost some prestige, and he had a new city a-building. And as a final contribution, he and his successors continued to sacrifice at Esagila whenever they were in Babylon, and the building subsidies to the temple (no doubt in part diverted to the maintenance of the priests) continued to be forthcoming.[17]

The Seleukids thus did everything they could to honour all of the various gods of their empire, as well as honouring their own traditional Greek gods. So they played up their imagined ancestry from Apollo, promoted the newly revealed shrine of Apollo at Daphne, and provided rich gifts to other Apolline shrines in old Greece. In Babylonia not only Esagila at Babylon was honoured but so were the gods of other Babylonian city-temples, at Borsippa, Nippur, and Uruk, for example.

In some ways the Ptolemies attempted to take over control of the temples in Egypt by such means as installing statues of themselves in temples; statues of Arsinoe II were sent to many of these temples. The Seleukids made no such attempt; instead they accepted whatever rites and rituals normally took place in the temples of their territories, and accommodated themselves to them – as in the continuing subsidies to Esagila. Another case in point is the temple of Atargatis at Bambyke in north Syria. This was a temple sufficiently well-established that when Alexander conquered north Syria its chief priest, Abd-Hadad (who was technically the 'husband' of Atargatis), attempted to take the royal title for himself, probably following the pattern of the kings of the Phoenician cities who had been tolerated by the Persians and continued in office under Alexander.[18] His attempt was suppressed, probably when Alexander passed by once more on his way east; he would hardly wish to have such a power, even so minor one as in a single town, in his rear at such a time. The temple, however, was unaffected. Seleukos I converted the town of Bambyke into a Greek city, naming it Hierapolis, 'Holy City', but did nothing to affect the procedures in the temple. His second wife Stratonike, probably when her second husband Antiochos I came to rule as king in Syria from 281, visited and patronised the temple. Atargatis was a goddess with a variety of functions, including protection of crops, and protection of women in child-birth, and as such was a very suitable goddess for the attention of the wife of the king (indeed, she was the wife of two kings, and the daughter of another).[19]

Stratonike's visit is recorded only much later in the fanciful novel about the Syrian goddess (that is, Atargatis) by Lukian of Samosata. Stratonike was the object of much male attention, and appears to have become a powerful symbol of her sex, both as a powerful woman, an attractive woman, an object of desire, and the subject of male fantasies.[20] Lukian records that one of the devotees at the shrine, supposedly a royal Friend, but with a non-Greek name, went so far as to castrate himself, either in an attempt to gain her attention, which it surely would have done, or to cope with his apparently uncon-trollable desires. (The story has its unlikely elements, such as the name of the castratee, but the practice was not unknown, and appeared at Rome later.)

The rituals within the temple were suitably exotic, and perhaps were made exaggeratedly un-Greek – or anti-Greek – but they continued to be cele-brated in the traditional way without Seleukid interference. The temple was of course enclosed within the new Greek city, but this was the extent of Seleukid operations. The city itself would be governed by the local Greek elite rather than by the priest; the temple was allowed to go its own way, with the result that it was still operating in the traditional manner in the Roman period, when Lukian's account was composed, and when the imposed Greek name of the city was no longer in use.

Devotion to gods, Greek and non-Greek, is to be expected of kings in the ancient world, as it is of their subjects. They were no more immune from the general superstition than the lowliest peasant, and yet, men in positions of power were rather more cynical in their uses and manipulations of religion. They fully appreciated the loyalty of local communities to their local temple and they could use this, as Ptolemy did in Egypt, to attract those com-munities' loyalties. In Syria, for example, the devastation wreaked by the Assyrian conquerors in the eighth century had not been repaired by any sub-sequent occupier of that land until Seleukos I began founding his cities after 300 BC. In the meantime local shrines and temples had provided Syrians with the necessary focus of loyalty which had enabled them to survive both as indi-viduals and as communities, self-consciously Syrian, through their loyalty to Syrian gods and goddesses. Atargatis at Bambyke is a prime example, as is Yahweh at Jerusalem; there are numerous others.[21] These local shrines and temples had survived under the enveloping blanket of the time and of the great, all-powerful empires; the same may be said of Babylonia and Asia

Minor, where Alexander and the Seleukids found well-entrenched temples counting on and receiving local loyalties.

It was therefore intelligent politics for the Hellenistic kings to attend to the needs of the temples in their kingdoms. In the process the priests of those temples suffered what might be described as a corruption of power. The power and wealth of the kings was quite capable of enlisting the priests on the governing side, which brought them into the governing system, by providing them with status and wealth, though this was probably to the detriment of their relations with their local communities. This became especially noticeable in Egypt, where from about 200 BC the Ptolemaic kings made agreements with the temple priesthoods in many parts of Egypt, agreements which are uncommonly like international treaties, and which were designed by the kings to attach the priesthoods to the governing power, and so deprive the Egyptian rebels of the priests' religious and political leadership. The temples thereby became rich, and dependent on government subsidies, and largely ceased much of their protection and advocacy of the local Egyptian peasantry. From the king's point of view, however, this did not altogether work, for one of the main reasons for the prevalence of Egyptian opposition to the Ptolemaic government which is obvious during the second and first centuries BC is that the temples no longer stood in a mediating role between the government and the people.[22] By enlisting the priesthood in support of the monarchy, the Ptolemies had exposed both to Egyptian despair and anger.

The Seleukids seem to have managed the process differently, and more successfully. They were assiduous in attending to the Babylonian temples, but the foundation of cities such as Seleukeia-on-the-Tigris did leach some of the strength from the prime local city, Babylon. On the other hand, it is clear that the prime southern Babylonian city, Uruk, flourished under Seleukid rule, and so did its temples.[23] In Syria for most of the dynasty's period of power the same may be said. Stratonike's experience at Bambyke, for example, is a good example of the royal patronage of a local temple; coupled with the enclosure of the temple within the new Greek-type city of Hierapolis, this is simultaneously royal patronage for the temple and its domestication under royal authority.

Such patronage might similarly be used as an instrument of foreign policy. Even while Lysimachos ruled in Asia Minor with an iron fist, Seleukos, his wife Apama, and his prime general Demodamas gave rich gifts to the temple at Didyma and to the city of Miletos in whose territory the temple was – and both were within Lysimachos' kingdom. Statues of Seleukos and Apama his wife were put up in the temple; probably any local doubts concerning the story that the oracle had predicted that Seleukos would become king were thereby stifled. This sort of influence was useful later when Seleukos went to war with Lysimachos.[24]

The Hellenistic period was for many areas a time of increasing wealth, and the temples, both Greek and non-Greek, profited from gifts and the devotion of loyal believers as well as the kings; as a result many temples became very wealthy.[25] Since most temples were also part of several kingdoms, and since a good deal of the wealth may well have been provided by one or other of the kings, the kings clearly came to regard the temples' wealth as a reserve upon which they could draw as necessary. This was not something the temples' priesthoods and the local inhabitants accepted at all easily.

Many temples were in fact in a way local banks, and their monetary reserves, held in the form of precious metal and coin, were often regarded by the local community as an emergency reserve, something to be drawn on when times were bad: drought, flood, privation, civil war. Consequently when a king demanded a heavy contribution to his expenses – usually for a war – there could be local resistance. But the kings had the military power, and were not shy of using it against temples. In the nature of the historical experience, this could scarcely happen until the temples had accumulated considerable wealth, and so not until the end of the third century do we find any examples of this – by which time the accumulated wealth of the Akhaimenids and Alexander, inherited by the kings, had evidently been largely dissipated.[26]

There were, of course, exceptions. Alexander's intentions at Tyre were to 'visit and worship' the temple of Melqart in the city; the resistance of the Tyrians would suggest that they had strong suspicions that he wanted to do rather more; looting the temple would be quite likely one of his aims, but letting the king in to sacrifice at the temple would also be an acknowledgement of his suzerainty.[27] The Phoenician cities had maintained an ability to acquire a good deal of local wealth during the Akhaimenid Empire, and Alexander's aim of extending his empire eastwards required a great deal of cash. This was clearly also one of his aims in invading Egypt.

Alexander's cash problem was evidently solved when he captured the main Akhaimenid treasuries at Susa, Persepolis, and Ekbatana. The proof of this, in a way, quite apart from the extravagant behaviour of many of his newly rich commanders (Philotas' practice of using gold nails in his boots, for example), is at Ekbatana, where a century later Antiochos III was able to remove silver tiles from the local royal palace to the value of 4,000 talents.[28] This rich resource had not been required by earlier kings, and Alexander had clearly left the tiles in place. That Antiochos did so, however, indicates that his resources were already stretched after only a short campaign. (It is to be noted also that this action provoked no local opposition.)

It is in the time of Antiochos III that there are several examples of temple treasuries being appropriated by the kings. Antiochos himself removed those tiles from the palace in Ekbatana as part of his campaign into the eastern part of his empire. At the end of his reign he was returning to those eastern parts and attempted to seize the treasure of a local temple in Susiana; the local people resisted to such effect that they managed to kill the king himself, who was probably, as usual, in the forefront of his attacking forces.[29] This need of cash, of course, was a result of the Roman confiscation of Antiochos' own treasury, to the extent of 2,500 talents, to be followed by a contribution of 12,000 talents spread over the next ten years. If Antiochos was to shore up his battered empire he had both to campaign to bring back under control those fragments that were breaking away, especially in the east, and he had to gather money to finance the campaign. In attempting to seize the wealth of the temple in Susiana, he clearly believed that he was acting in the interests of the empire as a whole.

In Greece in the same period King Philip V was conducting desperate campaigns to expand his Macedonian kingdom and his own royal authority. Confronted with an alliance between Rome and several Greek states, of which the main one was the Aitolian League, and unable to make any progress, Philip resorted to the desperate measure of capturing and sacking the Aitolian main shrine at Thermon.[30] This provoked cries of horror in Greece, yet it had the effect Philip wanted.[31] The Aitolians made peace, breaking their alliance with Rome, and, having made peace with Aitolia, Philip was then able to make his own peace with Rome the next year. No doubt Philip also kept the loot from the temple.

The motives of Antiochos and Philip in attacking and raiding temples were therefore different: Antiochos simply sought the money, Philip had a political aim in view, though he was not backward in seizing the resources at Thermon. The civil war in Egypt between 207 and 186 produced by the rebellion of the Egyptians of the south, also resulted in the looting of some of the temples (by both the rebels and the royal forces).[32] This was no doubt one of the motives of the royal rewards allocated to the temples and the priests during and after the war.

Then there is the case of the relations of the Seleukid kings with the temple of Yahweh at Jerusalem. Widely touted as a case of Seleukid persecution, and generally condemned even by modern historians, this episode requires much more consideration. There were in fact two episodes. During the reign of Seleukos IV, the king's minister Heliodoros (the later murderer of the king) is recorded as having seized treasure to the value of several thousands of talents from the Jerusalem temple. The historian of the Maccabees, who relates the story, garnished it with elements of fantasy, while at the same time paying detailed attention to the treasures that were taken (and no doubt exaggerating greatly their value).[33] Despite the elements of invention involved in the story – Heliodoros is claimed to have been stopped from looting the temple treasury by a divine apparition – it seems unlikely that the whole story was invented; we must expect the victim, of course, to have exaggerated his losses, and it is possible to explain the raid in purely political terms. It occurred not long after the confiscation of Antiochos III's treasure by Rome, as a result of which the Seleukid treasury was virtually empty. A large treasure in a temple was an enticing prospect, and Antiochos III had already attempted to refresh his treasury from the temple in Susiana. Sources for the period are rather poor, but one would expect that contributions, forced or otherwise, were expected from many temples. A century earlier, during the First Syrian War (274–271), Babylon and Babylonia had contributed heavily to the Seleukid war effort, to the extent that the local Babylonian chronicler complained of widespread poverty.[34] That is, Heliodoros' raid on the Jerusalem temple was not a matter of religious persecution, but a forced contribution by subjects to the king's treasury, a practice which is unlikely to have been confined to the temples.[35]

The second occasion of a collision between the Seleukid king and Yahweh is described in much more detail, and took place over a much longer period than a single raid in a single day. In 170, Antiochos IV went to war with Ptolemaic Egypt. At the same time there was a dispute in Jerusalem over the acceptance in the city of certain Hellenic institutions, including the establishment of a gymnasium where, in accordance with Greek but contrary to Jewish customs, men exercised naked. In order to have this pro-Hellenic policy accepted, the conservative high priest Onias was driven out, and a more amenable high priest, Jason (note the Greek name), was installed. This was accompanied by riots. A garbled version of what was going on reached King Antiochos, who interpreted it as a rebellion. From his point of view this may well have been an accurate description, since the high priest was appointed by the king, and the deposition of Onias was an insult to him, at least. Judaea, of which Jerusalem was the centre, lay very close to the king's strategic communications. His army was in Egypt, his main base was in north Syria, and a rebellion on his flank in this way was clearly dangerous. He reacted as kings do to such threats. On his return from Egypt late in 170 he sent his army into Judaea. The temple was, of course, looted in the process.[36]

This was the first stage in what developed into a rebellion in Judaea against the Seleukid kingdom which lasted for several years before being put down. Since control of the temple in Jerusalem was crucial to control of the country, it changed hands several times during the conflict. This cannot be described as a persecution, except by one who was fanatically Judaist, or unless one was

a warlike advocate for Jewish independence. It was no more a religious persecution than were Antiochos III's raids on the Iranian temple, or Philip V's
raid at Thermon. Indeed, it is frequently remarked that the very idea of
religious persecution was something any Greek or Macedonian would regard
with incredulity. (And in fact, in examining even the Jewish sources, it is clear
that persecution was what was being imposed by the Maccabean rebels on
their fellow Jewish citizens, rather than by the Macedonian kings.)[37]

It may be said, therefore, that Hellenistic kings certainly treated temples
with care and generosity, but they also regarded them as resources to be
exploited when necessary. (One can also argue that by releasing the large
treasuries held in temples, they were inadvertently stimulating their economy,
just as the release of the Akhaimenid treasure hoards by Alexander was the
proximate cause of the widespread increase of prosperity in the third
century.)[38] It was evidently expected that the temples would contribute to the
royal treasury whenever a crisis developed, and if this was refused, the kings
clearly felt that they were entitled to use force to appropriate the treasure
to their own use. From a social point of view, they were acting perfectly
reasonably; from a religious point of view the victims necessarily complained
of some sort of persecution; they were in fact arguing from irreconcilable
positions.

It was the power to do such things which was the basis for the general
population to regard kings as akin to divine. It was not that the kings were
themselves taken to be divine – their appetites and actions and disasters and
general behaviour, and their deaths, made it all too obvious that they were not
– but that they wielded powers of life and death and destruction, of favour and
encouragement and enrichment, which were like those which might be
supposed to belong to the gods. Of course, this might well have an effect on
the kings themselves, as it clearly did later on some of the Roman emperors,
but it is not altogether clear that any Hellenistic kings accepted worship as
divine.[39] There were certainly temples in which dedications to kings were
placed. For example, statues of Ptolemy II Philadelphos and Arsinoe II
Philadelphos were placed in a temple in Alexandria, and of Arsinoe in other
temples throughout Egypt, and in other places to which the Ptolemies had
access, for example in the Aegean islands – but this was usually after her
death. Such statues are not, however, necessarily an indication of divinity. As
the Athenian hymn in honour of Demetrios Poliorketes put it, such statues
were 'wood and stone'.[40] Similarly, there are kings who had been given
surnames which implied an approach to divinity – Antiochos II Theos, for
example, or Antiochos IV Epiphanes, but on examination some of these are of
very limited scope. Antiochos II, for example, was given his surname by the
city of Miletos, which he had rescued from the tyrant Timarchos the Aitolian,

who had seized power there. This was a gesture of gratitude by the city; otherwise it does not seem that this name was used anywhere else, though it has been taken up as his surname by later historians; his achievement in rescuing the city from a tyrant was clearly, to the citizens, a godlike act. Antiochos IV's title of Epiphanes ('God Manifest') was perhaps self-awarded, but his accession to the throne was violent in more ways than one and it may be that he felt the need to camouflage that by a divine nickname; his achievement in defeating the Ptolemaic kingdom might be regarded as godlike. There is no evidence that anybody regarded him any way as like a god; indeed, Polybios regarded him more as a clown.

The Antigonids of Macedon do not seem to have gone in for acquiring epithets of a religious nature, though nicknames appertaining to their appearance or careers were awarded, probably by others – as in the apparently favourable reception accorded to Demetrios Poliorketes by the Athenians in 307.[41] The Attalids confined themselves to indicating their internal family affinities – Philadelphos, Philopator. For much of their career the Seleukids restricted themselves to non-religious terms, Antiochos II as 'Theos' being a distinct anomaly. Victories for Seleukos I and II (Nikator and Kallinikos) and 'Megas' ('the Great King') for Antiochos III were clearly non-religious, if only just. 'Epiphanes' crops up four times altogether, but most kings of the dynasty avoided religious names of that sort.

The Ptolemies, by contrast with their contemporaries, regularly chose religious themes for their self-descriptions, alternating with statements of family affection – Epiphanes, Euergetes, even Neos Dionysos, mixed with Philadelphos, Philopator, and Philometor. These cannot be taken seriously as indications of self-divine status. No one would accept that Ptolemy XII was a 'new Dionysos' and such a description did not prevent him from being evicted and reinstated. (He was not of the direct royal line, and was made king only as an emergency measure; maybe choosing such a surname, harking back as it did to the glory days of Ptolemy II, was a statement of hope more than anything else, and an attempt at legitimisation.)

Installing a statue in a temple was not an indication that a king was thought of as in any way divine, any more than was his adoption of a religious term as a personal epithet. For the ordinary population the king was akin to a natural force, a power of nature. He was something who remained at a great distance, his actions were unpredictable, often irresponsible, his needs could affect adversely a whole population, his arrival in an area could well be devastating. He thus behaved in much the same way as the gods might. They sent thunder and lightning, floods, volcanic eruptions, earthquakes, just as kings might send armies or seize temple treasures. So if prayer, or fawning, or flattery, could dissuade him from any adverse action of this type – even a visit – it was clearly worth attempting. The installation of a king's statue in a temple may thus be no more than the appearance of the picture of a saint in a Christian church – a wish for his intervention, if it came, to be benevolent.

The most explicit apparent linkage of a king and a god appears to be in the Athenian hymn which was chanted when Demetrios Poliorketes entered the city in 291. He is referred to as 'the dearest of the gods', 'son of Poseidon and Aphrodite', but it was also pointed out that 'the other gods are far away ... [but] you are not made of wood or stone, you are real'. Therefore 'bring us peace ... for you have the power'. In other words, a king had the divine power to inflict punishment, wreak vengeance on his enemies (some of them Athenian in the case of Demetrios), and at the same time to protect and enrich his subjects. He is not divine himself, but he does have power which is akin to that of a god.[42]

On the other hand, worship of dead kings was a normal characteristic inherited from the classical Greek past. Herakles, once more, was the original case law to becoming divine, along with Asklepios and Dionysos, but worship had been offered at Samos to the contemporary hero Lysander, the Spartan victor in the great Atheno-Peloponnesian War a century before, at least in that city.[43] Such offerings were more in the nature of thank offerings than a recognition of the divinity of a person – and a king who had wielded godlike powers while alive, but was quite likely to become divine after his death, and would then wield even greater powers. In the same way, in Smyrna as early as the first years of the second century, the city of Rome had a temple named for it; no one, surely, would regard Republican Rome as divine.[44] At that very time, we also have a record from Seleukeia-in-Pieria of an annual priesthood for the successive Seleukid kings, in which the deceased kings were regarded as objects of devotion;[45] and at Antioch-in-Persis the city dated its events and decrees by the name of the priest of the royal family. In a decree of that city of about 206, concerning the recognition of a festival at Magnesia, the priest Herakleides son of Zoes was described as 'the priest of Seleukos Nikator and Antiochos Soter and Antiochos Theos and Seleukos Kallinikos and King Seleukos (III) and King Antiochos (III) and his son King Antiochos'.[46] That is, a cult of the deceased kings had been long established and was extended to include the living kings. The dynasty was clearly seen as a continuing entity, a means to linking various parts of the kingdom together, and the elevated kings were seen as capable of extending their power to assist their current member, and presumably his subjects.

In Asia Minor a few years earlier, Antiochos III's wife, Laodike, was honoured in a temple at Sardis, established as a result of a direct request to her by the city.[47] Of course, the city was doing its best to conciliate the royal family after having been the headquarters of a rebellion, and clearly regarded

Laodike as a useful channel for communicating with her husband, just as Smyrna was keen to use Roman power to deflate the overwhelming presence of Antiochos.[48] Her cult was also established at Laodikeia in Iran, but in this case at the initiative of a local Seleukid governor on the instructions of the king.[49] It does not appear that anyone thought that Laodike was divine, but that, as the king's wife, she was powerful; she was able to act apparently autonomously at Iasos, for example, to provide a supply of corn at a time of dearth – exactly the sort of beneficial action which implied godlike power.[50] One therefore conciliated such power in any way which seemed appropriate.

It is clear, however, that the deceased kings were considered divine. When alive they wielded godlike power; once dead, they could be addressed in the hope of using those same powers for good, or to avert evil, or even perhaps to punish an enemy. That is, they continued to be regarded in the same way while they were divine as when they were alive. They were not worshipped, but they were seen as divine.

The relations of kings to the gods was thus complicated, but was based essentially on the exercise of their royal power. They may have found it amusing, exasperating, exciting, or annoying to be regarded as having divine power, since that would imply that they had such powers, which, of course, they knew they did not have. Constantly subjected to flattery, any king with any common sense would discount such offerings as a statue, or the establishment of a cult by private citizens, or in a temple, for what it exactly was, a sort of bribe. On the other hand, it is clear that all the kings of whom we have any knowledge of their religious beliefs cleaved to the belief that the Olympian gods were worth conciliating, and in particular attended to those gods who had graduated from unearthly life to divine status – Herakles, Dionysos, and so on – which is what they and their ancestors would achieve, or had achieved. The difference was that Herakles and company did so by their own achievements, while most kings achieved divinity simply by being kings, having merely inherited the position and the power; the process had clearly become devalued.

After death, of course, earthly kings had no control over how people regarded them, whether or not they were taken to be divine; this was left up to their descendants, and to the institution of their cult, a priesthood of which was an office regarded as socially most acceptable, but more because of its social prestige than for its religious content. Since ordinary people did not really regard the Olympian gods as benevolent deities capable of interfering in people's lives in any way other than capriciously, this attitude inevitably transferred itself to the kings, whose power might be regarded as divine-like, but who were also to be regarded as uncontrollable forces, whose effects on ordinary lives could be as mercurial as those of any god.

Chapter 3

Kings and Kings

The relationship between the many Hellenistic kings begins, as usual, with the first generation. Alexander's successors were a group of men who had grown up together and, even when involved in political disputes, could regard each other as friends. Seleukos and Ptolemy were in dispute over the spoils from Antigonos Monophthalamos' empire, but when Seleukos decided that he should not in fact attack Ptolemy, he announced that he would not do so, giving as his reason that Ptolemy was his friend.[1] Of course, there was a good deal more to it than that, including the fact that, if he attacked, Seleukos would very probably be defeated, but it made a good propaganda point. At the same time, there seems every reason to accept that Seleukos did regard Ptolemy, who had assisted him significantly in the past to gain his own kingdom, as his friend. Two of the main antagonists in the wars which followed Alexander's death, Lysimachos and Demetrios, met companionably on the coast of Asia Minor for Lysimachos to admire Demetrios' great ships as they sailed by.[2]

However, this friendship did not extend very far; it was a personal matter, and did not extend into political affairs. In the drastic and chaotic early years after Alexander, many other men who could claim to be his successors had acquired independent power, and had been ruthlessly eliminated by their rivals, men they might have regarded as friends. And there seems to have been no friendship at all involved in relations between these successors and the family of Alexander. Admiration for the man did not extend to indulgence to his relations, all of whom were murdered – his mother, his sister, his wives, his sons.

It follows that it is clear that the relations between kings might be considered friendly on a personal level, but such friendship was never allowed to interfere with their political aims. When Ptolemy VI had been ousted from Egypt by his brother, he went to Italy, where he was helped by Demetrios, the Seleukid heir who was a hostage in Roman hands;[3] later Demetrios seized his ancestral throne to make himself king (in the course of which he had his nephew murdered). In Italy he and Ptolemy had been friends; in power several years later Demetrios tried to seize Cyprus from Ptolemy by subterfuge, and then Ptolemy involved himself in a plot to overthrow Demetrios, which ended in the latter's death in battle.[4]

One of the results of the initial condition of friendship among the antagonists, which originated probably in the institution of royal pages in Philip's and Alexander's court, of which most had been members, was that the kings regarded other kings as their only equals, politically and socially. One of the customs practised by Hellenistic kings was royal marriages. This was one area where the examples of Philip and Alexander were of little use. Philip's marriages had been frequent and numerous, but his last had brought his assassination. In the Hellenistic period, royal marriages took place between kings and king's daughters; and king's daughters expected to marry kings. This rule, if it was one, was frequently honoured in the breach, but there are sufficient examples to establish it as a shaky social convention. Intermarriage between the several dynasties very quickly produced a social caste spread over the whole of the Mediterranean and the Middle East, from Sicily to Baktria, and even India. As a result most kings, at least in the eastern Mediterranean, were related to each other; it is likely that a similar social custom operated in the Far East among the kings in Baktria and India. It was especially true of the Seleukids, whose kings were prolific in daughters and who, unlike the Ptolemies after Ptolemy I, were willing to bargain them off to rather less important dynasties. This meant, of course, that those minor dynasties were raised somewhat in the social scale, which left their daughters available to be married back into major dynasties. For example, the marriage of Stratonike, daughter of Antiochos II, to Ariarathes of Kappadokia was accompanied by Ariarathes taking the royal title; in Cyrene, Magas' marriage to Antiochos I's daughter Apama also brought him a royal title.

Relations between kings, in other words, were complicated, and the familial connections reverberated all through the royal network. When Magas, the King of Cyrene, died in about 250 BC, he left a wife and a daughter, Apama and Berenike. The death of this minor monarch, the first of his line, and as it turned out the last, created a widespread political crisis. Apama was the daughter of Antiochos I and of Stratonike his wife; Magas was the son of Ptolemy I's second wife by an earlier marriage; Berenike was betrothed to Ptolemy II's son, the future Ptolemy III; Apama was also the sister of Antiochos II, who had lately been married to Ptolemy II's daughter, another Berenike, but in the midst of the crisis he deserted her and returned to his first wife, Laodike, who was not the daughter of a king, for he had married her before he became the heir presumptive of his father; Apama's other sister was Phila, the daughter of Seleukos I and Stratonike (later Antiochos I's wife), who was married to Antigonos II Gonatas, who in turn was Stratonike's brother. (Phila was thus her husband's niece.) Antigonos intervened in the crisis in Cyrene, for he had no wish to see Ptolemy II enlarge his power by taking over Cyrene, and he had witnessed the effect on Ptolemy II a quarter of a century before of Magas' shift into independence. He sent his half-brother Demetrios 'the Fair' as a new suitor for Berenike, to take the place of the younger Ptolemy, whose suit was not favoured by Apama. And Demetrios was in fact the son of Demetrios I, Antigonos' and Stratonike's father, and Ptolemais, a daughter of Ptolemy I and therefore a sister, or perhaps half-sister, of Ptolemy II. Amid all this marital complication it is fairly astonishing to discover that Demetrios the Fair and Berenike the princess were not actually related.

It is cases like this which make it clear that such marriage linkages and friendly relationships had little or no effect on the conduct of international affairs. Demetrios the Fair, in fact, was murdered by Berenike – or perhaps on her orders – while in Apama's bedroom. Since he was regarded as a king, it is probable that he had in fact married Apama in preference to Berenike. Berenike's betrothal to Ptolemy depended on her bringing Cyrene to him as a dowry; with Apama and Demetrios in power, Berenike's marriage was unlikely to take place – until she killed the new king, that is. Berenike then married Ptolemy, who inherited the Ptolemaic throne only a year or so later. It seems probable that becoming the wife of the Egyptian king and so enjoying the luxury of his wealth and his palace had been Berenike's aim all along.[5]

King Antigonos II Gonatas may or may not have reacted to the death of his half-brother, but not long after he was certainly involved in an undeclared war with Ptolemy, and the death of Demetrios cannot have done anything but pour fuel on the fact of their enmity. What happened to Apama is not known, but when Ptolemy III succeeded to the throne in 246 he at once launched an attack on the Seleukid kingdom; he discovered that his sister Berenike had been murdered, probably on the orders of Laodike, Antiochos II's wife, who had been widowed by that time. Ptolemy III lamented his sister's death, and claimed that he had been going only to visit her; it just so happened that he had a navy and an army with him at the time.[6]

In such a complicated genealogical interrelationship no statesman could possibly allow family sentiment to interfere with his ambitions; this would be a recipe for paralysis. The relationships between kings had to be essentially political, that is, they took the form of diplomacy and warfare, disputes and intrigues. It is frequently considered that the Hellenistic age is one of constant warfare; this is clearly not true when one considers the actual wars which took place; at the same time, it is evident, at least from the sources which survive to inform us, that the relations between the several kings were largely based on hostility. Ptolemies fought the Seleukids in nine 'Syrian Wars', but these were spread over two centuries, and the intervals of peace between the wars were often two or three decades. The Ptolemies also fought the

Antigonids, usually at sea, but often also on land through proxies or allies. But again, any detailed consideration of the actual warfare shows clearly that the intervals of peace were long. That is, the hostility of the kings towards each other was a political relationship. It is very difficult to find a case where a war was begun purely for personal reasons: it took much more than that.

The international situation, from the time of the rise of Antigonos Monophthalamos from 316 onwards, can be best characterised as repeated attempts at hegemony which always compelled other powers to link together to prevent it, though this often took some time to develop. So Antigonos' attempt at hegemony from 316 to 301 compelled Ptolemy, Seleukos, Lysimachos, and Kassandros to ally with each other repeatedly until they brought him down in 301 at the battle of Ipsos. This was followed by a near-hegemony of Lysimachos who was brought down partly by Seleukos, and partly by the enmity of Pyrrhos of Epeiros and the cities of Greece. Seleukos' subsequent attempt was overthrown with his murder as he was about to claim control of Macedon in 281; he was murdered by the eldest son of Ptolemy I, so it is evident that fatherly friendship influence had not affected the son. Ptolemy I, II, and III exercised near hegemonic power at sea by the use of their navy for the next forty or fifty years. To maintain this power they had to fight the Antigonids and the Seleukids repeatedly during that time, and their power was clearly overstretched by the end of it. Their pretensions to power fell apart in the last decade of the third century with the massive internal rebellion which detached a large part of the Nile Valley to form an independent pharaonic kingdom, and this was followed by joint attacks by Philip V and Antiochos III on the Ptolemaic possessions outside Egypt. This was another classic case of the weaker powers uniting to pull down the stronger, and taking advantage of a momentary weakness in the hegemonic power.

Such alternations of periods of war and peace did not, of course, preclude intrigues and other preparations for a future war. The situation was such that all sides realised that another war – Seleukids versus Ptolemies, Ptolemies versus Antigonids, Attalids versus Antigonids or Bithynians, and so on – would probably occur in a relatively short time. (This is, of course, characteristic of such multi-state configurations.) In particular, the process and conventions of making peace almost ensured that a new war would break out within a few years. At the end of any war a conference was usually held in which peace terms were worked out. This was frequently between high advisers for each king, the meeting taking place in the main city of one of the protagonists.[7] The negotiations were only preliminary, and peace was only actually made when the two kings involved took oaths to observe it – that is, the oaths signified the ratification of the peace terms; until that point the terms could still be rejected or renegotiated.

The significance of the process, especially the oaths the kings swore, was that after the peace agreement they could not fight each other for as long as they both lived, or they would be foresworn; it also meant that when one of them died the other felt free to launch a new war. Thus Ptolemy II and Antiochos I made peace at the end of the First Syrian War in 271; Antiochos I died in 261 and Ptolemy II launched a new war next year, making peace in 253. Antiochos II died in 246 and a new war was being prepared when Ptolemy II died a short time later; Ptolemy III invaded Seleukid Syria later that year. The same sequence can be observed at the deaths of Ptolemy III and Ptolemy IV and on into the second century. In 205, at the death of Ptolemy IV, the regency government in Alexandria sent out envoys with the news and to announce the accession of the new king; the man who went to Antiochos III was charged also to request that the peace made in 217 should continue. Antiochos made no promise, a response which in the context was very threatening.[8]

In the intervals of peace it was possible for any king to expand his power over neighbouring territories, or to secure alliances with neighbours or more distant kings, so long as no overt attack was made on the 'enemy' or his allies. All the kings of the greater dynasties – Antigonids, Ptolemies, Seleukids – made a practice of securing allies among the Cretan cities. Crete was always a useful source of mercenary soldiers, and Ptolemy II had established a naval station in the east end of the island at Itanos; Antiochos II had then established an alliance with a city very close to Itanos, clearly as a threat.[9] In reply Ptolemy had to fortify Itanos and garrison it; so for the price of an alliance and a subsidy, Antiochos had compelled Ptolemy to expend resources to a much greater extent.

In 214, Ptolemy III interfered almost openly in favour of Akhaios, sending his son Magas with reinforcements and money, and hiring a group of Cretan mercenaries who were supposed to extract him from the siege of Sardis (but who instead sold him to Antiochos). This was extremely close to a clear disruption of the peace that the two kings had approved only three or four years before, when Antiochos III and Ptolemy IV had made an oath-bound peace agreement; Ptolemy's intervention ceased to be secret once the Cretans had changed sides and Antiochos probably had a good case to attack Ptolemy as an oath breaker. In fact, the episode did not break the peace, but this was perhaps largely because Antiochos won the contest in Asia Minor, and appreciated that if open war did break out it would have to be fought in Syria, and so Akhaios would be able to survive for a few more years. But it seems unlikely that anyone would have blamed Antiochos had he declared war.

Wars between the Great Powers were one thing: wars between a Great Power and lesser powers were rather different matters. It was extremely unlikely that the lesser power would survive if the king fought on to the bitter end. As a result, few did. It would make sense when attacked by a Great Power to make only a token resistance, and then submit. Territory and treasure and prestige might be lost, but it was extremely unlikely that the kingdom itself would be extinguished. This might be because resistance ended in a timely fashion, or it might be because the lesser power was able to call in the assistance of allies, or possibly because the Great Power became distracted by some other problem. An early capitulation, after a degree of resistance, might in fact bring local popularity to the lesser king; his people would not relish the prospect of a long fight, which would almost invariably take place within their kingdom. But the main reason for the kingdom's survival, and that of the king, was that kingdoms had become established entities in the international system and it was clearly regarded in some way as wrong for a Great Power to deliberately destroy a whole kingdom.

The Seleukid kingdom was surrounded by numerous lesser powers, in Asia Minor, in Iran, in the Far East, none of which any of its kings attempted to extinguish. In 212, for example, Antiochos III invaded one of the Armenian kingdoms. He besieged the king's palace, from which the king, Xerxes, escaped. Thus the scene was set for a long siege, with Xerxes periodically raiding the besieging forces. Hellenistic kings and armies were not good at sieges, and when they settled into one it usually took a long time before a result arrived. Xerxes could have conducted a guerrilla war harassing his enemy for as long as his people could bear it.

For Antiochos this was a very minor matter. He had a larger expedition in mind, so that his invasion of Armenia was only a preparatory expedition designed to remove any threat to his rear while he went off further east. Xerxes sued for peace, having clearly realised that if Antiochos captured his palace he would lose all credibility at home. He came into Antiochos' camp to negotiate terms. It is said that Antiochos was advised by some of his council to seize Xerxes and so finish the war that way. Antiochos refused, partly no doubt because his honour was involved, but also partly because by making peace with Xerxes he would be able to place him under obligation.[10]

Xerxes and Antiochos made peace. Xerxes promised to deliver arrears of tribute, 1,000 horses, and 300 talents; then by taking the oath of peace both kings could be certain that the other would keep the peace until one of them died. Xerxes continued as king for some years. One of the rewards he gained was a female relative of Antiochos, called Antiochis, as his wife (she was probably Antiochos' sister); she was not pleased, or perhaps she detected in Xerxes some nefarious plan to harm her brother; eventually she murdered him and returned to Antiochos.[11]

Therefore, a victory by a Great Power over a lesser power, and a subsequent formal oath-bound peace treaty, established a political ascendancy for the former which could only be renewed once one of the participating kings was no more. Cyrenaica had become independent of Ptolemy II in 275 and the peace agreement lasted until Magas the Cyrenaican king died in 250. His successor, who was his wife Apama or his daughter Berenike, or Demetrios the Fair – the sequence is unclear – had no agreement with Ptolemy and no allies to defend them.

The obvious protector, Antiochos II, was bound to keep the peace with Ptolemy II after their peace treaty in 253. Internal disputes resulted in the murder of Demetrios by or on behalf of Berenike, and this was one of the triggers for the Ptolemaic takeover of the kingdom. (Demetrios had been sent by the Macedonian King Antigonos Gonatas, but apparently Antigonos was not prepared to go to war with Ptolemy to defend him or avenge him; his murder had severed any links.) In this case the result was the full incorporation of Cyrenaica into the Ptolemaic state, though as a going concern. The Ptolemaic kingdom in effect annexed the king – Berenike – while in theory the kingdom remained unassimilated, with Ptolemy becoming its king when he married Berenike. But then, driven by the need to develop what was probably a very precarious control, political adjustments were made, and Ptolemy made separate agreements with the several cities of the former kingdom, the port city of Apollonia was separated off from Cyrene, and time-expired Ptolemaic soldiers were settled in many of the cities. The result was the transformation of an independent kingdom into a series of cities dependent on the Ptolemaic king.[12]

By contrast, the Seleukid kings were apparently perfectly happy to exercise suzerainty rather than annex an enemy kingdom – as in the case of Xerxes of Armenia, where the murder of Xerxes also resulted in the increase in Seleukid authority. This lasted until the death of Antiochos III, and only then did the two satraps he had appointed shift into independence, prudently moving their government centres further away from Seleukid territory as a precaution. Suzerainty rather than incorporation had been Seleukid practice from the beginning. Even Lysimachos, a much more controlling king than most, had accepted defeats of parts of his army by men who then made themselves kings in Bithynia and Pontos, on the North Anatolian coast. These kings were then accepted as independent states by Seleukos I when he defeated Lysimachos. In the same region the first ruler of Pergamon, Philetairos, performed a notable service for Antiochos I when he recovered Seleukos' body after his murder, and he was then left in virtual independence in his well-fortified castle.

As a result of this policy, eventually the Seleukid kingdom was bordered on the north by a long string of independent kingdoms which were in fact all tributaries of the Seleukid king. Of course, these agreements had to be renewed with every king, and not all of them got around to it. In the case of Kappadokia, Seleukid policy promoted the local chief, Ariarathes, as king, and his marriage to the daughter of Antiochos II in effect recognised Kappadokia as an independent kingdom and Ariarathes as king, but under Seleukid suzerainty.

In another case, when Antiochos III marched into Iran in 220, King Artabarzanes of Media Atropatene succumbed quickly to a threatened attack by Antiochos III. Despite having supported the rebel Molon, Artabarzanes was permitted to retain his kingdom. By this time Media Atropatene had been in existence for over a century as an independent or semi-independent state, but one which had long accepted Seleukid suzerainty as a means of survival, while the Seleukids had accepted Media's existence as an easier option than invading a difficult and mountainous country. It must be assumed that Artabarzanes and his predecessors had had earlier agreements of this sort with previous Seleukid kings; Artabarzanes was probably a direct descendant of Atropates, who had been confirmed in place (as satrap) by Alexander's regent Perdikkas in about 322. The family had raised itself to the status of kings, but had managed to maintain a certain independence ever since Alexander's death. Artabarzanes was thus able to submit quickly simply because he was returning to a condition which his ancestors had long accepted.[13]

In moving east on his great expedition in 211–206, Antiochos encountered the Parthian kingdom which had occupied one of the Seleukid provinces, Parthia. There had, presumably, never been any agreement between the two kings so far; Antiochos had to fight a difficult war, but as a result he recovered the lost province, driving the Parthian king back beyond the Kopet Dag Mountains and into the desert whence his father, the first king, had come to conquer the Parthian province.[14] So far as can be seen (for the next section of Polybios' account has not survived), Antiochos compelled the Parthian king to accept his suzerainty, and seized part of his territory (the former province), but had not seriously attempted to extinguish the kingdom. Whatever peace agreement had been made and ratified would place Parthia under Antiochos' suzerainty, but would also recognise Parthia as a separate kingdom. Certainly Parthia remained at peace with Antiochos and his successors for the next forty years. It may therefore be presumed that the suzerainty agreement reached by Antiochos in 208 was renewed by his successor Seleukos IV after 187.

The ancient sources concentrate very much on the hostilities which took place between the kings. This was, of course, much the most publicly noticeable of their activities, as well perhaps as their most irresponsible, and perhaps a concentration on their warfare is not really quite so misleading as might be expected or supposed. But the mutual relationships of the Hellenistic kings were not merely marked in wars and intrigues but at times also in alliances.

It is as well to clear up one point before moving on. It is often commented that arranged marriages between kings and other kings' daughters amounted to a marriage alliance. In the sense of the man and woman were then living together it was of course an alliance of a personal sort. In the sense of a political alliance there is no evidence that these royal marriages had any effect beyond the immediate moment. An early example is the marriage of Seleukos I to the daughter of Demetrios Poliorketes, Stratonike. This was certainly a political move, in that these two kings were politically isolated at the time the marriage was arranged, and were faced by an association of their rivals in what amounted to a political alliance which threatened both Seleukos and Demetrios. In particular, the three others, Lysimachos, Ptolemy, and Kassandros, were allied against Demetrios, while Lysimachos and Ptolemy were both in dispute with Seleukos. The two isolated kings made an alliance – a political alliance – in reaction to the apparent threat to each of them, and this was in a sense confirmed when Seleukos married Stratonike.[15]

In political terms their need for an alliance passed quickly. Seleukos and Ptolemy seem to have made some sort of agreement to leave each other alone – at least the urgency of any dispute faded away – while Demetrios became deeply involved in affairs in Greece, where Seleukos had no vital political interests. Demetrios had seized control of Kilikia, and this appeared to be a threat to Seleukos' territories in Syria. In 294 Seleukos, Ptolemy and Lysimachos combined to seize several parts of Demetrios' territories.[16] A year later Seleukos repudiated Stratonike by handing her on to his eldest son Antiochos as his wife, and packed both of them off to rule his eastern territories.[17] By this time Demetrios had made himself king in Macedon and was building a great armament with the intention of campaigning to recreate the empire of Alexander. He was once more a threat to all the other kings, including Sekeukos – with all of whom he had multiple grievances by this time – and three of the others combined once more to pull him down. He set off on his campaign anyway, only to be eventually captured by his father-in-law, and was kept in a gilded captivity in Syria until he died.[18]

As a political alliance, therefore, the marriage of Seleukos and Stratonike was a clear failure, if one considers it as a political arrangement intended to last. It was evidently successful in signalling to the other kings that it would be dangerous for them to attack the new allies, but within only a short time the two were pursuing policies with no relation or reference to each other, and any threats to them had faded. Within a few years of the marriage they were at enmity, and Seleukos was in part instrumental in bringing Demetrios down.

Any political arrangements between them lasted little longer than the marriage ceremony.

The nearest relationship there was to a long-standing apparent alliance was that between the Seleukids and the Antigonids, which began in about 277 with the betrothal of Phila, the daughter of Antiochos I and Stratonike, to Antigonos Gonatas, the son of Demetrios, and their marriage a year later.[19] Both of these kings had a mutual enemy in the form of Ptolemy, whose fleet dominated the eastern Mediterranean, including the Aegean, thereby threatening Antigonos' position in Macedon and Greece. The two were also both threatened by the Galatians. The latter, Celtic invaders, had overrun Macedon until driven out by Antigonos, while another branch had invaded Asia Minor and were being battled by Antiochos and his army. Such was the confusion of the time that briefly the two kings had fought each other at sea, but had soon rapidly decided that they had much more serious wars on their hands.[20] They negotiated a settlement of any problems they had, and the marriage of Antigonos and Phila was arranged, as a ratification. Yet the marriage did not actually take place until Antigonos had succeeded in driving out the Galatians and making himself king in Macedon; it had not been Antiochos' intention to render direct assistance to Antigonos in Macedon. These two dynasties never fought together against their enemies, even though both were threatened above all by the Ptolemies for the next seventy years. On occasion they were both fighting one of the Ptolemaic kings at the same time, but they never coordinated their military or naval activities.[21] The relationship between them was nevertheless close enough for another royal marriage to be agreed in the 240s between Demetrios II and Stratonike, the daughter of Antiochos II.[22] And still another in the 170s between King Perseus and Laodike, the daughter of Seleukos IV.[23]

Four marriage links between the dynasties were not enough to make them political allies, though it was perhaps enough to create a political friendship, which is by no means the same thing. The nearest they came to a direct alliance was in that partition agreement between Antiochos III and Philip V in 203. The Ptolemaic kingdom, their mutual and long-standing enemy, was in the process of collapsing in the face of a great native Egyptian rebellion. Both Antiochos and Philip eyed the situation greedily. Each had old claims to parts of the Ptolemaic Empire. They made an agreement, which remained secret in its details, a factor which only fed rumours about what had really been agreed, but which seems to have gone into some detail about which parts of the Ptolemaic state each should seize. But this did not amount to an alliance; it is exactly what it appeared to be, an agreement to partition Ptolemy's territories.[24] In the wars which began each fought for his own hand, to seize the lands he wanted. There was no co-ordination of military activities, and no co-ordination of political activities. Antiochos began his war in 202, but Philip waited a year, during which, of course, much of the Ptolemaic military power was concentrated on fighting Antiochos' invasion of Syria. And both made separate peace treaties, though in fact Philip may never have made a peace treaty with Ptolemy since he was soon involved in a war with the Roman Republic, at the end of which he had lost whatever he had gained in the war with Ptolemy. Antiochos III fought on until 195, when he was able to make a treaty by which he gained the territories – Phoenicia and Palestine, and the coastal cities of Asia Minor – he had sought.[25] Had there been an alliance Antiochos would have been obligated to help defend Macedon against the Roman attack; he did nothing – and when Antiochos was attacked by Rome in turn, Philip took the Roman side.

The relationship between the various kings was therefore always at a distance, a diplomatic arrangement, the delivery of a daughter in marriage, or a war. Royal marriages did not mean more than a momentary political agreement; an alliance existed only if it was convenient for both parties, and only for the period of the war being fought. It is striking that beyond the first generation after Alexander there is no record of any of these kings meeting each other. That first generation, the time of Antigonos Monophthalamos, Seleukos, Ptolemy, Kassandros, and Lysimachos, consisted of men who had made themselves kings but who had in fact also grown up together. They all knew each other, and it must have seemed reasonable when they had a dispute to discuss the matter in person. This practice gradually evolved into diplomatic meetings, what in the modern age we call summit meetings. So Antigonos met Kassandros and Lysimachos in 313 at the Hellespont in a failed attempt to make peace, but the details were being worked out by their agents;[26] he met Ptolemy later in the same year at Ekregma on their mutual border, and again failed to make peace.[27] And then, of course, there were the occasions when Demetrios met Seleukos, and Lysimachos had joined Demetrios in admiring the latter's ships. Lysimachos and Kassandros frequently worked together, and were in fact neighbours in Macedon and Thrace, and were regularly allied against Antigonos I; it is highly likely that they consulted each other regularly, though there is no record of when or where they met.

Yet after this first generation there is no record of any of their successors meeting each other. The only meetings between kings were between the king of one of the Great Powers – Seleukids in particular – and subordinate kings. So Antiochos III met Xerxes of Armenia, though it is noticeable that it was only when the latter had been defeated that the meeting took place. When he invaded Baktria in 208, Antiochos III besieged the Baktrian King Euthydemos in his city at Baktra (just as he had done with Xerxes), and after the siege had lasted for some time – two years, we are told – negotiations began. But the two kings never actually met each other, conducting their negotiations through an intermediary. Euthydemos stayed in the city, Antiochos stayed in his camp. The closest the families came was when Euthydemos' son Demetrios came out to ratify the agreement in a meeting with Antiochos. He was offered Antiochos' daughter in marriage, but this never took place.[28] It is clear that Euthydemos and his son were being very careful not to become too entangled in Antiochos' family, and Euthydemos by keeping his distance was not placing himself in a situation of subordination. Nevertheless the agreement did reduce Baktria to a subordinate ally of Antiochos for the next several years; that is, in the end, Euthydemos admitted defeat, and then Antiochos did go away.

This pattern of arrangements between kings continued all the way through to the destruction of the Hellenistic world at the hands of Rome. Marriages between the three major royal families took place in 195, when Antiochos III's daughter Kleopatra Syra married Ptolemy V, in 174, when Seleukos IV's daughter Laodike married the Macedonian King Perseus, and on several occasions between 150 and 120 between Seleukids and Ptolemies.[29] In fact, this latter marriage practice continued through until after the Seleukid kingdom had been extinguished; the last occasion was when the Ptolemaic Queen Berenike IV was searching for a husband and lighted on a Seleukid, called Seleukos Kybiosaktes, married him, but then had him murdered after only a few days because she didn't like the way he smelled, or so she is reported as saying – but by that time, of course, the Seleukids had no power and her husband therefore had no political influence; this is a much more convincing reason than any olfactory unpleasantness.[30]

These royal marriages clearly had no long-lasting political content, though at the time they were concluded it is reasonable to suppose that the two ruling kings were friendly towards each other, even politically aligned against another. On the other hand, at least two notable marriages – that of Berenike to Antiochos II, and that of Kleopatra Syra to Ptolemy V – were in fact concluded as part of peace settlements. Extracting a royal princess in marriage from the Ptolemaic family, as Antiochos II did, counted as a major diplomatic triumph, and rather suggests that he was in a particularly strong political and/or military position when the peace was being negotiated. Handing over a Seleukid princess in marriage to another king, however, was by no means unusual, and Ptolemy V could not regard his marriage to Kleopatra Syra in the same way as a major diplomatic triumph.

These marriages were therefore concluded not as parts of the diplomatic or political process of alliances, but because the Seleukids, the Ptolemies, and the Antigonids regarded each other as the only suitable marriage partners for their children. It was not a diplomatic but a social process, a mark of prestige.

The Ptolemies in particular appear to have regarded their daughters as far too precious to be married out, and several of them were never married at all; the Seleukids, on the other hand, were much more willing to use their daughters as rewards to subordinate kings.

The most extraordinary sequence of marriage events took place in Syria between 150 and 139. In 152 the bastard son of Antiochos IV, Alexander Balas, had instigated an uprising against his cousin King Demetrios I.[31] This claim had been supported, directly or indirectly, by the Pergamene king Attalos II and then also by Ptolemy VI, each, of course, for his own reasons. It took two years for Alexander to make any real progress in extending his power out of Ptolemais-Ake, but in 150 Ptolemy threw his own diplomatic weight on Alexander's side, presumably because it was only with some direct Egyptian help that Alexander was going to succeed. Ptolemy's gesture was to marry his daughter Kleopatra Thea to Alexander.[32]

This was a highly unusual, even unique action. Ptolemaic daughters were regarded as extremely valuable in dynastic terms. They carried with them, in Ptolemaic political theory, a latent claim to the kingship, which could become active in a husband when they married (so Berenike IV's successive husbands became kings). The solution to the dilemma this posed was generally to marry brothers to sisters, which kept the dynastic position within the family, and either to kill off surplus children or to keep daughters unmarried. Until Ptolemy VI's gesture, only one Ptolemaic daughter had been married out into another family in the previous 120 years. That had been Berenike, the daughter of Ptolemy II, who had married Antiochos II. As a marriage it had been disastrous; politically, when Berenike was murdered, it gave her brother Ptolemy III a perfect excuse to intervene in Syria and conduct a victorious war of conquest. After that few would want a Ptolemaic daughter in marriage, and never since had a Ptolemaic daughter been married outside the family. So Ptolemy VI's delivery of his daughter, even though she was a younger daughter to the pretender to the Seleukid throne was a political gesture of the first importance. (The elder daughter, Kleopatra III, eventually married her uncle, Ptolemy VI's brother.) Ptolemy VI was taking a gamble, since if Alexander succeeded he might well use his marital status as a means of aiming for the Ptolemaic throne. In actual fact, of course, Ptolemy did not make the gesture until Alexander was on the verge of success; he was not going to waste such an asset on a man who might still fail. Clearly Ptolemy did not believe in the possibility of Alexander claiming the Egyptian throne. He already had a son, and a brother, so Kleopatra Thea's latent claim was extremely distant.

Kleopatra's value now lay in the Seleukid scheme of things, as the wife of the king. When Alexander was attacked by an army recruited by Demetrios' eldest surviving son, Demetrios II, and Ptolemy and Alexander fell into dispute, Ptolemy had no compunction about retrieving his daughter and then marrying her off to Alexander's enemy, Demetrios II.[33] Kleopatra clearly had no say in the matter, at least at this point, but her political importance in the Seleukid system was clearly demonstrated by these marriages. Not only that but she proved to be extremely fertile. She already had a child, a son, by Alexander, and soon she had three children by Demetrios. Her transfer from Alexander to Demetrios was followed by all three men fighting each other, in which Ptolemy was killed, and after which Alexander was murdered. This left the weakest of the three, Demetrios II, as the king.[34]

Kleopatra was being used by her father as a symbol of his supremacy over the Seleukid kings. Her marriage to Alexander was a sign that, whatever disputes there were about his legitimacy, Ptolemy accepted that he was the son of Antiochos IV and so a legitimate Seleukid king. When Alexander tried to break this dependency, Ptolemy had shifted his support to Demetrios II, and then it was only the fact of his death in battle which prevented him from enforcing a subordinating peace treaty on Demetrios. He had already occupied the territory of Palestine and Phoenicia which had been lost by his father in the Fifth Syrian War treaty in 195, and there is no doubt that he intended to keep it. His brother and successor Ptolemy VIII had no such ambition, and the Ptolemaic army in Syria was quickly withdrawn, with the result that the disputed provinces remained Seleukid.[35] At the same time, Ptolemy was content to see the Seleukid state dissolving into civil war and suffering hostile invasions from the east. His personal relationship with his niece's husband was one of indifference.

Demetrios II could not command the full loyalty of his subjects. The infant son of Alexander was promoted by rebels as an alternative king (Antiochos VI), so Kleopatra saw her only son being used in a rebellion against her husband. Demetrios II could not prevail in the civil war, and eventually turned away to deal with a parallel crisis which was developing in his eastern territories. While he was away Kleopatra solved the problem of the civil war in Syria by calling in Demetrios' younger brother, Antiochos, marrying him and so making him king – Antiochos VII.[36] Meanwhile, Demetrios II was captured by his enemies, though this seems to have occurred some time after the marriage of his wife to his brother.[37]

This tangled story was not in fact over for several more years. Antiochos VII waged war in the east to recover the kingdom's lost territory, and when it seemed he was winning, Demetrios II was released, clearly as a spoiler in the hope that he would destroy Antiochos' Syrian base.[38] This plan miscarried because Antiochos was killed in the meantime; Demetrios returned to reclaim his place as king in Syria. Kleopatra would have nothing to do with him. But then he was contacted by her sister, another Kleopatra (III) who was ruling

Egypt, and who suggested that he should marry her and make himself king in Egypt. Her own husband, Ptolemy VIII, against whom she was fighting, thereupon took a leaf from Ptolemy VI's actions and sent another pretender, another Alexander (Zabeinas), whose parentage was variously suggested with little intention of plausibility.[39] The purpose was to sabotage Demetrios' Syrian political and military base, but the main intention was to further Ptolemy's campaign to return to Egypt. Demetrios was eventually murdered. Kleopatra then discovered that her eldest son by Demetrios expected to become king in his place, and she had him killed. After several more years the next son, Antiochos VIII, showed the same ambition, but this time the poisoning plot was turned against her, and he insisted that his mother drink the poison she had prepared for him.[40]

In addition, while held in Parthian captivity Demetrios II had been presented with Rhodogune, the daughter of the Parthian king, as his wife, and by her he had had two children.[41] These, as children of a Seleukid king, clearly had as good a claim to the kingship as Alexander Balas. And, when Antiochos VII was defeated by the Parthians, his son and a daughter of Demetrios II were captured.[42] The son could have been used as a Parthian puppet; the daughter went into the Parthian king's harem, and any children they had could also lay a claim to the Seleukid kingship. None of this happened, so far as we know, but it all brought the Parthian monarchy into the diplomatic complexity of the Hellenistic world, and added to the difficulties faced by the Seleukids.

In this tangle of marriages and murders, plots, and civil wars two items stand out. First, it is evident that in her capacity as a daughter of Ptolemy VI, Kleopatra Thea's person was especially valuable, and this value transferred to the Seleukid dynasty as a result of her series of marriages. This, in fact, was not new in the Seleukid family; one of the reasons for the marriage of Antiochos II and Berenike, the daughter of Ptolemy II, was that Antiochos' first wife, Laodike, had not been of royal birth; Berenike was, and was therefore a more valuable match. Second, the prestige gained by Kleopatra Thea as a result of her Seleukid marriages was enough to put her into a position of political power such as no earlier Seleukid royal wife had held. It was clearly her own decision to summon and marry Antiochos VII, and later to abandon Demetrios II, just as it was her decision to murder her eldest surviving son, and to attempt to murder her next son; the purpose was clearly to be able to retain the exercise of royal power for herself; if either boy gained power, she lost that power.

Her revenge was posthumous. She had children by both Demetrios II and Antiochos VII; they fought each other in a dynastic civil war which lasted for twenty years (113–95), and this enmity carried on into the succeeding generations. The result was the final disintegration and destruction of the Seleukid kingdom, even before the Roman advance extinguished the last remnants and the Ptolemaic kingdom.

The relationship of kings with other kings was one which was founded in warfare, and this is apparent only in part because of the bias of the sources we possess. Most kings were related to each other, literally, as a result of their complex intermarriages, but also diplomatically in the intrigue which went on without cease during the intervals of peace. The lack of trust between individual kings, except when fixed by an oath-sworn peace treaty, is very obvious (and may be one of the main reasons they never met each other). Encounters with lesser kings, after all, implied and produced conditions of political dependency, and this was clearly what Ptolemy VI was attempting to achieve with Alexander Balas and Demetrios II. This might be possible with many kings, such as Xerxes of Armenia, or Ariarathes of Kappadokia, but to attempt the imposition of Ptolemaic power upon the Seleukid kings does display too great an appetite.

Kings had to rely on their armies, which were primarily recruited from their own subjects, in defending their positions against enemy kings, and this is presumably the reason many minor kingdoms were able to emerge and to remain independent. Once a kingdom had existed for a generation it was an accepted part of the political and diplomatic landscape, and even in defeat it was very unlikely to be suppressed. It may be that the most secure relationship of one king to another was one of subordination and suzerainty, which provided protection for the lesser power.

Chapter 4

Kings, Wives, and Children

Philip II and Alexander the Great provided a political model for their successors in their treatment of their women and children, but this model was followed only by those of the generation of Alexander himself. Philip married seven or eight women, in a sequence spread over a relatively few years – four of them in his first four years as king. He collected a princess from every conquest he made, though in fact only two of them appear to have been of both personal and political significance: Olympias, an Epeirote princess whose brother became king of Epeiros, and who was the mother of Alexander and his sister Kleopatra; the last wife was Kleopatra daughter of Attalos, who was also the only one of his wives who was Macedonian. When she gave birth to a child, this was one of the triggers for the final dispute in which Philip himself was killed.

Alexander famously refused to marry before setting off on his great expedition, supposedly for fear of becoming domesticated when there were lands to conquer. A better reason would be that he had seen that his father's marriage to a Macedonian woman had been instrumental in promoting his murder. Alexander could not afford to put himself in a similar position by choosing one Macedonian woman as his wife out of the many available, for this would instantly align him politically with a Macedonian faction, with the others feeling resentful. Marriage with Alexander was a route to civil war.[1] On the other hand, while he was on campaign he certainly did not restrain his sexual appetite. He married at least three, perhaps four, women: Roxane, the daughter of Oxyartes, a Baktrian noble, and Parysatis and Stateira of the Akhaimenid royal family; he may also have married Barsine, also of the Akhaimenid royal family, but who was also the widow of the mercenary commander Memnon, whom he had defeated. None of them, it must be emphasised, were Macedonian.

Alexander was therefore following his father's practice of collecting wives from conquered communities. He had defeated Memnon in Asia Minor, and so his widow was a prize of war.[2] Roxane represented his brutal conquest of Baktria.[3] Parysatis, a daughter of Artaxerxes III, and Stateira, Darius III's daughter, symbolised his conquest of the Great King Dareios III, and therefore his conquest of the whole Akhaimenid Empire.[4] But the marriage of these last two women had a further purpose. As the daughters of the last two Great Kings of the Akhaimenid line, they carried within them an inheritance package. With the male members of the Akhaimenid family now extinct, these two women were the final representatives of the great imperial dynasty, and Alexander's marriage to them was an indication that he had not merely conquered the empire, but had now inherited it by marriage with the last female members of the dynasty. (This may have been also one of his purposes in marrying Barsine, who was also of Akhaimenid descent – if he did marry her; if so, this was a very early sign that his ultimate purpose was to secure control over the whole empire.) The only exception was that his friend and lover, Hephaisteion, was married to another daughter of Darius, Drypetis, but the groom died shortly afterwards.[5]

In a sense this can be seen as a development of Philip's marital policy, if perhaps more narrowly and precisely focused. In no case, however, can Philip's wives be seen to have carried with them any sort of a claim to the thrones of their homelands. The marriage with Olympias had a clear political purpose in that it reassured her brother King Alexander that Philip was not about to invade his territory. Similarly, the marriages to two women of the Thessalian nobility, including Nikesipolis, a niece of the Thessalian hero Jason of Pherai, did not provide Philip with any sort of a claim to that country, but they did represent a strong supportive connection with that nobility. Combined with his clear political decision to respect the formal autonomy of Thessaly, even though he clearly ruled the country, the marriages had obvious political content. As an indication of the highly political content, whereas Nikesipolis provided him with a connection with the family of Jason, the other Thessalian wife, Philinna, was connected with Jason's Thessalian enemies. Rather as Alexander's marriages to the Akhaimenid women annexed them to him rather than to anyone else, so Philip was annexing the most prominent Thessalian women, rendering them unavailable for a Thessalian husband to use them against the Macedonian domination.

In none of these marriages is there any hint of personal feelings. It is known that the relations of Philip and Olympias were stormy, to say the least, but Alexander appears to have avoided such marital storms, probably by largely ignoring the women and hiding them in the harem. He was certainly sexually active, indeed bisexual, but his marriages were too carefully considered political arrangements to have any personal content. The wives were, in accordance with Greek custom in some places, secluded once married. None of them played anything but a passive role in the events of the years after Alexander's death.

Royal marriages, therefore, were political events. (See Chapter 3 for the limitations on this.) In certain circumstances they might provide the husband with a claim to his wife's ancestral territory, as was the case for Ptolemy III on his marriage with Berenike, the heiress of Magas the king of Cyrene. And yet at the same time there is no evidence that royal marriages had any greater significance in political terms than at the moment of the marriage ceremony, when they presumably indicated a political alignment of the families of the two participants. They did not amount to long-term political alliances. Philip II was not allied with King Alexander of Epeiros, either when Alexander's sister married Philip, or when Alexander himself married their daughter Kleopatra (his niece) nearly a generation later. The political content of Philip's marriages with the two Thessalian women – one from the family of Jason, the other from a noble family probably opposed to Jason – depended upon the fact that Philip had conquered Thessaly; this was his authority to control that country, not the fact that he had married two of its nobles' children.

Philip had children by several of the women he married: Alexander was the son of Olympias, Arrhidaios was the son of Philinna of Larissa in Thessaly; he may have had other sons, who died in infancy, by accident, or in war.[6] If so, we know the names of none of them, nor of the precise circumstances in which they died, if they ever existed. It does demonstrate quite clearly, however, that Philip was sexually extremely active – and not all of his children were necessarily born of his wives. He had at least three daughters: Kynna was the daughter of Audata of Illyria, Kleopatra was another child of Olympias, and Thessalonike was the daughter of Nikesipolis.[7] He also had a child by his last wife Kleopatra; Alexander ordered that both mother and child be murdered, probably any other sons were also despatched, then or earlier – though Arrhidaios lived on. Alexander himself had two or three children: Alexander (IV) by Roxane; Herakles by Barsine (the widow of Memnon); and possibly a son called Argaios, whose mother is unknown.[8] None of these sons survived the fighting and murders of the decade or so after Alexander's death, though Herakles was not actually murdered until about 308. Of Philip's children only Thessalonike survived into the period of the successors. Of Alexander's children, all died in the wars of the successors.

The marriages of these two Macedonian kings were, in other words, both a tempting and a discouraging example for his successors to follow. Several of the successors adopted Philip's practice of successive marriages, though it was unusual for them to have several wives at the same time (as Philip and Alexander both had), but they certainly cynically manipulated their position for sexual gratification and for political advantage. It was also normal for many of the kings to maintain concubines.

The one king of Alexander's successors who was of Philip's generation, Antigonos I Monophthalamos, married only once, which was presumably the practice among other prominent Macedonians of his generation.[9] The next generation, however, the contemporaries of Alexander, sometimes followed Philip's and Alexander's examples. Lysimachos and Ptolemy had several wives successively, or in Ptolemy's case perhaps simultaneously; on the other hand, Seleukos married twice and Kassandros married only once; the most prolific was Antigonos' son Demetrios Poliorketes, who married at least five times; like Philip, he was married to several of his wives simultaneously. Most of these men, along with ninety or so other prominent Macedonians, were forcibly married to Persian noblewomen by Alexander's decree in 324 in a mass wedding ceremony at Susa at the same time as Alexander married Parysatis and Stateira. It is reported that of all those marriages only that of Seleukos and Apama continued after Alexander's death.[10]

Multiple marriages might indicate excessive sexual appetites, and this is no doubt the case with some of these men. Demetrios, for example, was notorious for his sexual indulgence, having relations not only with his wives, but also with several courtesans. On the other hand, most of the marriages of these men were politically inspired. Antipater, for example, had been regent for Alexander the Great while the king was on campaign, and for fifteen years he was the substitute king in Macedon. He had at least six sons and perhaps five daughters, and possibly more. In the years after Alexander's death, these daughters were married off to several of the competing commanders. One (whose name we do not know) married Alexander of Lynkestis, one of the upland regions of Macedon which it was necessary to keep onside to be able to control Macedon itself.[11] Phila was married to Krateros, who was in fact killed within a year of his marriage.[12] Nikaia was married to Perdikkas, the joint regent who took control of the Asian empire while Antipater ruled in Macedon.[13] Eurydike was married to Ptolemy once he had put away Artakama, his Persian wife.[14]

This was only the start. After Krateros was killed, Phila married Antigonos' son Demetrios.[15] Perdikkas was killed in 321, and Nikaia then married Lysimachos.[16] Demetrios later, while still married to Phila, also married Eurydike of Athens, Deidameia, the sister of Pyrrhos, King of Epeiros, Lanassa the daughter of King Agathokles of Syracuse, and Ptolemais, the daughter of Ptolemy I and Eurydike, Antipater's daughter (though by this time Phila had committed suicide).[17] Lysimachos, having married Nikaia, later married Amestris, a Persian lady who was the widow of the tyrant of the city of Herakleia Pontike; as her husband Lysimachos took control of the city, and once having gained that, he put her away; then he married Arsinoe II, the (much younger) daughter of Ptolemy I.[18] The demand for these women as wives continued even into their middle age – Antipater died in 319 and many of his children will have been born twenty or thirty years before, yet they were still in demand ten and more years after his death. This can only have been because their father's great renown carried on into his children.[19] His eldest son, Kassandros, for example, was able to establish himself as ruler, and later as king, in Macedon, with substantial local support, largely based on his father's reputation.

Ptolemy was another serial husband. Having dismissed his Persian wife, Artakama, he married one of Antipater's daughters, Eurydike, and had several children by her. She brought with her, however, an attractive, and probably younger, companion or lady-in-waiting, Berenike, who eventually supplanted Eurydike in Ptolemy's bed. For a time Ptolemy maintained both women as continuing wives, but when Berenike's son displaced Eurydike's as Ptolemy's chosen heir, Eurydike decamped, taking refuge with Ptolemy's political enemy, Seleukos.[20] The final member of this polygamous group was of the next generation, Pyrrhos of Epeiros. He apparently took his marital practices from Philip's and Ptolemy's examples; he had taken refuge with Ptolemy for several years during his exile from Epeiros, and his first wife was one of Ptolemy's daughters, Antigone, but she died fairly soon. He then married Lanassa, the daughter of King Agathokles of Syracuse, and after a campaign against enemies in the Balkans, he copied Philip II of Macedon and collected a princess from each of the two defeated kings. At this Lanassa removed herself, taking with her the island of Kerkyra which had been her dowry. She went off to Demetrios Poliorketes and married him, presenting him with the island.[21]

The actions of Eurydike and Lanassa in leaving their royal husbands after being so insulted was a mark of the expanding ability of these high-born ladies to assert themselves.[22] Philip II's Epeirote wife Olympias had acted in a similar way when Philip married Kleopatra, daughter of Attalos; she left his court and returned to her home, though she was persuaded to return later; Alexander had gone with her, and as the only suitable heir to Philip (for the moment) he was essential to Philip's plans. Politically Olympias and Alexander came out of this court contretemps as victors.[23] This female assertiveness is a phenomenon which was new in the Hellenistic period, though there had been signs of a similar independence of action by women in the Akhaimenid royal family, and Philip's mother Eurydike had been forward in manipulating the Macedonian succession.[24]

This female assertion, or 'woman power', as McCurdy termed it, is generally celebrated, or regarded with amazement, depending on the sex and width of view or sympathy of the historian. It is, however, restricted to a very small number of women, all of whom were royally born and wealthy and able to assert themselves – usually against an oppressive, neglectful, or wandering husband – because of their independent wealth, position, and prestige. The possible independence of women lower in the social scale would entirely depend on themselves, without the use of powerful relatives. The celebration of 'woman power' in the Hellenistic period is less than convincing as a general phenomenon.

The marriages of their daughters were arranged by the Hellenistic kings and this always remained part of their prerogative, but the women involved were extremely conscious of their own social status, and did not brook either opposition or competition – Olympias was one of the originals in this. It was this, rather than the sexual competition from younger princesses, which compelled Lanassa to leave Pyrrhos. Eurydike no doubt felt even more annoyed at being supplanted by one of her own ladies at Ptolemy's court. There is never any indication that their fathers took serious exception to their treatment in these cases, and it was clearly the ladies' independence and appreciation of their social position which compelled them to desert their husbands.

Pyrrhos was the last of the seriously serial husbands. The generation which followed Ptolemy I, Demetrios, and Pyrrhos tended to be monogamous, at least in terms of their legal and open marriages. This did not prevent these men from taking advantage of their powerful positions in sexual matters. For example, Ptolemy I's son, Ptolemy II, had three wives, but successively rather than simultaneously, and was reputed to have had many children with many women, but he also ensured that none, or perhaps very few, of those 'illegitimate' children survived.[25] His father had the same appetite, but left the product alive in the main.

Ptolemy II's marital history also brings forth another element in these royal marriages, one which may have had an echo of the preceding Egyptian royal marriage customs, or, perhaps more likely, may have been one of the elements which Ptolemy inherited from Alexander and from the preceding Akhaimenid dynasty. His elder sister, Arsinoe, was married to Lysimachos, and she agitated and schemed to have her children preferred before Lysimachos' eldest son, Agathokles, the son of Antipater's daughter Nikaia. She succeeded sufficiently well that in 283 Lysimachos turned on Agathokles and ordered his execution.[26] This action proved to be a political disaster; Lysimachos' authority within his kingdom was sensibly reduced by the resulting public hostility and distrust. Rebellions and secessions began, and Lysimachos was then defeated in battle by Seleukos, who had clearly been waiting for just such an opportunity, and had given refuge to Ptolemy's estranged wife Eurydike and her children (though Eurydike had willingly handed over her daughter Ptolemais to Demetrios a few years before). Arsinoe took her children and fled in disguise, first to Ephesos, and then to Macedon. There, her half-brother, Ptolemy Keraunos, was making himself king (having murdered his host, Seleukos). Arsinoe, as the widow of Lysimachos, who had also been king of Macedon, seemed to Ptolemy to be a prize worth winning, and he persuaded her to marry him. He then immediately murdered two of her children (the eldest of whom, though he failed to kill him, had a good claim to be Lysimachos' successor as king in Macedon). Not surprisingly, this brought the marriage to a swift end.[27]

Arsinoe, now having nowhere else to turn, returned to her original home in Egypt, to take refuge with her (full) brother Ptolemy II. She has been reckoned as one of the newly independent royal ladies of the Hellenistic period.[28] However, her career until her return to Egypt looks more like one in which she was buffeted by the unpredictable winds of fate rather than showing any mark of real independence – her intrigue against Agathokles was of a very traditional type of court intrigue, not a sign of her independence; still less was it a mark of her political ability or sense, for the result was to send her fleeing for her life in disguise and the ruin of her husband's life and kingdom. She had, as Lysimachos' wife, clearly had considerable influence over her husband in the matter of the succession, though this was bedroom influence, and it turned out to be a disaster both for her husband and herself; in Macedon, Ptolemy Keraunos had clearly thought that, despite their close relationship (they had the same father), she was worth marrying, presumably because she was the widow of the former king of Macedon and would thus assist him in holding the Macedonian kingship he had so recently seized. She was therefore being valued because of her marital career and her ancestry, rather than for herself and her abilities, and certainly not for any independence she had displayed. She had not, for example, displayed the sort of independent action of her stepmother Eurydike (who had deserted Ptolemy in anger) or of her older contemporary Lanassa in leaving any of her husbands.

In Egypt, however, perhaps drawing on her experience of marriage to her half-brother, she now persuaded her younger brother Ptolemy II to become her next husband (she was several years his senior).[29] At least that is how it is usually portrayed, though it is rather more likely that Ptolemy himself was the moving spirit. This was a marriage of full siblings.

Near-incest had been part of the royal marriage pattern among Macedonian kings at least since Alexander II of Epeiros married his niece, Olympias' daughter Kleopatra. It had occurred occasionally in the Akhaimeid royal family – Dareios I married his full sister, for example. Sibling marriage is supposed to have been part of the essential pattern of marriage for the pharaohs, and this has been supposed, rather lazily, to have been one of the sources of this apparently revived phenomenon. It is, however, not clear that the Egyptian royal custom was understood by these Macedonian kings. Investigation does show that, at least among the later pharaonic dynasties (say, from

700 BC), there were no full-sibling marriages among the pharaohs, and no marriages of close relations among the last two native independent dynasties (the Saites, and the 28th Dynasty, of which the latter were well enough known to the Macedonians to feature in the myths surrounding the conception and birth of Alexander). The marriages of these late pharaohs with nieces and aunts, usually from different mothers, was not uncommon, but this was also the case among the Akhaimenids – not to mention the marriage of Philip's daughter Kleopatra with her uncle Alexander of Epeiros. There are no instances of full-sibling marriage among the pharaohs for several hundred years before the time of Ptolemy II.[30]

   There is therefore no indication that full-sibling marriages were the result of any influence of the practices of the preceding pharaonic regime on the Ptolemies; indeed, there is little evidence that the Ptolemies had much detailed knowledge of pharaonic Egypt, even if they decorated Alexandria with miscellaneous pharaonic art works.[31] They were certainly surrounded by monuments from the past, the priests of the temples had influence, which was usually exerted to benefit themselves, and Ptolemy I commissioned the Egyptian Manetho to compile a history of the preceding Egyptian dynasties. But this account is little more than a list of those dynasties, with occasional anecdotal narratives; in no part of the surviving text is there any reference to pharaonic marriage practices.[32]

   It is much more likely that the marriage of Ptolemy II and his sister Arsinoe II was only the final step in a whole series of incestuous marriages which had become part of the pattern of Hellenistic royal marriage since Alexander's time, and it was therefore an independent development within the Hellenistic dynasties; and so it must, first of all, be seen as a political action. The essential element in the use of sibling marriage was that the daughter of a king carried with her, so to speak latently, the ability to make the man she married king. This had been one of the reasons for Alexander's marriages to Parysatis and Stateira, the daughters of Akhaimenid kings, for, by marrying both ladies, Alexander prevented any other man from doing so. Arsinoe was the daughter of Ptolemy I, and so, by this theory, she carried with her a latent claim to the kingship; she was also the widow of both Lysimachos and Ptolemy Keraunos, both of whom had been kings of Macedon, while Lysimachos had been the king in Asia Minor as well. Ptolemy Keraunos, the eldest son of Ptolemy I, and the half-brother of both Ptolemy II and Arsinoe, had left Ptolemy I's court with his mother Eurydike, and it was only when he managed to gain the kingship in Macedon that he, by a letter to Ptolemy II, renounced his claim to the Egyptian throne; but by marrying Arsinoe at Kassandreia, it was likely that he was reserving his position on that once again

– after all, as Ptolemy I's eldest son, he no doubt regarded Ptolemy II as a usurper.

So in Egypt, by marrying Arsinoe, Ptolemy II was acting above all to safeguard his own position, even though by then Keraunos was dead. (There were other sons of Ptolemy I and Eurydike he might fear could challenge or supplant him.) Furthermore, in the international context of the 270s, Antiochos I had inherited from his father Seleukos the rule over Asia Minor, and had a strong claim to Macedon based on his father's conquest of Lysimachos. By marrying Arsinoe, Ptolemy II established his own claim to both territories. Her experience of the political conditions in Macedon and Asia Minor may also have been useful, but Ptolemy had plenty of other sources of information on this, and by the time they were married – probably in about 276 – her first-hand information was well out of date, and conditions in those two countries had become very different.

These political aspects of the marriage may well have escaped many contemporaries, just as they have escaped many historians. Instead, what they focused on was the incest. At least one poet, Sotades, so enraged Ptolemy II by his mocking comments on the matter that Ptolemy drove him out of Egypt and is then reputed to have had him murdered, locking him in the sarcophagus and throwing it into the sea.[33] The apparent strangeness of the union has led at least modern historians to conjecture that it was Arsinoe's doing, the product of her propensity for intrigue and her supposed forcefulness, and that somehow she compelled her brother to marry her, presumably in order to put herself in a position of power; it has often been assumed that it was she who was then the guiding element in Ptolemy's international policies until she died in 270. In the normal way of historical interpretation this idea has now been effectively challenged.[34] There is no evidence that Ptolemy's policy changed when he married Arsinoe or that it changed after she died.

It was, of course, necessary for a king to father children, specifically sons, one of whom would inherit his position. And yet the kings were constrained to a large degree in their choices of wives. For eighty years the only sibling marriage was that of Ptolemy II and Arsinoe, and since Arsinoe was about 40 years old, perhaps more, when the marriage took place, it is not surprising that no children resulted from the marriage – if indeed they had sexual relations at all. Other kings also married wives who were close relatives (Antigonos Gonatas married his niece Phila in the same year that Ptolemy II married Arsinoe), but the normal practice was to secure one from another dynasty. This practice has been labelled 'marriage alliances', though in fact, as has been seen in the previous chapter, the political alliance part of this description scarcely existed.

An example is the marriage of Seleukos I with Stratonike, the daughter of Demetrios Poliorketes. This took place very publicly in a spectacular meeting between the two kings at Rhosos on the border of Kilikia and Syria in 299, only two years after Demetrios' father Antigonos had been killed in battle, against Seleukos among others. (Demetrios had, on his way to the meeting, seized control of Kilikia, including a large treasure stored in one of the castles there, from Pleistarchos, the brother of Kassandros, who had been another of his enemies at the battle of Ipsos.) It is presumed that Seleukos' first wife, the Persian lady Apama, had already died, though this is not certain, but monogamy was a Seleukid habit. The marriage with Stratonike was preceded by negotiations, which have to be presumed since they are not recorded, but, as in the case of all summit meetings, details had been sorted out beforehand so that the actual meeting, which was held on board one of Demetrios' great warships, was merely the ratification.[35]

The marriage certainly took place as part of a political arrangement. Seleukos and Demetrios had each been left politically isolated by alliances organised between Ptolemy, Lysimachos, and Kassandros. They therefore made their own alliance in reply, and the marriage of Seleukos and Stratonike was a public mark of this political change. At no point, however, did the two kings operate together in any political way, and several years later, when Demetrios fell into serious difficulties in the Aegean region, Seleukos seized the opportunity to take Kilikia from him.

Stratonike, as Demetrios' daughter, had a particular status all her own. Many of the Macedonian subjects within Seleukos' territory had been soldiers in the army of Antigonos and Demetrios, and Stratonike may well have had some influence over these men; certainly she could transmit any message to them from her father.[36] This is probably one of the reasons why, soon after Seleukos' seizure of Kilikia, an action which presupposes a new hostility between the two kings, Seleukos handed on his wife to his eldest son, Antiochos, and then sent both of them off to Baktria as his viceroys. Antiochos was given the title of king and was recognised as Seleukos' intended successor. It may also be assumed that Stratonike had taken part in the family negotiations which produced this result.

The very strict, local, and temporary limits of a so-called marriage alliance are illustrated further by the peace treaty between Ptolemy II and Antiochos II concluded in 253 at the end of the Second Syrian War. One of the clauses of the treaty was that Ptolemy's daughter Berenike should marry Antiochos. Antiochos was already married, to Laodike the daughter of a major family in Asia Minor, a marriage he had contracted before he became heir to his father, so it would seem that he had made a relatively free choice in the matter. There is no evidence that he divorced or set aside Laodike (though it has been assumed that this had happened, largely from an inscription which records the transfer of an estate to her at the time of the new marriage, and which is therefore regarded as a divorce settlement, though this is never stated).[37] Laodike continued to live at Ephesos; Berenike was installed in the palace at Antioch-in-Syria.

Berenike had a son, but within a relatively short time Antiochos had gone back to Laodike, and when he died in 246 he was living at Ephesos with her. (Conspiracy theories have flourished, including one that Laodike poisoned Antiochos and procured the murder of Berenike; the former is unlikely; the latter is quite possible, though the actual deed was done by two citizens of Antioch.)[38] Theories have been developed that the marriage with Berenike was a means for Ptolemy to exert influence within the Seleukid kingdom, and that Berenike's child was intended to become Antiochos' heir. There is no evidence for any of this. Berenike was certainly supplied with a large and rich dowry, and she was conducted very publicly to her marriage, yet nothing political which resulted can be ascribed to the marriage, to Berenike herself, or to Ptolemy's influence on Antiochos.[39]

Within Ptolemy's territories it appears to have been assumed that Berenike's child, inevitably named Antiochos, would succeed to the kingship, and at least one inscription, from Kildara in Asia Minor, supposes this.[40] But no matter what the peace treaty might have said (we do not have a text), or what might have been assumed by Ptolemy's officials such as Tlepolemos at Kildara, there was no way by which Ptolemy could insist, particularly since Antiochos had two sons who were near-adult by the time he died. Ptolemy II had died not long before Antiochos, and his successor, Ptolemy III, Berenike's elder brother, took a small force into Syria when he heard of Antiochos' death. Presumably this was intended to prop up Berenike's child's succession, or perhaps merely intervene in the process, but both she and the child had been murdered by the time he arrived.[41] This expedition was actually more a matter of Ptolemy initiating a new Syrian War (the Third) than concern for the succession; he might have attempted to impose the child as a new Seleukid king if the child had lived, but he must have known that the rest of the kingdom would not have accepted this, and that he would have to fight Antiochos' other sons if he was to impose his nephew as king in Antioch.

No matter what Ptolemy III's intentions, Ptolemy II, who had negotiated the original marriage treaty, was experienced enough to understand that neither he nor his son would be able to regulate the Seleukid succession. Berenike's marriage to Antiochos II was therefore in no sense either a political alliance or an interference in the Seleukid system of succession. The marriage must therefore be explained in another way. There are in fact two possible reasons for it which carry some conviction. One is that it may be that Ptolemy was handing over his daughter as the price for peace; the course of the war is very unclear, but it is known that Ptolemy himself, an unmilitary man, had to move to Palestine at one point because of the danger;[42] another reason is that Berenike may have been particularly acceptable to Antiochos because he had married 'beneath' him, and it was thought more socially acceptable that the Seleukid king should have as his wife a more exalted lady.

We do not know the real reasons, as these speculations make obvious, but to begin with, Antiochos was not the eldest son of his father. That had been an older son called Seleukos, who had been executed by his father for some unknown cause in about 267.[43] By that time Antiochos was already married to Laodike, and he continued to be married to her when he became king. Berenike, daughter of a king, was socially some distance above Laodike, who was merely the daughter of one of the Macedonian lords established in Asia Minor. Kings should marry king's daughters; it may well have been social snobbery which induced Antiochos to marry a second time.

Antiochos' mother, Stratonike, had been married to Seleukos I and then to his son Antiochos I. She was the subject of rumours and myths circulated into later historians' accounts. There was the story that she was handed over to Antiochos I when a doctor diagnosed that Antiochos was suffering from love-sickness, of which Antiochos was supposed to be unaware (at the age of 30!).[44] There was the story, already mentioned in the previous chapter, that, when she visited the temple of Atargatis at Bambyke in northern Syria, a man castrated himself, either in her honour or because of his sexual attraction for her.[45] This has provoked two historians to label her as one of those women to whom such stories were attached, whether or not they had any basis in fact – the lovesickness story is fairly nonsensical.[46] But these stories also indicate that Stratonike was regarded as an individual woman in her own right, not just as the wife of the king or the mother of a king. It is known that after her second husband's death in 261 she lived on at Sardis in Asia Minor, dying in 253. She was clearly another of those independent and capable Macedonian women, liable to make her own decisions and go her own way, in the tradition of Lanassa and Eurydike.

Such women emerge repeatedly as political players in Hellenistic history. Stratonike's daughter Apama was married to Magas, and as a result of the marriage Magas made himself king in Cyrenaica; when Magas died, in about 250, it seems clear that Apama was able for a time to determine the political direction of the kingdom, possibly making Demetrios the Fair her husband and king.[47] Another Stratonike, the youngest daughter of Antiochos I and Stratonike, was married to Demetrios II, the son of Antigonos II of Macedon, who became king in 239; she was supplanted in his affections by another, left him, and returned to Syria, where she proposed marriage to her nephew,

Seleukos II. When refused she caused a riot in the city and had to be captured and executed to prevent further trouble.[48]

It is surely significant that the instances of these independent women are confined very largely to the Seleukid and Ptolemaic dynasties. The third Hellenistic dynasty, the Antigonids of Macedon, certainly produced such women – Antipater's daughter Phila, and her own daughter, the first Stratonike, are the prime examples – but they did not flower into independent activity until they had left Macedon. None of the wives of the Antigonid kings showed such an independent spirit, even when they came from the Seleukid dynasty. The Antigonids and the Seleukids repeatedly intermarried: Antigonos II was married to Phila, the daughter of Seleukos I and Stratonike, Demetrios II was married to Stratonike (as noted above), Perseus was married to Laodike, the daughter of Seleukos IV. Yet none of these ladies emerges from the sources as anything other than the king's wife. Only Stratonike showed an independence, but only by leaving her husband after he married another.

The reason is presumably that Macedon was a much more conservative society, and that women were kept in traditional subjection, and seclusion, even among the royal family. When the second Stratonike left her husband – not something one would expect of a Macedonian wife – she returned to Syria and immediately caused trouble with her independent views and ambitions. Yet it does not appear that she caused similar problems in Macedon, where she had rather more reason to be annoyed. A comparable case would be Phila, the daughter of Seleukos I and Stratonike, and the granddaughter of Demetrios I, both people of independent spirit. Yet, once married to Antigonos II, any independence she had displayed earlier evaporated, at least in public. We, of course, know little or nothing about her life as the king's wife. Her husband did not confine his sexual attentions to his wife, and acknowledged at least one bastard son; this was what had annoyed Stratonike; Phila evidently put up with it. She was, however, the recipient of praise by Aratos of Soloi, who also composed her wedding hymn.[49]

Several Seleukid and Ptolemaic ladies were even more publicly active than the two Stratonikes, but it was above all out of the Seleukid family that the most notable of them emerged. As part of the peace treaty at the end of the Fifth Syrian War in 195, Kleopatra, the daughter of Antiochos III, was married to Ptolemy V. Both of these were very young, Ptolemy probably younger than his wife. When Ptolemy was murdered in 180, Kleopatra, whom the Alexandrians nicknamed 'Syra' for her origin, became regent for her three children, and operated as such successfully for four years before herself dying. Given recent Ptolemaic succession problems it took some care and ability for a woman to survive the immediate crisis and then to live out her own life. Her predecessors as kings' wives, Berenike II, wife of Ptolemy III, and Arsinoe III, wife of Ptolemy IV, had both been murdered by aspirant regents soon after their husbands died.[50] The success Syra enjoyed as a Seleukid *de facto* ruler of the Ptolemaic Empire is demonstrated by the mess made of that government by her successors as regents.

Kleopatra Syra's granddaughter, Kleopatra Thea, was used by her father Ptolemy VI as a means of advancing his political agenda during the Seventh Syrian War, as discussed in the previous chapter. As a teenager she was married to the Seleukid usurper Alexander I Balas, but when he and his father-in-law came to political blows, she was summarily removed from his bed and presented to his rival Demetrios II.[51] It may be this experience which stimulated her independence, which had not been particularly noticeable until then (though at her transfer to Demetrios she was still no more than 17 or 18 years old). When Demetrios II went on campaign in the east, she was left in control of the Seleukid dynasty's position in Syria, and it was her summons which brought Demetrios' younger brother Antiochos to Syria, where she married him – and so far as we can see it was her decision – and thereby made him king as Antiochos VII.[52] She had children by all three of her husbands: her son by Alexander Balas died under a surgeon's knife. Two other children were captured by the Parthians.[53] She murdered another.

Kleopatra Thea was the dominant political personality in the Seleukid kingdom for twenty years, and took careful measures to maintain her power. When Demetrios II was killed, her eldest son, Seleukos V, claimed power: she had him killed.[54] The problem with this, of course, was that when her next son, Antiochos VIII Grypos, made the same claim, he knew exactly what to expect, and turned the tables; she is said to have been compelled to swallow the poisoned drink she had prepared for him.[55] Her influence lived on after death, however, for she had made it her business to despatch another son into exile in Greece, and he was able to come back later and dispute the throne (Antiochos IX Kyzikenos).[56]

One of Kleopatra Thea's legacies to her adopted kingdom was therefore another twenty-year civil war between the children of two of her husbands. On the other hand, she had presided over the ending of earlier civil wars, and it was in part her doing that the Seleukid kingdom had survived that crisis, even if much diminished. Her reputation rests too much on the lurid details of her personal life, which, to be sure, are startling enough; her political activity is less obvious, but she was clearly capable of decisive action. And at the end, as she took her own poison, still aged only about 45, she might have reflected that she was leaving the kingdom in peace, and in the hands of a new king who was not one of those who, unlike her husband, gloried in war, and yet, as she could at that moment attest, he was certainly capable of taking difficult decisions.

In the Ptolemaic family, the women tended to operate more within the dynastic system, and within the palace, rather than in the wider political sphere; Kleopatra Thea could only have been as active and prominent as she turned out to be by moving out of Egypt. The marriage of Ptolemy III with Berenike (II), the daughter of Magas and Apama, united the kingdoms of Egypt and Cyrenaica, and Berenike appears to have been one of those women who attracted male admiration even from a distance, and the subject of admiring poems from Callimachos and Thekritos. In this she was rather like Stratonike, but she effectively disappeared into the palace at Alexandria after her marriage, with very little effect upon the outside world.[57] Of course, giving birth to at least six children, all between her marriage in 246 and late 239, will have preoccupied her to some degree, though this circumstance does not seem to have stopped Kleopatra Thea.

The death of Ptolemy III in 222 left the kingship in Egypt to Ptolemy IV, who married his full sister, Arsinoe III, in the first fertile sibling marriage of the dynasty. Of the six children of Ptolemy III and Berenike, two had already died, and those two were married. Ptolemy IV evidently feared that his relations were a threat. One was his uncle Lysimachos, the other his brother Magas – both were killed by an agent of Ptolemy's chief minister Sosibios, undoubtedly on the instructions of the king. Their next victim was Berenike, who apparently had a power base of her own in the court, and had the wit and nerve to act, as her killing of Demetrios the Fair had demonstrated. In the most bizarre circumstance imaginable the regent Sosibios conducted an almost open debate in the court about killing her; it was finally decided that she must die.[58]

The new king and his wife were the only members of the royal family left out of their parents' five children. There is a revealing moment when Ptolemy and Arsinoe both appeared in the midst of their army just before the battle of Raphia against Antiochos III. It was as much the appearance of Arsinoe which inspired the army as the knowledge that they were being commanded, in form if not in fact, by Ptolemy.[59] When Ptolemy died, still young, in 205 or 204, leaving the throne to his underage son, Ptolemy V, Arsinoe was supposed to be the regent for her son. However, she faced competition from her husband's long-standing ministers, Sosibios and Agathokles, who had exercised power during Ptolemy IV's reign – for he had turned out to be lazy and on pleasure bent – and in order to retain their power they organised the killing of Arsinoe.[60] This time an accident was staged – Sosibios was not going to repeat the debate – and Arsinoe died in a palace fire. The killings of Berenike and Arsinoe are the most compelling testimony for the power of these women within the court system, but that they could be murdered with impunity, and the acts accepted by the rest of the royal court, is a further testimony to the constant dangers they faced, and the very limited power they wielded. It must be noted, however, that one of the reasons Berenike was killed was that she had herself shown that she was capable of murder.

Ptolemy V survived a series of regents of varying competence, but his kingdom only just survived a simultaneous major rebellion in the south of Egypt and defeat by Antiochos III in the Fifth Syrian War. The dynasty was rescued, paradoxically, by the peace treaty which ended the war with Antiochos, one of the terms of which was that Ptolemy should marry Antiochos' daughter Kleopatra Syra. She was able to act as regent for her children when Ptolemy V was murdered.[61] She had three children, two boys, both unhelpfully called Ptolemy, and a daughter called, unsurprisingly, Kleopatra. The mess her successors as regents made of the administration of the kingdom suggests that she was a powerful and capable woman, able to command the loyalty and obedience of the men of the government system. She was presumably fully aware of the difficulties of her position, but was adroit enough, and perhaps tough enough, to survive until her natural death.

The practice of sibling marriage in the Ptolemaic dynasty therefore only became of genetic importance with the marriage of Ptolemy IV and Arsinoe III. It was then practised only occasionally. One measure taken by the regents of Ptolemy VI after his mother's death was to marry him to his sister Kleopatra II. Her potency was such that when he died his successor, his brother Ptolemy VIII, quickly married her; the existence of a daughter of Ptolemy VI and Kleopatra II, Kleopatra III, was also clearly a danger to him, so he married her as well.[62] Ptolemy VIII was widely disliked and Kleopatra II emerged as a major force in her own right, at one point driving her husband out of the kingdom; similarly forceful was Kleopatra III, her daughter-niece, who not only governed the kingdom herself in the name of her children but conducted a war which may be reasonably called the last Syrian War (the Ninth) in 103–101. These women were clearly adept at political manoeuvring, but these later disputes spilled over out of the dynastic arena and into open civil warfare, to the distress of their subjects. And, of course, the final Kleopatra – VII – struggled for two decades to maintain the continuity of the dynasty and the independence of her kingdom, eventually in vain.

Sibling marriage in the Ptolemaic dynasty was therefore only an occasional resort, and often an emergency measure. The reason for these sibling marriages lies in the dynastic necessity of conserving the dynastic continuity, and excluding non-Ptolemies from the inheritance. In this in fact the dynasty eventually failed, mainly because of the frequent dynastic murders, and in 80 BC the inheritance had to go to Ptolemy XI, who was not really genetically part of the dynasty; similarly Kleopatra VII and her brother were, in Greek eyes, the products of irregular marriage. The marriage practices of the dynasty had been unsuccessful. (It may also be noted that the intermarriages do not seem to have seriously degraded the abilities displayed by the members of the dynasty; Ptolemy VI, the son and great-grandson of sibling marriages, was one of the more capable of the Ptolemaic kings; his brother Ptolemy VIII was also a very competent man, even if widely disliked.)

The exclusivity implied by these sibling marriages also became part of the policy of the Seleukid dynasty. Until the marriage of Antiochos III in 221, all the marriages of Seleukid kings had taken place with princesses from outside the dynasty, with none related more closely than first cousins. Antiochos, however, adopted the sibling marriage policy in the 190s by marrying his eldest son, Antiochos the Young King, to his daughter, Laodike.[63] When the Young King died before his father, Laodike was remarried to the next in line, who became Seleukos IV. After Seleukos was assassinated, his younger brother took power as Antiochos IV, and became Laodike's third husband (and contrived the death of her son by Seleukos).[64] She had children by all three of her brothers.

Antiochos IV was ultimately succeeded by his nephew Demetrios I (the son of a sibling marriage), and he married another Laodike, who was probably his sister. She had been married first to the Macedonian King Perseus, and when Perseus was defeated and captured by the Romans, she had been sent back to Syria, where she was when Demetrios arrived to claim the kingship.[65] The intervention of the Ptolemaic Kleopatra Thea, herself the product of a sibling marriage, into the Seleukid dynasty paradoxically brought this sequence of Seleukid sibling marriages to a halt, and so far as we can see it was not revived, though the succession of husbands for Kleopatra herself has the same air of maintaining the dynastic continuity – though it was also, as has been noted, the result of a series of political emergencies. It was probably just in time that the sibling marriages ended, since by the time of that last marriage, the inter-breeding had probably become dangerous, a factor which had been evaded by the Ptolemaic practice. There is, of course, no evidence to suggest that this cessation had been deliberately decided on the part of either dynasty. Whatever genetic knowledge existed in the chancellories of both dynasties, it was social rank which determined marriage partners at this level, not the prospects of, or the dangers of, interbreeding.

Sibling marriage, therefore, was a good deal less prevalent than its noto-riety might suggest. It did not exist at all in the Antigonid dynasty, nor does it seem to have occurred in the minor dynasties of Asia Minor, Greece, and elsewhere. On the other hand, marriages of uncles and nieces, half-brothers and half-sisters, and between first cousins, became fairly common, simply because of the social requirement that kings must marry princesses of their own rank. The Attalid dynasty deliberately escaped such practices, making a virtue of choosing wives not only from non-Attalid women but also from non-royal women, though Eumenes II married the daughter of Ariarathes IV of Kappadokia, and she was then married to his brother after Eumenes' death.[66] Neither had children by her, which resulted in the dynasty resorting to the succession of the sons of Eumenes' concubines, and its eventual extinction.

The exclusivity of the Ptolemaic dynasty was such that after the first generation, no Ptolemaic princess was married outside the family, with the exceptions of Berenike (a younger daughter) going to Antiochos II – a marriage which could fairly be called a disaster for both families – and Kleopatra Thea (another younger daughter) being sequentially married to three Seleukid kings. Exclusivity ended when the daughters of Ptolemy VIII were married to a series of Seleukid kings after Kleopatra Thea's death. The Seleukid practice, on the other hand, was quite different. From the start, when Seleukos I's daughter Phila was married to Antigonos II Gonatas of Macedon, it was normal Seleukid practice to send princesses off to marry other kings, often of lesser renown. The dynasties of Pontos and Kappadokia, that of Ptolemy, and the Antigonids, were all presented with princesses as wives, sometimes more than once. This in effect widened the scope for recruiting wives for Seleukid kings, since daughters of such unions were obviously high-born relations. Antiochos III, for example, the fifth generation of the family, by which time exclusivity was certainly setting in, was married to Laodike, the daughter of King Mithradates of Pontos.[67] Pontos was a minor kingdom, and as such would not normally have been within the scope of the recruitment of a princess for a Seleukid king, but Laodike was in fact Antiochos III's first cousin, due to an earlier Seleukid princess being given to an earlier Mithradates.

It is difficult to find information on the lives of Hellenistic queens, and it is even more difficult to do so on the subject of their children.[68] We can probably list most of the children who were born, at least in the major dynasties, but their lives are generally opaque, and in many cases even their names are not known. It is probable that a considerable number of babies were stillborn or died as infants (two children of Ptolemy III and Berenike died in infancy, for example); Hellenistic kings clearly had access to the very best medical attention, and the best supplies of food, but this would hardly guarantee that every child lived.

Those children who survived were educated within the Palace, and here we do have some information. Philip II employed Aristotle as a tutor for Alexander, and he was joined by boys from the corps of royal pages who were attached to the court. These included Ptolemy, Seleukos, and Lysimachos, and others of their generation, and this was one of the foundations both of their friendship and of their rivalry. Philip's example in this as in many other things, was followed by the successor kings. Ptolemy II employed Apollonios of Rhodes, the poet, as tutor to his children, and it seems that Eratosthenes of Cyrene, a contemporary of Berenike, who probably knew her as a child, was used in the same way.

The boys would need some training in military matters, such as swordplay, horse riding, and wielding the sarissa, the Macedonian weapon – Ptolemy V, a delicate youth, is said to have been accomplished in hunting, riding, and fencing – and many kings fought in battle.[69] The girls were provided with an education alongside their brothers, and their curriculum clearly included more than such traditional women's accomplishments as sewing and weaving. Arsinoe II corresponded when adult with her former tutor, Strato of Lampsakos, apparently on scientific subjects;[70] Berenike II employed Eratosthenes to educate her children, and a place for educating the royal children was, of course, one of the main purposes of the Museum at Alexandria. In general, it would seem that both sexes were treated more or less equally in the general education, in music and mathematics, and so on, at the level of the royal family. Literacy, after all, was universal among the royal families of the time.

From the dynastic point of view, the purpose of children was either to inherit the throne or to be useful marriage pawns in the diplomatic game which was played throughout the eastern Mediterranean. This created several dilemmas. The casualty rate among children was high, perhaps not so high among the royal families as among the ordinary population, but royal children did die in infancy. It was therefore necessary for dynasties to produce more than one son, though daughters were to a certain extent optional. However, more than one son could mean competition for the succession. In the Seleukid family the eldest son of Antiochos I, Seleukos, was executed in 267, and the only reason one can suppose is that he was aiming to replace his father as king. Only twenty years later, in 246, the two sons of Antiochos II quarrelled over the succession, Seleukos II, the elder, was generally recognised as king, but his younger brother Antiochos, nicknamed Hierax, 'the Hawk', possibly with the encouragement of their mother Laodike, operated in Asia Minor as king.

This problem was not absent in the Ptolemies as well, though it took rather longer to emerge – the issue was clearly present in the mind of Ptolemy IV when he ordered the killing of his uncle and his brother. Ptolemy VI and Ptolemy VIII, brothers, disputed the succession over a period of at least twenty years between 168 and 145. The issue became even more fraught in the later decades of both dynasties, with civil wars – that is, dynastic wars – a frequent occurrence in Syria and Egypt from about 120 onwards.

The problem does not seem to have existed in either the Antigonid or the Attalid dynasties, both of whom had public reputations for family harmony. In 160, Eumenes II was reported to have died in an accident at Delphi, and, to great public amusement, his younger brother Attalos II immediately married his sister-in-law; the amusement came when it emerged that he had been misinformed, and Eumenes II was still alive. The lady then calmly returned to her first husband.[71] But immediate remarriage of widows was a common requirement; among the Antigonids the minority of Philip V, whose father Demetrios II died unexpectedly in battle in 129, was covered by his cousin Antigonos, nicknamed Doson, who had quickly married his predecessor's widow, and it may have been this which was the prime reason for the two remarriages of Laodike to her brothers Seleukos IV and Antiochos IV. Antigonos performed successfully enough in his first year as regent to be elected by the army as king, in a process which replicated the accession of Philip II to power, and like Philip with the rightful king Amyntas, Doson carefully guarded his ward.[72] He then conveniently died just as Philip was about to reach his majority. By contrast, when the Seleukid Antiochos IV was in the same position, he assumed the title of king – without any form of election, it seems – and married his predecessor's widow, thereby becoming the stepfather of her son. Five years later he organised the boy's killing.[73] When he himself died his son became Antiochos V, under the guardianship of the regent Lysias, but when the rightful king Demetrios I arrived in Syria, he ordered the killing of both the boy and the regent.[74]

The problem of the succession, therefore, was always a difficult one, and tended to provoke violence among members of the royal families.[75] The complication between Eumenes II and Attalos II was sorted out amicably (at least so far as we know), but such an outcome was extremely unusual, even unique, and murder was much more common. The selection of an heir was one of the prerogatives of any king, and he was not necessarily bound to choose his eldest son. Ptolemy I preferred his eldest son by his second wife Berenike, who became Ptolemy II Philadelphos, to his eldest son by Eurydike, Ptolemy Keraunos. To ensure that his choice really did succeed, he made Philadelphos joint king in the last two years or so of his life. Seleukos I had done this already, making his eldest son Antiochos joint king, when he was married to Stratonike. Seleukos' next action illustrated his apprehension of the possible danger in this process, for, once an heir was selected, and installed as joint king, he was clearly liable to anticipate the death of his father. Seleukos dispatched Antiochos (and Stratonike) to be his viceroy in the eastern territories, where, as it happened, Antiochos may well have been able to point out that he was half Baktrian, as the son of Apama. This separated the two kings by a major distance, and prevented legal disputes. (The whole sequence of events is an illustration of Seleukos' political inventiveness). Antiochos when king made his eldest son joint king, but then had him killed, seemingly for presuming on his inheritance.

Installing a chosen heir was not necessarily the safest thing for a king to do; but not choosing an heir could be just as dangerous, since if there was only one son he would be the obvious choice anyway, but if there were several of them one might carry through a *coup d'état* to anticipate or derange his choice.

The transition from one king to another was always a dangerous moment, and there are vanishingly few occasions when a crisis did not occur. The early successors of Alexander more or less managed the issue – Lysimachos being a major exception – but from then on succession crises were constant. This, of course, was one of the major causes of the decline in power of all the kingdoms, though it has to be said that, until the emergence of the sacralised kingship of mediaeval Europe, no other policy solved the problem. The only way through the issue that most people could see was to murder competitors, an unpleasant process, and one which sets a limit to our understanding and appreciation of family affection within the royal Hellenistic families.

Chapter 5

Kings and Palaces

Kings and palaces go together, and have done since the institution of kingship developed. The Hellenistic kings therefore inherited in this an age-old custom and institution. As a result, every kingdom had at least one palace, and the larger kingdoms had several.[1] It is quite likely that the Akhaimenid palaces had some powerful influence upon the succeeding Hellenistic kings, though in many cases the Hellenistic kings were much more mobile than some of the Persian Great Kings. These men did move regularly between the three main cities of Persepolis, Babylon, and Ekbatana; there were several palaces in Babylon, and these continued to be used by Alexander and then by the Seleukid kings; they had been inherited by the Akhaimenids from the preceding Babylonian dynasty which had ruled from *c.*620 to 539. So by the Hellenistic period the palaces in that city had been used as royal power centres for at least three centuries, perhaps longer. There were other palaces at Pasargadae, the original Akhaimenid centre, originating perhaps with the successes of Cyrus the Great in the sixth century, and at Susa, another pre-Akhaimenid royal centre. These continued in use in the Akhaimenid period, just as did those at Babylon.

It seems likely, given that the Persian kings were very recent arrivals on the royal scene when Cyrus the Great captured Babylon in 539, that it was the royal palace there which had provided the general model for the great Persian palace at Persepolis, and that of the Median kings at Ekbatana. The former 'Palace of Apries' (Wahibre = Psamtik I, 664–610) who reigned at Memphis in Egypt had also been inherited by his successors of the 26th dynasty, by the Persian governors, by the pharaohs of the 27th to 30th dynasties, and then by Alexander and so by Ptolemy I. This therefore provided another compelling model for royal living and working alongside those at Babylon and Persepolis.

This is not necessarily to say, as is often assumed, that the Persian and Egyptian palaces – there were others – provided the direct model for Macedonian and later Hellenistic buildings. They probably did not have to, for royal palaces, after all, have the same function whether Persian, Macedonia, Roman, modern European, or in a democratic republic. They were a combination of several elements: a domestic home, on a large scale to be sure, but they were the places where kings and their families normally lived; slave and servant quarters; barracks for the guards, and a secure refuge for kings; offices in which the kings and their bureaucrats worked and kept their records; the royal treasury; temples to communicate with the gods; reception rooms in which visitors are greeted and entertained; dining rooms of several sizes, from intimate to banquet size.[2] Given this collection of factors and functions, all of which were necessary if the kingship was to operate effectively, the difference between the various palaces is a matter of architecture, personal preference, and social customs, and the search for preceding models seems vain.

The size of the greater Hellenistic kingdoms made it necessary for there to be several palaces spread throughout the royal territories. Not all these buildings necessarily qualify as 'royal'; each provincial governor needed a palace as well, and would probably occupy a 'royal' palace if the king was absent. Of course, if the king came to visit he would occupy the governor's palace, quite possibly expelling the governor for a time, and the building would temporarily become 'royal'. But certain palaces were distinctively royal, and would be reserved for royal use. The three Akhaimenid buildings already mentioned are examples. In the Hellenistic period, the varying sizes of the kingdoms had its effect on the sizes of the kings' pretensions, but there were multiple palaces in all the greater states. One result of this, and of the architectural and administrative inheritance of the fragments of Alexander's empire which developed into kingdoms of themselves, was that the Hellenistic palaces were as often based on the smaller palaces of the provincial governors as on the monsters of the Akhaimenids. There were also other palaces on which the Hellenistic kings could model their own buildings. Of particular relevance would be palaces developed by the Macedonian kings. Archelaos had built a new palace at Pella in about 400 BC and this was extensively and repeatedly rebuilt by Archelaos' successors as Macedonian kings; its original form is unclear.[3]

Elsewhere in the Greek world the Syracusan tyrant Dionysios I developed a palace on the Ortygia island/peninsula in the city not long after.[4] The palace was destroyed when the Dionysian monarchy was overthrown by Timoleon in the 340s, but it was rebuilt by Agathokles, and this was then used and rebuilt by Hiero II.[5] Access to the island was restricted by a fortified gate and wall, and this restriction continued under Roman rule, so emphasising that the Roman Republic had taken on the role of the Syracusan kings after the conquest in 212; nothing of the building survives but conjectural reconstructions of it have been made based on the several source descriptions and some possible fragments found in excavations.[6]

The curious semi-state in Karia which the satrap Mausollos semi-detached from Akhaimenid rule in the fourth century had a major palace at Halikarnassos.[7] None of this building survives, and even its precise site is uncertain.

It was probably located on a headland overlooking the harbour entrance, but also looking out to sea (and so very similarly sited to the palace at Syracuse on its island). It is said that the palace overlooked a 'secret harbour' where Mausollos could assemble a fleet without being detected; it might also have been useful for a quick getaway if it was needed. It is probably buried under the Hospitaller Knights' castle.[8]

It seems unlikely that Dionysios I would have had an Akhaimenid model in mind for his palace, but Archelaos and Mausollos could well have taken the governors' palaces in Asia Minor as the basis of their buildings – Mausollos, of course, was himself technically an Akhaimenid governor. Of course, it is always possible that these rulers and their architects could think up the plan for themselves. Given the needs of the rulers, any palace is always likely to be similar to any other, for it was largely a matter of function dictating form.

So the Hellenistic kings, if they needed a model for their palaces, had several they could use: Akhaimenid royal buildings or Egyptian palaces, Akhaimenid governors' palaces, and several Greek buildings in Macedon – which they knew from their early lives – Sicily, and in Greece, where there was a palace in Thessaly; there was another in Cyprus.[9] As it happened, they tended to adopt the example set by Ptolemy I in the great new city supposedly laid out by Alexander, and named for him. The great palace at Alexandria became the most renowned of Hellenistic palaces, and was built on a new site in a new city, and must be reckoned the first Hellenistic palace. Ptolemy's, or his architect's, inspiration is not known, though it has to be pointed out that Ptolemy knew the palace at Halikarnassos, having taken part in Alexander's siege of the city in 334, and of course was familiar with palaces in Macedon, and by the time he took control of Egypt he had seen the great Akhaimenid palaces, not to mention that at Memphis, which was his government centre until Alexandria had been built.

The palace at Alexandria was constructed on Ptolemy I's orders and is the best known of the Hellenistic palaces, since it was discussed by several commentators, notably Strabo, though his comments dated from the early Roman period. The palace itself has now vanished under the waters of the Mediterranean, so any 'reconstruction' has to be based on descriptions of a building which was then three centuries old.[10] There are other details which emerge incidentally from accounts of events in the palace, but in total it is difficult to produce a full and accurate description.[11] Ancient commentators tend to emphasise the splendour and wealth on display, and to minimise the fact that any palace was also a government workshop. The palace seems to have been a series of buildings covering a substantial area; these included a large audience hall, barracks for the guard, and so on, all in a large ornamental park; in total the palace occupied almost a quarter of the city. Intellectuals and writers were attracted by the idea of the Museum, the house of the Muses, whose library was supposed to contain a copy of every book ever written, but this was located some distance from the main palace buildings. In fact, the Museum was another government workshop, a school in which the children of the king and their friends were to be educated by the chief librarian, and where research materials for the use of the government were concentrated.[12]

The palaces at Syracuse, Halikarnassos, and Alexandria were all located on the coast. At Syracuse it was on the Ortygia Island, with access securely controlled by a fortified gate in the wall; at Halikarnassos it was on a promontory overlooking the city and its harbour; at Alexandria on a peninsula, which was also walled off from the city, though with a good deal of the palace buildings, including the Museum, outside that wall. It was also separated from the city by an area called the Basileia, which occupied a quarter of the city area, and which included temples, the zoo, gardens, and the Museum, imposing a clear separation between the city and the innermost palace; the name indicates clearly that the Basileia was part of the palace complex and subject to the king's authority, and not that of the city council. All these palaces also had a private harbour close by, supposedly for the royal fleet, but it could also be used for a quick royal escape in emergencies.

The Alexandria palace may or may not have formed the model for other palaces of the Hellenistic period (and the succeeding Roman); but most of these were situated inland, which is one major point of dissimilarity. Several of these other palaces were being developed at the same time as that in Alexandria, and so the precise similarities would likely be only generic, not specific. These other buildings would have been built anyway by the other kings, and, like that at Alexandria, several were being built before the royal titles were taken by Alexander's successors. The occupation of a palace was a necessary part of royalty's position, power, and function, and they scarcely needed a model to copy; the idea of the palace would be quite sufficient to inspire one to be built.

For example, the Alexandria palace was supposedly planned by Alexander, which is certainly possible, since he was present when the basic city plan was laid out, and the palace's layout conformed to the rectilinear city plan, but it was built on the orders, and thus to the eventual plan and requirements, of Ptolemy I, who gained control in Egypt in 323.[13] But he used Memphis, and the 'palace of Apries', as his government centre until about 311 (an inscription of that year reports that the government had moved to Alexandria by that time).[14] However, the palace complex was not completed for several more decades, and in fact was probably altered and adapted and rebuilt throughout the Ptolemaic period. The Museum, for example, was not founded until after Demetrios of Phaleron arrived at Ptolemy's court, sometime after 307, and who then persuaded the new king of the utility of such an institution, though, of course, the temple of the Muses, where the scholars were sent, already existed – this therefore is an example of a building changing its use, and this was probably fairly common.[15] Indeed, it is highly likely that no palace was ever 'completed'; many kings would feel the need to change or expand what they had inherited, not to mention the need for repairs and maintenance.

While the initial building in Alexandria was being constructed, Seleukos I had conquered Babylonia and Iran, countries which contained several defunct Akhaimenid palaces (Persepolis, which was in ruins after Alexander's sack, Babylon, Ekbatana, and others). He had established a new palace for himself in his new city at Seleukeia-on-the-Tigris.[16] In the years between 307 and 301 Antigonos Monophthalamos was living at his new city of Antigoneia in Syria, where a palace was built, and was advanced enough in construction by 306 to be the setting for his assumption of the kingship;[17] he had earlier occupied the governor's palace at Kelainai in Phrygia, and this was maintained as a royal palace by Lysimachos and the succeeding Seleukids.[18] There were several other such palaces in Asia Minor – Daskylion, for example, and the ruins of Halikarnassos. In Macedon Kassandros' new cities of Kassandreia and Thessalonike no doubt included royal palaces, and he had the use of those at Aigai and Pella.[19] In Sicily, Agathokles was rebuilding the palace on Ortygia at the same time. The Ptolemaic kings periodically travelled the length of Egypt, even as far south as Aswan; naturally they travelled by boat or barge – an enormous and spectacular barge, lovingly described in an exerpt from Kallixeinos in Athenaios, was in fact a floating palace. The king and his entourage were evidently intended to live on board during the voyages, but it was so unwieldy that, like its companion monster built as a flagship for the fleet (the Forty), it stayed in harbour at Alexandria.[20] There may also have been palaces in the major towns. Memphis certainly had a palace, and it seems probable that there was one at Ptolemais, and perhaps one at Thebes.[21]

That is to say, palaces proliferated as these kings became fully established, but in all cases they will have taken years to build. Whatever plan was made at the beginning, it was no doubt changed, and/or extended, possibly radically, during the construction phase, and even when it was 'finished', change and rebuilding will have continued. It cannot be believed, for example, that the palace at Babylon, built at the latest in the sixth century BC (and perhaps based on a still earlier version) was still viable or comfortable as a royal palace in the third century.[22] The temple of Esagila in the same city was being continually repaired and rebuilt; it is very probable that the palace was undergoing the same process.

Elsewhere the former Akhaimenid palaces at Pasargadae and Persepolis were no longer in use. Persepolis had been burnt down by Alexander, though possibly Pasargadae was used by the governor of Persis (or later local kings). The palaces at Susa – two have been located – were presumably used by the Seleukid governors; the larger palace fell out of use in the third century BC, the smaller would therefore be that used by the governor. They were close to the city's acropolis, which was the scene of fighting several times in the Seleukid period; no doubt they suffered damage.[23]

From archaeological investigations, the palace of the Macedonian kings at Pella is probably the best known of those in use in the Hellenistic period. This is one of the largest of Hellenistic palaces, half the size of that at Persepolis, and exceeded in size only by those at Alexandria and Ai Khanum in Afghanistan. Palace size is often difficult to estimate since the buildings were usually set in extensive grounds. That at Alexandria is estimated at 200 hectares, for example, and that at Ai Khanum at 87 hectares, but both included large open spaces, courtyards, or gardens. At Pella the area is 'at least 60 hectares', but the buildings occupy only about a third of that.[24] Enough of the buildings at Pella have been excavated to detect most of the functions to be expected – though all this is only interpretation, of course, not definitive. There are reception areas, some (minor) religious elements, and administrative offices. The royal apartments contained bedrooms, bathrooms, and private dining rooms, and there were apartments for guests. It is also known that it contained a large library, which was looted by Aemilius Paullus and taken to Rome in 168. The whole was enclosed within the city wall, and built on a hill which might be considered to be the city's acropolis – which therefore might be regarded as yet another of the palace's functions.

The original building was, as noted earlier, probably built about 400 BC by King Archelaos, but Philip II was the main driver for its expansion. The library is presumed to have been in large part the collection made by Antigonos Gonatas, the only king of the Macedonians who could pretend to serious intellectual activity. It was enlarged later, probably by Philip V. It thus, by this interpretation, mirrors the characters of the Macedonian kings over a period of over two centuries: Archelaos' ambition, Philip II's achievements, Gonatas' learning, and Philip V's restlessness and jealousy of other kings.[25] The Macedonian kings also had palaces at Aigai and at Demetrias, both reconstructed and/or expanded by Philip V, as at Pella, and probably another at Thessalonike, just as the Ptolemaic kings had a palace at Memphis, possibly one at Pelusion, and maybe even one somewhere in the south of Egypt, Thebes perhaps. The palace at Demetrias was smaller than that at Pella, but probably much the same size as Pella's was in Antigonos II's time. Again it was built around (three) courtyards, but this one was fortified much more sternly than that at Pella. Demetrias was, of course, a new city when Demetrios founded it, on or close to the coast, and since Demetrios was at odds with most of his neighbours, the city was vulnerable to attack. Philip V again expanded it somewhat.[26]

Since the kings moved about, and will have taken with them not only an army – they were generally on campaign when they moved – but part of the administrative apparatus of the kingdom, they required palaces in which they and their necessary entourages could be accommodated all through their territories. Those in Macedon and Egypt have been noted; in the Seleukid kingdom they are known to have existed at Seleukeia-on-the-Tigris, Babylon, and Ekbatana, Susa in Susiana, Baktra in the Far East, at Antioch and Seleukeia-in-Pieria in Syria, and probably at the military centre at Apameia; in Kilikia there was one in Mopsuhestia, which was eventually burnt down, with one of the kings inside it, by the enraged citizens; in Asia Minor there were palaces at Kelainai and Sardis. Another probably existed at Lysimacheia in Thrace, and Seleukos I may have inherited another from Lysimachos at Ephesos, though that city passed back and forth between his family and that of Ptolemy throughout the third century – Antiochos II's first wife Laodike lived there, presumably in a palace, during her separation from the king. There were probably others. But, of all these palaces, only the Macedonian examples have been excavated.[27]

The Seleukid kings' need for a series of palaces was due to the size of their kingdom. The main palace was eventually at Antioch, but this apparent priority may be merely because it remained the last palace under royal control as the dynasty expired, and it eventually became the headquarters of the Roman governors of Syria. Antioch was built on the site of the defunct city of Antigoneia, founded by Antigonos Monophthalamos, which was deliberately dismantled by Seleukos after his victory over Antigonos. The stones were said to have been used to build Seleukeia-in-Pieria, a telling symbol of the transfer of power and authority from one king to the other.[28] Therefore Seleukeia-in-Pieria had been intended to be the main city of Syria, and indeed perhaps of Seleukos' empire.[29] The city contained the mausoleum of the first kings, for example. However, it fell to Ptolemy III in 246, and was kept by him at the peace which ended the Third Syrian War in 241, which was again a deliberate matter of humiliating the enemy. Captive and under enemy control, the city inevitably ceded its priority in Syria to Antioch, with the result that Antioch's palace rapidly became the more important. By the time Seleukeia had been recovered by Antiochos III in 219, Antioch had been established as the government centre, and a large palace area had been developed.

In a curious reverse of this history, the palace of the governor of Ptolemy's province of Koile Syria at Ptolemais-Ake was used by several Seleukid kings once that region had become theirs after 200, and above all it was the scene of the proclamation of Alexander I Balas in 152, and of his marriage to Kleopatra

Thea. She later used it as her main palace during the 120s, and it was the last place under the control of Kleopatra Selene in 70 when Tigranes campaigned to take over the whole Seleukid inheritance. There seems to be no description or excavation of this building, and it was probably originally the palace of the governor of the Ptolemaic, then the Seleukid, province of Koele Syria.

The functions of the palaces are partly revealed in their plans, where these are known. Most included rooms leading off the main rooms or the court-yards which are interpreted as 'androns', rooms which had a variety of pos-sible uses, including functioning as dining and meeting places. These were therefore rooms where the king and his Friends (*philoi*) met, talked, and enter-tained each other, rooms which in many cases were usable for fairly small-scale meetings. These Friends were the instruments in many cases by which the kings implemented their decisions; as will be seen in the next chapter, they performed a whole variety of functions, including that of military com-manders, provincial governors, diplomats, and in effect anything the king wanted to have done was done by them. It was a varying selection of these men who formed his council.

The palace as a workplace was thus also a place where kings ensured that the men who were their Friends were brought together with him and others who formed the group of administrators, perhaps as a bonding exercise, more certainly where they were given instructions. It is known, for example, that Antiochos III participated in a Macedonian armed dance with his Friends in one of the palaces, which was quite possibly a regular event;[30] Antiochos IV's exploits in the streets of Antioch, such as standing for election in what he thought of as a Roman fashion, might be considered extensions of that prac-tice towards the population of the city.[31] All the Hellenistic kingdoms' gov-ernments operated in much the same way, and it is reasonable to assume that one room, not probably one of the ordinary androns, would be set aside as a council meeting chamber, where formal discussions took place. It is always best to designate, and furnish, such a special room, in order to ensure a degree of formality and precision to the meetings, and it is reasonable to assume that the kings understood this.

Other elements common to all palaces were the courtyards, sometimes several of them; some were in the residential area, others were for more public occasions. They could number anything from one to six in any particular palace, and might or might not be surrounded by a peristyle. It was usually off these open spaces that the smaller rooms, for storage, offices, and so on, lay. They were, of course, not simply open spaces, but architecturally necessary to bring light to the adjoining rooms, and fresh air as well in the Mediter-ranean heat.

The Attalid kings seem to have had just one main palace, at Pergamon. This was originally probably the building used by Philetairos, the first of the dynasty, who was originally a financial official of Lysimachos, and so the palace was a version of the governors' palaces established by his Akhaimenid predecessors. For a century this was effectively the only place the Attalid rulers controlled, hence its dynastic importance. It was also, very obviously, a fortress, built on a dominating hill, surrounded by steep sides and protected by solid walls. The dynasty faced numerous militant enemies throughout its existence. When Eumenes II finally, from 188, gained undisturbed control of much of Asia Minor, they will have inherited older palaces – at Kelainai, Lysimacheia, and Daskyleion – but these do not seem to have been maintained as royal palaces; Pergamon had always been the centre of their power and it remained so.

The Pergamon palace was built on the craggy hill which had housed the treasury which Philetairos had first guarded, and then controlled. Gradually, the whole hilltop was built over, though the main development seems to have come, not surprisingly, after 200 BC.[32] It has been well examined, and the site provides evidence for much of the ideological content of Hellenistic kingship. Within the walls there is, of course, the house in which the king and his family lived, together with separate quarters for the women of the household, and for the slaves and servants. There is also a building in which the guards were quartered, for there is no point in having a fortified palace unless you are going to have men to guard it. Again, these residential areas were under more or less constant constructional change and maintenance; at least five successive palaces have been detected, beginning with one on the northernmost spur of the rock, which was replaced by barracks and the arsenal, and which was presumably the palace of Philetairos; palaces IV and V (II and III are mainly extensions of the first) date from the first half of the second century, and were built when the dynasty was in its pomp. These were built along the eastern wall of the hill, leaving a considerable space before them for monumental buildings. One (IV) is identified as 'residential', and the other (V) as 'official'.[33]

There were at least two temples on the site, one of which is aligned differently from every other building, and was probably present on the site when Philetairos took control. It then became dedicated to Athena Nikephoros, as perhaps an early celebration of victory; the other was to Dionysos, who had been adopted as the divine ancestor of the dynasty. The Athena temple was originally that of a local deity which had existed on the site well before the Attalids, and probably before even the Persian conquest. It was therefore a local deity, and preserving and beautifying its temple was a gesture to the non-Greek population of the surrounding Mysian countryside, as well as a means of honouring the deity of the place. The great library, which rivalled that of Alexandria, was housed close to the Athena temple. It was given by Mark Antony to Kleopatra VII, though it is not altogether clear that the books were actually delivered to Egypt; some of them at least remained at Pergamon to be sold off later.[34]

The dynastic temple was, of course, Greek, and was a proclamation that the Attalid dynasty appealed particularly to the Greeks of the cities of the coast of Asia Minor. This was all the more necessary because the dynastic progenitor, Philetairos, was probably not Greek, but Paphlagonian. The main Dionysos temple was below the main level, beside the theatre which was carved into the hillside; there was also a smaller family/dynasty shrine on the upper level.

Palaces were therefore not simply living and working quarters, they were also dynastic statements of power, of divine favour, and of military strength. The Museum at Alexandria was centred on a temple to the Muses; the citadel at Pergamon featured a huge sacrificial altar, the Altar of Zeus, decorated with elaborate sculptures celebrating the victory of the dynasts over the local barbarian enemy, the Galatians. At the Macedonian palaces the religious element was much less emphatic, but it is presumed that all of them contained a shrine dedicated to the dynasty.[35] There were temples close by at both the Pella and Demetrias palaces, though that scarcely signified much, given the ubiquity of temples in all Greek cities. But the Attalids had less legitimacy as royalty on their side than the Antigonids, and perhaps as a dynasty were much less confident in their powers – they only acquired a substantial area of territory after 188 – and perhaps they needed the boost that the emphasis on temples at Pergamon gave them.

Palaces were also citadels of power, not merely bureaucratic and administrative, but military as well. This is all too obvious at Pergamon with the palace perched on a fortified hill, and a substantial barracks on the most obvious place; the Syracusan palace similarly included a sizeable barracks. Even where a palace was situated within a city, as at Demetrias, it was separated from the general population by walls. At Syracuse the southern half of Ortygia was occupied by a barrack complex capable of housing 10,000 soldiers.[36] At Alexandria the palace was on a peninsula walled off from the rest of the city, and separated from the nearest part of the city by the Basileia, the royal part of the city – a double isolation, though, as Theokritos' poem on the Adonis festival shows, access to the Basileia was easy on festival days, and probably during the rest of the year as well, though it could probably be isolated fairly easily as well.[37] The palace at Antioch was separated from the city by the river, and was built on an island;[38] it was sufficiently isolated from the city so that when Alexander Balas became unpopular, he was accused of hiding himself away in the palace, 'lounging among his bevies of concu-bines'.[39] At Syracuse the palace's situation was much the same, at least under Agathokles, when it was fortified and isolated from the city by a separately reinforced gates and wall. At Demetrias the palace was fortified and lay on one side of the city, which was also separately reinforced. These buildings were clearly capable of being defended against external attack, and against internal threats as well. At Cyrene, the acropolis (which presumably contained the palace in Magas' time) was fortified as strongly against the city as against the outside world.[40]

At times, of course, it was the guards in the palace who were the danger, as at Seleukeia-on-the-Tigris, during the Seleukid dynastic war between 246 and 227. At a time when the royal authority in the area was divided and had sensibly diminished, the guards of the palace repeatedly broke out into what the local chronicler refers to as rebellion.[41]

It is perhaps customary now to emphasise that aspect of Hellenistic royal palaces which might be called the social-ceremonial. This is summarised in the curious term 'theatre of royalty', and the proximity of actual theatres to some royal palaces has led to the suggestion that what the kings were doing in their public appearances at the palaces was staging a performance, perhaps to bedazzle their subjects.[42] The problem with this, on a practical level, is that most palaces are nowhere near theatres. It is certainly the case that the palace at Pergamon, on top of its crag, had a theatre carved into the flank of that stone hill, but given the normal shape of Greek theatres this would have been an obvious site for one, even if the palace had not been already there; nor is there any obvious physical connection between the two. Given that the palace was fortified, it would have been militarily dangerous to have easy access by way of the theatre. It is also apparent that the theatre at Aigai in Macedon was close to the royal palace, for it may have been there that Philip II was assassinated in 336.[43] The main source for this interpretation and theory, however, is an incident in the life of Demetrios Poliorketes, when he gathered the citizens of Athens together in the theatre, ringed the people with armed guards standing on the highest points in a manifestly threatening manner, and appeared through the main actor's entrance himself to pronounce Athens' fate.[44]

This incident, however, owes rather more to the flamboyant personality of Demetrios than it does to any idea of royalty as indulging in a theatrical display. At neither of the two greatest of Hellenistic palaces, at Alexandria and Antioch, is there any sign of a theatre close to the palace, and in neither case was it practical to build a theatre large enough to contain the local citizenry. At Alexandria in 205/204 a coup was staged within the palace, involving only officials and the guard; the citizens of Alexandria had no part in it – this could certainly be classified as 'performance', but was held in secret.[45] Similarly, neither the Pella nor the Demetrias palaces had theatres close to them, so if any theatrical display took place it did so within the palace. The theatricality of Antiochos IV, with his elections and his roistering in the streets of Antioch, is more busking than elegant display[46] – or, as with Demetrios in the theatre at Athens, menace. It is best to regard meetings which may well have taken place between the king and his people in theatres as having taken place in such venues simply because they were the most convenient; the theatre's acoustics made it sensible to use such a place if a large audience was to be addressed orally, but kings did not indulge in such meetings for any reason other than to enforce, or reinforce, their authority.

The idea of public performance of a sort by kings, of course, does not require a physical theatre, and the theory is intended to be a general statement rather than a series of particular performances. At Antigoneia in 306 Antigonos Monophthalamos staged a ceremony of receiving the news of his son's victory at the battle of Salamis in a way which particularly attracted attention. The messenger, his diplomat Friend Aristodemos of Miletos, walked slowly and deliberately up to the palace from the coast, while Antigonos put on an act of nervous impatience; on the news being announced a diadem was produced and Antigonos was proclaimed king.[47] The audience may have been taken in – and Diodoros the historian certainly seems to have been – but then the whole thing was clearly a pre-arranged performance – the audience was a select group, probably mainly of the king's Friends, who were guaranteed to support him anyway; the citizens were not involved, still less consulted. There were undoubtedly other performances of a similar type by other kings, from funeral ceremonies to the proclamation of new kings, as in the secret coup at Alexandria in 205/204.

But these events were either pre-arranged, or at least expected. To regard such events as central to the conduct of a monarchy is to accept superficiality as substance, and to ignore the reality of work and the continuing exercise of authority. The palace was much more than a site for public performances – and most such ceremonies were inaccessible to any people who might be impressed; those who could attend did so because of their positions or their wealth, and would not be impressed at all. The 'theatre of royalty' is only a minor factor in the purpose and life of a palace.[48] This is not to deny the existence of ceremony in royal affairs, but only to insist on its relative unimportance.

The king, it has to be emphasised, was the centre of all events, all work, all ceremony, everything that happened in the palace, and the palace was where all this took place. Further, the 'palace' was wherever the king was, whether he was inside a building or not. Without his presence the population of the physical palace was much reduced, and the activity which normally took place was much quieter. That is, the government centre of the kingdom remained with and around the king, wherever he was. In Antiochos III's great eastern expedition, Antiochos left his wife Laodike in control at the palace at Antioch, and so overseeing the routine administration. She evidently ran what administration was left in Syria and the western provinces, but she still had to refer major decisions to Antiochos on the march.[49] That is, she controlled only part of the administration, no doubt that part which was largely routine; Antiochos took the rest on the road with him; this division probably also took place under Antiochos IV, when Lysias remained in Syria while Antiochos campaigned in the east. This was the halfway stage in the development of an institutionalised administrative system in which the government became rooted in one place – yet kings still took most of the senior personnel with them. In the Hellenistic period only the Ptolemies in Egypt went any further in developing a permanent and stationary administration.

(It is worth noticing, however, that the position of Laodike in Antioch while Antiochos III was on campaign in the east made it unnecessary for the king to appoint a minister to take charge of the administration. His early experience at the hands of Hermeias had no doubt been sufficiently unpleasant that he did not appoint anyone to such a position at any time during his reign who was not a member of his family – and he clearly trusted his wife and his sons; Antiochos IV did not have that hang-up in leaving Lysias in control.)

The increasing size of some of the palaces, notably those in Macedon, which have been excavated and can be seen to have expanded during the Hellenistic period, might suggest that the administration had expanded also. In fact the enlarged size, which seems to have been developed at Pella and at Demetrias in the reign of Philip V, is more likely to be due to the king's vainglorious self-regard. The elaboration of the palaces was an aspect of ceremonial, by which the king constructed impressive buildings for the sake of impressing – another aspect is the production of great processions full of soldiers and displays of wealth. The grandeur of the Alexandrian palace seems to have had something of this sort about it, and the deliberate expansion of the Pella palace, overlooking the city of which it was part, is another example. This, if anything was, was an inheritance from the Akhaimenids, who also went in for impressive grandeur. But it was still not the essence of the palace and its function.

The minor monarchies which had already existed before the Hellenistic period – in Sicily, the Spartokids in the Crimea, in Epeiros – had of course developed their own palaces, and these may well be one of the sources for the layout of the palaces of the Hellenistic kings. The increasing numbers of minor kingships which proliferated on the fringes of the greater kingdoms also meant that new palaces were developed. Even the briefest of kings worked at this; the new city of Seuthopolis in Thrace was developed by King Seuthes II of Thrace, who was a contemporary of Lysimachos. The city included a small palace, placed in the corner of the city, and walled off from the rest of the citizenry in the usual pattern, even though Seuthes' kingship seems to have faded as soon as he died.[50]

The Spartokid kings of the Crimea had their palace at Pantakapaion, walled and crowded with buildings. This seems to date from 350–325, and so was contemporary with the increasing regard to kingship which resulted from the achievements of Philip II and Alexander. The date also suggests that the palace was more likely to have been based on Philip's building than on any other.[51]

Similarly Magas' brief kingdom of Cyrenaica had a royal palace on the acropolis at Cyrene; when Ptolemy III gained control of the area he deliberately made Ptolemais the government centre, and the governor's palace was built there, in his name city, thereby reducing the power and influence of the city of Cyrene, which was the centre of opposition to Ptolemaic rule;[52] Cyrene duly faded. The Ptolemais palace is large and grand enough, but it is situated in the centre of the city, and had no obvious defences, not even a continuous wall around it; it was clearly not a royal palace, but one for a governor, who was apparently thought to be in much less danger from the citizenry than a king.

We can expect that a palace was built by King Pyrrhos in Ambrakia, which city he developed as a dynastic centre. It is not clear if earlier Epeirote kings had a palace anywhere; they were probably peripatetic, moving between the tribes which constituted the federation, to the formation of which they owed their position as kings; they were thus constrained by their position and had very limited royal powers. Pyrrhos, however, succeeded in gaining control of Ambrakia as a personal possession and so he could build there, but there must have been royal houses in other parts of the kingdom. The Bithynian kings built up the city of Nikomedeia, and probably constructed a palace there. The Mithradatids presumably also did so at some unknown place in their kingdom, perhaps at Sinope, once they had gained control of that city. The seceding Judaeans in Palestine had a palace in Jerusalem by the 140s, but this was probably the house of the high priests who preceded the Hasmoneans (who, of course, owed their authority in part to holding that position as well). This was only a few years after establishing a quasi-independence, and by 134 Simon Maccabee had a country house at Dok on the hills above Jericho.[53] Later the extravagant King Herod built a new palace in Jerusalem, and developed palaces at Jericho, and on the hilltops at Herodion and Masada, though all these were relatively small sites and buildings by comparison with the other palaces discussed here – and were unusually heavily fortified.[54] Every king had to have his palace, though Herod's were about the same size as a governor's palace in the greater kingdoms.

The palace at Ai Khanum in Baktria I have saved to the end, because it is a particular problem. It is in an odd geographical position, it appears to be extremely elaborate, and it is one of the largest of Hellenistic palaces, but it does not have the real feel of a royal palace. To be sure, it has many of the elements of a royal palace, such as a large courtyard, many smaller rooms, and it is close to a theatre, above all, its sheer size deserves to be emphasised. Of all the known palaces in the Hellenistic world, only that of Alexandria is larger. Ai Khanum is almost twice the size of the Babylon palace, three times that of Pergamon, and half as large again as that at Pella. But examining the plan of the city as a whole, it is evident that the palace constituted a far larger proportion of the area within the walls than would be healthy for a well-conducted economic establishment. It and the other main public buildings – the gymnasium, the theatre, the 'arsenal', and more – occupy almost half of the level ground alongside the river, while the rest of the city is partly occupied by the 'citadel', and a third of the area is separated off by walls. There are, of course, a few large houses, which in Roman times would be called villas, inside and out of the city, but none of the smaller houses which one would expect to have been located, though it has been assumed that they existed on the relatively small area of the upper city, and perhaps in the northern part of the lower. In short, the city has the look less of a normal city, and more of a large palace separated from the surrounding countryside. It may be noted also that the theatre, of the normal Greek type, is relatively small for a city the size of Ai Khanum; if it was constructed to accommodate the city population, that population was fairly small in relation to the city area – though if there was a substantial (Greek-speaking) rural population, they might fill the space.

The plan of the palace is also curious when compared with that of other palaces, which we know were rather more certainly royal headquarters. Rachel Mairs has discussed in detail the inner layout, in which entrances are regularly offset, blocking lengthy internal vistas, corridors give no access to rooms, and most of the space is devoted to large open courtyards.[55] Part of the building – about a quarter – is interpreted as the treasury, and the number of rooms is relatively few when compared with, say, Pella.

Geographically, Ai Khanum – its ancient name is still unknown, despite numerous guesses, and the royal builder and occupant, or occupants, if any, are also the subjects only of guesses – certainly had access to well-cultivated and productive farmland.[56] The city was also positioned in such a way as to make it defensible, though the wall separating the city from the surrounding land looks relatively flimsy, is long and vulnerable, and in fact shows evidence of having been breached. On the other hand, economically the palace looks much more like a fortified counting house. The discoveries of seals, pottery, lapis lazuli, and metals within the palace buildings strongly suggests that the palace's purpose was to hold and store the product of the local mines, particularly the lapis lazuli mines in Badakhshan, upriver along the Kokcha – 75kg of the stone, unworked, was left in the treasury when the city was abandoned.[57] The treasury could also contain the local tax take from the area, in cash and kind, which would be gathered in preparation for forwarding on to, probably, Baktra or Qunduz. That is, this complex was not necessarily a royal palace but at the most the palace of the local governor. It is certainly large enough to be a major royal palace; this does not make it one.

Every kingdom had to have its palace or palaces, and if it was an especially large kingdom, several. They could be the scene for display and ceremony, and the kings' wishes could be directed in part to the elaboration and decoration of the places they inhabited, but this is only on the surface. Such buildings will have undoubtedly impressed the king's subjects, who were perhaps partly envious and partly proud of his power and display, but anyone who visited or even saw a palace from a distance, knew perfectly well that it was a place of work, and under a king such as Antigonos Gonatas it was a place in part directed to the work of ensuring the well-being of those subjects. Unfortunately, too many kings considered life in a palace to be theirs by right; that way lay inevitable destruction for any dynasty.

Chapter 6

Kings and Governing

Kings owed their power and position to their command of an army. In primitive Macedon it was the army which acclaimed a new king;[1] in the more extensive Seleukid and Ptolemaic kingdoms assembling the whole army together for such a ceremony was impossible, but remnants of army acclamations continued to be staged. When Ptolemy V succeeded to the kingship as an infant, his regents assembled the royal guard, some bureaucrats, and a few citizens in a weak facsimile of an army acclamation.[2] Of course, this was done in part because they did not wish to be opposed (the regents had concealed the previous king's death and had murdered his well-liked wife), and only those present were their supporters.

And yet the Hellenistic kings were not pure autocrats, despite the fact that they are too often regarded as a species of absolute monarch. This may have been the theoretical position, given that there was a near total absence of any constitutional restraints on royal power, but a moment's thought indicates that if a king owed his position to acclamation by his army, no matter how exiguous the practices of that ceremony remained, he was not therefore absolute. And in a large kingdom, with the army scattered widely in garrisons, on the frontiers, and on campaigns, absolute power and control based on the army were out of the question – quite apart from the fact that the armies tended to be made up of the king's own subjects, with a clear stake in the kingdom, in lands and possessions, and in their families' lands and possessions. Riding roughshod over such a population was more dangerous for the kingdom than for his victims. In 143 Demetrios II in Antioch was besieged in his palace by the population when he turned his mercenary force on them and tried to extract extra taxes in order to pay the men, and then he had to face a rival king as well.[3] It was, of course, quite impossible for one man to rule even a relatively small kingdom like Macedon. All kings had only limited power due to geography and the limits on human capacity. Further, the army acclamations in fact disappeared, and kings normally owed their position to heredity – which was a precarious basis for their authority: kings needed support, and again, they also needed help.

None of the Hellenistic kings or kingdoms had any sort of constitutional government; any suggestion of that is no more than a modern theory constructed by historians and constitutional experts who had been trained in studying modern European constitutions. Even modern European constitutions are a relatively recent invention; perhaps the earliest would be that constructed by the Dutch in their revolution against Spain, though the most obvious one is that of the United States. (Magna Carta is not such a document.) Examining and explaining the British 'constitution' has been an absorbing pastime for such experts for centuries.

So the first thing to understand about the supposed absolutism of a Hellenistic king is that no such absolutism actually existed, whatever the theory, ancient or modern; every king had only limited power. Geography, in the sense of the sheer size of some of the kingdoms, of course, was one limitation. But there were also limits to what the king could do even close to or in the palace. Even a powerful monarch like Philip II or Alexander the Great required to be surrounded by men to whom he could give delegated authority. These men therefore had to be able to act independently of the king, and had to be supported by the king by his delegated authority. These were the agents used by kings to extend their own power to the rest of the kingdom. They acted in part because of their willingness to participate in the exercise of the king's power, but also for the rewards provided. Such rewards were almost invariably assignations of land, estates, which would support them in the style to which kings wished them to become accustomed. That is, the king became surrounded by men whom he had raised up, but who had then become wealthy and powerful in their own right, largely by his favour.

Many of these men actually inhabited the court, either living in the palace or in their own houses close by. At Pella in Macedon the large palace was honeycombed with rooms, only some of which the king could use and only some of which would be part of the government system; others were clearly guest suites. And near to the palace in the city outside were large luxurious houses in which it is supposed that the king's men lived. Such men were thus close by and available should he need them.[4]

The name used for these men was *philoi*, 'Friends', clearly originally a fairly informal term used in the Macedonian court long before Philip II and Alexander. In the Hellenistic period it became the standard term for men who were close to the king. It became almost a title of nobility, though kings did apparently attempt to control who used the title. In keeping with the general tenor of Hellenistic society, it tended to become a hereditary position, or at least the sons of Friends had relatively easy access to the court, and thus to gain the title of Friend for themselves. And, as these things are inclined to, the group of Friends also tended to develop a hierarchy. By the second century BC there were 'Friends', 'First Friends', 'Honoured Friends', 'First and Honoured Friends', and 'Kinsmen'.

At the Ptolemaic court the various titles took on a certain rigidity. Possibly this was because of the long periods of regency between 220 and 190, whereby the holders of these titles became accustomed to a ranking system. Certainly by the time of Ptolemy V in the 190s there seems to have been a fairly strict hierarchy of four grades. A generation later another grade was added appearing about 145 BC and so probably an initiative of Ptolemy VI who died in that year; yet another grade was added in about 120, and so by Ptolemy VIII. This elaboration was succeeded by a simplification and in the first century BC there were no more than three grades.[5]

How strict this hierarchy was in other courts is not clear. It was within the remit of any king to award such titles, and aiming to satisfy the aspirations of courtiers is probably the reason for the elaboration at the Ptolemaic court. But other courts were clearly less rigid. The Seleukid court went through so many upheavals in the second century BC and it seems unlikely that any strict system could have survived, though there are records of men with the title Kinsman and First Friend. Similarly the Attalid court was much less organised than the Ptolemaic and considerably smaller than the others. It seems unlikely that the Antigonid court, also fairly small, went beyond a single category of Friends.

These men who were regarded as royal Friends were the pool from which the king usually – but not always – chose his senior administrators. This complex apparent hierarchy in fact only seems to have existed – if it did – late in the Ptolemaic time of power, and might be seen as an example of a system elaborating itself as its power failed.

The ranks of the administrators, however, were not necessarily filled with men who were regarded as royal Friends. For there was also a parallel group of men who were appointed to particular offices of state – governors, ministers, envoys. Generally speaking these would be Friends, but not always, and is not always easy to decide who was a Friend and who was not. Among Ptolemaic courtiers there was a division between those who attended the court more or less full-time and those who were appointed to government or administrative positions in the empire. This was the distinction made by Polybios in discussing the decision made by Theodotos the Aitolian, who governed Koile Syria in the 220s, to switch sides and join Antiochos III during the Fourth Syrian War.[6] He was, of course, operating in a time when the court was an especially poisonous place, and further, he was a mercenary, able to look at the situation at Alexandria with a detached gaze. Those clustered at the court were, to Theodotos' view, merely in search of gifts or sinecures. Such men might be those whom sociologists would call 'favourites', men who had access to the king on a regular, perhaps informal, basis, and whose advice the kings valued.

There was also another set of men, who might be counted as royal Friends, but whose path to royal favour and employment was by way of the institution of royal pages. This is another of the court institutions which had been inherited from Macedon, quite probably another of those measures which began more or less informally, for it was common practice, in Greece and Rome as well as Macedon, for boys to be brought up in households other than their parents'. If that household was royal they became royal pages. The pages had various fairly elementary duties, such as serving the king at his meals or holding his horse when he mounted; they also acted as his guards, particularly at night, when they slept across the doorway to his bedchamber – guards presumably in the sense that they could sound the alert if a problem arose, but it was more likely they were there, sleeping across the doorway to the king's bedroom, as servants rather than active guardsmen. One or two of the pages were the king's own sons, and the whole group therefore grew as a particular set of boys of similar age, and were bound together in friendship and shared experiences. For non-royal boys the advantage was to become the friend of a boy who might become king, in which case he would almost certainly become a favoured Friend and counsellor.

They could be regarded as, and have the title of, royal Kinsman, and would be addressed by the king, and would address him as 'brother'. In addition, the tutors of the boys, who might be one man or several, were addressed as 'father', and were described as the king's 'foster father'. For non-royal boys, of course, this would quite probably gave them a much better education than they could get outside the court. This was a separate, perhaps parallel, set of men which would overlap with the Friends, and with the administrators, but were clearly in a much more favoured position to approach the king than most of the rest.

These were the men, therefore, whom the kings relied on as their instruments when they decided to implement their policies. They could be governors of provinces, that is, satraps, for the old Akhaimenid term remained in use; they could be commanders of forces, either in an independent role or in command of parts of the full royal army. They could be employed as envoys to foreign kings, or to cities inside or outside the kingdom. They could be employed as explorers, though this task became less common as it became assumed that after Alexander there was nothing left to investigate. They could also be employed within the palace in all sorts of administrative capacities. The sources of the period are littered with examples of all these tasks and offices.

It is difficult to sort out whether these tasks were regarded as successive, in the sense that a man might progress along what Roman historians regard as a '*cursus*'. Very few men are ever recorded in more than one job, so it is impossible to decide if there was anything like a career structure, though on the whole, it seems unlikely, given the fact that the king had the power to choose who his Friends should be, and therefore who should do what task. Occasional examples of men employed in different tasks do appear; for example, Diognetos, probably one of Antiochos III's 'Kinsmen', was employed in the delicate diplomatic task of securing a bride for the king, and was later employed as commander of Antiochos' small fleet.[7] But some men were repeatedly used in the same type of task. Hegesianax of Alexandria Troas, one of Antiochos III's envoys to Rome, was sent there several times, and clearly became a Roman expert at the court.[8] His colleague Menippos went to Rome as an envoy in 193, and then commanded the Seleukid forces in Boiotia and Thessaly in 192–191.[9] Both men were also courtiers, Menippos was responsible for putting up statues of the king at Delos and at Pergamon; Hegesaniax was recalled later as having refused to join Antiochos in the Macedonian armed dance (presumably, being from Alexandria Troas, he had no previous experience of it).[10] The king's 'foster brother' Antipater was employed to negotiate a truce with Ptolemy IV in 217, having commanded in the Raphia battle, and later he commanded the Tarentines (light cavalry) at the battle of Panion in 200. He was employed again to negotiate with the Romans in 188, both to secure a truce after the battle of Magnesia, and then to negotiate peace terms at Rome.[11]

The king had a powerful Royal Council, which he was expected to consult on all important matters. Repeatedly in the sources the council is cited, and it seems clear that minutes were often taken. Alexander is repeatedly recorded as discussing matters with his council, and Polybios, for example, is able to give in detail accounts of the debates within several councils, particularly in the first years of Antiochos III's reign.[12] (It may also be that bowdlerised versions of these council meetings had been published, and that he was relying on those.) By this time it is clear that there was a set procedure, with the most senior member speaking first, and the king summing up and giving a decision at the end of the meeting, and he was expected to make a decision in accordance with the majority view. If he did not, and went against the majority, he might find himself without support; in that case he might lose, or be defeated, in whatever action he hoped to take, and his power would be that much reduced.

It is clear from the several records of royal council meetings that this was one of the key institutions of all the kingdoms. It may not have been able to overrule a decision by a determined king, but since he relied on members of the council to implement whatever he had decided, it was clear that the members had the power to drag their feet over, or divert, whatever activity the king required of them. Members of the council would probably be chosen for exceptionally difficult tasks, especially if they had argued in favour of what was decided. It is also clear that on a number of occasions one man other than the king exercised a dominating influence. At the beginning of Antiochos III's reign this was the position of Hermeias, and in Demetrios II's first year he was dominated by the Cretan mercenary Lasthenes; at Alexandria Sosibios appears to have dominated the court in the last years of Ptolemy III and during the reign of his successor. These men were not necessarily Friends, but may be classified as 'favourites', that is, men who had been selected from outside the ranks of the Friends and the council as the king's prime adviser or minister; all three of those mentioned were in fact from outside the kingdoms whose kings they served.

These men became exceptionally powerful if the king was weak, or if the king was a child. It may well be therefore that their apparent power was only filling in the gap created by royal weakness. They were, however, once in position, very difficult to get rid of. Of those who are known, several were only removed by being murdered, sometimes by the king personally since no one else could be trusted to do the job, because the minister was well guarded, or the potential assassin was a client of his. In Seleukid history the prime example is Hermeias, Antiochos III's minister at the beginning of his reign. But Hermeias had enforced his position by arranging the condemnation and killing of his rival Epigenes. Hermeias' advice was frequently sensible, though at times it seems to have been implemented only against the wishes of the council. His power was such that only Antiochos himself was able to kill him, and then only by getting him alone by means of a ruse.[13]

In Ptolemaic history, prime examples are Sosibios, minister of Ptolemy IV and V, and his successor Agathokles. Both owed their positions of prominence to their descent: Sosibios' father had been chief of the guard under Ptolemy II; Agathokles was descended from Ptolemy I through his daughter Theoxene, the wife of the Syracusan tyrant-king Agathokles. Sosibios remained in power as the favourite of Ptolemy IV for twenty years, but when the king died he was instrumental in murdering the king's widow, Arsinoe, who, it is presumed, had been designated as regent for her infant son, Ptolemy V. Sosibios died soon after this, so far as we know from natural causes, and his power was inherited by Agathokles. But Agathokles, like Hermeias, attempted to rule alone, and in the interests of his own relatives; he must have been suspected of having had designs on the throne himself, given his ancestry; he was murdered by the Alexandrian mob in a riot.[14] From then on for a dozen years the regency was held by a succession of men who were able to gain power because they commanded part or all of the army. It was in this period that the Egyptian revolt in the Theban region developed into a direct challenge to the power of the Ptolemaic system. Having generals in control does not necessarily guarantee efficiency in government or victory in war, in fact all too often having the opposite result.

Sosibios was a member of a prominent family, three generations of which held important government positions under the Ptolemies: his father Sosibios was from Taras, and his sons, Sosibios and Ptolemaios, were active in diplomacy in the early years of Ptolemy V.[15] There were other 'official families' which can be traced in both the Seleukid and the Ptolemaic courts: Tlepolemos was governor in Lykia in 246, his descendant (probably a grandson), another Tlepolemos, was commander of the garrison at Pelusion when he seized the regency, also in Ptolemy V's minority.[16] One of the most notable families was that of Thraseas, whose line can be traced through five generations from the early third century to the late second, first working for the Ptolemies, then for the Seleukids.[17] There were no doubt other aristocratic families of the same sort, though the sources only rarely reveal them.

One aspect of these men is that in many cases they rose to power within a court in which they were foreigners. The first Sosibios was from Taras in Italy, Agathokles was a descendant of the king of that name of Syracuse, Thraseas' family came from Pamphylia, Tlepolemos was apparently of Iranian origin. In the Seleukid kingdom Hermeias was Karian and Lasthenes was Cretan. A tabulation of the origins of Friends suggests that Macedon and Greece supplied the majority of them to both courts.[18] That is, both kingdoms actually recruited capable man wherever they could be found, no doubt holding out the opportunity of both exercising power and getting rich. Asia Minor – a large diverse area – also supplied large numbers of such men. Among the Pergamene courtiers, however, the great majority came from Pergamon or Asia Minor. (There are certain difficulties with these figures, however. The classification of 'Macedonians' is ambiguous, since descendants of Macedonian settlers in the kingdoms retained that designation in future generations as a sort of honorary distinction; also the lists only include those whose origin is known; there were at least as many whose origin is not stated.)

Governing the provinces was perhaps the next greatest task for the king's Friends after giving him counsel in the royal council. Macedon was possibly small enough that the king could attend to most local matters personally, though when he controlled land outside the Macedonian kingdom and Thessaly, he certainly employed governors. Athens, for example, was subject to Macedonian control for much of the third century, and appears to have been governed with as light a rein as possible. The city remained self-governing, though Attika was held by a number of Macedonian garrisons, one of which occupied Peiraios.[19] By the 230s, this garrison was not sufficient to defend Attika against attacks from Achaia orchestrated by Aratos of Sikyon, though Aratos was not successful through these raids in persuading Athens to join his League. In the end a subscription was raised to buy out the Macedonian garrison. Aratos is said to have contributed a good deal of his own money to the fund, only to find that Athens was as ungrateful for this as it had been hostile to his raids. (It seems probable that Aratos' contribution was in fact Ptolemy's money.) By this time it is clear that the senior Macedonian in Attika was in fact the garrison commander, who, as it happened, was an Athenian mercenary soldier, Diogenes.[20]

At Corinth, by contrast, Antigonos Gonatas had installed a distant relative, Alexander son of Krateros as governor. Alexander's ambition led him to detach his viceroyalty from Antigonos' control, move into independence, and make himself king.[21] Such an event was clearly one of the dangers of delegating responsibility at a distance, and this was a problem which was faced repeatedly by the Seleukid kings. During the third century Baktria broke away, as did Asia Minor, both under men who had been appointed as governors. Baktria remained independent under the short dynasty of the rebellious governor Diodotos I and his son Diodotos II, and then developed into a rather disorderly, fragmentising, and aggressive kingdom.[22] A rather nebulous province called the Upper Satrapies was liable to be hijacked by its governor – Molon in 222, and Timarchos in 160.[23] It was out of this region that the army commander Philip attempted to displace Lysias as regent for Antiochos V in 164.[24] The problem here was that the large territory of the Upper Satrapies governorate, which was essentially upland Iran, required a large garrison, and the governor therefore felt that he had the power under his control to lunge for the kingship. As it happened none of these men ever succeeded, not that this prevented other ambitious governors from trying.

Asia Minor had broken away under one of Antiochos III's relatives, Akhaios, who had in fact been sent into the region to reclaim it from Attalos of Pergamon, who in turn had conquered it from a rebellious Seleukid, Antiochos Hierax. (Seleukid Asia Minor was thus separated from the main kingdom for over thirty years; in effect it must count as an independent state, a condition it resumed after 188, when the Attalids annexed it, courtesy of Rome.) Attalos was the representative of a new dynasty, originating with Philetairos, an official of King Lysimachos, who had ingratiated himself with Seleukos I at the latter's victory. Whether any of the Attalids ever counted as Friends of any Seleukid king is unlikely, but they certainly existed as one of several aristocratic dynasties who occupied large areas of Asia Minor. The third generation (Eumenes I) took the royal title; Akhaios, a member of another of these dynasties, did the same: others did not get the opportunity, but several continuing families can be identified.[25]

The Ptolemies faced the same problem of over-mighty subjects in disaffected lands, not so much in Egypt as in their other regions. Cyrenaica had a tendency to drift into independence under early Ptolemaic governors and Magas took the royal title to signify his independence; Cyprus similarly had a tendency to be placed under a governor for a long time to such an extent that one governor made himself wealthy enough after a long tenure that he was able to rescue the Egyptian treasury;[26] in Koele Syria, a military region, more than one commander deserted to the enemy in time of war.[27] In the Aegean Ptolemaic control of the numerous cities was always precarious. In at least one case a son of Ptolemy II Philadelphos, referred to as Ptolemy 'the Son', appears to have been induced into rebellion before being killed off by his military commander, the Aitolian mercenary Timarchos.[28]

Ambition in a royal subordinate was to be expected, but was also clearly dangerous. It perhaps reached the nadir of its negative effects in the disintegration of the Baktrian kingdom. This had remained under Seleukid control from the time of Seleukos I's conquest in about 305, until about 255; at that time it was placed by Antiochos II under the governorship of Diodotos. He remained in place for twenty years, for some time as a loyal governor but exercising increasing independence, and was succeeded by his son, also Diodotos, who was confident enough to claim the royal title.[29] For whatever reason he was overthrown by a man who may well have been one of his own provincial governors, Euthydemos, who held the kingdom and passed it to his son, Demetrios, but after that a plethora of kings are recorded. Demetrios led an expedition into India, but it seems to have been impossible for one man to control both Baktria and its Indian provinces. The number of kings recorded in the region after Euthydemos has run into the dozens.[30] Most of them, it must be assumed, must have been provincial governors who had made themselves into kings; their issuing of coins in their own names, and bearing their portraits, indicates that they were independent. Perhaps they felt that they were safer in their own particular mountain valley than operating as someone else's governor. And, of course, once the habit of taking independence develops it is difficult to eradicate. The inevitable result was the eventual conquest of all Greek kingdoms in the region by outsiders, nomads from the north, Parthians from the west, Indians from the east. A divided kingdom always invited invaders.

One of the main reasons for such rebellious behaviour by subordinate governors was probably that these men had their own substantial estates, possibly in the territories they were governing, which had been presented to them by the king. One example is Akhaios, the rebel against Antiochos III in Asia Minor. He was the grandson of another Akhaios who was probably a younger son of Seleukos I.[31] As such he was presented with a substantial area of central Asia Minor, where he is attested in an inscription.[32] That is to say, Akhaios II was posted as governor to a region in which his family already had large estates. This may well have seemed a good idea, since it would give him an interest in recovering it from Attalos I, and provided him with substantial personal resources for his use. Further, not only was he wealthy locally, but he was married to the daughter of the king of Pontos, his father Andromachos was another official of the Seleukid dynasty, and his sister Laodike had been the wife of Antiochos II, who had presented her with a substantial estate in the northwest. This concentration of family interests in Asia Minor may have been a reason for his appointment to recover the land, but it was also clearly too much for him, and must have been one of the main reasons inducing him to rebel.

Below the level of the provincial governors there were two types of administration: what may be termed 'urban' and 'rural', and the urban administration also fell into two types. Much of the Seleukid kingdom was sown with cities. The first group of these were old foundations, either Greek or Persian or Babylonian or even earlier, and had existed for long before Alexander's conquest. The second group were new cities, established by Seleukos I and his successors, and these were administered in a rather different way from the old. The Ptolemaic kingdom did not have such a concentration or number of urban settlements, but there were cities in parts of the kingdom, such as Koile Syria, Phoenicia, and Cyrenaica; the Ptolemies also for much of the third century controlled in various ways many of the cities along the Asia Minor coast, and many of the Aegean islands, who would usually count as *poleis*. In this case the overwhelming majority of cities predated Alexander.

The old cities and the new were contrasted not simply in age. The old cities had long had their own indigenous government systems, a mixture of oligarchies and democracies of various hues, varied by the occasional tyrant, and governed by a series of elected local officials chosen on an annual basis. They were also generally walled, and their populations were prickly when it came to being interfered with by a king. The cities had therefore to be treated very carefully by the kings; a rebellious city was not only dangerous in itself, and behind its walls it could resist attack strenuously, but its example might well persuade others to join it. The kings therefore generally adopted a version of the policy promulgated by Antigonos Monophthalomos, in his declaration at Tyre, a policy which has been called 'the freedom of the cities'.[33] The idea was that kings would not intervene in urban affairs, leaving them to govern themselves, but they would protect the cities, and in return they would be given presents, in lieu of taxes. That is, the relationship between kings and cities was conducted on the basis of separation, the cities retaining much autonomy at least in internal matters, and contact between the two, the king and the cities, was by means of envoys, maintaining the illusion that the cities were technically independent states.

This generally worked well enough, though the cities were always liable to take umbrage at something a king did. Generally it was not worth a king's effort to attack a city which had drifted out of his control. This meant that in certain areas, such as western Asia Minor, there was a discreet, and at times not so discreet, competition between the kings to gain the allegiance of various cities. The Ptolemies used their naval power for much of the third century to dominate the coastal cities; the Seleukids used their land power to dominate the inland cities; there was a constant low-key competition for the allegiance of cities in the borderland.[34]

This system had certain advantages for both kings and cities. The cities retained a considerable area for independent action, were free of garrisons by the licentious soldiery, and their taxation remained fairly light and under local control; at times they might find the king being particularly generous in presenting them with gifts, such as notable buildings, or contributions to a prominent temple. For the kings there was a guarantee of a more or less regular income from the cities, who were expected to present a gift to the king on more or less regular occasions, such as the anniversary of his accession, his birthday, the birth of an heir, his wife's birthday, to celebrate a victory, and so on. The gifts are usually described as a gold crown, which were, if they actually took such a form, no doubt melted down and the metal placed in the king's treasury. Perhaps just as important the king was relieved of the duty of placing a garrison in all the cities, either to control it or to defend it. The cities were numerous enough so that had he to do so his field army would have melted away – and, of course, were he to withdraw his garrisons from the cities he would probably find it extremely difficult to get them back in. So the kings gained a modicum of non-tax revenue, and did not have to spend it on fortifications and garrisons.

The new cities founded by and after Alexander were dealt with differently, on the pattern of the treatment of cities within the Macedonian kingdom. These places had a certain degree of self-government, but only in very local affairs, such as regulating the market and the temples. They were subject to the same regular taxation regime as the rest of the kingdom, and their male citizens were subject to service in the royal army. They cannot under any circumstances be considered to be like the traditional Greek *polis*, which had much more independence of action, particularly in foreign affairs, and some of these had survived as the 'old' cities. Within Macedon, however, there were also Greek cities which had to be treated with the same kid gloves that had developed among the old cities of Greece and Asia Minor – in Thessaly, for example, and along the Macedonian coast.

This may have been the pattern which Alexander the Great and Seleukos I – the two main city founders – had in mind, but in fact for Seleukos it turned out to be inadequate. (And in fact Alexander's cities were very few, though later large numbers of cities claimed to have been founded by him. In fact it seems that he founded not more than four or five cities during his lifetime.[35]) Antigonos I and his son Demetrios founded a few cities, as did Ptolemy I, but between them Alexander, Antigonos, Demetrios, and Ptolemy only managed about a dozen cities; Seleukos I and his son Antiochos I founded something of the order of thirty.

Establishing a new city was a major task, involving acquiring the land, organising the layout, arranging for the initial building, including the city wall and the positioning of the acropolis, financing all this, and above all, finding the new inhabitants. When Seleukos in 300 BC began establishing ten new cities in north Syria he could not possibly have done all this work himself. We do not know to whom he delegated the task, but many men must have been involved, one man presumably to oversee the whole task for each of the new cities, an architect and planner for each site, and others sent out to search for and recruit the colonists. (And this is not to mention the men who did the actual work, quarrying, building, constructing streets and walls, and so on – though many of them will have been the colonists themselves.)

Some of the problems involved had emerged with Seleukos' first new city, Seleukeia-on-the-Tigris, which he founded soon after recovering control of Babylonia in 311. This was planted on the River Tigris, at a point where the Royal Road from Iran reached the river, and therefore in a highly important strategic location, which was probably the major consideration in choosing the site. It was also only a day's journey from the historic centre of Babylonia, Babylon itself, and again this was evidently a major factor. In area, Seleukeia was more or less the same size as Alexandria-by-Egypt, which was being built at the same time. (Ptolemy I had moved his administrative centre to that city about the time Seleukos was founding his own great new city.) Seleukos had trouble with the priests of the main temple Esagila in Babylon, who did their best to sabotage the process by imposing a curse on the new city (see Chapter 2). Seleukos detected their lie – their opposition must have been obvious – and persuaded the army to begin the initial work 'spontaneously'. It is unlikely that the army was happy at the thought of becoming builders' labourers, but if it had been explained to them that they were thwarting the machinations of a group of Babylonian priests the soldiers may well have enjoyed the joke; the army was probably doing no more than break the ground; it was surely not involved in anything large-scale such as the actual building the city.[36]

We do not have this sort of detail for the cities of Syria, where it seems quite likely that the local native Syrian inhabitants welcomed the idea of the wide-scale urban development which he initiated. In the one settlement which existed in the North Syrian region, at Bambyke, it appears that the temple priesthood were quite happy to have their town boosted in size, re-named Hierapolis, and the temple enclosed within a Greek-type city.[37] Most new cities were inevitably founded where a village already existed; this can be most easily seen in the plan of Beroia (Aleppo) where the contrast between the new grid pattern of streets and the old meandering streets of the village is quite clear.[38] North Syria was widely sown with villages; since one of the requirements for a city was access to water, and this was obviously something which inevitably had attracted village settlement, it can be taken as certain that a village already existed on the site of every city.

Peopling the new cities required the migration of large numbers of people from old Greece and other areas. Antioch, for example, received colonists from Athens, Cyprus, and other places, as is evidenced by the gods which were worshipped in the city.[39] Seleukos must have been able to offer the colonists substantial inducements – land, a house, lower taxation, or perhaps none for a time, internal self-government, protection, as well as the initial financing. He was so successful that by the time he died all those cities in Syria were in existence, populated, and functioning. (The total number of people who moved to Syria in those two decades was perhaps in the region of 500,000.) But since the new inhabitants were mainly Greeks – Syrians were also attracted to the new cities, but were not admitted to the citizenship – the king had to be careful not impose too rigid a governing regime upon them. Of all the successors to Alexander, Seleukos was the most fertile in political invention, and he came up with a means by which the apparent contradiction between royal control and self-government could be resolved, but in a different way than in the royal relationship with the old cities.

Each one of the new cities had assigned to it one of his Friends, usually a man who either came from the city or who moved to live there, perhaps with the assignment of a royal estate nearby. These men had the job title of *epistates*. Their task was to be the link between the royal administration on the one hand, that is, the court or the king, and the city on the other. Any prob-lems the city faced could therefore be taken to the king for resolution, and any requirements could be communicated from the king to the city (the expec-tation of a gold crown, for example, or a congratulatory decree). The essence of the system was ease of communication between the two.

One of the conditions of settling in the new cities was that, as in every city in old Greece, the male inhabitants were expected to undergo military train-ing as *ephebes*, and then to be available in an emergency to defend the king-dom. This mobilisation would be the sort of message the king might have to send by way of the *epistates*. Since all the Greek new cities in north Syria were quite clearly planted in order to defend that territory against the king's potential or actual enemies, Lysimachos in the north and Ptolemy I in the south, this requirement will have been both self-evident and understandable.

From the point of view of the governing institution of Friends linking the cities and the court, the *epistates* was a major innovation, and one which proved to be highly successful. One of the results was a continuous loyalty which bound the cities to the dynasty, for none of these cities ever staged a rebellion unless the central government had broken down.[40] The process of foundation was also a major stage in the development of the Seleukid government system. It allowed the king to foster and plan the foundation of a whole series of self-governing cities, but at the same time to know that they were under his more distant control; he was the *ktistes*, the founder, a role which gave him an indefinable position of influence in each city, one which was inherited by later kings. This was not quite the royal control which was exerted over Macedonian cities, nor was it the formal and recognised freedom 'of the Greeks' which Antigonos I had envisaged in his declaration. It was instead a creative response to a difficult situation, and one which was highly successful – so successful that in fact it became the basis for relations between emperor and cities in the Roman Empire.

In keeping with the extensive delegation of responsibility for government at the local level, the Seleukid kingdom relied in the rural areas partly on assigning large estates to the king's Friends, who would therefore be responsible for transmitting taxation revenues to the king's treasury, but also on a hierarchy of administration which was clearly designed as a check on the holders of those estates. These were men who had gained the king's favour in one way or another as a Friend, as the son of a Friend, or as a favourite, but who could not necessarily be expected to remain totally loyal. It was the ambition of every Friend and favourite to keep any gains awarded them, and most of them operated in a very independent way once they had gained wealth of any sort. They expected to be able to pass on any estate they had been granted to their offspring, and once heredity had been established, it was extremely difficult for the king to alter the situation.

A parallel administration was therefore required as a check on these estate holders, but this also had to be composed of men who had distinctly limited responsibilities, and therefore few opportunities for personal enrichment. This system in the Seleukid kingdom is evidenced in two inscriptions, one from Asia Minor and one from Palestine. Until the discovery of the Palestinian inscription it was assumed that the administration in that region had been developed by the Ptolemaic rulers before 200 BC and that its elaboration was the result of Ptolemaic bureaucratic procedures. But the Palestinian inscription demonstrates that in fact the Seleukid administration in Palestine was very similar in organisation to that which had been revealed by the inscription from Asia Minor. Essentially it consisted of the transmission of instructions in the form of letters down through the layers of the administrative hierarchy.

The Asia Minor inscription is that in which King Antiochos II delivered a large estate in northwestern Asia Minor to his first wife Laodike.[41] Setting aside the purpose of the gift, the inscription provides a view of the royal administration which had been set up in the area. The process of the transfer began with a letter from the king to Metrophanes, the satrap of the Hellespontine province, in which the estate was located, describing the estate and its boundaries. Metrophanes then wrote to the *oikonomos* Nikomachos, the financial official of the section of the satrapy in which the estate lay. Nikomachos then wrote to the hyparch of that territory, who marked out the estate on the ground as it had been described in the king's original letter. Also included in recording the transaction were the men who had to inscribe all these documents in two copies, which were to be set up at the sanctuaries of Apollo at Didyma and Artemis at Ephesos, the manager of the estate and the keeper of the royal archives at Sardis; the record of the transfer was to be inscribed on *stelai* to be set up in the two temples at Didyma and Ephesos, and also at the sanctuaries at Sardis, Ilion, and Samothrace.

This single document therefore lays out the layers of the royal administration, from the manager of the estate through the financial officials of the section of the satrapy – the hyparch and the *oikonomos* – to the satrap and then on up to the king and the royal administration established in Sardis. It implies that there were officials in all the royal estates, financial officials and hyparchs in each section of every satrapy, a satrapal administration in each satrapy which was separate from the royal administration which was established in Sardis. How many sections of each satrapy there were is unknown, but it has been suggested that there were seventy or eighty hyparchies.[42]

The inscription from Palestine implies a much less ordered administration. Antiochos III wrote variously to the governor of Koile Syria, Ptolemy son of Thraseas, to two men identified as *dioiketai*, to an official named Marsyas who was concerned with the illegal billeting on villagers by men of the army, and copies of various of these letters went to at least seven other officials.[43]

It may be supposed that the differences between these two indications of administrative methods result, at least in part, from the fact that both regions involved, Asia Minor and Palestine, had been governed by other kings before being seized by the Seleukids. That is, it is possible that the Seleukid kings simply took over the administrative systems which Antigonos I and Lysimachos had operated in Asia Minor – which may well have been originally the Akhaimenid system – and that set up by the Ptolemies in Palestine. This, of course, implies that the Seleukid kings ignored inefficiencies and made no attempt to organise or reorganise the local administration. This might be the case with the Palestine example, because Ptolemy son of Thraseas had been the Ptolemaic governor of Koile Syria and was then reappointed to the same position by Antiochos III; he could well have continued operating a system he presumably already understood. We simply do not know the Seleukid approach to this issue, though it seems unlikely that a messy administrative system, which is what it appears to be, was simply allowed to continue.

The Asia Minor case implies a fairly clear system of administrative hierarchy. In Palestine, however, there were evidently overlapping, possibly competing, responsibilities, and the administrative hierarchy was at times ignored by the king. In Asia Minor the line of communication was clear; in Palestine the king wrote directly to Ptolemy the *strategos* (governor), but also to several subordinate officials, bypassing the governor.

The reason for assuming that the Palestine administration was in essence Ptolemaic is that it is well documented and appears very different in philosophy and intention from that of any of the other kingdoms. Ptolemy I found when he arrived as satrap in 323 BC, shortly after the death of Alexander, that Alexander's administration, intentionally divided between several men because of the wealth of Egypt and so its liability to be used as a strategic redoubt, and an independent power, had in fact collapsed in the face of the fact that one of the men, Kleomenes of Naukratis (and so an Egyptian Greek) had controlled the treasury, as well as becoming extremely wealthy himself.[44] Having eliminated Kleomenes, Ptolemy organised a detailed administration in which a largely Greek and Macedonian bureaucracy was devoted to extracting as much taxation revenue from the rural population as possible. He had some excuse at least at first in that he was under constant threat for the next twenty-five years, usually from enemies more powerful than he was; he also had the expense of building Alexandria, the site and plan of which had been determined by Alexander and, since Alexander's conquest of Egypt was Ptolemy's rationale for governing the land, his plans could not be changed. This administration relied on quotas of produce being delivered by each village. Each village and its headman, and a mass of clerks was used to check that each village was in fact both capable of delivering what was required and did deliver it. This may well have been a system inherited from the Akhaimenid past, which would be based on the preceding pharaonic regime. It is, after all, a basic system typical of all rural-based empires.[45] On top of this there was a Greek-manned administration based in Alexandria, staffed by Friends of the king and their clerical subordinates. Having recruited the clerks, of course, the system tended to run itself.[46] It produced vast wealth for the king, but at the cost of profoundly alienating a rural population which had been initially welcoming of the Macedonian conquest. Rural rebellions began as early as 245, when extra expenditure and therefore extra taxation was imposed during the Third Syrian War (reduction in expenditure by the court and the government does not seem to have been an option). From then on rural disorder was endemic, rising to a full-scale rebellion from 207–186, in which a rival pharaonic kingdom was established in the south of the country. It is unlikely that the peasantry in the south found their burdens eased, but at least they were paying over their produce to an Egyptian king, not a Greek-speaking Macedonian.

This administrative system has been delineated in detail by modern historians, based on the surviving papyrus records. It has been bedevilled by the assumption that it had some relationship to socialism, and comparisons have been made with the oppressive socialist system in Soviet Russia. Studies in the 1930s were admiring, later studies have been less so. The Roman Emperor Tiberius summed up the system, which the Roman government had inherited from the Ptolemaic past and maintained, when he remarked to one over-zealous governor that he wanted his 'sheep to be shorn, not skinned'. It has also been assumed that the Ptolemies merely adopted the traditional pharaonic and Akhaimenid governing systems. In fact it looks much more that Ptolemy I imposed an essentially Greek method of administration on top of the earlier methods of extracting as much from the peasantry as possible. It was certainly much more successful than any earlier system in extracting wealth from the peasantry, so long as it can be accepted that the cost was repeated and eventually virtually continual rural unrest and rebellion. Such a system is in fact uneconomic, since the cost of putting down the rebellions were probably greater than the gains made from the tax-extraction system and certainly so during the twenty years of internal war between 207 and 186. Admiration for the system must be tempered by the fact that it was unpopular, uneconomic and extremely oppressive. It has to be said that by comparison with the Seleukid system it did produce a greater quantity of wealth, but at the same time it did force the population into a condition of hostility to the governing system, which did not happen under the Seleukids.

Chapter 7

Kings and People

Two stories were told of Demetrios Poliorketes when he was king in Macedon between 294 and 288. In one he accepted written petitions from citizens and put them into his cloak, promising, at least by implication, to deal with them later; he was then later seen to throw them into a river he was crossing;[1] dethronement followed soon after. A pleasant story of arrogance rewarded.

The other story is also told of Demetrios, but of Philip II as well, and again of the Emperor Hadrian. An old woman intercepts the ruler as he is travelling by and hands him a petition. He brushes her away saying he's too busy, to which the unanswerable answer is 'Then stop being king.'[2] Quite possibly the story is true of all three men, but that seems fairly unlikely, and quite possibly both of these stories are inventions and have attached themselves to particularly spectacular and arrogant kings. Rather, their repetition is a clear indication of what was expected of a king by his ordinary citizens and subjects: attention to their own problems and the adoption of measures designed to relieve those problems. (Demetrios is said by Plutarch to have turned back to attend to the old woman's complaint.) If a king did not so attend, he did not deserve to be king, was the popular opinion. The people had requirements of a king, just as the king expected them to support him, serve in his army, and pay their taxes.

That these stories were told of two Macedonian kings is not only an indication of people's expectations, but they also bring out the contrast between that kingdom and the others. Macedon was relatively small and compact compared to the other great kingdoms, and its people were relatively unified in origin and language. It was a kingdom which had existed for several hundred years by the time of Philip and Demetrios, and its political culture was familiar and understood – hence the annoyance at Demetrios' cavalier way with the petitions and his plea of being 'too busy'.

The other kingdoms were much more diverse in population and very much larger in geographical extent. The Ptolemaic state had a basic population of several millions of native Egyptians, which was overlaid by a ruling set of very many fewer Greek-speakers, immigrants from Greece and Macedon and other places, and their descendants, and to this Egyptian population were attached those of the empire, Cypriots, Cyrenaicans, inhabitants of Asian cities – Greek-speakers – and Aramaic-speaking Syrians, of which these last were themselves divided into Jews, Phoenicians, and others. The Attalids ruled over Greeks and Macedonians, both natives and more recent immigrants, and a variety of native Asia Minor peoples, including Mysians and Phrygians. But the Seleukid kingdom was even more highly diverse than these, but was also composed of compact and distinct blocks of peoples – Babylonians, Elymaeans, Medes, Persians, Baktrians, and others – some of whom had been imperial peoples in the relatively recent past and who were self-conscious enough of this condition to be at times impervious to any sort of Hellenisation. In retrospect it is astonishing that the Seleukid kings managed to hold onto their empire for as long as they did. It clearly took considerable political skill.

That skill began with identifying the central element in the culture of the group, and in almost all cases this came down to religion. Almost all the subject peoples of Asia and Africa had been without any sort of independent political organisation of their own for several centuries. (The only group which had had any sort of self-government had been the Phoenician cities; the Egyptians had had a native-born pharaoh for some decades in the period before the Macedonian conquest.) The recourse of all these groups had been to concentrate on their religion, the worship of their own particular gods, so that the chief priests of the small temples and shrines became the effective chiefs of the communities; and this identification of the group with the god was a means also of self-identification and of differentiation from other groups roundabout, and from their rulers. Therefore by honouring the local shrines and temples, the kings could bring these communities onto their side. It also helped that the Seleukids, if less so the Ptolemies, were rescuing many of these peoples from earlier foreign rule, substituting their own, equally foreign, rule, but one which appears to have been more sympathetic.

And yet, whatever sympathetic policies the kings displayed to their subjects, their rule rested essentially on their control of armed force. And this was not simply a matter of being in command, but had a tradition behind it, a sort of constitutionality which, if not written down in documentary form, was generally understood.

In Macedon, which had been the origin of the greater kingdoms, the army had been the quasi-constitutional basis for the king's authority. It was the assembled army which acclaimed a new king, particularly in a disputed succession, or at a time of particular confusion. Philip II owed his royal position to such an acclamation.[3] He toured the country after becoming king, speaking to meetings of the people in an attempt to secure their support and to provide reassurance;[4] it was the army in Babylonia in 323 which insisted that Philip

Arrhidaios and Alexander's unborn child be made joint kings.[5] In 306 when Antigonos I was organising his own proclamation as king, he waited until his son had won a great victory, and was then acclaimed by his courtiers – but it was the victory which counted, and Demetrios, the actual victor, was proclaimed king as well.[6]

As Antigonos' fudge indicates, these new kingdoms could not operate in the same way as Macedon. Thus Kassandros and Antigonos Gonatas – and even briefly Pyrrhos – could use the assembled army to have themselves acclaimed as kings, but the other kingdoms were far too large and diffuse to use that method.[7] Heredity was of course part of the mix when it came to the acclamation of a new king, and it was always one of the fundamental bases of royal authority, so it was this which emerged as the defining element in the royal succession among the other dynasties, the military acclamation having been largely shed over the years.

And yet the army, in whatever kingdom, still remained the basis of the actual power of the kings. Antigonos Monophthalamos, perforce, claimed the title of king by virtue of his command of an army, Ptolemy I could claim the same because he had successfully defeated several attempts to remove him from Egypt with the support of his own Macedonian army, and Seleukos I could do so because he had defeated Antigonos, having persuaded large elements of Antigonos' army to join him. Remnants of the practice of military acclamation therefore survived in an attenuated and distorted form, and the process could be used, or misused, usually in an emergency. When Ptolemy IV died, his successor was proclaimed by the regents for his infant son (his self-appointed regents) to a select group of the royal guard in a facsimile of a military acclamation.[8] When Demetrios II of Macedon was killed in battle, there was a repetition of Philip II's near-usurpation, but in a rather more elegant and considered manner: Philip V, the son of Demetrios, was too young to rule, so his adult cousin Antigonos Doson took command of the army in the emergency. After a year Antigonos was proclaimed as king at a military meeting.[9]

Normally, however, by this time an acclamation was not required. In 223, when Seleukos III was murdered in Asia Minor, his younger brother Antiochos III succeeded without question, even though he was in Babylon, separated from his brother's army by a thousand miles.[10] No army acclamation took place, unless there was a guard present on the occasion, as is very likely. The Attalids in Pergamon do not seem to have required a military acclamation either, and in fact the origin of the dynasty was emphatically non-military. The succession was rarely in doubt within the family until the very end, when one claimant, Aristonikos, disputed the will of Attalos III, in which the kingdom was bequeathed to Rome.[11]

The point of an army acclamation was originally that the army was the assembled male population of Macedon. The meeting of king and army and the former's acclamation was thus an implicit contract between the two, the king would defend the kingdom by his abilities as commander and diplomat; the army would fight for him. The dispersion of the army in the greater kingdoms made such an acclamation impossible to organise, and such an implied contract impossible to effect. Yet at the same time an acclamation of sorts was something which was required by a man attempting a usurpation. When Antiochos III's cousin Akhaios defeated his rival Attalos I and drove him back into his ancestral kingdom, Akhaios' army wanted to proclaim him king, but he refused. Later when he saw that Antiochos III had major difficulties and seemed liable to be eliminated by a rival rebel, he marched the army eastwards with the intention of invading Syria and seizing the kingship; when the army he commanded – the same men as had attempted to make him king earlier – realised that this was more than a mere expedition against the local barbarians, Akhaios had himself proclaimed king, but acclamation by the army failed to follow; the troops refused to go with him to invade Syria, where they would have to face the main Seleukid army; so, although he was accepted as king by the army in Asia Minor, Akhaios' prospects of a wider empire had vanished.[12] The contract as the army understood it, therefore, was limited to their homeland – and the army fought hard to support Akhaios when he was attacked by Antiochos. His rival Molon had, like Akhaios, rebelled first, and only when he had won a victory did he have himself acclaimed king by the army he commanded.[13] Sixty years later Timarchos, seeking to remove Demetrios I, went through the same process, with the added twist of seeking the approval of the Roman Senate; he got it, but it was no use to him.[14] The generally accepted political theory, or perhaps accepted practice, of the greater monarchies was therefore that a fraction of the army could act as the representative of that general population, just as in Macedon the army in assembly acted as representative of the whole population. It was a very rough and ready matter, and clearly produced a situation which permitted the sort of usurpations which mass acclamation had partly been designed to avoid. Molon, Akhaios, and Timarchos all had, if the army acclamations were the validating principle in making a man king, as much legitimacy as Antiochos III or Demetrios I – and Demetrios had in fact seized the throne by violence.

Thus the practice adapted from ancestral Macedon had to adjust to the actual situation of the expanded geography of the greater kingdoms. The end of the active participation of the army in the process of the royal succession also meant that the army ceased to have any real effect in the government of the state. In 315 Kassandros had used his Macedonian army – only a part of the whole, for he was fighting a civil war – as a jury to condemn Olympias for her recent murders of members of the Argead royal family and of large numbers of the Macedonian nobility. She was not allowed to speak in her own defence before being condemned and killed, but the process clearly bore some semblance to legality – or, at least, it was acceptable at the time. In the next year Antigonos Monophthalamos used the army as a sort of referendum on his new policy of freedom of the cities by announcing it in a speech to the assembled troops at the siege of Tyre.[15]

The impossibility of the army of the greater kingdoms being able to act as an active political element in the state – as opposed to being the occasional passive instrument in an acclamation – left the kings as effectively absolute rulers, at least in theory (but see Chapter 6). It followed therefore that the people had no direct relationship with the kings, and had no say in the person of the king, or in the government of the state.

So much for theory. In practice, of course, things were not so stark. Kings could not possibly rule alone, and for major decisions usually convened a council of Friends; governors were required for provinces, *epistatai* for cities, and so on – the government was effectively diffuse, a condition made more extreme by the slow communications available; to send instructions, or reinforcements from Syria to Baktria, say, was a journey of months; if the king went himself it would take even longer, since he would be travelling with a large following and would need to attend to local issues along the way. In addition the people were never slow to voice their opinions, and the kings knew perfectly well that it was necessary to conciliate and please the people if their rule was not to seize up. It was also necessary for them to be able to enforce their decisions, even against popular resistance.

They did this, crudely, by monopolising armed force.[16] It is a notorious fact of Ptolemaic history that the great rebellion which began in 207 and which detached a large area of Upper Egypt into an independent pharaonic state for two decades, was linked to the mobilisation of 20,000 Egyptians into the army in 217 to fight at the battle of Raphia. The theory is that these men, trained to arms, were then able to use their acquired military expertise to defy the Ptolemaic government.[17] This is a very shaky theory, not least because of the ten-year delay in the rebellion's arrival, and that the link between being armed and going into rebellion is hardly persuasive, but the point is well made nevertheless that the Egyptian native population was sufficiently angry to revolt.[18] One of the reasons for the Seleukids' relative success in avoiding such native rebellions is that their army did not usually include such large native contingents. Medes were certainly recruited into the cavalry by Seleukos I in order to fight Antigonos Monophthalamos, but not apparently in large numbers later, and most non-Greek or non-Macedonian troops came from outside the empire – Arabs, for example, at Raphia, or Dahai from the Central Asian deserts.[19] These were, however, only auxiliary troops. The main force of all Hellenistic armies in whatever kingdom was always composed of sarissa-wielding infantrymen, Macedonians or their descendants, and Greeks or their descendants, and when manpower was in short supply inside the kingdom, Greeks and Macedonians were recruited as mercenaries, together with men from parts of Asia Minor, such as Pisidians, who were apparently treated as honorary Greeks for the occasion.[20]

Therefore the inhabitants of the great kingdoms to which the kings had to devote most of their attention were the Greek-speaking inhabitants. These were, at least in the Seleukid and Ptolemaic kingdoms, and to some extent also in the Attalid, either immigrants or the descendants of immigrants, and they remembered their origins. They used Greek or Macedonian names, their institutions had Greek or Macedonian titles (such as the *adeiganes* at Seleukeia-on-the-Tigris, who were the magistrates of the city), and in some cases they called themselves 'Macedonian'. And it was this element of the population which formed the greater part, and at times the whole, of the armed forces available to the king.

This was the section of the population to which the kings therefore had to attend most carefully – their 'constituency', as it were. The native groups were not ignored, but in the two greatest non-Greek groups, Egyptians and Babylonians, it seems that royal attention to the local religion for a long time proved sufficient to conciliate any bruised feelings. This was successful enough that the Babylonians remained loyal to the Seleukids through thick and thin, while the Egyptians put up with the Ptolemies for a century before the great rebellion came – earlier risings, as in 245, were easily dealt with. But the Greco-Macedonians needed more careful attention, simply because they provided the men for the armies.

Keeping the allegiance of the Greco-Macedonians required royal attention and work. Several of the Ptolemies became negligent in this, notably Ptolemy III and Ptolemy IV, allowing the power (but not the title) of the king to be effectively usurped by men such as Sosibios; and it happened with the Seleukids at times as well.

An unpopular king could therefore expect trouble. The Seleukid Demetrios I had made himself unpopular by killing the child Antiochos V and the regent Lysias, even if his claim to the kingship seemed legitimate. Further, he had acquired an enjoyment of hunting while in his hostage exile in Italy, and he carried on with it when king in Syria, probably to the neglect of his duties, or so it was perceived. His absence from the palace was thus noted and criticised.[21] When his successor Alexander Balas was holed up in the palace at Antioch and rarely emerged, he was also criticised – in effect for doing the opposite of Demetrios. These stories suggest not so much inattention to his work as unpopularity among a certain part of the population which led to the exaggeration of certain personal characteristics in the king. It is also inaccurate, for we are also given a picture of Demetrios I at the entrance to the palace where he is attending to visitors: the Macedonian pretender Andriskos was able to approach him personally and asked for his help in his intended usurpation, only to be rapidly deported.[22]

Thus, in his general work the king had to deal mainly with individuals rather than military men, and this would include ordinary citizens, though it would be difficult to separate these two categories, which were usually combined in every person he met. The right of petition, to ask or require the king to attend to an individual's grievance, remained a constant throughout the Hellenistic period, and on into the Roman, as the story of Hadrian ignoring a citizen's petition demonstrates, whether that occurred or not.

For any king of a fairly conscientious nature, and one with some active political instincts, paying full attention to such people and their petitions was clearly necessary. Demetrios Poliorketes did not last long once the story of the discarded petitions got about; and the Seleukid Demetrios I was also soon overthrown by the usurper Alexander Balas, whose success required that some considerable support came from the population who were technically Demetrios' own subjects; but then Alexander forfeited that support by his own negligent behaviour later, and by his failure to hold the kingdom together.

An aspect of this necessity to attend to the people's wishes was the kings' activities in legal matters. The city councils and the provincial governors were the first resorts in legal disputes, but the king was always the court of appeal of last resort. Little is made of this in the sources, which indicates that it was taken for granted rather than that the writers of our sources did not consider it important. But Antigonos I Monophthalmos is known to have been conscientious in this matter.[23] The masses of evidence in Egyptian papyri concerned with legal disputes indicates clearly the large part such things played in everyday affairs.[24]

Most of the people with whom the kings had to deal, of course, were those of wealth and power, their Friends, their governors, the royal council. At Sardis in 212 King Antiochos III captured the city, which suffered badly in the process, and he had seized and executed Akhaios, who had been supported by the Sardians until the end. Antiochos' army occupied the public buildings and some of the private residences in the city – no doubt those of prominent people who had been Akhaios' supporters. After some time the city council, which apparently had not been abolished, though it had perhaps been purged, petitioned to be allowed to set up a regular celebration in the name of Antiochos' wife, Laodike. Antiochos responded favourably, and in response to this friendly overture, he withdrew much of his occupying force from the city; on top of this he provided materials for the reconstruction of the damage the city had suffered in the fighting. It seems probable that those who had actually suffered most were the poor and the ordinary citizens, but Antiochos had responded not to their suffering but to the intervention of the city council.[25] No doubt one of the factors in the minds of everyone involved was the possibility that unless they did something about it, those suffering most would turn on their oppressors.

Rebellion was, of course, the ultimate sanction available to the ordinary population. In 245, Ptolemy III, victoriously promenading through conquered north Syria, and sending detachments of his forces into Kilikia and Mesopotamia, suddenly had to return to Egypt when a rebellion broke out among the native Egyptian population. The rebellion was suppressed, but for the first time a Ptolemaic king publicised the loot he had acquired in his campaign – 40,000 talents' worth (so he claimed), and the return of 'Egyptian gods' from their 'foreign captivity', presumably held abroad since Akhaimenid times (if the claim was actually true).[26] This was a clear appeal to the Egyptian rather than the Greco-Macedonian population, and the implication was surely that the Syrian loot would be used to lighten the tax burden on the Egyptians, which burden appears to have been the mainspring of the rebellion.

There were thus essentially two main parts of the population of the kingdoms to which the kings paid especial heed. The first and closest and most individual, and probably the most influential, were the wealthy, the king's Friends, the city councils, the governors, and the great landowners – all of these being overlapping categories, and very largely composed of Greco-Macedonians. The second was the rest, the poor, the farmers, the soldiers, the shopkeepers. The first group tended to look to the king largely for posts, commands, gifts, with which to increase, or perhaps revive, their wealth. The second, mainly 'natives' but not entirely, were unlikely to be favoured by material gifts, or estates, except on very special occasions, but might expect tax reductions, the possibility of loot if they were soldiers, justice in a dispute, or just to be left alone. The wealthy could react to personal bad treatment or indifference by the king by treachery, absence from court, even rebellion; the only real recourse for the poor was riot, or in extreme cases, rebellion, or, in Egypt, perhaps the sort of mass refusal to obey or a mass insistence on the king's full attention which a king would probably call rebellion. The Egyptian peasantry had developed a process of withdrawal and refusal to cultivate their lands as a means of bringing pressure on the government.

The division between these two sets of people was by no means always clear, nor were the two groups themselves homogeneous. The wealthy might have their lands – this was the main standard of wealth – in different provinces or cities, and while each man and family no doubt had their lands generally in a single region, they could empathise with the men from another province in their relations with the king. The wealthy would tend to stand together, though no doubt their ranks were riven also by jealousies and rivalries. If a rebellion developed they would be the crucial element locally, with their support it would go ahead, if they refused to do so, it would fail at the start. This is why the various attempts at usurpation require to be considered as widespread conspiracies: only once support was guaranteed could a rebel governor make a serious attempt at the kingship. The poor were, however, divided rather more obviously. The most noticeable division would be between Macedonians and Greeks on the one hand, and 'native' Syrians, Babylonians, Iranians, Egyptians, and so on, on the other. But they were also divided between city dwellers and countrymen, and the city men would have a strong loyalty, perhaps above all, to their cities.

The king was much more vulnerable to enmity from the wealthy than from the poor – despite the fate of Demetrios Poliorketes. It was the courtiers who had access to him, perhaps on a daily basis, even in private. It was necessary to keep them on-side by providing what they required. When that failed, the king was in immediate danger. Ptolemy V was killed by a courtiers' plot when he casually implied that he would tax the rich in order to finance a suggested war.[27] In the Seleukid empire two types of civil warfare occurred: those between men of the royal family, which happened once in the third century (rebellions by Antiochos Hierax and Akhaios) and then constantly in the last half-century of the dynasty's life (between kings), and, second, those in which a member of the elite aimed to usurp the throne – Molon and Timarchos, for example.

This second version did not happen among the other greater dynasties, the Ptolemies, the Antigonids, or the Attalids. This is not to say that, as the fate of Ptolemy V made clear, the courtiers were constantly supportive, but, at least for the Ptolemies, the grumbling and constant threat of a rising by the native Egyptian population tended to restrict discontent among the rich to internal court matters. Perhaps the same factor operated with the Antigonids, who were constantly threatened by invasion from over the northern borders; similarly, the Attalids were surrounded by every other kingdom in Asia Minor, most of whom were at least passive enemies, and this will have operated to enforce support for the kings. Even so, Philip V of Macedon had to conduct a nasty purge to remove some antagonistic courtiers, and some members of the Attalid royalty deliberately fostered the madcap adventure of the Macedonian pretender Andriskos, which eventually involved the monarchy in another war when he had made an unexpected success of his pretences.[28]

So, once more, the exception is the Seleukid kingdom. Here there were repeated risings aimed at either replacing the ruling dynasty by the leader of the revolt, or in a few cases possibly the overthrow of the monarchy altogether. The basic contrast is with Egypt. In both lands the kings had encouraged the immigration of Greeks, Macedonians, and others who could pass for them (such as various groups from Asia Minor), and had settled them in relatively compact groups. In Egypt these men were often retired soldiers of the royal army, and were settled above all in the few cities (Alexandria especially) and in parts of the countryside, especially in the reclaimed land of the Fayum, southwest of Memphis. It was on these men and their descendants that the regime depended to supply soldiers in the time of war – though they also extensively recruited mercenaries in extreme emergencies, as in 217 and 202. They were generally loyal because they were surrounded by, and massively outnumbered by, the non-Greek Egyptian population, which was taxed to the limit and repeatedly demonstrated its hostility. Hence they looked to the king and his government for support, jobs, handouts, and protection.[29]

In the Seleukid scheme, however, the immigrants were placed in many cities, usually newly founded, and were constituted in imitation of the independent cities of Greece. The origin of the immigrants was much the same as those going to Egypt, but they were much more widely spread through the kingdom, with significantly large populations at the extreme ends, in Asia Minor, and in Baktria, both areas which repeatedly manifested an intention of breaking away into independence.[30] The concentration of immigrant manpower in Syria was divided between numerous autonomous cities; these remained loyal to the dynasty as founders, though of course every city had a conspicuous acropolis which was presumably garrisoned by part of the royal army.[31]

To a large extent these cities were normally loyal. They faced the same factor of native alienation and intermittent hostilities as in Egypt, but the light hand of government assisted them in their loyalty, and the hostility of the native groups in the Seleukid kingdom was much less than in Egypt. But the wide geographical spread of the Greek-speaking population and the existence, alongside and 'above' them, of a class of wealthy landowners and officials could provide a combustible mixture. For it was the Greeks of the cities who provided the military manpower both for the kings and for their internal enemies, and it proved to be alarmingly easy for rebels from the elite to recruit an army willing to fight against the king.

The kings therefore were operating in a social atmosphere of some anxiety, and there were risings in both the Ptolemaic and Seleukid kingdoms frequently enough to keep everyone alert. The death of Seleukos I in 281 triggered trouble of some sort in Syria. Exactly what happened is not known, but it seems to have taken place in the cities which Seleukos had recently founded, and it is a reasonable guess that increased autonomy was the aim.[32] A generation later a dispute over the succession and a Ptolemaic invasion produced the sort of chaos which the cities had surely feared. In Antioch the candidate for the succession was Antiochos, the infant son of the deceased Antiochos II and his Ptolemaic second wife Berenike: they were killed by men of the city on instructions from his first wife Laodike.[33] In Kilikia, the governor Aribazos attempted to escape through the Taurus Mountains, but he was captured and killed by the local people.[34] Here was native enmity, a lethal royal succession dispute, and alarmingly effective local action all combined with a successful Ptolemaic invasion, the collection of problems which formed the nightmare which every kingdom surely feared.

In the next generation, between 246 and 212, there were rebellions by members of the elite in Parthia, by the governor Andragoras, in Media by Molon and in Elymais by Molon's brother, in Asia Minor by Antiochos Hierax and later by Akhaios, both of whom were members of the royal family; in addition the kingdom suffered invasion by nomads into Parthia, by the Ptolemies in north Syria, and by Attalos I of Pergamon into Asia Minor. One of the reasons Antiochos III, who became king towards the end of this series of disasters, received strong support was that he led the revival of peace and order in the kingdom.

Given the repeated conflicts within the ruling group of the Seleukid kingdom, it is perhaps surprising that there were not also occurrences of exasperated annoyance among the lower classes. The apparent outbreak in Syria in 281/280 was not repeated, though one group, the 'Kyrrhestai', assumed to be the military contingent produced from the city of Kyrrhos, went into mutiny, and then rebellion, at the same time as Akhaios and Molon were rejecting Antiochos III as king. They were treated with kid gloves at first, but being obdurate, they were eventually crushed.[35] Apart from that it was not until a similar period of elite quarrelling in the 140s that another outbreak of civic annoyance appeared.

The civic conflict occasioned by the appearance of Alexander Balas as pretender/usurper culminated in a war in north Syria between three kings, the rivals Alexander and Demetrios II, and Ptolemy VI of Egypt. In the process some of the cities were destined to become involved, and in 145 there is an indication that the four great cities of the region – Antioch, Seleukeia, Apameia, Laodikeia – became leagued together as the 'brother cities', though this did not last long, and whatever their purpose, they had no effect on the conflict.[36] After the defeat of Alexander Balas in 145, a group in Antioch promoted the idea of Ptolemy as king of Asia as well as Egypt, but he ultimately

declined.[37] After his and Alexander's death later in the year, Ptolemy's hench-
man Diodotos persuaded his home city of Apameia to join him in his
usurpation – or it may be he took control of it and then used it as his base.[38]
In Antioch riots had to be put down by the Cretan and Jewish mercenaries
hired by Demetrios II, which resulted in widespread destruction in the city.[39]
All this may be construed as demonstrations of citizen power, but it looks
much more like anger and fury at the continuation of the civil warfare.

The people involved in these events were the inhabitants of the cities and so
were mainly Greco-Macedonians. But at the same time one group of native
Syrians, the Jews of Judaea, broke out into rebellion and eventually organised
themselves into an independent kingdom.[40] This took a generation and more
to work out, and was only successful in the wake of a massive and costly military defeat, with horrifying losses of Greco-Macedonian military manpower,
suffered by Antiochos VII in 129, which provoked a great display of grief and
mourning in Antioch. But it was the first of an increasing number of local-
ised bids for independence by Syrian – as opposed to Greco-Macedonian –
groups. These included the old cities of Phoenicia, who declared their independence successively between 129 and 111, but also by the non-urbanised
regions where Greeks were few – Judaea is an example.[41] Other mountainous
regions such as the Lebanese mountain area, the Bargylos hills, or the desert
edge regions like Emesa, detached themselves. In the generation following
the achievement of independence by the Jews, a good half of 'Greater Syria'
(from Gaza to the Taurus) ceased to remain under Greco-Macedonian rule.[42]

The Egyptian rebellion of 207–186 was a similar type of rising as that
mounted by the Jews later, both centred on the local god and his temple –
Thebes and Jerusalem. Conciliation of such places and their priests and
believers had been one of the priorities of all the kings in Asia and Egypt from
the beginning. Seleukos I had continued the subsidies to Esagila in Babylon
and there are repeated notices in Babylonian sources of Seleukid kings sub-
sidising, sacrificing at, or honouring in other ways, temples in several
Babylonian cities.[43] Ptolemy I had centred his power at first in the old Egyptian capital at Memphis, and he and his successors had striven to bring the
temple priesthoods on their side. The Attalid capital-fortress at Pergamon
preserved the pre-Attalid temple on the site and adorned it. The chief reason
to do this is shown by the consequences when the policy failed – in Egypt in
207, in Judaea in the 160s.

At the same time, all kings paid attention to fostering the religion the
Greeks had brought with them. Temples were built in all the new cities, cults
developed, both of the kings and their families and of synthetic gods like
Serapis. One of the ways of bringing the wealthy classes on-side was to award
them prestigious priesthoods, of which the Ptolemies had a whole series

ranked in a hierarchy. An example of the use of such appointments is the priesthood for Laodike, the wife of Antiochos III, which was awarded to Berenike from Telmessos in Lykia. She was the last representative of a little dynasty descended from Lysimachos and Ptolemy I, and installed at Telmessos by Ptolemy II in about 280; her principality had been seized by Antiochos in his campaign along the south Anatolian coast, and the priesthood was a measure of the need he clearly felt to conciliate her.[44]

As the power of the kings faded, particularly among the Seleukids, the basic local loyalties of their subjects emerged, rather like solid submerged islands appearing as the Macedonian tide receded, and in the process revealed the essential antipathy of many of these peoples towards foreign rule. The emergence of these local states, independent and resilient, demonstrated clearly the long-term failure of the conciliation policy even more than had the Jewish and Egyptian rebellions. In Egypt, the geography of the country worked against the success of local independent movements, but rural unrest, by definition hostile to the Ptolemaic government, was constant. In Asia Minor the Roman takeover led to the disintegration of the Attalid kingdom into a series of minor local polities, many under local rule by 'native' authorities. In the Seleukid kingdom, dozens of minor states, kingdoms, cities, tetrarchies, and so on, appeared even before the Roman arrival, a development accompanied by foreign invasions. The nightmare of the collapse after 246 was repeated on a vastly greater scale.

The process of the withdrawal of the power of the kings had, of course, happened to a degree from the beginning of the Hellenistic period in Asia Minor, with the independence of Bithynia and Pontos and Kappadokia (and the Galatians), though the whole region was so saturated with Greek influence that it is difficult to classify these movements in the pseudo-nationalist terms which can be applied in Syria. The same may be said of the disintegration of Seleukid authority in Iran, where the regions in the south – Persis first, then Elymais – drifted into independence, as did the Parthians, in effect, in the north. Yet the essential point about all these shifts into partial or complete independence is that they were based, like the disintegration in Syria, on particular local non-Greek groups, often centred on a temple or shrine, groups which, while rejecting Seleukid political authority, generally welcomed Greek cultural influences. Several Parthian kings took the epithet Philhellene, for example. The group which seems to have had most success in rejecting, or perhaps ignoring, the opportunities for Hellenisation seem to be the people of Persis. The Jews of Judaea struck out at the Seleukids when they seemed to interfere with their religious practices, but eventually Judaea became a fairly typical Hellenistic state, very much in imitation of the Seleukid kingdom they were rejecting.[45]

Then there is Egypt. The trouble which in 245 brought Ptolemy III back to Alexandria from his Third Syrian War adventure was a clear signal that the Egyptian population was disenchanted, to say the least, with the king's government. The 207 rebellion resulted in part from a return to Ptolemaic complacency under Ptolemy III and IV – and the kings lost their empire in the next years as well, basically from the same cause. (218 was not in fact the first occasion when Egyptians had been armed in defence against an invasion; Ptolemy I had done so much earlier;[46] that he did not reap a rebellion whereas in the later case it did happen, is a measure of the deterioration in conditions of the Egyptian peasantry, and perhaps also the alienation of the Egyptian priesthood, which tended to become the leaders of Egyptian opinion; it is significant that this rebellion took place almost immediately after the death of Ptolemy II Philadelphos, who had been instrumental in increasing taxation, imposing new taxes, and making the whole system more 'efficient'.)

These contrasting rebellions, by the Seleukid elite and by the Egyptian peasantry, indicate the fundamental problems of both kingdoms, but in the context of this chapter they are also signs of the state of relations between the kings and their subjects. In Egypt the repeated rebellions by native Egyptians show that such relations could probably not have been worse, the main problem being the overly efficient extraction of taxes, usually taken in the form of the produce of the peasantry. In the Seleukid case it was the liability of members of the elite to rebel which was the problem. And in both kingdoms the Greco-Macedonian populations of the cities had a tendency to exhibit disaffection more in riots than full-scale rebellion; Alexandrians were particularly prone to assert themselves in such a way. The temporary success of several pretenders to the throne – for they had all gained control of some cities as well as getting support from fellow members of the elite – rather suggests that, given a lead, the people of the cities were quite likely to join in the rebellion.

All this is inevitably somewhat general, for the source material which we can study tends to focus overwhelmingly on members of the elite, with the landowners, city magistrates, governors, or priests. It is possible to name some rebels, notably in the Seleukid elite, but among the general population, Greco-Macedonian or native, a few leaders can be named, but it is not possible to investigate with any depth the causes of the rebellions, or why groups might support a particular rebel. It can be said, for example, that the Seleukid elite rebels normally aimed at the kingship, but it is rarely possible to discover exactly what provoked them to such a step, other than general ambition, which might indeed be quite enough; but we are never able to find out why their followers joined them, though if the rebel chief had command of the army of his region, he might both seem to be a winner and therefore worth joining, and at the same time be able to compel the participation of those who were less than keen. When Molon fought Antiochos III the rebel army switched sides when the king seemed to be winning. The case of Akhaios in Asia Minor might be thought to contradict this, but in fact we have no idea why the army which Akhaios commanded first promoted him as king then refused to follow him when he did take the title. They were certainly induced to march towards Syria by being told that they were to campaign in Pisidia but they refused to continue when they discovered that Syria was the actual destination, and the reason given is that they refused to fight against 'the king'. This sequence of events suggests strongly that the Asia Minor army was wedded to the idea of a separate kingdom in Asia Minor. That is to say, it seems quite possible that pretenders were liable to lie to their followers to persuade them to support them. Even so most of them continued to back the rebel leader long enough to indicate that they had a loyalty to him. For a time – at least so long as he seemed to be winning – this overrode any such loyalty towards the legitimate king.

Similarly the tax burden on the Egyptian peasantry was heavy enough to provide a plausible reason for rebellion, especially when combined with the death of one king, the accession of another, and the latter's absence from Egypt, and the Ptolemaic government was to all appearance stifling and interventionist, but this may not be the whole story. The height of the Nile flood is sometimes blamed for triggering a rising, but Egyptians had ways of coping with such events based on millennia of experience of the river. Yet to cope they did require to hold reserves of food and seed, and the tax gatherers were voracious. The motives of individuals involved in such peasant uprisings are almost impossible to discover.

So all that can be suggested is that the recurrent rebellions imply that the kings did not have good relations with the people, or perhaps in many cases, any relations with them, quite probably because they knew little about their lives, the besetting problem of any ruling group. Yet in the Seleukid system the Friends of the king who were based in the cities surely knew of conditions there, which may be one reason why rebellions in the Seleukid cities were so relatively infrequent.

In that connection there may be noted the festivals and processions which all dynasties put on periodically. Ptolemy II's 'grand procession' in the 270s, which is described in extravagant detail in an extract from Kallixeinos of Rhodes preserved in Athenaios, and Antiochos IV's equally extravagant display in the festival at Daphne in 166, are the best-known cases, but there were others throughout the Hellenistic period, right through until the displays by Kleopatra for her lover Mark Antony in the 30s BC.[47] In addition, there were numerous local festivals, games which could become extravagant displays, and religious festivals at many places. These were staged for a variety of reasons: pride of wealth, royal boasting, religious devotion, diplomatic messages to potential enemies, are the most obvious, but one purpose was also to entertain and distract the city populations. Athletic games, another manifestation of religious devotion, multiplied during the period, in part in order to attract free-spending tourists. And all these were in large part aimed at the urban population; they were the Hellenistic version of the policy of 'bread and circuses' in the Roman Empire – as a means of distracting the people of the city of Rome. This was obviously part of the purpose of such shows, but the frequency of rebellion suggests that it was only partially successful. It does seem to have worked with their immediate audiences, the people of the cities, who generally went little further than brief riots, but such displays would have little effect on the men of the elite, and they did not take place in the sight of the rural population.

Despite attempts, it is not really possible to connect the kings with the ordinary people of the Hellenistic kingdoms which is why much of this chapter has been centred on the army and the elite. We do know the names of large numbers of individuals thanks to the survival of Babylonian documents and Egyptian papyri and Greek inscriptions.[48] But what we do not know is much beyond their names and perhaps the work they did. Their thoughts, ambitions, political and social attitudes are generally a blank, and unless further and more detailed sources emerge, we never will know of them.

Chapter 8

Kings and Cities

Cities were one of the main institutions through which kings ruled their kingdoms, and the relationship of kings with cities was perhaps one of the most important of the Hellenistic period. A large proportion of people living between the Zagros Mountains and Sicily, and between the European mountain ranges and the Sahara, were urban dwellers. And if they did not actually live within the city walls they probably lived in a city's territory, its *chora*. Cities were numbered in hundreds, and it was politically, socially, and economically a constant concern for the kings to ensure that these places were well treated, or at least fairly.

The kings were not helped in this by the priorities set by Philip II and Alexander the Great. In his concern to consolidate and expand his kingdom Philip had founded cities here and there – Philippi and Philippopolis, for example; these were generally planned and placed for good strategic reasons – Philippi was near the goldfields; Philippopolis was in conquered territory.[1] Beyond these actual cities, which was a less than precise term in Macedonian usage than in Greece, Philip fortified new and older towns, especially along his new frontiers, in, for example, the Magnesian Peninsula (where Demetrios later founded Demetrias), and along his northern and northwestern borders.[2] In at least one case he moved the population of a town in Pieria to a new site which was strategically more important to him.[3] On the other hand, Philip was also extremely destructive towards certain existing cities, notably those in the Chalkidike Peninsula which had become members of the local league, many of which were destroyed during his war of conquest against the league.[4]

Alexander had founded one small city, Alexandropolis in Thrace, even while Philip was alive, to join the other cities founded by Philip to control that area.[5] Alexander later balanced this, like Philip in the Chalkidike, by the destruction of the ancient and notable city of Thebes in his war of succession against the 'rebellious' Greeks.[6] During his great conquering expedition in the east, Alexander continued this mixture of conquest and destruction. He is reputed to have founded dozens of cities, though the number of actual cities he founded is very few, probably no more than four or five.[7] Many places which received garrisons of Macedonian and Greek soldiers could therefore later claim to have been 'founded' by Alexander – but if they did receive a garrison it meant the place already existed as a village or town. Alexander also contrived the destruction of ancient but recalcitrant cities such as Halikarnassos, Tyre, and Gaza, the great Persian imperial city of Persepolis, and cities without number in Baktria and India.

This destructiveness was a bad model for Alexander's successors to follow, and the narrow focus of strategic need in founding new cities could never be enough for them; they had to widen their perspectives in considering new foundations. The process of destruction continued during the wars between his successors. Babylon was severely damaged in fighting between Seleukos and Demetrios, Tyre was besieged and sacked a second time; Ptolemy destroyed the fortifications of all the cities in Palestine when he withdrew in 311, and several cities in Asia Minor suffered the same fate. So any city founded by Alexander had very little chance of surviving for very long during the wars and disputes which followed his death. For example, his most notable foundation, the city beside Egypt which became called Alexandria after him, may well have been founded by him in the sense that he had chosen the site and appointed the architect, but only a start on the building had taken place while he was alive or even for several years after his death. The real founder of the city was Ptolemy I, who is said to have built the walls and temples, and he only moved himself and his government to the city more than ten years after Alexander died.[8] Even then it will have remained a gigantic building site for many more years – the Egyptian name for the place was taken up by Greeks under the name Rhakotis, which in Egyptian means 'building-site'; it later became the name for part of the city.[9]

In another example the Alexandria which was founded in Margiana in Central Asia appears to have been destroyed by nomad attack during the succession wars; it had to be refounded in the 280s by Antiochos I.[10] Other Alexandrias were in fact usually existing 'native' settlements which were boosted by the imposition of a Macedonian garrison and given a new name, or adopted the name later. Examples are Kandahar in Afghanistan and Muhammerah at the head of the Persian Gulf; Alexandria Troas was originally an Antigoneia.

Destruction of a city was usually a short-term response to what the warlords will have considered military necessity. The founding activity by Philip and his son was, by contrast, much more relevant to their successors in the longer term. It provided a pattern on which they could rely for their own work, and a precedent which they could cite. These two kings had many motives in founding their new cities. Philip's prime aim seems to have been the defence of his kingdom and the preservation of his conquests, hence the new cities and fortifications along his frontiers, and the city foundations in Thrace. But even there he had other aims as well – the holding of the frontier, and the organisation and, perhaps just as importantly, the Macedonisation of Thrace, an area the size of the Macedonian home kingdom. The first aim, guarding the frontier, proved to be more or less successful, but it was never proof against attack from beyond the frontiers at times of internal problems in the kingdom; the Thracian conquest, however, was lost during the successors' wars, and later attempts at controlling the region – by Lysimachos, by Antiochos II and Antiochos III – proved to be just as ephemeral. Even Rome took a long time to gain control, and used the more effective and subtler method of a client Thracian kingdom to tame the land before annexing it.[11]

Alexander followed his father's lead and his few foundations were generally strategically placed with a view to controlling very wide areas of territory. Alexandria-by-Egypt was clearly positioned where it was in order to safeguard Egypt from attack from his enemies in Greece: it guarded one of the main entrances to Egypt from the sea at the mouth of the Canopos distributary of the River Nile – the fort of Pelusion performed the same function at the mouth of the other distributary on the east. At the same time, Alexandria functioned as a link with Greece – it was positioned at the nearest point of Egypt to Greece – and the sheer size of the planned city was such that it functioned also as a giant economic power generator. Egypt had welcomed Alexander a good deal more enthusiastically that any Greek city ever did, and the country's wealth made it absolutely essential for him to continue to control it. It had been invaded by others, Persians and Macedonians, at least three times in the two decades before Alexander's arrival, so establishing a major fortified city on the coast was thus a strategic necessity for him.

Alexandria-in-Margiana similarly controlled an important river valley and the water thereof, and thereby also dominated the surrounding territory; the fact that the nomads instantly attacked it when his back was turned indicates its importance, as does the evident priority ascribed to its recovery and re-foundations by Antiochos I. Muhammerah, at the head of the Persian Gulf, similarly performed the function of guarding the approach by sea into Babylonia – and Babylonia was the other very rich province which he had conquered; but Muhammerah had also to be repeatedly refounded by later kings, not because of invaders, but as a result of being founded in an area subject to floods.[12]

Alexander's strategic purposes in founding cities were taken up by his successors, and this was inevitably, given their wars, one of their main motives, though they usually had other priorities as well. Ptolemy I certainly developed Alexandria, but he did so only partly because it performed the function of a guard on the entrance to Egypt. His other reasons included homage to Alexander, whose embalmed body he had diverted into his own hands and which was eventually entombed in his name-city; he also regarded the city

as an economic asset, promoting trade by sea with the rest of the Mediterranean, and as a naval base from which he could defend Egypt (this had, of
course, also been implied in Alexander's purposes) and whence he could
launch attacks against his enemies by sea. His son Ptolemy II Philadelphos
extended this to use his navy to dominate the Aegean. Alexandria was the
fleet's main base, with subsidiary bases at several places in the Aegean area,
including Thera, Itanos in Crete, and Samos.

Elsewhere Ptolemy I was extremely chary of establishing cities: only two
seem to have been successfully attributed to him: Ptolemais in Upper Egypt,
and Ptolemais in Palestine. Both of these were in fact existing towns which he
expanded. Ptolemais in Palestine had been one of the Persian imperial bases,
Ake, from which at least one Persian invasion of Egypt had been launched.[13]
Ptolemais-in-the-Thebaid was in fact founded well to the north of the city of
Thebes, and is described as the largest city of that area, and the same size as
Memphis. It was thus evidently intended as a city which would rival Thebes
in importance, and would perhaps draw life from it as the Egyptian population moved to it. It was hardly successful in this, but was presumably – the site
itself has not been excavated – a major government centre for the whole
region; it was certainly a centre of communications with oases in the Western
Desert. Ptolemy's foundation was thus quite likely to have been very largely
inspired by his defensive needs and the necessity of gaining control of a region
which was always recalcitrant in the face of the Greco-Macedonian
government.[14]

Two of Alexander's successors were especially ambitious to restore his full
empire, stretching from Macedon to India, Antigonos Monophthalamos and
Seleukos Nikator. They were inveterate enemies from 315, when Antigonos
drove Seleukos from his satrapy of Babylonia, until 301, when Seleukos was
one of the coalition which finally destroyed Antigonos' kingdom, and Antigonos himself, at the battle of Ipsos. Yet both men appreciated, perhaps more
than anyone else in their time, the value of cities for their power and authority. Ptolemy valued one city in particular, Kassandros in Macedon developed
just one city, or perhaps two – Kassandreia and Thessalonike (in the conquered and devastated Chalidike).[15] Although the latter also vindictively refounded Thebes to demonstrate his antipathy towards Alexander's memory.[16]

Lysimachos founded only one, so far as we can tell, though he did enlarge
existing cities and renamed them. The one city which he appears to have
founded, and which had his name, Lysimacheia in Thrace, was in fact one of
these re-foundations, on the site of the destroyed Kardia.[17] His attempt to
rename Ephesos after his wife, Arsinoe, after enlarging the city, had no result,
and the new name soon vanished – Arsinoe herself, in flight after the battle

of Koroupedion, had to pass through the city in disguise, while her maid, dressed as Arsinoe, was killed.[18]

Antigonos and Seleukos were more radical in their approaches, the latter in particular. Both of them developed particular policies towards cities which, in unwitting combination, became the established policy towards cities for every king and emperor for at least the next five or six centuries; and Seleukos founded dozens of new cities, some of which remained major urban centres for even longer than Antigonos' own policy lasted.

To some degree Antigonos' work on cities was at first only tentative, and very similar to that of Alexander. Garrisons established throughout Syria used Macedonian names for the places they were stationed, and many were enlarged and founded as cities later by Seleukos and given Seleukid royal names. For example, 'Pella', at the site of a Syrian town called Pharnake, was founded as a new city and given the royal name Apameia.[19] Some places were simply renamed by Antigonos, and then renamed (by their inhabitants, or by a later king), for example, Antigoneia Troas became Alexandria Troas under Lysimachos.[20] Antigoneia-in-Bithynia became Nikaia after the Bithynian kingdom was able to establish its full independence.[21] In some cases Antigonos could refound cities by bringing small settlements together to form a major urban centre – Smyrna was an example, as was Antigoneia Troas – and in other cases he could enlarge old cities to create one which was an economically more useful size.[22]

The long war Antigonos fought against Seleukos was marked by unusual attention to Syria, a neglected area under the Akhaimenids, but where Antigonos founded his name city. With enemies in Egypt and Babylonia, it had been become necessary for Antigonos to establish a firm presence in north Syria. The city was designed, it seems, to become his main governing centre, and he spent much of his last years there, was proclaimed king there, and founded celebratory games at the city. To the east he planted Macedonian garrisons at Edessa, Karrhai, and Ichnai to hold the line of the Balikh River and block the routes from the east (and Seleukos did the same on his side to control those same routes from the west, along the line of the Khabur River).[23] Antigonos' motives were therefore various: frontier defence, revival of older settlements, a new capital city, occupation and control of conquered land; motives very similar to those of Philip (who was Antigonos' contemporary, of course). The Macedonian names of these places (both of Antigonos and of Seleukos) imply less than formal foundations, and the planting of garrisons of Macedonian soldiers seems the best explanation.

Seleukos had a much greater problem. Unlike Antigonos his empire was acquired piecemeal, sections being added at considerable intervals, first Babylonia and Iran in 312/311, then Mesopotamia as far as the Khabur River by 307, then the Far East (Baktria and eastern Iran) in his eastern expedition in 305–303, then northern Syria in 301, and finally Asia Minor in 282–201; he was on his way to occupy Thrace and Macedon when he was murdered in 281. He used cities, newly founded or expanded, or native sites taken over, or existing garrisons enlarged, as his primary means of imperial control. This appears from the very beginning, when he founded the great new city of Seleukeia-on-the-Tigris in 310 or a year or so later. This was a city designed to rival in size and wealth and importance the new Alexandria which was being developed by Ptolemy in Egypt, and probably also it was aimed at rivalling Antigonos' Antigoneia-on-the-Orontes in northern Syria as well (if he had begun that city by then). It was also designed to provide a new focus for economic power in Babylonia, as a government centre for the region, and was planted at a much more strategically important place than Babylon itself, close to the Bisitun Pass leading into Iran – though between them these two cities controlled the two river routes along the Tigris and Euphrates.[24]

The strategic motive seems most evident in the string of cities across northern Iran which were founded or enlarged or taken over by Seleukos. One was called at Apameia (after Seleukos' wife), but it is only vaguely located. One, the Iranian town of Rhagai, was named Europos (close to modern Teheran). As it happened, the Macedonian town of that name was Seleukos' birthplace, but it was accompanied by several others which also had names suggesting that the Greco-Macedonian inhabitants had already adopted the city names for themselves – Charis, Kalliope, Hekatompylos – and so had been named before Seleukos began his city-founding and naming campaign, and therefore before 310.[25] Thus Seleukos' work here was mainly to organise and enlarge the Macedonian garrisons, making them into true cities, and to fill in the strategic gaps; this would be the best explanation for his being credited as founder. His son, Antiochos I, either while he was his father's viceroy in the east, or as king himself later, continued the work with two cities named Laodikeia after Seleukos' mother – Laodikeia-in-Media and Laodikeia/Nihavand.[26] Further east, Seleukos again confined himself to settling matters down, confirming and no doubt encouraging places already founded; reinforcing them, organising their government; his son ruled here from 292 onwards and much of the work was no doubt done by him. As in Media and northern Iran, this work was essentially a process of consolidation; it seems highly unlikely that there were many new colonists available to populate the new foundations in the area even after Seleukos had secured control and communications were open; he was, after all, defeated in his Indian war, and was compelled to cede Arachosia and surrounding areas to the Indian emperor Chandragupta Maurya. Baktria was thus a precarious frontier region, hemmed in on the south and east by Indian territory, and on the north by nomads.

It was when Seleukos gained control of northern Syria, from 301, that his city founding activity became truly exceptional. Other kings, and Seleukos in his earlier career, had founded two or three cities, or even half a dozen; Seleukos in Syria established a dozen, apparently within a year or so of taking control, and then oversaw their development, their building, and their peopling during the next twenty years. Some were native Syrian settlements which were enlarged and Hellenised (Hierapolis-Bambyke), more were places where the earlier Macedonian garrisons had brought in new, often Macedonian names, and some of these were given royal Seleukid names to replace them (such as Pella which became Apameia); some were new foundations from the ground up, with perhaps no more than an existing Syrian village to be enclosed (an example is Beroia). The whole activity saw the rapid urbanising of the territory in Syria which Seleukos had acquired in 301, and so successfully that most of the cities have continued in existence to this day.[27] For two decades after Seleukos' acquisition of the area, it must have been like Alexandria but on a vastly greater scale, a great 'building site'.

The purpose of Seleukos' work in Media had been to consolidate his control; in Syria it was partly to establish his control over the country, but even more it was primarily defensive. He had acquired a land which was effectively without any worthwhile means of defence, and was vulnerable to attack by his enemies from the south, from the north, and from the sea. By planting and populating his new cities he made any invasion much more difficult (though in the event not impossible); the positioning and size of the cities was above all designed to foil any invasion from the Ptolemaic territory in Palestine and Phoenicia ('Koile Syria') after he and Ptolemy had quarrelled over their respective shares of the Syrian spoils from Antigonos' brief kingdom. This in turn compelled Ptolemy to develop an adequate defensive system in Phoenicia, designed to deter a Seleukid invasion, though it was more precisely done by military works – there was a line of defended cities along the coast, and again it was not wholly successful.

It was the immediate successors of Alexander – Antigonos, Kassandros, Seleukos, Ptolemy, Lysimachos – who did the main work of planting and development of new cities, far more so than Alexander himself, who surely had little time for such work. Their own successors, particularly Antiochos I and Antiochos II and Demetrios to some degree, continued this work, but to a much lesser extent, and this was mainly work on the re-foundation and enlargement (and renaming) of existing settlements, though, to be sure, the sources for this are poor. Much of the work, once Antiochos I had moved west after his father's death, took place in Asia Minor, where the Galatian invasions had rendered much of the region unsafe and vulnerable to their raids.[28] By the mid-third century the impetus for new founding had died away, even in the Seleukid Empire – which was racked by the civil war from 246 to 220 – and partly perhaps because of the reduction in the availability of colonists from Greece. The main reason, however, was because the political situation was such that founding new cities was no longer an appropriate response to threats and problems.

All the founding kings operated under powerful political pressures and their attitudes towards cities were overwhelmingly based on securing political and military advantage. Even before the practice of founding (or refounding) new cities had developed among the successors of Alexander they had all faced the difficulties inherent in relations between over-mighty warlords and the determined independence of the old Greek cities in Greece and Asia Minor (and Cyrenaica). Here the brutality of both Philip and Alexander was soon seen to be counter-productive, but the sheer difficulty of warlords who were based in Macedon or Asia or Egypt in controlling the cities of Greece, which were numerous, fortified, and independently minded, was daunting in the extreme.

Ptolemy, for example, burnt his fingers in Cyrenaica, where he faced an early rebellion after responding to an appeal for help and then his troops overstayed their welcome; in the end he sent his half-brother Magas as governor, a man with only a fraction of the burning ambitions of the greater warlords, and Magas evidently came to an amenable arrangement with the Cyrenaicans, so much so that he ruled the region, as satrap and then as king, for half a century and more – but hardly as Ptolemy's vassal.[29] Kassandros and Lysimachos tended to use their military power to dominate the cities in their regions, but they also came to see the usefulness of founding new cities and tolerating the older ones. But it was Antigonos who developed the most useful and far-reaching policy, even if it did not provide him with real physical control over the Greek cities.

Antigonos' policy is described, in brief, as 'the freedom of the Greeks', or more precisely, 'the freedom of the cities', which he proclaimed at Tyre, ironically during his siege of the city in 315.[30] This was designed to attract the support of the cities in Greece and the Aegean area, many of which had been alienated from Macedonian rulers by Alexander's and the later warlords' policies. It was, in the immediate term, aimed at persuading the Greeks not to support Kassandros, but when Ptolemy adopted the same policy by his own proclamation it soon became standard for all the kings. In essence it pretended to leave the Greek cities free rather than establishing direct rule over them; in actuality it offered protection in exchange for tribute. Antigonos promised that he would not garrison those cities which were his allies, but he did expect them to provide funds for his trouble in providing defence for them. Some Greek cities saw through the pretence; others understood that this might well be the best option for them in a dangerous and violent world. Above all, this became the policy pursued by most Hellenistic kings towards the existing cities, and it was later also adopted as the basic policy of the Roman Republic (if somewhat erratically and greedily in some cases) and its succeeding imperial system. Rome, of course, had a policy of establishing its own colonies to hold down its conquered territories, very like that of Philip II; in this it was replicating on a small scale the activities of King Seleukos.

Antigonos' policy of apparent conciliation stumbled on more than one occasion. It had been announced, for example, while he was besieging Tyre. This had been occupied by Ptolemy in defiance of him, and when Ptolemy announced his own version of the policy of 'the freedom of the Greeks' neither he nor Antigonos relinquished their grip on the city. Ten years later Antigonos' son Demetrios laid siege to Rhodes after a curious diplomatic dispute which provides a case study in dispute-escalation; this was hardly an action consistent in any way with his announced policy. And the repeated campaigns of Kassandros and Demetrios in Greece were as negative from the cities' point of view as the attack on Rhodes. Despite the announced policy, to which all the kings proclaimed their adherence in the end, their actions towards the Greek cities amounted to direct control and domination. Athens fell under the control of Antigonos Gonatas of Macedon, who planted several garrisons in forts around the city to maintain that control.

Seleukos I's strategy of founding new cities in the almost empty countries he had acquired was therefore an alternative, in a sense, to Antigonos' policy of 'freedom' for the cities. Diplomatically the policy of 'freedom' allowed kings to accept the distant support of friendly cities without having to expend troops in garrisons; meanwhile the process of new foundations neutral-ised Seleukos' enemies, since conquering north Syria in the face of a dozen or more defended cities would be time-consuming and militarily and economic-ally ruinous. The citizens therefore provided Seleukos with military man-power, an expanded tax base, and at the same time defended his conquests. In all the new cities he established an autonomous government, and attracted settlers to them, who provided the manpower for his increasing armed strength. The new cities thus approximated to the creation of independent cities who were allies of a king, though rather more reliable than most. The two policies therefore moved in parallel, with the result that the diplomatic situation of the two sets of cities became similar.

Seleukos' main purposes in founding his cities in Syria, even beyond physical defences, was to attract colonists, whose men could be recruited into his army. Without a population, even fortified, Syria was a liability, vulnerable, open to invasion, and producing no taxes. Founding new cities in the country, each within its own walls, performed the first function; their existence attracted settlers, above all from Greece, who were provided with land, homes, and the possibility of future prosperity. The land thus became defensible; the settlers produced taxes; their military obligations increased the size of Seleukos' army. As a policy, this was clearly a masterpiece. At the same time, Seleukos carefully ensured that the autonomy which the new cities had was strictly limited to internal affairs. Two institutions in particular were established so that he and his successors always maintained control.

In the building and planning of each city, the acropolis was deliberately located in one corner of the site. This meant that the garrison dominated the city, and at the same time it maintained its own access to the land outside, and so would be very difficult to isolate in the event of an internal rebellion, and so it was virtually impossible for the citizens to rebel successfully. (Rebellions, as noted in the last chapter, were very rare in Seleukid cities, but was this because of loyalty to the kings, or fear of the acropolis garrisons?) Second was the institution of the *epistates*, a post to which one of the king's Friends was appointed, already discussed in Chapter 6. Usually he would be a man from the city itself, and his purpose was to maintain a line of political connection between the city and the king. This ensured that any problem could be defused or dealt with before it became serious – another possible restriction on any rebellious activity. And finally, of course, the king was counted as the *ktistes*, the city founder, which gave him and his successors considerable, if vague, influence and authority.

The kings had, as was long ago remarked, taken upon themselves a great deal of work and expense in founding cities, and Seleukos in particular in establishing a dozen cities all at once, could surely have been overwhelmed. The work involved has been listed as the king having to 'find land and settlers for it, build the wall, supply food, seed-corn, cattle, and tools to give the people a start, remit taxation till the city found its feet, ... give a constitution, ... settle the city laws ...'.[31]

Of course, no king did all this personally, though he would be ultimately responsible for all of it. One of the crucial necessary qualities for a king was the ability to delegate. Seleukos delegated the government of the eastern territories to his son, and governors (satraps) had fairly wide-ranging powers. It is altogether likely that he delegated the supervision of much of the work of founding his Syrian cities to his Friends. It is a pity we do not know of any of them by name, but of one place, or perhaps two, we do know something. The date of the foundation of Ai Khanum in Baktria is not known, but it is thought to have been during the reign of Seleukos.[32] There is an inscription from the place naming the founder as a man called Kineas, who, given the timing and the place, was evidently acting on behalf of Seleukos, though since his rule of the east lasted a quarter of a century this is less than precise.

There is also one other city whose founder may be known. The old Mesopotamian city of Nisibis is recorded as being 'founded' by 'Nikator', which is the epithet applied the Seleukos.[33] But kings are normally identified by their names, so the founder's name is often reckoned really to be 'Nikanor', who is also recorded as founding an 'Antioch' – Nisibis was given the dynastic name of Antioch-in-Mygdonia.[34] The issue is difficult, and endlessly debatable, but it does seem that the king was not the direct founder, but was operating through another, possibly this Nikanor. If so, that is the second of Seleukos' cities whose actual founder is known by name, and may be taken as a demonstration that he successfully delegated his authority in the matter to subordinates.[35]

This, as well as the sheer likelihood of such a proceeding, is reasonably good evidence that the 'hard work' which Seleukos undertook in founding the cities was shared with a considerable number of other men. At a guess a plan of operation was laid out by Seleukos, who would be responsible for choosing the sites, and one or two Friends were assigned to each new city, with the king supervising and intervening where necessary, and no doubt making periodic inspections. The distribution of the cities in Syria indicates clearly an overall plan: four large cities, all named for members of Seleukos' family, formed a quadrilateral of four fully fortified sites placed to block any possible Ptolemaic invasion; the other, smaller cities occupied the lands between that greater group and the Euphrates, where the city guarded the only bridge over the river.

The other contribution by the king was financial. The treasures collected by Alexander from the accumulated hoards of the Akhaimenid kings had been released from their stores, largely by Antigonos in financing his campaigns, but there were still large quantities available for each king to spend. Seleukos not only gained the greater part of the kingdom of Antigonos, he also acquired much of his treasure. We know of at least two treasuries – at Pergamon (acquired only in 281) and at Quinda in Kilikia. More deposits were no doubt collected at various places in Syria – at Antigoneia-on-the-Orontes, for instance – and in Asia Minor to add to those he had obtained in the east. This, together with the regular product of taxation, was the source used to finance the building of the cities, and Seleukos clearly had sufficient resources even before acquiring Asia Minor to set about founding the Syrian cities.[36]

When he appointed his son Antiochos as joint king and gave him responsibility for establishing and maintaining control over Central Asia, one of the tools Antiochos had to use was city foundation. (Antiochos may therefore be counted as one of Seleukos' city-founding instruments, though since he was appointed joint king, it may be presumed that he was acting to some extent independently, and that he would use his own squad of Friends to do the detailed work.) Alexandria-in-Margiana, for example, as already noted, was refounded, strengthened, and repopulated, and renamed Antioch-in-Margiana. It seems probable, though deficient sources make it difficult to decide the issue, that Antiochos also established the Seleukid frontier along the Jaxartes River, using Demodamas of Miletos as his military commander. Certainly Demodamas is credited with re-establishing the seven altars by that river which Alexander had built during his campaign – and which were close to a city or fortress founded by Cyrus the Great, and one of Alexander's foundations Alexandreschate, which may or may not have survived the turbulence in the region after his departure.[37] Alexander had crossed the river to defeat a nomad band; it seems likely that Demodamas and Antiochos did so as well, but soon after, the boundary on the river retreated to the line of mountains south of it, abandoning a good stretch of territory to those very nomads, probably a result of the move into independence led by the governors Diodotos I and II, which was in turn a result of the dynastic civil war of the 240s and after.

This process of founding new cities more or less ended as the first generation of kings died off, except among the Seleukids. One reason must be that for Egyptian and Macedonian kings there was no need for new cities, their lands being fully occupied and defended already, and their lands more or less fully urbanised. But the Seleukid kingdom still had large areas of non-urbanised land. The frenetic pace of city foundation of Seleukos I's reign was not repeated, but Antiochos I did continue the work in Asia Minor, which Seleukos had conquered in the year before his death. By this time however – the 270s and after – it was really no longer possible to recruit the necessary settlers. These had, so far as can be seen, mainly come from Greece, always a land of overflowing population. Any new city would need several thousand settlers, that is to say several thousand men – 5,000 or 6,000 citizens are noted in later cases – plus their wives, plus their children, and perhaps their slaves, as an initial foundation population.[38] The dozen cities established in Syria by Seleukos I must therefore have absorbed between 250,000 and 500,000 immigrants between 315 and 280, which included any who had settled there under Antigonos, and in addition to any Syrians who moved into the new cities from the surrounding countryside; meanwhile others had also migrated to Egypt and Asia Minor. Such a flow of people could not be continued forever.

The practice of founding new cities, therefore, even in the Seleukid kingdom, only lasted until perhaps 260, roughly the end of the reign of Antiochos I. After that point any migrants, of which there were fewer, would be

able to settle in the existing cities. The practice continued of renaming existing cities, usually by awarding them a dynastic name, an event which involved
reordering their constitution and their laws. Seleukos I had so treated two of
the Syrian cities which had originally been towns inhabited by native Syrians:
Hierapolis-Bambyke and the river crossing point at Thapsakos, which was
probably taken over as a new city and given the name Seleukeia; to distinguish
it from all the other Seleukeias it became known as Seleukeia-Zeugma,
'Seleukeia-the-Bridge'; the suburb across the river on the east bank received
the name Apameia, the name of Seleukos' wife; the two settlements were thus
linked in the same way as the king and the queen.[39] This renaming tactic was
also used by other kings; Lysimachos, for example, at Ephesos-Arsinoe.

The existence of a well-established urban society within Lysimachos' kingdom, particularly along the Aegean coast, meant that he scarcely needed to
adopt Seleukos' expedient of widespread new foundations. The western coast
lands of Asia Minor, and a good deal of the western interior, were studded
with cities which had existed for centuries. Such was also the case in Greece,
and in southern Italy and Sicily, with the result that new cities were rarely
needed in those areas. In the eastern territories, in Asia and Egypt, the situation was much more varied. Egypt, for example, certainly had urban settlements which could be classified as cities. Memphis was the 3,000-year-old
imperial capital of the pharaohs; in Upper Egypt Thebes had an equivalent
status; both of these were large enough to count as major urban centres;[40]
most of the administrative regions of Egypt – the nomes – had an urban
centre as their governing base. Few of these, if any, were recognised as cities,
that is, *poleis*, by Greeks and Macedonians, though they were urban in size and
government, and most of the population in Egypt actually lived in villages.

The territories acquired by Seleukos were infinitely more varied. Babylonia
had been an urban society for as long as Egypt, perhaps longer, and its cities
were as self-governing as any Greek city, though, again, Greeks would scarcely
recognise them as *poleis*.[41] The Seleukid government was more amenable,
however, and Babylonian urban self-government continued. Baktria was also
an urbanised region, at least partly, and was eventually to be regarded as so
citified as to have a 'thousand' cities.[42] Even in regions which were scarcely
regarded as urbanised, there were ancient and well-established cities. For
example, the old kingdom of Elam, east of Babylonia, contained the city of
Susa (which was awarded the name Seleukeia);[43] and along the great route
through northern Iran connecting Babylonia and Baktria there were a series
of urban settlements – Ekbatana, Kangavar, Rhagai, and others, though they
were not usually recognised as *poleis* by Greeks simply because they were not
governed in the Greek manner; like the Babylonian cities they had had a

sufficiently effective and acceptable system of civil government that the Seleukids continued it.

There were therefore three broad types of cities which Hellenistic kings had to deal with. There were those founded as new by the kings themselves, whose relations with the king were regulated by the presence of an *epistates*, by the existence of a garrison, by the fact that the king or an ancestor was the founder, and by a general loyalty expected of the inhabitants. Then there were the pre-existing Greek and Macedonian cities, which were largely confined to Greece, the Aegean coasts, and the Ionian Sea lands. These might or might not be content to subject themselves to a king, an attitude dependent on the alternative, which might be the near presence of another king, though switching allegiances was dangerous, and only to be carried out if the new king was an effective protector. Such cities would indicate their alliance with the king towards whom they leaned by an agreed treaty, which was usually inscribed on a stone set up in the city.[44] They would make regular presents of 'gold crowns' at notable moments – on the occasion of a victory gained by the king, for example, or his birthday, his marriage, the marriage of his eldest son, the accession of a new king, to commemorate a victory, and so on. Such cities were not formally taxed, but the crowns were an effective substitute.

The third group of cities comprised the great variety of the pre-existing cities developed by the native populations before Alexander's conquest. Every country to which Alexander and his successors penetrated had some of them – Phoenicia, Egypt, Babylonia, Iran, Baktria, India. Their internal constitutions were similarly varied. They might be ruled by a governor appointed by a king, they might be controlled by the priests of a temple, or they might have no obvious government, consisting perhaps of an agglomeration of villages, each of which had its own chief. The existence of these places therefore constituted a major governing problem for the new kings. Not surprisingly, approaches varied.

The approach used by many Seleukid kings was twofold. In most cases the original city was accepted as it was, and its internal autonomy and organisational government was allowed to continue, with acceptable indications of loyalty – tax payments, attendance at royal audiences, possibly the presence of a garrison. This was the general approach in Babylonia, and at Jerusalem until trouble there provoked the intervention of Antiochos IV. The second approach is that adopted by Antiochos at Jerusalem as a result of his intervention – to remodel the internal constitution in such a way that a governing system friendly to the king was installed. In most cases this would bring to power a Greco-Macedonian oligarchy, which would be reinforced by hellenised natives. The signal that this had happened – not always necessarily as a result of some trouble – was the imposition of a dynastic name, which would then be the official name of the city, even though the old native name usually continued in use locally. The Seleukids did not apply this change systematically, but over two centuries and more of their power significantly large numbers of the existing cities received the treatment.

This was not a policy the Ptolemies favoured. Ptolemy I established himself in Memphis for a time after he gained control in 323, and it was there that for a decade or more that he placed Alexander's sarcophagus. It might have seemed that he had intended the city to be once again the imperial capital of Egypt, but it was clearly only a temporary arrangement until Alexandria was fit to be occupied. But by merely using Memphis in that way he had effectively recognised its political importance, and his successors generally respected that importance, for example by staging a crowning ceremony there at the accession of new kings, though it seems this did not take place until the reign of Ptolemy V, by which time it had become urgently necessary to conciliate Egyptian opinion, and putting the king through a crowning ceremony derived from pharaonic ritual was one method of doing this: many later Ptolemies used the same ceremony.[45] Neither Alexander nor Ptolemy I nor Ptolemy's successors made any serious attempt to alter the internal government of Egypt. Even in settling Greeks in the country the Ptolemies tended to organise them in villages, as in the Fayum, which was reclaimed land. These may in fact have been fairly large as villages go – one of them, Kerkeosiris, had a population of 1,500 or so – but they were never allowed to develop as *poleis*.[46]

Babylonia was the economic heart of the Seleukid kingdom, and had demonstrated an early loyalty to Seleukos I when he was under great pressure from Antigonos and Demetrios, and again when the Galatian War was on. It would have been folly to disturb the position there too seriously. There is therefore no indication that at any point any Seleukid king attempted to change the government system of Babylonia. The Babylonian cities continued to be self-governing in their own way, and the only major change was in the foundation of a new imperial city at Seleukeia-on-the-Tigris. One or two cities were awarded dynastic names, and this may well indicate that they were reorganised on Macedonian urban lines, but the ancient Babylonian urban centres remained essentially untouched.

The effectiveness of royal control of the cities – or influence over them – depended on the effectiveness of the royal regime overall. A dynastic dispute, or an invasion, brought any threatened cities to rely on their own resources. The Phoenician cities appear to have had ambitions to shift into independence, and Arados in particular made repeated efforts to escape from Seleukid overlordship, until it had final success in 130/129, in the aftermath of the great Seleukid disaster in the east under Antiochos VII.[47] The Babylonian cities, however, made no such attempt and at times displayed a self-sacrificial loyalty to the Seleukid dynasty.[48] However, they fell without any obvious resistance into Parthian hands in the 130s, by which time there had been civil war in Syria for a decade. Seleukeia-on-the-Tigris, on the other hand, did put up a strenuous resistance.

Because the cities were generally fortified they became the prime targets in any war, but they were also liable to surrender to avoid a sack by an enemy army. When Ptolemy III invaded north Syria in 246 the whole Seleukid position collapsed and Ptolemy was able to take control of every city as far as, and beyond, the Euphrates.[49] It is clear from Ptolemy's account that Seleukeia and Antioch welcomed him with appropriate ceremony – they clearly did not realise that this was a war.[50] But when Antiochos III invaded Ptolemaic Koile Syria in 218, he had to move slowly and several of the cities resisted him.[51] When he attacked his rebel cousin Akhaios in Asia Minor in 216–212, he had to fight his way along the main road from Syria to the western cities, and Sardis was eventually besieged, taken, and sacked.[52] Resistance or surrender in fact generally depended on the presence or absence of a royal garrison, and often of a senior general or the king himself. Cities, given the option, tended to surrender at the first summons rather than display any too obvious loyalty to the attacker's enemy. This might, however, then incur the wrath of the returning king, as when Ptolemy IV reproved the Palestinian cities for surrendering too easily to Antiochos III's army.[53]

The willingness of cities under threat of attack to surrender is indicative of the fact that they could not be assumed to be loyal under all circumstances to any particular king or dynasty. Most of the time they had no choice in the matter, being garrisoned and thus under obvious military domination. But those without garrisons – generally the older Greek cities – were fully capable of changing their allegiance. The campaigns of Antiochos III in western Asia Minor provide plenty of evidence that the cities there only surrendered to main force.[54]

This is true also of the cities which were founded by the Seleukid kings and garrisoned by their troops. In Syria, where the number of cities, the obligations of the population, and the strength of the garrisons might have produced an expectation of loyalty, the cities either rebelled or surrendered to enemies several times – a rebellion of some sort in 281, rapid surrender in 246, a rebellion by Kyrrhos in 220, mass surrender from Gaza to Antioch in 145, and serially surrendering to Tigranes in the 80s. The cities were not consistently loyal. On the other hand, these events mark a breakdown in the dynastic governing system, upon which the cities relied for their defence; the cities might well react to such a collapse by assuming that the loyalty they expected from the king no longer existed. As the kings recovered, there is no sign that punishments were awarded; even Ptolemy IV went no further than reproving the cities of Palestine for surrendering to Antiochos III.

It may have been with the aim of bolstering the cities' loyalty that Antiochos IV (a usurper in some eyes, even a madman in others) began a policy of extending minting privileges to many cities, particularly in the Syrian region. This meant that mints were established in some cities where they had not been before, and in others were extended, all to produce royal currency in silver, and local bronze coins. The mints would also produce a profit for the cities themselves and no doubt for the king. Antiochos' purpose is not, in fact, known, but it can be assumed that it was intended to a large degree for his own benefit more than that of the cities, whose gains were incidental. It may have had the result of increasing civic autonomy, or at least civic consciousness, and it is noticeable that it is from then onwards that many cities tended to become more assertive.[55]

The intervention of cities in the internal political processes in any of the kingdoms was rare, and, again, tended to happen only when the royal authority was in dispute or had collapsed, occasions when the cities tended to be left to their own devices. Ptolemy III was able to gain control of Seleukid north Syria in 246 for this very reason. In 146/145 there were three contenders for the rule of the same area, and two of the great cities of Syria banded together as 'brother-cities', apparently in an assertion of neutrality in the war in which three kings were simultaneously contending for control. Antioch in fact made some attempt at intervention by claiming to recognise Ptolemy VI as the Seleukid king, but Ptolemy, after thinking about it for a time, refused. The city is credited with being the arbiter in the choice of a new king in 85, when Tigranes of Armenia moved in, but this may only be a later civic legend.[56] In Egypt, Alexandria was a turbulent city in the first century BC, seating and unseating kings. Such difficulties might lead to the seizure of civic power by a tyrant, as at Kassandreia in the crisis of the Galatian invasion of Macedon, but such men had relatively little support after the crisis, and could be dislodged by a victorious king with little difficulty.[57] The Babylonian cities made no serious resistance to Parthian control in the 140s, and in fact Babylon itself surrendered to a mere message sent by the Parthian king.[58]

The civic consciousness of the new Hellenistic cities was much less assertive than might have been expected from a population which was overwhelmingly of Greek or Macedonian descent. This did not apply in the older Greek cities. The old rivals Athens and Sparta repeatedly attempted to overthrow Macedonian domination to reacquire their ancient ability to act independently - with little ultimate success – and groups of smaller cities banded together in leagues – the Aitolian League was explicitly developed for self defence against Macedon. These older cities were always more likely to act independently, if they could, than the new colonial cities, but they had little power to effect change. The kings had largely organised a government system which worked and which most cities could accept and work within. In crises, however, they rarely displayed any obvious loyalty towards the ruling dynasty, but looked generally to their own safety first; no doubt the kings felt betrayed.

The relationship between kings and cities was one of the two crucial elements in public affairs in the Hellenistic period – the other being inter-royal relations. It was a relationship with many elements of, if not enmity, at least competition within it. The balance between royal authority and civic authority was never still, and the weakest of the two turned out in the end to be that of the kings, whose authority depended too much on the individual capacities of the holders of that power. But when the relationship of cities to power moved from the Hellenistic to the Roman it became very clear quite rapidly that equality and balance were not concepts understood by the Roman warlords or later the emperors. The cities in many ways had been softened up by their Hellenistic experience in preparation for the more rigorous Roman approach. Autonomy for the cities in the Roman Empire was much less than that in the Hellenistic kings.

Chapter 9

Kings and War

The ancient sources imply that the main business of kings was warfare, though this is more the result of their omission of other activities than from any full consideration of the range of royal actions and responsibilities. In this the sources were not, of course, entirely wrong, but since we do not have an accurate breakdown of how the kings spent their time, we must take leave to doubt such a sweeping impression. Once again, it is necessary to return to the examples set by Philip II and Alexander the Great. Their Macedonian kingdom was clearly threatened by all their neighbours, Greeks from the south and the Aegean coast, and barbarians from over the landward borders – Thracians from the northeast, Illyrians and others from the north, Epeirotes from the northwest. This constant and continuing problem compelled every Macedonian king to wage war on a more or less regular basis, particularly at the commencements of their reigns. Philip II had to fight hard for several years to establish his control over the borders of his kingdom, and Alexander had to do the same twenty years later, though the memory of his father's recent successes and his own speed and decisiveness meant he was free from such problems fairly quickly. But under his successors the difficulties revived.

Alexander's death in Babylon was followed, notoriously, by fifty years of warfare of gradually diminishing intensity, in which numerous kings, would-be kings, and commanders died, not to mention their soldiers and their would-be subjects, until just half a dozen contestants were left. But by that time it had become clear that the new rulers and kings were being compelled to spend rather more time on administration than on war, though war still remained one of their major activities.

Kings relied on their armies for their basic authority to rule, a factor which has been repeatedly emphasised in this book (notably in Chapter 8). As such every Hellenistic kingdom was a military monarchy, and such coronation ceremonies as existed at first involved an acclamation by soldiers, or at least an early expedition with the king in command, even if only theoretically. Over time, this military emphasis varied and in some cases it sensibly declined. The first generation of the successors – Antigonos Monophthalamos, Seleukos I, Ptolemy I, Lysimachos, Kassandros – lived in such an unstable and violent world that they had little option but to fight each other, at least until the destruction of Antigonos' kingdom in 301 BC. From then on the intensity, or perhaps frequency, of warfare was replaced by equally intense diplomatic contests and intrigues, interrupted by occasional wars. For example, Seleukos I can be seen to have been fighting virtually constantly from 312, when he regained control of Babylonia, until 301, when he participated decisively in the destruction of Antigonos – wars in Syria, in Babylonia, in Iran and Central Asia, in India, and finally in Asia Minor. But from 301 until his death in 281, he appears to have remained for much of his time in Syria, and perhaps in Babylonia, without indulging in major warfare except in his last year. He did seize control of Kilikia from Demetrios in 294, though without much, or perhaps any, fighting.[1] But there is no trace of him fighting for the next ten or so years, until Demetrios invaded Syria in 285, when Seleukos carefully refrained from tackling the invader head on.[2] In the years 312–301 therefore Seleukos campaigned constantly, while between 301 and 281 he fought only three relatively brief wars, in two of which there was little fighting, and an extensive campaign and a single battle in the other. The same calculation can be made for Lysimachos and Ptolemy I, but for Kassandros and the succeeding kings of Macedon for the same three decades, until Antigonos Gonatas established his firm control in the kingdom, warfare remained a constant preoccupation – the results of the near presence and invasions of barbarians and of the Macedonian borders.

Indulging in war was to some extent a personal choice for any particular king. Antiochos III, for example, can be seen to have gone on campaign in almost every year of his reign, though he did not necessarily have to fight – the very presence of his army could at times overawe his chosen opponents.[3] To be sure, he had a huge empire to rule, and he faced many and difficult problems in it, with hostile neighbours on many fronts, but some of his wars were clearly of his own choice, so we must assume that he felt that warfare was one of his duties as a king, while at the same time it was an activity which pleased him. Between 246 and 219 three successive Seleukid kings fought constantly to recover lost territories, and to subdue rebellions; then, from 219 to 188, Antiochos III campaigned annually to expand the territory he had inherited. The range of his military activity spread from Greece and Thrace to the borders of India. Whatever justification he advanced for this constant activity – it is generally assumed that his programme was one aimed at the restoration of the bounds his kingdom had reached at any time in the past – it was clearly something that the king enjoyed and which he therefore undertook.[4] He is recorded repeatedly as taking a full part in the actual fighting.[5]

By contrast, the Ptolemaic kings, if not actually more pacific, were much less likely to take part in war personally. It is difficult to find more than half a dozen occasions when a Ptolemaic king between the last years of Ptolemy I and the reign of Ptolemy VI (say between 290 and 164), left their kingdom to go on campaign. It was considered worthy of comment when Ptolemaic kings went on campaign – Ptolemy II went to Syria during the First Syrian War, for instance, at a moment when it appears that the campaign was going badly for his troops, though he did not take command and he scarcely advanced further into Syria than Gaza.[6] Ptolemy III's first year as king was spent supervising a campaign in northern Syria, but he soon returned to Egypt, leaving the role of commander to generals.[7] And, in fact, on examining what he actually did in north Syria it is clear that he was nowhere near any of the fighting; he perhaps went no further inland than Antioch, having staged ceremonial entries into that city and into Seleukeia-in-Pieria.[8] Ptolemy IV's presence at the battle of Raphia in 217 was evidently one of the reasons for the Ptolemaic victory, his presence inspiring the army, and caused great surprise, but he did not command.[9] And so on. Ptolemy I had been an active campaigner for much of his life, and Ptolemy VI campaigned for ten years inside Egypt to restore internal peace, but when he ventured into Syria on campaign he ended up being killed in battle.

One of the consequences of royal power being based so obviously on the military was that it was often necessary for a king to achieve a military victory soon after his accession, just to 'prove' his military credentials. This is one of the reasons for the frequent wars which follow such accessions – and it is one of the many marks of royal authority which transferred into Roman imperial and monarchic practice. The creation of the new kingdoms all through the Hellenistic period almost invariably followed the achievement of victory by a local leader who then proclaimed himself king. This happened with Pontos, where victory was gained by the local commander Mithradates over a general of Lysimachos.[10] Also with Bithynia, where the local chieftain Zipoetes also defeated one of Lysimachos' commanders.[11] In Cyrenaica Magas attacked Ptolemaic Egypt but was prevented from reaching it by a rebellion by the local Libyan nomads, probably stirred up by Ptolemy II; his victory over these was his royal baptism.[12]

The need to go on an early campaign was not only the result of the requirement for a victory at the beginning of a reign. It was also the result of the diplomatic arrangements which had developed during the Hellenistic period. Any peace treaty between kings expired on the death of one of the parties to that treaty; as a result a newly enthroned king was immediately liable to be attacked. This was not invariable or inevitable, and a powerful king was likely to be safe from attack by a minor power, but where there were outstanding issues between dynasties – as over Syria between the Ptolemies and the

Seleukids – a new war was almost inevitable at the start of a new reign. Simple tabulation demonstrates this for Syria:

281 Death of Seleukos I	First Syrian War began 274
261 Death of Antiochos I	Second Syrian War began 260
246 Death of Ptolemy II and Antiochos II	Third Syrian War began 246
223 Death of Seleukos III 222 Death of Ptolemy III	Fourth Syrian War began 221
204 Death of Ptolemy IV	Fifth Syrian War began 202
176 Death of Ptolemy V 175 Death of Seleukos IV	Sixth Syrian War began 170.[13]

It may well be that it was a mark of the instability of a kingship that a king felt it necessary to go on frequent campaigns. The contrast here is between the Seleukid kingdom and the rest. The Antigonids of Macedon certainly waged war with relative frequency but their kingship appears to have been well grounded in local loyalties. The Attalids of Pergamon had the unusual origin in an opportunistic bureaucrat, and their military credentials were for a time minor, but once they had extended their power over the local area beyond the city of Pergamon, they soon conformed to the normal pattern, and each new king had usually to fight his Galatian neighbours early on in order to restore the peace between him and them. In 263 Eumenes I, who succeeded in that year defeated Antiochos I, or an army commanded by one of his generals; Attalos I, who succeeded in 241, fought the Galatians and was 'proclaimed king' as a result; Eumenes II became involved in Rome's war with Antiochos III, and fought at the battle of Magnesia, even being credited with a substantial part of the victory.[14] The Attalids' Galatian problem was again the result of the acceptance of time-limited peace treaties, and several of the kings became active and sometimes successful commanders. The Ptolemies, on the other hand, rarely needed to lead their armies themselves, but at the same time did tend to take on a war soon after an accession.[15] Ptolemy II, Ptolemy III, and Ptolemy IV all began wars with the Seleukids soon after their accession; Ptolemy V and VI were both infants at their accession, but their kingdoms were nevertheless involved in wars soon after.

The Ptolemies' habit was to direct operations from a distance, from their capital in Alexandria, employing commanders to conduct operations in the field, or at sea. This was in part due to their need to hold Alexandria and Egypt firmly, as Ptolemy III discovered, but also because their wars generally took place in several different regions, and so local governors was already in command. So in the Aegean it was usual for a commander of the Ptolemaic fleet in the region to act as local viceroy, and then to take up the military –

or rather naval – command when the fighting began; Philokles in the 280s, Patroklos in 267, Khremonides later in the 260s, and each man had the power and authority to seize and hold new bases; Patroklos in particular took control of Itanos in Crete, the island of Thera, and Methana on the coast of the Argolid, which became permanent Ptolemaic bases, to add to Samos.[16] In Syria Antiochos III faced subordinate commanders in all his invasions, Theodotos of Aitolia in 221 and 218, Ptolemy son of Thraseas in 202, and Skopas, another Aitolian, in 200–199, but only at the climactic battle of Raphia did he face the Ptolemaic king.[17] When Ptolemy III was recalled to Egypt soon after embarking on his invasion of Syria as a result of a peasant rebellion, he demonstrated that the Ptolemaic practice of concentrating on holding Egypt was fully justified; at the same time the incident revealed a weakness in the Ptolemaic system which their enemies would eventually exploit. By making oath-bound peace treaties they staved off the day of reckoning, but when it came that reckoning was final.[18] In the Fourth Syrian War (221–217) Ptolemy IV only appeared once on the battlefield – much to the troops' surprise – at the Raphia battle.[19] Neither of these men could be considered as in any sense a warrior. Ptolemy VI, on the other hand, had to battle hard to recover full control of Egypt in the 160s, and eventually died fighting in Syria.[20] He is the exception who thereby proves the rule, for it was necessary for him to gain full control in Egypt before he could embark on any foreign adventures, or even if he was to survive as king. In this in a way he followed the example of Ptolemy III who had so swiftly returned to Egypt when the rebellion began.

Every Seleukid king indulged in a war soon after his accession. The only exceptions were Seleukos IV and his brother Antiochos IV, and again, there are particular reasons for their abstentions. Seleukos, who was already joint king on his accession, had built up a military reputation before acceding to the throne, which occurred in the aftermath of the defeat of his father by the Romans; he had commanded for his father in Thrace, and against the Romans in Asia Minor, and in and after the battle of Magnesia, so he had no need to prove his military capabilities.[21] Further, his accession was not challenged by any enemy since the terms of the treaty of Apameia had made it unnecessary, and he had been left in charge in Antioch while Antiochos III campaigned in the east, so when the news of Antiochos' death arrived he was already in full control. Antiochos IV as king was in the peculiar position that for five years he was technically the guardian of his nephew-cum-stepson, though he was also acting king and had the title; having rid himself of the boy, however, in 170, he was soon involved in a successful war against Ptolemaic Egypt; one of the reasons given out by the Egyptian regents in launching this war (the Sixth

Syrian) was that the death of Antiochos the boy king had rendered the Seleukid kingship vulnerable.[22]

A new king could in fact almost rely on being attacked; he scarcely needed to search for a war to prove himself. This was one function of the diplomatic system, in which a treaty expired with the death of one of its participants. This allowed the surviving king, presumably better seated on his throne and more experienced by then, to attack his newly emplaced neighbour with some hope of success.

It did not always work. Antiochos III invaded Ptolemaic Syria in 221, only to be defeated;[23] Ptolemy III's invasion of Seleukid Syria in 246 was at first successful as the enemy collapsed into internal confusion, but he then had to turn back to Egypt to deal with the peasant rebellion. At the end of the war, which lasted for five years, by holding on to the city of Seleukeia-in-Pieria in the eventual peace treaty he ensured that another war would certainly result, even without the stimulus of the death of one of the royal parties to the peace. That is, the balance between the two kingdoms was such that only a collapse by one of them could produce anything close to a victory. This was the reason Ptolemy III was able to conquer north Syria in 246, though he lost most of his conquests (except the city of Seleukeia) when the Seleukids partially recovered. It became the turn of the Seleukid king to exploit the enemy collapse after Ptolemy IV died in 204 amid the outbreak of a great rebellion among the Egyptians.

There were also, and always, even if such an eventuality did not come along to provide a war, the barbarian neighbours of all the kingdoms who could provide victims for an ambitious king. The existence in the centre of Anatolia of a discordant group of Galatian principalities could be relied on to provide a target for any king whose territories adjoined them, though the Galatians themselves rapidly came to accept the diplomatic practice of a treaty lasting until one of the parties expired. They also held faithfully to their original alliance with Bithynia for almost half a century, through at least three Bithynian reigns, while at the same time taking an instant advantage of the deaths of any and all Seleukid and Attalid kings.[24]

Elsewhere the Ptolemies waged war on the desert nomads, and against the Nubians of the kingdom of Meroe south along the Nile; Macedonian kings could attack and be attacked by Balkan tribes; Seleukid kings could attack almost anyone who was their neighbour, from Thracians to Baktrians and Indians. Antiochos III made a serious and sustained effort to conquer Thrace, though this was one of the issues which brought the Roman war upon him.[25] In the Hellenistic world, it is sometimes assumed that war was constant and without rules;[26] in fact it was much more intermittent than that, and the rules were perfectly clear, particularly the diplomatic rules, to everyone involved. As a result there were long stretches of peace for all kingdoms and kings.

The military education the kings received was less than helpful to them in their roles as army commanders. They were trained to arms in much the same way as the other young men in their kingdom, learning to wield the Macedonian sarissa, to handle a sword, to control a cavalry horse in a charge, and perhaps even how to command soldiers.[27] This last achievement was however much more likely to be learned after they became kings, in a sort of on-the-job training.

Antiochos III, for example, became king at the age of 18 or thereabouts. His elder brother Seleukos III had clearly enjoyed warfare, but had indulged himself in it perhaps too recklessly, for he had suffered a serious defeat, and had then been murdered by two of his commanders.[28] There is no hint anywhere that Antiochos had had anything but the most basic military training such as would be given to any young man in his kingdom, and he had no experience of actual warfare or of command when he became king – at the time he was in Babylon, in the region which was one of the most peaceful in the kingdom. Further, his early command experiences betrayed his lack of knowledge and experience: in the initial offensive in his first Ptolemaic war in 221, he simply marched directly against the enemy in the Bekaa Valley and there he was stopped abruptly in his tracks by the well-sited Ptolemaic fortifications and defence. However, he certainly learned quickly, and in particular he soon discovered that avoiding such direct and disastrous confrontations was preferable, if possible, and he quickly found a less dangerous and expensive campaign method, a lesson he perhaps transferred from his experience at the hands of his minister Hermeias, who had so entrenched himself in power as to be immovable except by murder, by the king himself; to do so the king had to indulge in the sort of conspiracy which usually resulted in a king's own assassination.[29]

He thus soon learned that it was much better to manoeuvre the enemy out of his way than to fight him, and that the best way to do this was to subvert his command system. He had to face a major rebellion at the beginning of his reign, by Molon, his viceroy of the eastern provinces; by emphasising his superior kingship he eventually persuaded the rebel forces to accept him.[30] In his war in Syria his initial defeat was followed by his attack on the city of Seleukeia-in-Pieria, in which, when his first attempt to bribe the Ptolemaic commander failed, he found that the more junior officers were less scrupulous. In the eventual attack there was thus very little fighting.[31] This became his method of warfare, seeking out his opponent's political or diplomatic weakness, which could then be exploited, providing him with victories without much, or sometimes any, fighting.

Just as with Antiochos III, relatively few Hellenistic kings had much experience of military affairs before their accession. Antiochos I was an exception: he had been his father's cavalry commander even at the age of 20.[32] When he was sent off to govern the eastern provinces, he certainly indulged in warfare in bringing Baktria and its neighbouring territories back under his dynasty's control. Antiochos III ensured that his eldest son, Antiochos 'the young king', and after his early death the next son, who became Seleukos IV, both gained considerable experience in command.[33] But the next series of Seleukid kings – Antiochos IV, Demetrios I, Alexander I, Antiochos V, Demetrios II, Antiochos VII, Alexander II – were either very young or otherwise militarily inexperienced when they succeeded, and none of them had any military experience at all on their accessions.

None of them had had much chance to gain such experience. Two of them were dispatched as successive hostages to Italy (Demetrios I, Antiochos IV); three were too young at their accession to have any had possibility of command (Demetrios II, Antiochos V, and Antiochos VII); two were usurpers (Alexander I and II – though Alexander I Balas had been involved in some mountain warfare in the Taurus). This pattern of inexperienced youths succeeding lasted through to the end of the dynasty, and was clearly one of the many causes of the kingdom's eventual destruction.

One result of this was that the commanders against whom these inexperienced kings fought tended to be more experienced and competent. The usurper Tryphon, commanding in the name of the infant Antiochos V, had great difficulty in combating the Maccabee rulers in Judaea, for they had been fighting for many years, and had become cautious and careful.[34] The tables were turned later when the inexperienced and over-confident Maccabean King Alexander Iannai came up against well-commanded Ptolemaic armies and was driven from the field with contemptuous ease.[35]

Given the extreme lack of experience in military command of many of the kings on their accessions, it is therefore something of a surprise to discover that some of these kings became relatively successful in their command roles. For these inexperienced non-soldiers proved to be able to command armies and even win victories: Antiochos VII, who became king at the age of 20 and had, so far as can be seen, no previous military experience, was very successful for some time, as was Antiochos IV, whose life before his seizure of the throne had again been decidedly un-military. Demetrios II, after a difficult mentorship by the Cretan mercenary Lasthenes, held his own against Ptolemy VI, against Tryphon, and for a time he succeeded in reconquering Babylonia from the highly competent and experienced Mithridates I of Parthia.[36]

One basic reason for their successes in command is that commanding a Hellenistic army did not require much in the way of military expertise. It was quite possible to direct an army, and even to fight a battle, without much experience, because of the way the armies were constituted. Hellenistic (and Roman) armies were composed of clear and distinct units, sections of cavalry and infantry, and other units, each of which had its own distinct role and purpose in a battle, and so they had only to be set into motion.[37] In most cases, there were virtually no sophisticated manoeuvrings involved in a battle, unless (and until) the commander had gained greater experience and assurance, and direct and detailed control over his troops would hardly be expected of a neophyte. At Raphia, for example, in 217, in a battle between the huge forces of the Seleukid and Ptolemaic armies commanded by Antiochos III and Ptolemy IV – 70,000 men on each side – Antiochos set the elephants and the infantry attack in motion and then took personal command of the cavalry force of a few thousand men on one wing and led it in a charge.[38] The rest of the army he ignored. Ptolemy, having displayed himself to the army before the battle, along with his sister-and-wife Arsinoe, then disappeared into the midst of the infantry phalanx, only showing himself once more to rally his forces when under threat of defeat.[39] He no more commanded his whole army than did Antiochos.

In many ways the final demonstration of the relative ease of commanding a Hellenistic army comes with Andriskos, a man who had some basic military training – he seems to have been a mercenary – who conned his way to become usurping king of Macedon, in a superb display of effrontery. There he faced Roman forces and in his first battle he drove them out of the kingdom.[40] This was achieved by an army which had done no fighting to speak of for the previous twenty years, under a commander who had never risen above the rank of private soldier. It was, to be sure, composed of Macedonians who had flocked to join him on his claimed restoration of the monarchy (he called himself 'Philip VI'), but they were clearly able to form themselves into military units without much difficulty, that is, into the normal phalanx-with-cavalry formation, and Andriskos was obviously able to order them into battle. Of course, he was defeated later by a bigger and better Roman army, but the point here is how easy it was for somebody in authority to call an army into existence and put it into motion and then just let it fight. (There is no evidence that his conqueror M. Caecilius Metellus had any more military experience than Andriskos, and certainly none in a command position.)

Antiochos III's army was defeated at Raphia in 217 when its commander in effect deserted his command post to indulge in a happy cavalry charge, after which the army's various parts operated on automatic, with no reference to whatever the rest of the army was doing; but later it became a notably flexible military instrument. The king experimented with new weapons and new formations, but it was always difficult to innovate. Strategy was perhaps the most susceptible to an individual commander's work and intuition, and Antiochos III's capability of combining diplomacy and intrigue with a military campaign produced frequent successes. It must also have helped that in his later battles Antiochos commanded rather than taking a fighting part in the front line. But tactics at the level of a military campaign or a battle proved to be much more difficult to change.

The basic method of battle was much as it had developed ever since the invention of the phalanx. Philip II's innovation of a longer spear, the sarissa, was a success, but it was still phalanx-warfare, and this became ever less flexible than in the earlier versions – and others could, of course, imitate it. Cavalry on either wing could make a difference, as it did at Raphia when the Ptolemaic cavalry drove the Seleukid horse on one wing from the field.[41] (This was a battle fought at much the same time as Cannae, regarded as Hannibal's masterpiece, but one where he used exactly the same tactics as his Hellenistic contemporaries.) Every commander, Hellenistic or Roman, from Philip II until late antiquity, had to use a phalanx-plus-cavalry combination of forces in a battle.[42]

Innovation was thus difficult. The arrival of elephants was only partially successful at changing things, for the animals were liable to panic, and could be defeated without too much difficulty – at Gaza in 312 Ptolemy and Seleukos stopped Demetrios' elephants by laying out a carpet of metal chains and spikes which hurt the elephants' soft feet, so that they could not – or rather would not – advance; archers could fairly easily disable the animals either by shooting at their eyes or by shooting at their mahouts; their bellies were vulnerable to intrepid infantryman and their swords.[43] Nevertheless, both Seleukid and Ptolemaic kings invested a great deal of time and energy in acquiring and maintaining an elephant herd. Antiochos III collected elephants from two of the kings in his eastern expedition, and the presence of war-elephants in Syria forty years later, at the time of Octavius' visit, implies that the Seleukid kings were able to continue receiving elephants from the eastern lands; Ptolemy II organised elaborate and expensive expeditions into Africa to collect elephants, even though a modicum of experience showed that African elephants were much less amenable to training than the Indian animals. Ptolemy's expeditions involved establishing bases at several points along the Red Sea, sending expeditions inland to Nubia and Ethiopia, and constructing specialised ships to transport the animals. It is clear that he and his fellow kings regarded elephants as particularly useful.[44]

There were other military innovations. Antiochos III's army at Magnesia in 188 included a squadron of chariots (which proved unsuccessful) and a force of cataphracts – heavily armoured cavalrymen – which smashed through a Roman legion, though Antiochos still lost the battle.[45] On the other hand, the flexibility of his army had been demonstrated in Antiochos' eastern campaign between 211 and 205, particularly in the crossing of the Elburz Mountains as described by Polybios – and also later in the agile crossing of the Lebanon Mountains in 218.[46] By the time of these campaigns, Antiochos had also gained much experience himself, and had recruited able subordinates (often from his Ptolemaic enemies), but it was clearly his own authority as commander which gave the army its real effectiveness.[47]

Naval warfare was also subject to major development for a time. The basic warship before Alexander had been the trireme, but already in his time the Phoenicians had developed quadriremes and quinqueremes, and the enlargement of warships continued under Alexander's immediate successors. Demetrius Poliorketes was one of the drivers of this process, so that it was necessary for other kings with maritime ambitions to compete with him. The ships are identified by the number of rowers employed; the largest practicable versions seem to have been Sixteens, though the Ptolemies characteristically went further than anyone else, and Ptolemy III had a Forty built, but it was so large and clumsy that it was scarcely ever employed as anything but a floating palace.[48]

The one innovation of real effectiveness in Hellenistic warfare – apart perhaps from the use of elephants in the early battles at Gaza and Ipsos – was in fact the use of massed cavalry archers by the Parthians. It was this which was one of the sources of Antiochos' innovation of cataphracts, but the armour, which was essentially interlinked rings of mail, was heavy and expensive, and required a special breed of horse to carry the cavalryman. The light cavalry, thinly armoured, agile, and wielding bows of unusual power and range with great skill, proved to be the nemesis of the phalanx, especially if the phalanx could be caught and pinned down for any length of time so that the men suffered starvation and thirst. It is presumably these weapons which caused the defeat of Demetrios II in Babylonia in 141–138, though we have no details. The Parthians' tactics were not fully worked out, it seems clear, for some time yet; only at the time of the battle of Karrhai in 53 BC could it be said that their methods of warfare were really successful, and this included the innovation of bringing supplies of arrows carried on camels to the rear so that the archers could go on firing.[49]

For all commanders, once again, the test and model is Alexander, before whose military abilities those of all Hellenistic generals pale. It may be objected that he took over as king at much the same age as Antiochos III or Demetrios I and all too many of the other kings who succeeded him, yet he proved to be able to command and control his father's army from the beginning. One thinks above all of the extraordinary scene in his first battle with the northern barbarians in which he had the army put on a display of drill which so fascinated the enemy that their formation disintegrated as individual soldiers came out to watch; then, at his command, at the precise moment when the enemy was at its most vulnerable, he ordered the charge.[50] So if Alexander at age 20 could command in such a decisive fashion, why not the others? The answer is twofold. First, Alexander was a military genius, far more so than anyone else in the ancient world. Second, he was not new to command even at 20. He had the priceless example before him all his life of his father Philip, who if not quite a military genius in the same mould as his son, was an extremely competent commander; and Alexander had held independent command on several occasions before Philip's death.[51] Alexander, by the time of his accession, even at the age of 20, was therefore an experienced commander. Of his royal successors, only Antiochos I, Seleukos IV, and Antigonos Gonatas could be said to have had similar early command experience.

Some of the kings did display military competence beyond merely ordering an army into action. Few came anywhere close to Alexander the Great's achievements, but Philip V of Macedon was certainly competent above the average, as was Antiochos III. Ptolemy VI was an exception among Ptolemaic kings in being successful as a military commander, though he did manage to get himself killed in battle – and Antiochos III was rash and arrogant enough after thirty years of fighting to lead the attack, at the age of nearly 60, against unsurprised hillmen defending their temple and their wealth, and got himself killed.[52] The early Hellenistic kings had learnt their craft under Alexander and his father, but from then on the later generations of kings had mainly to pick up any expertise in the process of learning their craft, because these later kings tended to inherit power when young and this training was neglected in the early youth – probably, one cannot help assuming, because to have an obviously trained and capable heir was perceived to be dangerous for a ruling king. Ptolemy III employed his younger son Magas as his commander in Asia Minor in support of Akhaios, but when the king died, one of the first actions of his successor and his successor's minister was to kill Magas; this act then required several other murders because Magas had been well liked.[53]

Occasionally a king would emerge who was unusually competent as a commander, but he was rarely able to capitalize on his military ability to create something politically permanent. Alexander, for example, was scarcely a model of political sense, and it is not surprising that his empire collapsed into warring fragments as soon as he died. Philip II did have the political expertise, and his military ability was considerable, but his son only inherited the latter quality. Pyrrhos of Epeiros was similarly capable of winning battles, even defeating Roman armies, but was never able to convert that achievement into a solid political success.

This eventually led kings to employ professional soldiers to command their armies. The Ptolemies, unwilling to venture far from Egypt, had done this from the beginning with their fleets, and both they and the Seleukids had to appoint competent commanders to govern in military and/or distant provinces, though this had the effect of stimulating treachery, rebellion, or usurpation. No Hellenistic king, except for Demetrios Poliorketes, had engaged himself to command a fleet either on patrol or in battle. Ptolemy II Philadelphos employed a series of fleet commanders in the Aegean, men who also doubled as viceroys of the area, as already noted. The early kings had, of course, employed commanders, although we only too often hear of them because they were defeated, as was Diodoros, one of Seleukos' commanders, by the future King Mithradates I of Pontos, and Hermogenes by the future King Zipoetes of Bithynia.[54] These men were being employed to conduct subsidiary campaigns under the overall command of the king. At times the sons of kings were employed in a subordinate capacity. Antiochos III gave command of half his army to Antiochos 'the young king' at the battle of Panion in 200, and to his other son Seleukos in Thrace and in the campaign against the Attalids in 191, but he had retained the overall command of the campaign; this had been his method elsewhere as well.[55] But in the battle of Panion his opponent had been the Aitolian mercenary commander Skopas. The Ptolemies – again – placed viceroys in Koile Syria in command of the garrison forces there, and entrusted the defence of the region to them against Antiochos III's attacks. This should have been a powerful warning since in both Antiochos' attacks those commanders – Theodotos the Aitolian in 218, and Ptolemy son of Thraseas in 202 – deserted and took part of their forces over to the enemy.

Giving command to a subordinate was of course dangerous. Skopas was given command in Koele Syria in 200–199 in part because he was Aitolian, and not part of the Ptolemaic governmental and aristocratic system (but a predecessor, Theodotos, had also been Aitolian). And yet Skopas began to insinuate himself into that system after his defeat, until he was murdered, having been perceived as a threat to the regents of Ptolemy V.[56] The men who were ruling in Egypt at the time, in the name of the infant Ptolemy, were often generals: Ptolemy the governor of Cyprus, Tlepolemos the commander of the frontier fortress at Pelusion.[57] Command of an army was therefore seen, at least in the Ptolemaic system, as a possible route to political power, a route which was all the more open when the king was a minor. The Seleukid Empire was as liable to aristocratic insurrection in such circumstances as the Ptolemaic: Antiochos III's early years were dominated by a major rebellion in the east by Molon, the viceroy of the eastern provinces, and the secession of

Asia Minor under his cousin Akhaios, who reacquired the region in the king's name, but then made himself king.

Family members such as Akhaios were thus as dangerous as non-relatives such as Molon – perhaps more so in that they might claim some dynastic legitimacy. It took no more than a single victory to convince a rebel that he could make himself king. Antiochos I, Ptolemy II, and Antiochos IV all executed or murdered their sons or stepsons. The reasons are usually not recorded, but they are not very difficult to deduce: an ambition to anticipate their own succession in the case of the first two;[58] in the case of Antiochos IV, anticipating his own replacement by his stepson when he became adult. Giving command of an army to an ambitious son could result in a king's replacement. A notorious case in Baktria was the murder of Eukratides I by his son, a killing whose recorded account included a description of the son driving his chariot over his father's body and then refusing to allow it to be cremated.[59]

Suspicion of heirs was naturally widespread – it emerged in the new Maccabean dynasty in the second generation, as quickly as it had among both the Seleukids and the Ptolemies.[60] One result was the inexperience of military command which is so obvious in so many cases. Kings had a very troublesome dilemma: they could train their sons to command and so risk being over-thrown and/or murdered, or not train them and risk them failing in military adventures when they finally succeeded as kings. It was, in a sense, a good thing, from a dynastic point of view, that the Hellenistic armies which these young militarily inexperienced men inherited with their kingship tended to fight battles on automatic.

The civil war in Seleukid Syria in the 140s brought forth two non-royal commanders – Diodotos of Kasiana, who commanded on behalf of the infant Antiochos V, and made himself king (Tryphon) when the boy died;[61] and Lasthenes of Crete, recruited by the teenage Demetrios II to wage a war of revenge for his father's death and in recovery of his own throne. Lasthenes did not go so far as to make himself king, but he did single-mindedly accumulate a large treasure before abruptly leaving.[62] Since Demetrios II developed into a useful commander, Lasthenes' abilities had clearly rubbed off on him.

The disintegration of the Seleukid kingdom provided opportunities for much warfare. The occasional family member displayed some military com-petence, but they were clearly targets for their enemies and tended to die off quickly. Most, however, were exasperatingly incompetent. One commander, Herakleon, so resented that incompetence that he assassinated his king, but then found it impossible to secure control of the kingdom, and so decamped to rule a part of it, and established a minor dynasty which lasted until the Roman takeover.[63]

It is striking that, since war was clearly seen as one of every Hellenistic king's major activities, so few of them proved to be any good at it. Most could exercise a distant command, relying on the automaton which a Hellenistic army could so easily become, and because it was so relatively easy to do so, they felt no need to delve any deeper into military matters. For some, of course, the position of king was an invitation to luxury, play, and pleasure. Ptolemy III, for instance, pursued pleasure after his initial apparent success in north Syria in 246 single-mindedly; the result was a serious decline in Ptolemaic military and naval capability. Even those who took soldiering seriously were rarely more than competent. Overshadowed by the example of Alexander the Great, few could bring themselves to do the hard work of learning the military art. Perhaps they dazzled themselves with their own positions as kings.

This brief survey has inevitably concentrated on the experiences of the Ptolemaic and Seleukid kings, because that is where the information lies. But it is worth pointing out that no king or dynasty remained at peace for very long. Even minor states were beset by warfare. So these minor kings had almost as much opportunity to develop military skills as those in the greater kingdoms, but their lack of power – that is, military manpower – constrained them. Three of these may however be noted as being unusually successful. In Baktria, Demetrios I succeeded his father Euthydemos – Antiochos III's enemy in the siege of Baktra city – in about 190, and turned his army onto India. Since he apparently covered large distances, it seems likely that his army was largely cavalry; his invasion was the foundation of Greek and Macedonian rule in north-west India.[64] In the next generation Mithradates I of Parthia was king for at least thirty years, and towards the end he was able to conquer Iran and Babylonia from the Seleukids, but he waited until they were fighting a long and enervating dynastic civil war to do so; when he picked a quarrel with the smaller kingdom of Elymais, he found he had a much tougher fight on his hands.[65] And the third one is Mithradates VI of Pontos, who is usually considered in terms of his Roman War, but who was essentially a Hellenistic king. Whether he can be considered a successful ruler or not, he was certainly a capable military commander.[66] Then there is the comedy of the conflict between Attalos II of Pergamon and Prusias II of Bithynia. Mired in a long diplomatic dispute, they agreed to a conference at which each would have an escort of a thousand soldiers. Too trusting, Attalos turned up with his thousand; Prusias brought his tens of thousands. Attalos had in fact trusted too much in both Prusias' word and in Roman support, neither of which were forthcoming in the event. But having been chased back to his capital by Prusias' ragged army, Attalos, with Roman advice, set about organising his military forces – and it turned out to be quite easy to win.[67] It was necessary both to keep one's guard up and to have prepared a proper military force.

All of these men were successful royal warriors, even Attalos in the end, and their careers go far to reinforce the point being made repeatedly earlier in this chapter. All, like Antiochos III, had exceptionally long reigns, or had military experience before reaching the throne, or both. None of them stood out as a military genius, but were generally competent in command. The way to survive in the Hellenistic period as a king was, therefore, to live a long life (which many kings failed to do) and to gain some experience in command – the army would do the rest, so long as generally intelligent political preparations were made.

Chapter 10

Kings and Death

In a sense the Hellenistic period began with the death of a king, when Alexander the Great died in Babylon in 323. This was followed by the near farce of his funeral procession. According to one account it took several days before anybody could be bothered to prepare the body for burial, and then it was pronounced to be unaffected, and was then embalmed.[1] An enormous catafalque was constructed in Babylon in which the body in its sarcophagus was supposed to be carried to Macedon, to be buried alongside other members of his family at Aigai (the present Vergina). This was a decision by the regent Perdikkas, who disregarded the supposed stated preference by the dead king for burial at Siwah, the desert oasis in Western Egypt where he had had a powerful religious experience. Once completed the catafalque, under escort and commanded by one of Alexander's companions, Arrhidaios, began a slow movement towards Macedon.[2]

By this time two years had passed since Alexander's death and quarrels had already begun between the many commanders who had acquired – given or taken – local power as satraps. In particular Ptolemy in Egypt decided that he would carry out Alexander's apparent wishes to be buried in Egypt. At Damascus he intercepted the catafalque and diverted it southwards.[3]

A moment's thought, and a brief examination of the map of the Middle East, will show that Damascus is not on the route between Babylon and Macedon. That is to say, Arrhidaios had already diverted the catafalque from its intended route, and the only reason can have been that he and Ptolemy had concerted their intentions; Arrhidaios had turned south having crossed the Euphrates, presumably at Thapsakos. It follows that Ptolemy's interception of the catafalque was not a forcible diversion at all, but a planned hijacking, and Arrhidaios was involved in the conspiracy from the start. The story surrounding the interception that there was an argument and a stand-off for a time is pure flummery, presumably designed to save Arrhidaios' blushes.[4]

Ptolemy's motives were no doubt mixed, partly a wish to carry out Alexander's intentions – he had been in close attendance on the dying king in Babylon and probably knew at first hand of his desire for burial at Siwah – but also he cannot have failed to understand that possession of Alexander's body was a major propaganda victory. The episode also inaugurated the constant round of fighting which we call the Wars of the Successors, which lasted from Perdikkas' attempted invasion of Egypt to recover the body until Seleukos I's murder outside Lysimacheia, which marked the end of the last survivor of Alexander's successors.

The body had been embalmed at Babylon, and when Ptolemy got it to Egypt it lay in state in the temple of Ptah at Memphis for several years. When Alexandria was sufficiently advanced in building the sarcophagus was removed to the city which bore his name, where it became the centre for a mausoleum, the Sema (or Soma), in which the bodies of Ptolemies and their families were also installed after death, thereby partaking of his divinity.[5] There it is supposed to have remained until Octavian visited Alexandria in 30 BC, at the end of the final campaign which eliminated the very last of the successors' dynasties. He investigated and found that it lay in a transparent sarcophagus. He had the lid taken off and in a ghoulish moment put his hand on the face, to find that the nose broke off when he did so.[6] (Alexander therefore never did return to Ammon at Siwah.) The story itself, the transparent sarcophagus and the imperial actions, seems fairly unlikely.

The deaths of Hellenistic kings were all too often the result or the cause of violence. Given that many of them were active warriors, and took leading parts in military adventures in which they might head cavalry charges or command in infantry phalanxes, this is hardly surprising. Added to this was the constant risk of assassination, though judging by the occasional note we have of kings going out among their people, this was not something they felt too concerned about. Of course, they were never unguarded in these walkabouts, and in fact the danger of assassination came less from the ordinary people than from the members of the elite.[7]

Violent death was in fact a major variable between the dynasties. None of the Attalid kings died by violence, unless one includes the final pretender to the vacant throne, Andronikos – 'Eumenes III' – who died in battle. The early Ptolemies also evaded violent death, in part by delegating military commands to subordinates, but in the second century they became increasingly subject to assassination, and non-ruling members of the family had frequently died violently from the beginning. The first king of the dynasty to die in such a way was Ptolemy V in 180, almost a century and a half into the dynasty's history. In Macedon the Antigonids generally managed to survive to die of old age, though violent death was never very far away, particularly since they tended to lead in battle; in this activity two of them, Antigonos I and Demetrios II, died – but they at least escaped being murdered. But the prize for achieving multiple violent deaths must go to the Seleukids. So far as we can tell only two Seleukid kings managed to die more or less peacefully. The rest were killed in battle, or were assassinated; out of twenty-eight Seleukid kings, twelve were murdered and eight died in battle; three were deposed; and even one who probably died a peaceful death (Antiochos II) was rumoured to have been poisoned.[8] It is perhaps a measure of their commitment to violent solutions to their imperial problems that this should be the case.

It is much less easy to discover how members of the lesser dynasties met their ends, since the sources for these kingdoms are poor, but it seems safe to assume that violence met them fairly frequently. Among the family of Antipater who ruled in Macedon, two were murdered out of four – three out of five if Thessalonike, who acted as an officious regent for her two sons, who ended the dynasty, is included.[9] Taking the independent rulers of Asia Minor as a group, which would include Lysimachos, two of the dissident Seleukids (Antiochos Hierax and Akhaios), and the Attalids, two of these died in battle and two were murdered, out of ten kings. Among the Judaean kings four died in battle and two were deposed. In the double Spartan kingship, which had lasted several centuries by the time of the Hellenistic period, though surprisingly few had died even in battle before the Hellenistic, despite the repeated belligerence of the city and its kings, in this late period of the city's history four of the kings died in battle, five were murdered and one was deposed, out of nineteen kings; this emphasises that this was a time of instability and desperation at Sparta, an implication which is obvious even before consulting the details. The Epeirote kingdom was always unstable, being a federation of three tribes, and as a united kingdom it lasted not much more than a century. In that time there were ten kings, three of whom were deposed and then reinstated. Four were murdered, and two died in battle (both of whom had earlier been deposed). The last representative of the dynasty, the princess Deidameia, was murdered at the altar of a local temple. At that the kingdom was abolished, or perhaps simply dissolved. As a political device it can hardly have been counted as a success.[10] Among the Bithynian kings two usurpers were quickly deposed, one king died in battle and one was murdered, out of nine rulers. In Baktria, the rapid turnover and multiplication of kings – at least thirty-five within less than two centuries – implies an even more violent end for many of the kings than in the Seleukid family, though the fates of only a few of them are known.[11]

This is, clearly, an appalling record of violent deaths.[12] And yet the society which these kings presided over was not a particularly violent one. It had repeated and fairly frequent wars, of course, but in most of these wars the fighting was confined to relatively restricted regions, and most of them lasted only a fairly short time; they were also conducted intermittently, with halts in the fighting at least every winter for perhaps three or four months. So it does not appear to be that the society as a whole was responsible for the violent deaths of its kings – not that 'society' can be held responsible for anything so specific.

Instead, it is presumably the office of king itself which attracted the violence. It is striking that many of the murders were committed either by members of the murderee's family or by one of his officials or followers. Out of the twelve victims in the Seleukid family who were murdered, only one can be said to have been killed by outraged subjects – Seleukos VI, who was burned in the royal palace at Mopsuhestia in Kilikia when he imposed heavy and stringent taxes.[13] On the other hand, five of the murdered kings suffered at the hands of a close relative. One of these is doubtful: Antiochos II died at Ephesos in 246 and his wife Laodike has been blamed for poisoning him, though proof has not been produced,[14] and he may well have simply succumbed to the climate or to disease; blaming the wife is a fairly typical misogynistic reaction, and a claim of death by poison tends to suggest that the victim suffered a sudden death with no obvious cause, such as a heart attack or a stroke. On the other hand, Antiochos IV was certainly responsible for ordering the death of his stepson in 170; he was another Antiochos, and was technically king at the time;[15] of course Antiochos got one of his henchmen to do the deed;[16] Antiochos VI, another child, was murdered on the orders of his cousin Demetrios I in 162, though Demetrios also had someone else to commit the murder and insisted on not witnessing the death;[17] Seleukos V was murdered by his mother Kleopatra Thea when he was about to take power out of her hands;[18] and Antiochos IX was murdered by his cousin Seleukos VI – who in turn was the one later killed by his people in Mopsuhestia.[19]

Seleukid kings were equally in danger from their close associates who were not family. Seleukos I, the founder of the dynasty, was decoyed into a lonely spot in the Gallipoli Peninsula by a man he had befriended, Ptolemy Keraunos, and who he obviously still trusted; he was supposed to be going to see a curious tomb; Keraunos' aim was to make himself king in Macedon, which Seleukos was about to claim for himself.[20] Seleukos III was murdered by two of his mercenary soldiers while on campaign, one a Galatian, the other probably a Macedonian;[21] the reasons for the killing are not known, but it presumably involved some military scandal or incompetence.[22] Seleukos IV was murdered by his first minister, Heliodoros, who evidently hoped to make himself king by marrying Seleukos' widow;[23] the arrival of Antiochos IV, a man equally liable to be murderous, thwarted the murderer's intentions; he had the murderer executed, and then he married the widow himself. Demetrios II was murdered by the governor of Tyre when he landed there seeking refuge; once again his wife has tended to be blamed, though the timing of events refutes her involvement;[24] but the wife was Kleopatra Thea, who later that year did murder her own eldest (surviving) son, so, if she is blamed also for her husband's death, she has only herself to blame. Antiochos VIII, her next son, was threatened with death by her, and turned the tables by killing her himself. After a long reign Antiochos himself was killed by his army commander, Herakleon, who was exasperated by his failure to take any serious measures to win the long-standing civil war; Herakleon went off to found his own brief principality and dynasty in north Syria.[25] Alexander I Balas fled for refuge to an ally, an Arab chief, after being defeated in battle, clearly hoping the ally would protect him, but he was murdered by two of his own officers, at the instigation of the winner in the battle, Demetrios II.[26] In the midst of all this killing the death of the child king Antiochos V, the son of Alexander Balas and Kleopatra Thea, is attributed either to a medical operation which was unsuccessful or to a corrupt doctor deliberately killing the child during the operation on the instructions of Diodotos, the child's guardian-regent.[27] It is a measure of the intensity of propaganda among the competing kings in the 140s that the latter explanation is generally the one preferred. There seems no reason that the former reason should not be accepted – incompetent doctors are as liable to cause death as battles.

The Seleukids were, however, anomalous in this habit of killing their kings. The Ptolemies were much less murderous, at least for a time. Ptolemy V, in 180, seems to have been the first reigning king to be murdered, though in this case there is some doubt since it is said that he had been poisoned. On the other hand, his death happened suspiciously soon after he made an implicit threat to impose heavy taxes on the wealthiest of his courtiers.[28] These courtiers had succeeded in garnering much wealth to themselves during the king's minority, which came soon after a similar regency period during his father's minority, when the courtiers had also steadily enriched themselves. Between 221, when Ptolemy III died, and 163, when Ptolemy VI gained sole ruling power as an adult, the Ptolemaic government repeatedly fell into the hands of regents acting for kings in their minorities. Ptolemy IV's minority lasted for four or five years (222–218), Ptolemy V's minority for ten years or more (205/204–196/195), and after his death Ptolemy VI's minority lasted for fifteen years (180–165); there was also a long rebellion centred in Upper Egypt (207–186) and two destructive invasions of northern Egypt by Seleukid forces (170–168), and constant disputes between Ptolemy VI and his brother (Ptolemy VIII) over which one should rule. This is twenty-nine years of regency government out of forty-seven, and twenty-three years of internal warfare, added to which much of the reigns of Ptolemy III and Ptolemy IV had been times when the kings devoted themselves to pleasure, and left their real work to ministers, another time in which the courtiers could enjoy rich pickings.

During these minorities the government was unstable, time during which the cronies of the regents, and the regents themselves, were enriched; when Ptolemy V implied that he might well recover some of that filched wealth from them in order to finance a new Syrian War – that was when the king died. The periods of royal minority were therefore standing temptations to the unscrupulous to see that any minority was extended in time, preferably by the sudden death of the king as he reached the end of his minority. Among the Seleukids, minorities were relatively few, though deaths of kings while still young happened all too frequently. Only in the case of the murder of Seleukos V by his mother does the king's death seem to have been due to the king's intention of taking power from the regent. The lesson was learnt by her second son, Antiochos VIII Grypos, who, when he was ready to take power, ensured that she died.[29]

Among the Ptolemies, therefore, until the final decades of the dynasty only Ptolemy V could be said to have been murdered, and the accusation of poisoning renders such a verdict uncertain. On the other hand, the reign of his son was a time of vicious family dispute, and Ptolemy VIII had to wait for twenty years to gain power in Egypt. (He was assigned the kingdom of Cyrenaica to rule, but this was never enough for him, when he saw his brother controlling Egypt and Cyprus.) When he was brought to Egypt as king, after the death of Ptolemy VI in battle in 145, he was vindictive, driving out any prominent men who had supported his brother, or who had opposed his own accession. He was eventually overthrown by his wife (who was his sister Kleopatra II, the widow of Ptolemy VI), and she was as vindictive in her victory as he had been. In revenge, if that is not too weak a word for it, Ptolemy had their son murdered and his dismembered remains delivered to Kleopatra on her birthday.[30] (Of course, their unpleasant reputation in the sources may well be a reflection of the enmity they had provoked among the Alexandrian chattering classes, though some of the deeds they are accused of, and certainly their mutual enmity, cannot be gainsaid.)

By this time, the practice of killing off possible competitors for the kingship had become established in the Ptolemaic system, and once such behaviour has entered a family it is very difficult to expunge it. Ptolemy I appears not to have killed any family members, though his family life was sufficiently disorderly that one wife, Eurydike, fled the court when he showed a preference for the succession of his son by another, Berenike. Ptolemy II, however, according to his descendant Ptolemy VIII, who wrote up the family secrets and scandals, fathered several bastards on several mistresses – at least eight mistresses are known by name, one of which, Bilistiche, eventually became the king's official wife – and he saw that these bastard children were killed off, presumably to avoid succession disputes after he was dead;[31] this was thus not really any less unpleasant than Ptolemy VIII's own behaviour.

The question of the succession to a ruling king was always a likely source of violence. Two particular cases of family murder in the Seleukid family involved heirs to the throne. The eldest son of Antiochos I, called Seleukos, was executed by his father in about 267.[32] No reason is given, but it may be presumed that Seleukos was being too ambitious and urgent in his wish to succeed his father; that he was executed suggests that he had gone well beyond talk, and was into a fairly serious conspiracy; it must also be presumed that other conspiracy members died as a result, since it is unlikely that Seleukos would have been able to even begin to contemplate action against his father without assistance.

The other case was that of the son of Seleukos IV and his wife Laodike. Seleukos had been murdered by his minister Heliodoros, who was then killed by, or by order of, Antiochos IV. Antiochos was Seleukos' younger brother, and he then married Laodike (who was his sister). Two other children of Seleukos and Laodike had, in terms of heredity, better claims to the kingship than Antiochos. The eldest son, Demetrios, was in exile in Rome; the second son, Antiochos, remained with his mother, and Antiochos IV was thus in the position of guardian to his stepson, who, when he became adult, would clearly threaten Antiochos IV's position as king. Antiochos and Laodike had a son of their own, another Antiochos, and once he had passed the danger years of infancy, the son of Seleukos was killed by, or again on the order of, Antiochos IV.[33]

The reaction to these two killings was curiously different. So far as we can see the death of Seleukos the son of Antiochos I passed off with no obvious public reaction, though, to be sure, the sources are so poor that any reaction at all is not mentioned; on the other hand, had there been any major reaction it may well have resonated in later sources. The death of Antiochos the son of Seleukos IV was contrasted with the contemporary Ptolemaic monarchy when the Egyptian regents celebrated the triple monarchy of the children of Ptolemy V, as a supposed family harmony, at a time when the Seleukid court was in seeming disarray after the murder. Soon after, riding the tide of celebrations, they launched the monarchy into the Sixth Syrian War.[34] However, since they had already decided on the war this was no more than an opportune excuse. Otherwise there seems to have been no public outrage, no unpleasantness directed at Antiochos IV, who in fact became a fairly popular king. (He did, however, see to the execution of Andronikos, who had been given the task of killing the boy, an action which suggests that Antiochos was sensitive to public opinion, not to mention the standard reaction of such men in casting the blame away from themselves.[35]) The one item which might be considered to be a direct reaction to the boy's death came when Demetrios I arrived in Syria in 162 and immediately ordered that the child of Antiochos and Laodike, who was by that time King Antiochos VI, should be killed.[36] No matter what his dynastic justification, this killing was held against Demetrios.

All dynasties succumbed to such occasional crises. All that was needed was there be two sons of the ruling king, preferably close in age, and the existence in the court of intriguers who hoped that the younger would succeed rather than the elder and so give them access to power and wealth. This was the case during the last years of Philip V of Macedon, when his eldest son Perseus was threatened by the younger son Demetrios; elaborate theories have been developed involving interference by Rome in the Macedonian succession, but in fact it seems that Perseus had little difficulty in seeing off the challenge when their father died; Demetrios disappears from the record, quite probably killed by his brother.[37]

It was at the time of Ptolemy III's death in 222, however, that the practice of inter-familial killing took hold in that dynasty, with the murder of Magas, Ptolemy IV's brother, the king's uncle Lysimachos, and the king's mother Berenike II.[38] Magas had secured an influential position with the army, and had been sent on a diplomatic-cum-military mission to Asia Minor, so he was clearly seen as a capable man; hence he was seen as a threat to the new king, which was probably correct. Since Magas was supported and encouraged by his mother, logically she had to be killed as well. The killings were organised by Sosibios, but carried out by one or more of his minions, and clearly with the new king's approval. One of the reasons for murdering Berenike was probably that she had herself murdered her predecessor as ruler in Cyrenaica, Demetrios the Fair, and so was clearly capable of such violence. The thought in Alexandria must have been that she was already a murderess, and could well repeat the deed.[39]

The problem with acting in this way is that it becomes necessary to repeat the action at every accession, since the new king's siblings would obviously fear being murdered themselves, and so would aim to act to prevent their own killing by arranging the death of whoever they thought might threaten them; therefore, in the curious logic which was applied to royal homicides, they had to be killed first. So in 205/204, when Ptolemy IV died, his wife Arsinoe, who had been apparently nominated as regent for her infant son, was swiftly killed (Sosibios again).[40]

These two killing sprees (others died as well, such as Skopas the Aitolian and the exiled Spartan king Kleomenes, both of whom had tried to intervene in the regency) reduced the dynasty to the life of a single infant, Ptolemy IV, in 220, and again to the life of another infant, Ptolemy V, in 204. And this was in a kingdom beset by rebellion and about to be attacked by its two great power enemies. So much for Sosibios' statecraft. Despite all, Ptolemy V survived to adulthood, married, and had children before being murdered himself. But his children were, once again, infants – a factor probably well to the fore in the minds of the murderers – and there followed a decade and a half in which regencies continued to loot the state. Ptolemy VI, who did not manage to gain full control and power in the kingdom until 163, thus had to spend the next years repressing rebellions.

Life was therefore very dangerous not just for members of the royal family, but for everyone in the kingdom, when royal murders were indulged in. Supporters of a dead king, or family members, or courtiers, were obviously vulnerable in the aftermath of the killing, and the instability at the centre of government ramified outwards. Almost anyone could find themselves a target, while the instability also provided a splendid opportunity for the disaffected to further undermine the state.

In 145, when Ptolemy VI was killed in battle in Syria, his heir was, yet again, a child. In the same way that Antiochos IV took power in the Seleukid kingdom when Seleukos IV died leaving only a child as his successor, Ptolemy VIII, the uncle of the child, came to Alexandria to rule. His position was curious. He had been proclaimed king along with his brother and his sister many years before, but now technically he must also have been, at first, acting as regent for the new, infant, king. Like Antiochos IV, and like Antigonos Doson in Macedon a few years later, he married his predecessor's (and brother's) widow, in this case Kleopatra II (who was also his own sister – in another echo of Antiochos IV, whose wife was also his sister). So far this was normal for a Macedonian kingdom's succession crisis.[41] But Ptolemy VIII was generally disliked among large numbers of the Greco-Macedonian population, particularly in Alexandria, and he immediately conducted a purge of his brother's supporters, killed the boy he was supposed to be guarding (in his mother's arms at their wedding, so it is said – in which case this was a copy, perhaps deliberate, perhaps manufactured by the sources – of the action of Ptolemy Keraunos in 279);[42] he drove out many of the scholars of the Library, who were vocal in their opposition. The head of the Library, Aristarchos of Samothrake, died in 144 in Cyprus, perhaps as a result of his expulsion. It is probably this action which is at the root of the almost universal denigration of the king in our sources, written and publicised by men whose comradely feeling for the displaced Alexandrian intellectuals overrode their scholarly judgement.[43] Ptolemy went further, by installing a non-intellectual, 'Kydas the spearman', as librarian, presumably as a gesture of contempt directed at his opponents.[44] At the same time he made conciliatory overtures to other elements in Egypt, including having himself crowned at the old Egyptian capital of Memphis, and proclaiming guarantees of privileges to the priests of the temples, who retained a strong influence over the rural population.[45] The marriage with his sister soon produced a new child, Ptolemy Memphites, and not long after that he also married his niece, Kleopatra III, by whom he had five children. The king therefore married women who could be reckoned as able to make their husbands kings; marrying them both supposedly prevented anyone else doing so. But this marriage set the two Kleopatras (mother and daughter) against each other, and eventually, almost inevitably, it produced a new dynastic civil war.

This conflict brought the death of Memphites (killed by his own father), and further Egyptian rebellions, including at least one by a man who attempted to revive the defunct pharaonic kingship.[46] It also brought the threat of a new Seleukid invasion, when Kleopatra II invited Demetrios II to bring a Seleukid army to Egypt and marry her; this would make him king, and together they would then defeat and eliminate Ptolemy VIII. (One wonders how long Demetrios would have lasted had he actually made the journey.) As a riposte, Ptolemy sent a new pretender into Syria, Alexander Zabeinas, to raise a rebellion against Demetrios.[47] So the family dispute between the king and his wives in the palace in Alexandria had spread to incite civil wars in both the Ptolemaic and Seleukid kingdoms. In these conflicts, Ptolemy Memphites, Demetrios II, Kleopatra Thea, and Seleukos V all died as a direct result. The great survivors were Ptolemy VIII and his two wives.

It is tempting to suggest that the spread of the practice of family murder into the Seleukid family during the second century BC was due to the Ptolemaic example, and to the infection which intermarriage between the two dynasties brought, but in truth it was actually part of the continuing dynastic problem of the Seleukid succession which had existed from the very beginning. There had been killings in the previous century, though it was Antiochos IV's usurpation in 175 – 170 which brought the practice decisively into the Seleukid kingdom for every succeeding generation. Demetrios I clearly felt it necessary to kill Antiochos VI; Alexander Balas killed Demetrios' eldest son, Antigonos.[48] But two other sons of Demetrios I had been sent out of Syria for safety during the fighting, and they returned in succession, Demetrios II in 148, and Antiochos VII in 139. They had remained apart even in exile, presumably so that at least one would likely survive, but also perhaps for mutual protection against each other, though Antiochos' nickname of 'Sidetes' reflects the fact that he was living, for some time at least, at Side in Pamphylia, very close to Seleukid territory. Kleopatra Thea followed Demetrios I's example and dispatched two more of her sons – by different fathers – into exile in Greece in the 120s, and they also returned successively, but in this case as rivals and promoters of another dynastic civil war.[49]

These two, Antiochos VIII Grypos (who had killed his mother), a son of Demetrios II, and Antiochos IX Kyzikenos, a son of Antiochos VII, fought a twenty-year-long civil war. Neither was a capable commander or governor – though Grypos had earlier succeeded in driving out the pretender Alexander Zabeinas. Both men married women of the Ptolemaic dynasty, who evidently arrived with their fully formed sisterly hatred intact. When Kleopatra IV, the wife of Kyzikenos, was captured by her sister Tryphaina, the wife of Grypos, she was murdered; next year Tryphaina was captured by Kleopatra's widower and was also murdered in retaliation.[50]

Grypos later married a third of these sisters, Selene. When he was killed (by the disaffected general Herakleon) she married the survivor, Kyzikenos, who died within a year; she then married his son, her stepson, Antiochos X, by another woman.[51] She survived to be captured and executed by the Armenian King Tigranes, twenty years later.[52] Her first marriage had been to her full brother, Ptolemy IX, her second and third were to sons of her half-sister, Kleopatra Thea. Only with her fourth marriage, to Antiochos X, did she escape from marriage to a blood relative, though, to be sure, he was her stepson. Such was the penalty of being royal.

Ptolemy VIII's murderousness continued after he was restored to power in Egypt in 127, though he did manage to remain at some sort of peace with his two wives for another decade until his death in 116. However, that murderousness had once again made it very difficult for any other succeeding king to permit any sort of rival to live beyond the moment of his own accession. He himself managed to die peacefully, as did his sister-wife, Kleopatra II, but his second wife, his niece Kleopatra III, was eventually murdered by her son, to whom she was denying full power – a repeat of Kleopatra Thea's experience at the hands of Grypos (the two women were sisters).[53] From then on until the end of the dynasty every Ptolemaic king or queen except one died violently. Two kings died in battle attempting to make good their claims to the throne; the rest were murdered, usually by their relatives, son, mother, or stepmother. The exception, of course, was Kleopatra VII, who manoeuvred for almost thirty years to gain or keep the throne, before finally committing suicide – this might, of course, also be considered death by violence – rather than face being exhibited in Octavian's triumph in Rome, and then, if the fate of Perseus of Macedon was any guide, being starved to death in a noisome Italian prison.[54] She was the daughter of Ptolemy XII, who had similarly manoeuvred and murdered to keep the throne for almost as long as she did; he was the only other one of these last Ptolemaic kings not to be murdered, but both father and daughter were quite as murderous as their predecessors.

The end result, of course, for both Seleukids and Ptolemies, was the extinction of their dynasties and their rule. It is surprising in many ways that

Seleukid kings still existed at the end of the dynasty, given that so many of them were subject to violent death at a young age. One reason they survived was that Kleopatra Thea, even though she had as much blood on her hands as any other Seleukid or Ptolemaic ruler, had also produced nine children (by her three husbands), four of whom became kings and produced children themselves. This fertility ensured that the family always had someone available to inherit – or seize – the throne, though at the same time it also promoted repeated dynastic warfare, and several inter-familial murders. There were therefore still legitimate Seleukids alive and active in the first half of the last century BC, though they were still fighting with each other to the very end – which was to be suppressed and dethroned by Pompey.[55]

Among the Ptolemies, however, a combination of sibling marriage and family murder had already extinguished the legitimate line by 80 BC, with the deaths of Berenike III and Ptolemy X Alexander I; there were no 'legitimate' Ptolemies left, though there were children of marriages which were not recognised as legal by Greeks, and, of course, children of concubines and mistresses.[56] The succeeding kings were descended from an illegitimate marriage, or so it was in Greek eyes; this line expired with the son of Kleopatra VII and Julius Caesar, Caesarion, or Ptolemy XV, who was not even the son of an illegitimate marriage; the child was, of course, murdered at the orders of Octavian, who was the heir of Julius Caesar and therefore, by his action, demonstrated that dynastic marriage had entered the Roman imperial political system at its very beginning.[57] If there was any legitimacy left in the methods of Ptolemaic inheritance, Caesarion would never have been acceptable to the Egyptian Greeks as their king, any more than he would have been to the Romans.

It will also have become clear that the concentration of these kings and their wives on securing the succession for themselves or for their children, was a more lethal version of the attitude of Demetrios Poliorketes when he was seen throwing his people's petitions into the river; none of these last Ptolemies or Seleukids was attending to the well-being of their subjects; they were far too busy gaining or keeping their thrones. It is therefore not surprising that those subjects progressively removed themselves from allegiance to the neglectful kings. In the Seleukid kingdom this was done when cities and provinces and regions detached themselves into independence, either as free cities or as new states, as they frequently did from the time of Arados' move into independence in 129. In the Ptolemaic system the reaction was riots and rebellions and agricultural strikes. The arrival of Roman rule, even in the unpleasantly ferocious and greedy form of the warlords of the last years of the republic, might have seemed a little like a deliverance.

It will be evident from all this unpleasantness that the incidence of dynastic murder among these two dynasties increased radically in their last century. Death in battle had been much more common between 323 (the death of Alexander the Great) and *c.*220 (when there was a change of ruler in all three major dynasties). But from 220 onwards murder became the normal method of violent death. The incidence of violent death can be tabulated:

Years	Battle	Murder	Deposed	Suicide	'Peaceful'
323–280	5	6	1		1 (43 years)
280–220	6	4	1		3 (60 years)
220–160	2	7			1 (60 years)
160–100	4	10			3 (60 years)
100–60	2	3	3	1	2 (70 years)
Total	19	30	5	1	10

It will be seen that the greatest hazard faced by any king was being murdered, either by a family member, or by a close associate. The risk of being killed in battle declined over the Hellenistic period. It is also worth pointing out that the incidence of violent death among the minor dynasties was considerably less.

The death of a king created a difficult situation in any kingdom. Since this is the case even now, when it is possible to create an acceptable and accepted legal system of succession and to enforce it, it is all the more likely that in the Hellenistic period, when there was no such legal or fully accepted system, that trouble would erupt. It was usually necessary that the heir to the throne be physically present on the scene when a king died, and then to personally conduct the obsequies, which was part of the legitimising of the new king. In 281 Antiochos I was not present when Seleukos I was murdered, though it is possible he was on his way from his position as viceroy of the eastern provinces towards Syria. The absence of both king and heir from Syria at Seleukos' death may well have been the main cause of the trouble which happened in Syria at that time, whatever it was. In the event Philetairos of Pergamon secured Seleukos' body, cremated it, and sent it on to Antiochos at Seleukeia-in-Pieria, earning dynastic gratitude.[58]

The family obsequies was therefore a ceremony conducted by the new king designed to emphasise the transmission of authority from father to son. They consisted of a relatively simple ceremony, but they also required a noisy display of public mourning, which involved much weeping, wailing, breast-beating, and tearing of hair. This was in fact a completely artificial business, lasting a number of days decided in advance. It was decreed by the surviving members of the government – three days was a popular duration for this –

and the displays ceased abruptly when the government announced that the period of mourning was over. The absence of such demonstrations was a clear sign of political disapproval of the deceased – Berenike II, for example, having been murdered, could not be mourned, and her ashes remained outside the Sema, the Ptolemaic royal mausoleum in Alexandria, for ten years before being transferred.[59] There then followed the ceremonial presentation of the ashes of the dead king, encased in an urn, which was placed in the royal cenotaph; there followed the proclamation of the new king.

The artificiality of the display of public mourning is a reflection of the fact that the kings were little known to, or by, the general population. A royal death was thus seen very much as a family matter, especially no doubt when that death had been brought about by a member of that family, and the change of king had no direct effect on their subjects. That is, the royal family, and its extension the court as a whole, remained very much a separate organism, with little contact with the population. The display of mourning, like the great elaborate processions put on at times by the kings, was an opportunity for the participants to enjoy a show and participate in it, but it was hardly a genuine expression of grief. On the other hand, the death of a king could well presage a major political crisis which would undoubtedly affect the ordinary population; a display of grief might well therefore be an appropriate response, in anticipation of trouble.

The burial places of some of the kings are known. That in Alexandria was part of the palace area, an area called the Sema (or Soma), where the tomb of Alexander the Great had been placed by Ptolemy I after its fifteen-year sojourn in Memphis while the new city was being built. The tombs of Ptolemaic kings were placed close by, in a transparent attempt to appropriate the magic of Alexander's reputation to the Egyptian royal family. The Ptolemaic dead were brought together at the Sema by Ptolemy IV, forming, with Alexander's body, a distinct pseudo-shrine, again with the intention of emphasising the near-divinity of the family as a whole.[60] In doing this Ptolemy was rather late, for he was replicating the Macedonian process of royal burial, which had already been copied by the Seleukids. However, that they did begin with the burial place of Alexander the Great in Alexandria made their Sema different.

The earlier Macedonian kings, including Philip II, were buried in tumuli at Vergina in Macedon. Some of these have been excavated in recent years, and are seen to have been the sort of tomb one would expect from any Iron Age king, with plenty of rich gifts and memorials to see them on their way to, presumably, Hades, all covered by a heap of earth.[61] (The Galatian mercenaries employed by Pyrrhos are said to have rifled these tombs during the occupation of Macedon in the 270s, but what has been excavated does not show that all that much damage had been done.[62])

The early Seleukid kings were buried, or perhaps 'entombed' is the best description, at Seleukeia-in-Pieria in Syria, probably in or about a Doric-style temple that was built at the highest point of the city.[63] The capture and retention of this city by Ptolemy III in and after 246, at the beginning of the Third Syrian War, was thus a particularly egregious insult to the Seleukid dynasty. It can only have fired up their determination to recover the city eventually and to gain control of Phoenicia and Palestine, which Seleukos I claimed he had been deprived of by Ptolemy I after the destruction of the empire of Antigonos Monophthalamos, and whose possession would provide a major defensive glacis against any further Ptolemaic invasion.

It may be pointed out that, in case this chapter seems a little restricted in its subject, besides suffering death, the kings inflicted it. Their enemies in battle were killed, sometimes by kings personally; they were the court of last resort for some crimes, in which punishments included execution; they did not hesitate to order enemies killed by murder or assassination. But it was also their task to ensure that the government they ran was not interrupted by unnecessary personal or political disturbances. Kings, therefore, quite readily resorted to murder, execution, and assassination as a normal part of their governing equipment. In all this the kings of the Hellenistic period were no different from kings in any other time or place.

Chapter 11

Kings and Intellectuals

It was one of the marks of the Hellenistic monarchies that the kings patronised some of the leading intellectual figures of their time – though they would have called them 'philosophers', no doubt. Some kings, notably Antigonos Gonatas and Ptolemy Philadelphos, have gained a particular reputation in this area, which was mainly because of the eminence of the men they recruited. Other kings have no particular reputation for patronage of this sort, which is not to say that they were negligent in the matter.

As usual, it is necessary to go back to Philip II and Alexander the Great of Macedon for the earliest examples. In a curious sort of patronage, Philip called in Aristotle as tutor for his son Alexander. This also entailed Aristotle teaching, if that is the word, a set of Alexander's contemporaries, a group which probably included Hephaistion, Harpalos, Ptolemy, Seleukos, and Lysimachos, at least.[1] The odd aspect of this was that Aristotle came from Stageira in Chalkidike, one of the cities which Philip had destroyed during his conquest of the Olynthian League of cities in that area. Aristotle had thereafter lived in exile, out of reach of Philip. Yet Aristotle's father, Nikomachos, had been physician to Philip's father, though Aristotle himself had moved to live in Athens during Plato's lifetime. Whether one of Philip's motives was to make amends seems fairly unlikely; it is much more likely that Aristotle's reputation was such that Philip's capture of him as tutor for his son was regarded as an achievement similar to the capture of another city.

One of the more obvious motives of kings in relations with intellectuals was a sort of trophy hunting, the acquisition into their service, or at least their presence at their court, of men eminent in some area where they themselves did not shine. By the same token, one of Aristotle's motives in accepting the tutorial position could have been to embarrass Philip, a standing reproach, perhaps, for his past conduct, though this also seems unlikely. Quite possibly, Aristotle gained more out of the transaction than Philip, for he was able to persuade, or inspire, Alexander to send back to Macedon quantities of strange plants and animals from his great expedition, though it does not appear to have made much impact on his published work.[2] No doubt the pay was good, too.

On the other hand, neither Philip nor Alexander displayed any real interest in intellectual pursuits themselves; Alexander's favourite reading, even the inspiration for his work, remained Homer, but this is not a work likely to stimulate interest in wider affairs.[3] He did take a chronicler with him on his expedition, Kallisthenes, a relative and pupil of Aristotle's, but killed him before he was halfway through.[4] He is supposed to have begun his Asian campaign with 'a whole list of zoologists, botanists, and surveyors'. Certainly the last group had an effect on the understanding of the geography of his conquests; the effect of the others is more difficult to estimate, and probably insignificant.[5] The expedition did produce several other histories – Kallisthenes' account was, ironically, very laudatory of Alexander – but these were normally the personal reminiscences of the participants, none of which survive. One of these was by Ptolemy, regarded by Arrian as the most dependable of them all, but for the wrong reasons.[6] Even minor characters such as Nearchos of Crete and Aristoboulos the king's steersman produced monographs.[7] (Ptolemy's personal closeness to Alexander means his memoirs are more likely to be generally accurate than those of men such as Nearchos who were more distant from the king.) But Alexander was only responsible for these memoirs because of his astounding and extraordinary achievements, which reflected back on his colleagues, and not because he inspired intellectual activity himself.

Neither Philip nor Alexander were in the least systematic in their employment of intellectuals. Philip's use of Aristotle was perhaps as much to keep the hyperactive teenaged Alexander occupied as it was to stimulate his intellect – which, if he really did read little but Homer, was clearly pretty undeveloped. Aristotle, widely regarded in the Greek world as one of its greatest philosophers, might also have been a source of criticism and a centre for opposition had he been left at Athens, so Philip may well have felt that employing him would also silence him. It was suggested later that Aristotle was apprehensive of Alexander's wrath because of his guilt at the killing of his relative Kallisthenes; there was, it seems, a strong suggestion of antipathy between master and pupil: Alexander complained when Aristotle issued some of his lecture notes, delivered originally to Alexander, in public form, claiming that they were private; and Aristotle noticeably moved back to Athens when Alexander left on his great expedition. Alexander was known to harbour grudges for a long time: his tutor Leonidas, who had been parsimonious in his use of incense, was sent a huge quantity when Alexander took Gaza, a clear insult.[8]

Neither of these kings, who were, to be sure, rather too busy to be intellectually active in the philosophical sense, therefore provided an obvious model for their successors in the employment of philosophers. Their earliest successor, Antigonos Monophthalamos, was similarly less than engaged with the academic world. He has been supposed to have gathered a group of writers about him – Nearchos, Medeios of Larissa, who both wrote about

Alexander, and Marsyas of Pella, Antigonos' own half-brother – but it is not clear if Antigonos was actively engaged in their work, or inspired it, or improved by it. He is said to have enjoyed declamations in which he could deflate incompetent orators with quotations of Euripides, and music in which he corrected the harpists as they played, but these are hardly intellectual accomplishments. Antigonos therefore apparently liked to be entertained after a day's work, but he must have been an awkward audience to play to.[9] He apparently employed two of the most notable artists of the time, Apelles and Protogenes, to portray him, which would seem to have been more a matter of self-congratulation than artistic patronage. That is, Antigonos, another extraordinarily busy man, had little time for active intellectual pursuits, any more than had Alexander and Philip (who were his contemporaries).[10]

It is necessary, of course, to make some attempt to indicate what is meant by an intellectual and by intellectual pursuits; and having posed the issue, it is instantly clear that the answer is very difficult, not least because as a term it is too often a denigration, or alternatively a self-regarding description, implying arrogance. Of all the people mentioned so far in this chapter, only Aristotle could be described as an intellectual – that is, a man renowned for thinking rather than acting or doing – while the others fall into two groups. One is composed of the kings, who, as mentioned already more than once, were usually far too busy to intellectualise; the others were practical men who may or may not have had intellectual abilities and pretensions, but who had to make a living by practising a skill – music, oratory, painting, or some other similar avocation – in which above average intelligence is usually required.

The categories of 'intellectual' and 'artist', of course, overlap, and in these categories may be included a variety of others who would not normally be classified as either: doctors, for example, are rarely intellectual, though they do tend to be highly regarded, and may best be classified as craftsmen, though some rose above their craft into higher thought. So despite the limitations implied in the title of the chapter, it is perhaps best to widen those limits and to gather in such men as artists and notable craftsmen (such as Antigonos' painters, orators, and musicians) as well as the more obviously intellectual types. The boundaries are always porous, and it will be well to spread them as widely as possible.

The two kings of the generation after Alexander who moved forward from Philip's non-system of exploiting intellectuals were Seleukos and Ptolemy. Neither, however, did so, so to say, unprompted. Seleukos employed several men who made intellectual contributions of various sorts to the study of the world in which they lived. For example, Patrokles, who was posted to Central Asia by Seleukos, was employed by his son Antiochos to conduct explorations in the region. He investigated the Caspian Sea and certainly examined the southern third of it. He listened to local information, including references to a large bay (now dried out) and heard of rivers along which Indian traders reached the area. This was apparently accurately reported in the account he produced, but was misunderstood by others. He may have, and others certainly did, come to the conclusion that the Caspian was connected with the northern ocean. This became a geographical commonplace, despite the obvious ability of nomads to travel from central Asia to the lands north of the Black Sea; it was perhaps more a conclusion of the study than one based on autopsy and practice. Seleukos planned to cut a canal from the Black Sea to the Caspian and sail an expedition to India that way, so approaching that land from the north, but he died first. (If he had believed in the northern channel, such a canal would not have been needed.) Patrokles' explorations were therefore only limited, but the conclusions were evidently published.[11]

After his Indian expedition, which ended in defeat in 303, Seleukos dispatched ambassadors to the court of the Mauryan king, first Megasthenes, and then Deimachos. Both of these men produced descriptions of what they had seen, and the account by Megasthenes remained highly influential in later years, and was still being used by Arrian over four centuries later.[12] Their books do not survive, though they have been considerably excerpted by later writers, notably, of course, by Strabo.[13] It seems probable that the two men were in effect investigative agents of Seleukos rather than simply ambassadors and had been sent to explore the strange new empire with which he had collided, and by which his forces had been defeated – the empire had not, of course, existed when Alexander carved his bloody path down the Indus. Certainly Megasthenes travelled considerably around India, rather more so perhaps than an envoy assigned to a king would be expected to do. It seems probable that, as some of the Greek historians of the time claimed, the first Indian emperor, Chandragupta Maurya, had become familiar with Macedonian warfare while serving as a mercenary ('Sisicottos') in Baktria and as such he was clearly more dangerous than most of the barbarians.[14] (He might also have been able to communicate with Seleukos or Megasthenes in Greek.) The enormous power of the Mauryan Empire – 4,000 war elephants! – certainly merited investigation, and Megasthenes' tour might be reckoned complementary to Chandragupta's knowledge of the Hellenistic Far East.[15] Seleukos had acquired 500 of those elephants as part of his peace treaty with Chandragupta, and had won the battle of Ipsos with them.

Seleukos therefore employed men who might claim to be intellectual, if such a term had occurred to anybody at the time, but his purpose was emphatically both practical and political, as might be expected. Patrokles' explorations were partly aimed at defining the limits of the Seleukid kingdom; his colleague Demodamas operated for the same purpose along the Jaxartes

River, where one of the tasks that Seleukos gave him was to build, or rebuild, the set of altars constructed by Alexander on his northeastern boundary, on that river.[16] (Demodamas also wrote books, on India, and on Halikarnassos.[17]) This was also the site of the northeastern boundary of the preceding Akhaimenid Empire as defined by its founder Cyrus the Great; Patrokles and his colleague Demodamas, on Seleukos' instructions, were clearly defining the kingdom's outer limit in Central Asia, but Seleukos was also laying claim at the same time to be the successor of Alexander and Cyrus, while also seeking ways by which the empire could be expanded. Central Asia was a difficult and ill-defined region and deserved study.[18] Similarly India.

Megasthenes and Deimachos were dispatched to India with practical intent, therefore; Seleukos had made a peace treaty with Chandragupta Maurya, and the two ambassadors were clearly part of the process of maintaining that treaty and the subsequent peace, Chandragupta being by far the more powerful king of the two. And, as he was both powerful and a neighbour, it was important to gather information about his empire; the dual purposes of their visits were clearly matters of diplomacy and spying. No doubt Chandragupta was fully aware of this.

To some degree the implication of spying by Megasthenes and Deimachos is enhanced by the mission of Dionysios, sent by Ptolemy II to India sometime after the visit of the Seleukid envoys.[19] No doubt this was in part another diplomatic mission. Given the previous hostilities between the Mauryas and the Seleukids it made diplomatic sense for Ptolemy (at war with Antiochos I in 274–271 and with Antiochos II in 260–253) to investigate the possibilities of involving the Indian emperors Bindusara, Chandragupta's son and successor, who ruled from 297 to *c.*270, and/or Ashoka, his grandson, who ruled from *c.*270 to *c.*230, in a diversionary attack.

The route by which Dionysios reached India is a puzzle. Either he travelled openly through the Seleukid kingdom, in which case it would be unlikely he would reach his destination, or he travelled secretly, which is much more likely; alternatively, he could have sailed by way of the Red Sea and the Arabian Sea, landing at one of the ports near the mouth of the Indus. This is perhaps the most probable route – Ptolemy I had, after all, been with Alexander when he sent Nearchos of Crete to explore part of that sea route, and the Red Sea part of it was long known in Egypt, and exploited by Ptolemy II in his search for war elephants; the Indian-Arabian coasts were long known to Indian and Arab seafarers, and it was this section which Nearchos had sailed from the Indus mouth to the Persian Gulf for Alexander.

Ptolemy II had revived the old pharaonic (and Persian) exploitation of the Red Sea and was also active in sending out other explorers. In order to acquire elephants to confront the Seleukid superiority in these war animals, a series of explorations and expeditions ranged the length of the Red Sea, establishing or re-establishing a series of trading posts along its coasts.[20] One at least of these missions penetrated into Ethiopia. At least three men from Egypt explored upstream along the Nile Valley beyond Aswan. This was a region organised as a state and ruled from the city of Meroe – Dalion and Aristokreon travelled south beyond Meroe; Simonides lived in the city for five years and researched a book (or books) on it. Meroe was the centre of power in the middle Nile Valley and had been, and later was, an active enemy of Egypt; information about it was clearly as necessary to the Ptolemaic kings as information about India was to the Seleukids.[21]

Timosthenes of Rhodes had been employed by Ptolemy as an admiral, though we do not know any of his achievements. He was employed by the king to compose an account of the coasts of the Mediterranean, which he did by describing its ports starting at Alexandria and working counterclockwise round to Libya. His report, in ten volumes, was therefore entitled 'On the Ports'.[22] Whether he himself made such a voyage is not certain but it is clear that the book had politico-diplomatic purposes than being simply mercantile – after all, merchant sailors would already know of the ports, and he himself will have known at least the eastern Mediterranean coasts. Timosthenes' account can only have been for naval and military and political purposes, and the timing is interesting. It was produced in the later years of Ptolemy II, possibly in the 270s or 260s, just when the political situation in the western Mediterranean was changing with the expedition of Pyrrhos of Epeiros to Italy and Sicily, and when the collision between Rome and Carthage produced a seemingly never-ending war from 264. Ptolemy made diplomatic contact with Rome in 273, Pyrrhos died in 272 and his last post in Italy, Taras/Tarentum, fell to Rome in that year. By 269 a new king of Syracuse, Hiero II, had established himself in power there, and struck up good enough relations with Ptolemy II to present him with a particularly handsome ship, the *Syrakusia*. Ptolemy I and II were already geographical neighbours of Carthage. It was clearly necessary for the most powerful Mediterranean state to understand what was going on in the west, and this was no doubt part of Timosthenes' mission.

A ship, the *Isis*, sailed through the Straits of the Hellespont and Bosporos and contacted the Bosporan kingdom of the Crimea, where at least one man was so impressed that he had a picture of the ship painted on his wall. It was clearly a warship, though it is not altogether clear if it was a trireme or a quinquereme, and from its name it may be presumed to have been a Ptolemaic warship; the fact that it could and did sail to the Crimea had obvious naval and political significance.[23] These various expeditions can be characterised as diplomatic, exploratory, geographical, or, more helpfully, a combination of all these purposes. They were, like the earlier Seleukid missions into India, aimed at expanding and refining the knowledge of the world held by the kings, and at detecting any potential political or military threats or opportunities. It is noticeable, for example, that after Timosthenes' voyage to the west Ptolemy II steadfastly kept clear of the conflicts in that region, refusing a loan of 2,000 talents requested by Carthage, for example. His father had dabbled in the region more actively, marrying daughters to both Pyrrhos of Epeiros and Agathokles of Syracuse; Ptolemy II was much more cautious.

The result of these expeditions in intellectual terms came to fruition with the work of Eratosthenes. Educated at Cyrene while it was an independent kingdom under King Magas, and at Athens while Ptolemy II ruled in Egypt, he was induced to move to Alexandria under Ptolemy III, who had become ruler of Cyrenaica on his marriage to Magas' daughter Berenike – Eratosthenes and Berenike were quite probably already acquainted. From the Library at Alexandria he was able to coordinate much of the new information into a newly convincing mathematical system, chronological and geographical.[24] He was, of course, one of the stars of the Ptolemaic Museum in Alexandria, and became its librarian in 235, holding the post for forty years; it is with this institution that the world of the kings and that of the intellectuals truly intersect.

Ptolemy I's venture into the world of intellectuals turned out to be the most productive in terms of his own kingdom of any such ventures. He gave refuge to Demetrios of Phaleron, who had been the semi-constitutional ruler of Athens for ten years until Demetrios Poliorketes, son of Antigonos, took control of that city in 307. After a decade living at Thebes under Kassandros' protection, he fled to Egypt in 298, presumably by prearrangement with Ptolemy, who was keen to collect as many enemies of Demetrios as possible, and no doubt the philosopher thought that Ptolemy might be useful to him in his Greek ambitions.

Demetrios counted as a philosopher, which would be the nearest term for an intellectual among the Greeks. His rule at Athens was, at least to some of the philosophers, regarded as something of a model.[25] However, it was less highly regarded among the Athenians, who welcomed Demetrios Poliorketes with cheers when he arrived to oust Kassandros' power, and Demetrios of Phaleron personally, from their city.[26] The latter's reputation therefore remained high among those to whom a king like Ptolemy paid heed, and Demetrios could, of course, blame a much greater power for ending his rule in the city. Both were enemies of Demetrios Poliorketes. Ptolemy therefore took him up, perhaps in the first instance as a mark of his enmity towards the rival king.[27]

But Demetrios of Phaleron was more than a mere political exile. He was also intellectually ambitious, and he clearly saw in Ptolemy, the master of the richest kingdom in the Hellenistic world, a source both of support and funding. Ptolemy, in turn, quite possibly harking back to his early days as a pupil of Aristotle, took up the idea which Demetrios put forward of continuing Aristotle's system of making collections of almost anything, and then studying what had been collected. Whether or not the precise organisation, or even the exact origin, of the Museum and the Library in Alexandria came from Demetrios' brain, it seems clear that he was the intellectual originator, where Ptolemy was the earliest practical founder. At the same time, Demetrios himself was a capable organiser, as he had shown during his rule in Athens, and he could be left by the king to do the founding work – just as founding a city was usually assigned to a Friend of a king, though the latter would take the credit.[28]

The influence of Aristotle may also be distantly detected in the emphasis on scientific work which developed in the Museum. One of the earliest of those employed by Ptolemy I was Strato of Lampsakos, a younger contemporary of Demetrios of Phaleron, regarded later as a 'physicist'.[29] This was not the Phalerite's bent, but the Museum he provoked into existence was later renowned more for the scientific work done there than for philosophy, or even than its poetry.

The Museum could well have been a one-off event, a whim of Ptolemy I, though Demetrios was too much an organiser not to create something rather more permanent. But Ptolemy also used Demetrios as Philip II had used Aristotle, as a tutor for his children, and this became one of the responsibilities of later heads of the Library. His designated successor, Ptolemy II Philadelphos, was taught by a succession of intellectuals, among them Philitas of Kos, a philologist, Strato the scientist, and Zenodotos of Ephesos. The elder Ptolemy probably required his other children, certainly the sons and in all likelihood the daughters also – Arsinoe II was clearly one of the pupils – to attend those classes as well, but only Philadelphos appears to have caught the intellectual bug to any degree.[30] Arsinoe corresponded long after leaving Alexandria with her former tutor Strato, which does suggest an enquiring mind and a trained intelligence.[31]

Philadelphos was also an organiser, but above all a controller, responsible for developing the tight grip which the Ptolemaic kingship and government established over Egyptian society and its economy, for the king's benefit more than anything else, of course; it was this part of his character which, when turned to the intellectual legacy of his father, produced the Museum and Library. Philadelphos was, therefore, a ruler very much in the stamp of

Demetrios of Phaleron in Athens, who may be credited therefore with inspiring the work.

Until Philadelphos' work none of the relationships between the kings and intellectuals had resulted in anything permanent. It is not clear how far Demetrios of Phaleron had gone in founding the Museum, but he fell foul of Ptolemy I by advising him not to make Philadelphos joint king, and then of Ptolemy II by advocating the succession of his half-brother, thus ensuring the joint enmity of both men, and the installation of others in control of the Museum.[32] At Athens the succession of Socrates/Plato/Aristotle had established a sort of philosophical university, the Academy, and this proved to be the school for many of the later intellectuals – Strato, Zenodotos, Kallimachos, Eratosthenes, and so on, and this and similar institutions became established on a near-permanent basis in Athens and sometimes elsewhere. But they tended towards the informal, where the presence of a particular philosopher would attract followers and pupils, but where the group might well disperse after his death or retirement. The Academy, founded by Plato, did continue until the fifth or sixth century AD, and this was clearly the model Ptolemy and Demetrios had in mind, though it was, in their version, much more controlled, and was definitely part of the Ptolemaic government. One result was that those who were more freethinking tended to avoid the Alexandrian Museum; this is one reason the Athenian Academy continued.

The overall organisation was that of a temple of the Muses, but the realisation was less religious than practical. One aim was to collect copies of every book ever written, an aim perhaps originally confined to books in Greek, but this was soon extended to non-Greek books, which then suffered translation into Greek.[33] The clear intention was to provide information for governmental use. An example was the patronage of Ptolemy I for Hekataios of Abdera and Manetho of Sebennytos, priest of Heliopolis (close to Memphis), who separately produced histories of Egypt in Greek, the one from the Greek point of view, the other from the Egyptian. Manetho in particular had an academically ordering mind, and came up with the division of the Egyptian past into dynastic periods, a system which largely constrains the study of ancient Egypt to this day.[34]

This was one case of the collection of information about what the Greeks, even – or especially – those in Egypt, insisted in seeing as an alien society. It made sense in government terms to have some understanding, however, of the surrounding, taxpaying population, just as it made sense for the government to have some information about its neighbours further up the Nile Valley at Meroe. And Manetho was sufficiently involved in the need to link the new government with both the Greeks and Egyptians that he was involved in the creation of the Greco-Egyptian cult of Serapis, developed under the earliest Ptolemies.[35]

The Library also reached out to other ethnic groups, at least to those with a literary tradition. The Jews elaborated a story of the divinely inspired translation into Greek of their holy books, clearly playing on the general superstition of the Greek population to validate their own story.[36] This was less a quest for Jewish knowledge, however, and even less an interest in the Jewish religion – Hekataios of Abdera was hostile to them – than another case of investigating an alien subject population, for Ptolemy I conquered, and Philadelphos and his successors held, Palestine as a Ptolemaic province, while Jews were a considerable part of the population of Alexandria from the beginning.

The prevalence and constant repetition of the Jewish story has rather deflected the attention which was paid in the Library to other alien cultures. At the end of the third century Hermippos spent years studying Zoroastrian texts;[37] 'Chaldaean' texts were studied also, though they were probably already translated into Greek.[38] The library contained the reports from Dalion on Nubia, from Dionysios on India, and probably also copies of the reports of Megasthenes and Deimachos from India. This was a process going on simultaneously in the Seleukid kingdom, where Patrokles' reports on Central Asia were joined by the researches of Berossos on Babylonian history which were commissioned by Seleukos I.

These cases demonstrate a curious similarity with those of the explorers noted earlier in the chapter. In both cases the work done was only partial and limited. The explorers penetrated to India and Central Asia, to Nubia and Ethiopia, into the western Mediterranean and the Black Sea, but systematic investigation and continued engagement with these alien and distant societies did not continue. The tentative conclusions of Patrokles on the extent and form of the Caspian Sea were sufficient for Seleukos to plan, or at least to talk of planning, an expedition across it to reach India; completing the exploration does not seem to have interested him. Ptolemaic missions penetrated into Ethiopia, and probably an increase in trade resulted, but there was no real investigation of a potentially very interesting region. (However, an inkling of the cause of the annual Nile flood – a result of the monsoon in Ethiopia – was found, though once again this was not followed up.) In the same way, the students and translators in the Library were limited in their work because it stood in Greek guise. The Jewish writings, the work of Manetho, the Zoroastrian books, the Chaldean texts, were all translated into Greek, but never, so far as we can see, were they studied in their original languages. Understanding, such as it was, therefore, remained incomplete. Similarly, Greek understanding of the Egyptian population, its history and its institutions, remained partial and often merely superficial. That is to say, having gained a certain level of knowledge about all these regions and societies, no further or deeper investigation was made. In India, where Greek kings ruled for perhaps a century, only one of those kings, Menander, is known to have taken any serious interest in the local Buddhist faith, though at least one envoy from another king is recorded as making a dedication at a local Indian shrine.[39]

But the consequences of this multilingualism and superficiality were serious. The scholars, by operating with Greek texts only, allowed themselves to have forgeries foisted on them. Most of the Zoroastrian texts which Hermippos investigated, spending years annotating them, were either incomplete or forged, and much of the corpus of Chaldean prophecies and oracles were invented.[40] An example of this process is the Jewish account of the translation of the Septuagint into Greek related in the *Letter of Aristeas*, by a supposedly miraculous process of divine inspiration and intervention, a story all too clearly invented. By studying only the Greek versions, Greek scholars fell prey to these creations, or re-creations, or forgeries, as with Manetho's apparent systematisation of the dynasties of Egypt, which looks convincing though it was inaccurate and misleading. The Museum scholars were clearly very limited in their academic rigour.

That is, the work of the scholars in the Library of Alexandria was very liable to be diverted into essentially unproductive areas. This is something which happened from the beginning. The first librarian, Zenodotos of Ephesos, besides being tutor to Ptolemy's children (probably those of Ptolemy II, since those of Ptolemy I will have become adult before his appointment) spent his time correlating, annotating, and editing the *Iliad*, the *Odyssey*, and the poems of Pindar and Hesiod.[41] This was, no doubt, valuable work, and could only have been done once the Library had collected a large quantity of the various versions of these documents, but it was typically the work of a scholar in a library, and was evidently the sort of work which provoked satirists, such as Timon of Phlious, whose image it was that they were 'many ... who got fed, cloistered bookworms, endlessly arguing in the birdcage of the Muses'. Eratosthenes was attracted to Alexandria for the very reason of the Library's comprehensiveness, after what seems to have been a long period of reluctance, for by the wealth of information the Library had gathered, he was able to collate and make sense of much of it, but this scarcely inspired others (or indeed Eratosthenes himself) to go further. Kallimachos, though never the head librarian, performed useful, even necessary, work in devising a classification system for the Library's contents – clearly a systematiser like Manetho.[42] Both he and Apollonios 'the Rhodian' composed poetry redolent of the library, stuffed with unusual words and full of obscure academic references.[43] Apollonios' retelling of the story of the Argonauts was in effect a celebration of the extent and aspirations of Ptolemy's empire, as Jason and his men wandered over much of the Mediterranean, into the Black Sea, up the Danube, and over the Alps.[44]

Simply collecting the books, therefore, of which there were tens of thousands within a very short time, was not enough. Kallimachos' life's work of organising them into categories and providing a catalogue of the library's holdings was soon seen to be fundamental and necessary. Only when it was known what the library contained and where to find any particular volume was it of any use, just as a book without an index is only half-useful.

The kings could be quite ruthless in their approach to collecting. There is the notorious story of Ptolemy III Euergetes borrowing from Athens the original manuscripts of the plays which had won the prizes at Athenian festivals in the past with the promise of returning them once they had been copied; it was the copies which were returned, while the originals were retained in Alexandria.[45] (But it seems likely this is a confusion of two separate stories, one of copying Athens' manuscripts, the other of borrowing books from ships in the harbour, where the cleaner copies were sometimes returned;[46] note also Ptolemy III was in fact Athens' protector from about 230 onwards, and may have been able to exert pressure to secure his library loans.) At the same time, it is Ptolemy's father Philadelphos who must have found and financed the translations of the books of the Jews into Greek, if anyone did, not that this did much good for the relationships between Jews and Greeks.

The Museum/Library was thus an institution which, once it was established and operating, simply continued. Its existence and its form certainly reflected fame on the kings who had founded it, and the heads of the Museum became recognised and renowned, at least among their academic peers, but it seems unlikely that the kings found it particularly useful – clean copies of Athenian plays and revised versions of the *Iliad* were not really needed in their geopolitical endeavours. The Ptolemaic kings themselves could not usually claim to be of an intellectual bent, for, like all kings, their time was fully occupied elsewhere. In some cases, as with Ptolemy II Philadelphos and Ptolemy III Euergetes, their methods and tactics made them unpopular.

The organisation of the Museum partook of the same sort of top-down system which Demetrios of Phaleron had employed in his government of Athens, and which Philadelphos (and his father) employed in ruling Egypt. This perhaps was inevitable, both to avoid the dissolution to which the more informal philosophical schools were prone, and because it was clearly intended to be a governmental institution. But Demetrios made the elementary mistake of assuming that being in control of the Library and an adviser to the king gave him real power. As a politician who had been driven from power once already, he should have known better. The example lay before him of

Sotades, whose reaction to the marriage of Philadelphos and his sister Arsinoe was to produce a mocking poem; Philadelphos had Sotades murdered.[47] Demetrios had already made it clear that he considered that the succession of Philadelphos to his father had excluded the rightful heirs, the sons of Eurydike, Ptolemy's first wife, particularly Ptolemy Keraunos. He was dismissed, and it seems for a time he survived – he was after all a very eminent man – but the murders of some of those half-brothers appears (along with the death of Keraunos in Macedon, perhaps) to have compelled him to complain, at which he was imprisoned; he died, supposedly of a snakebite, in Ptolemy's prison. It is generally assumed he was in fact murdered.[48] Being in charge of the royal Library at Alexandria carried with it distinct dangers.

The example of the Ptolemies may have stimulated other kings to found their own libraries; it is more likely that the Ptolemies, characteristically, only did so with greater display, and that other kings quickly came to the realisation that they required a resource base of the same sort at their disposal. It is known that the Seleukids, the Antigonids, and the Attalids all had substantial libraries. The latter two did not secure full control of substantial territories until sometime after the invention of the Museum in Alexandria, but the library of Seleukos was likely to have been begun by 300 when Seleukos I gained control of Syria. Euphorion of Chalkis was librarian of the royal library under Antiochos III and possibly under his predecessors; the library was no doubt older than that.[49] (Since the Alexandrian Library cannot have been organised until Demetrios of Phaleron arrived in Alexandria after 298, it seems quite possible that a Seleukid library in northern Syria was already in existence before the Alexandrian version was established.) Berossos was commissioned by Antiochos I to compile his *History of Babylonia*, and he appears to have finished this by about 290 BC; it seems likely that he had begun the work a good deal earlier than that, possibly even before Ptolemy I had commissioned Manetho to do his history of pre-Greek Egypt.[50] These coincidences, or near coincidences, may be the marks of political competition among the kings, but they may also be a general recognition that a resource Institute would be a useful tool for any new monarchy.

The Attalids secured a major extension of their kingdom in 188, and it may have been then that they established a library at Pergamon which was intended to rival that at Alexandria. It is said that this rivalry resulted in the Ptolemaic government imposing an embargo on the export of papyrus from Egypt, though this could hardly have been the result of a librarians' dispute. The Pergamon library, apparently using vellum or parchment for its books, contained 200,000 volumes by the 30s BC, when Mark Antony presented it to Kleopatra VII (though they probably stayed in Pergamon).[51]

It was not necessarily through libraries that intellectual and cultural advances were to be made. Once the library was established it may well have escaped royal control, if the kings simply initiated it and then let it continue, and it would hardly be a priority for any king. It is significant that sources for the Alexandrian Library/Museum fade away after the flurry of evidence for its founding. We know the names of the heads of the library into the second century BC, though the later ones are increasingly obscure, and then their identities disappear; and the names are only known from a single papyrus, which appears to be a schoolboy's list.[52] Like many well established institutions under the patronage of government, it would appear to have become ossified. It seems unlikely that the diligent book collecting continued after about 200 BC, especially if it was costly, for by that time even the Ptolemaic government was strapped for cash, and, like all governments under such circumstances, it would be liable to dispense with 'inessentials', such as libraries and professorial salaries.

Rather than the kings using the libraries, royal contact with intellectuals was much more likely to be in person. Antigonos Gonatas, for example, attended the lectures of Zeno of Kition at Athens (probably between 296 and 287 when Antigonos had control of the city) but Zeno steadfastly refused Antigonos' repeated invitations to go and reside at his court in Macedon afterwards. On the other hand, Zeno did send some of his pupils to Antigonos' court: Persaios and Philonides are examples; Antigonos also attracted Menedemos of Eretrea and Bion of Borysthenes, philosophers of varying schools, to reside at his court.[53] (This variety might suggest that one of Antigonos' priorities was to be entertained by philosophical disputes, just as his grandfather had been entertained by musicians and orators.) Zeno was presumably particularly Antigonos' target because his philosophy was much concerned with political matters (but also, like Philip with Aristotle, by attracting Zeno to his court he would enhance his reputation among the literate classes). When Zeno died, Antigonos claimed to have lost his 'audience': what he meant is hardly clear, unless he believed that as king he was playing a part, but it may be that it was Zeno's influence which impelled the king to compare his office with a form of 'noble servitude'.[54]

There is some evidence that Zeno's political views changed over the years, no doubt as the power and stability of the new kingdoms became clearer after 300 BC. It seems unlikely that the philosophers' ideas about government had much influence on any of the kings, though an early exposure to philosophical ideas in their school days may have had some effect. The daily work of campaigning, travelling, difficult decisions, and replies to petitions, will have had little apparent relevance to the philosophers' ideas. It may be, for example, that Antigonos' reported diligence in ruling was more influenced by his father's carelessness in that regard, which had earned him expulsion from Macedon by his exasperated subjects, than by Zeno's lectures and political notions.

The influence of Ptolemy's Library and Antigonos' court was sufficient to inspire later kings to extend their own patronage to such men as philosophers and other intellectuals. It became part of the court system to have some philosophers present, though they may have been no more than decorations and trophies. At the same time, there was some serious work done. At Alexandria two medical men, Herophilos of Kalchedon and Erasistratos of Ioulis in Keos, investigated the human form by dissecting human corpses. They were able to describe and name many of the parts of the human body, though this does not seem to have resulted in any serious advances in medicine. Both carried out their dissections at Alexandria, apparently under conditions of strict secrecy, for fear of public anger. As a result the findings had only limited circulation, and the difficulty of medical investigations, in which the human body and person was necessarily an experimental subject, stultified any real progress in understanding.[55] This work, minimally publicised, had been done under royal patronage and protection. The limits of royal influence over others were thus demonstrated: carving up human bodies, even in the name of science, was one way of acquiring unpopularity.

Royal patronage was directed rather more overtly at artists and craftsmen. One might include Archimedes of Syracuse in this group, since his fame rested partly on his mastery of mathematics, but also particularly on the application of some of his achievements to practical aims: the Archimedean screw, the specific gravity theory which enabled the purity of gold crowns to be verified, and, of course, his invention of machines to hinder the Roman siege of his home city – for which he was killed. The basis of his creations, however, was not empirical invention, but always mathematics.[56] Euclid, based at Alexandria, but not part of the Library establishment, was more of the theoretical persuasion, as Ptolemy I discovered when he asked him for an easier way to understand geometry than working through the theory and was told there was 'no royal road' towards it.[57]

Kings always wished to generate favourable publicity, which was the basis of their patronage system. Antigonos I had sat for his portrait to Apelles and Protogenes, and other kings employed artists also to publicise their image – suitably improved on the reality, of course. Then there was the constant requirement by kings for sculptures of them and their families, again to publicise their existence, particularly to their more distant subjects, to whom copies of their portrait statues were sent.[58] The new cities – and city plans and their development were clearly intellectual activities in themselves – required the work of architects and sculptors for the public buildings and their decoration. For example, Seleukos I commissioned Eutychides to sculpt a Tyche for his new city of Antioch, which established the type which was copied in many other cities over the next century or so.[59]

The destructiveness of time and wars has removed much of the work of Hellenistic artists, though the coins produced for the kings, showing their portraits (again somewhat improved on the reality) were an interesting sub-category, though the artists are usually anonymous. Nevertheless it is clear that the major patrons of art were always the kings, and their requirements drove the changes which can be seen in the way their portraits developed. In Egypt royal patronage extended to the sculptors working in the Egyptian pharaonic tradition, with statues of, for example, Arsinoe II as an Egyptian princess, and Ptolemy II as an Egyptian pharaoh; these, and the bas-reliefs on temple walls, can only have been done by sculptors trained in the Egyptian tradition and method.

The increasing difficulties faced by all the kings after 200 BC may be one of the main reasons for the apparent reduction in intellectual patronage in the second century BC. The transfer of wealth westwards to Rome was at once a cause and consequence of this decline, and had the results of transferring such patronage westwards as well. In 168 Aemilius Paullus confiscated the library of the Antigonid kings as part of the booty taken from the defeated and dissolved Macedonian kingdom, and transferred it to Rome.[60] (He also took a prized ship, a Sixteen, which had survived for a century, preserved as a national monument: the Romans were intent on destroying Macedon not only as a kingdom, but as a society with a historical memory.) Rome had an ambiguous relationship with philosophers, as the alternating reception and expulsion of them from the city demonstrates. The library of the Attalid kings at Pergamon remained where it was until Mark Antony tried to transfer it to Alexandria; the Alexandrian Library, notoriously, suffered damage in the various episodes of fighting in the city, particularly in 48–47 when Caesar was fighting Ptolemy XIII.[61]

By this time the Ptolemaic kings had produced two rulers who might be considered to have had at least some intellectual pretensions. One was the final monarch, Kleopatra VII, who was supposedly adept at languages, it being claimed that she was the only one of her dynasty who could speak Egyptian. This may in fact be true, though as an intellectual achievement it is no more convincing than Antigonos Monophthalamos' critical abilities in music. But her great-great-great-grandfather, the much-disliked Ptolemy VIII, did have more serious pretensions in that direction.

This man has the reputation of being one of the more unpleasant of the Ptolemaic kings.[62] He constantly fought and intrigued against his more able brother, Ptolemy VI, in the hopes of gaining the Egyptian kingship. For two decades he had to be content with ruling only in Cyrenaica. When he finally gained the kingship in Egypt, when his brother was killed in battle, he spent much of the rest of his reign in dispute with his two wives (his sister and his niece) during which he is said to have murdered and dissected his nephew and sent it as a present to his wife. It is easy to discuss the man in condemnatory terms. To the Alexandrians he was seen as something of a joke, as when Scipio Aemilianus on a visit to the city walked through the streets with the king, who being fat found the pace humiliating (though his semi-transparent garments would seem to be sensible in Alexandria's hot weather, if perhaps unbecoming in a king; and yet it was normal to depict kings and queens in such dress in the Egyptian sculptural tradition). He is also said to have driven out by his persecution many of the intellectuals and artists from the city, including the head of the Library, Aristarchos of Samothrake.[63] All this would appear to have been to a large extent the result of his difficulties in maintaining his rule, and vocal opposition from a group of state-sponsored intellectuals was very easy to suppress; Ptolemy's conduct may well have suffered from exaggeration by his enemies and those of the Ptolemaic state.

On the other hand, this was the Ptolemy who finally gave up the dynasty's attempt to hold on to an overseas empire. He evacuated his brother's army from Palestine, where he could have held on to that territory, and abandoned the remaining naval stations held by the dynasty in the Aegean. Both of these measures will have had helpful financial consequences for Egypt. His expulsion of intellectuals and artists was no doubt another measure with useful consequences for the royal treasury in that the subsidies directed towards them were no longer paid. Yet this was the man who was able, during a turbulent reign, to write a commentary on Homer – a very 'library' enterprise – and to compose a book on his ancestors, which will have required a good deal of research.[64] Also he was responsible for the revival of an earlier enterprise of his dynasty, when an Indian sailor was rescued from a wrecked ship in the Red Sea, and arrived at the palace in a distressed condition. It was this Ptolemy who saw that he was cared for and interviewed, and who sent the Greek captain Eudoxos of Kyzikos to investigate the Indian's information about this winds and currents of the Indian Ocean.[65] This led to the Greek discovery of the monsoon winds, and to a new burgeoning of trade, not just in the Red Sea, but with India and eventually with territories beyond.[66] This trade may have existed already, of course, as the arrival of an Indian on the Red Sea coast of Egypt suggests, but it seems clear that the ships of the Mediterranean were much more capable, and capacious, than those of the Indian Ocean, and so were able to exploit the wind pattern more effectively, and by their greater carrying capacity to greatly increase the trade.

Chapter 12

Usurpations, Legitimacy, and Extinctions

The attraction of being a king stimulated considerable numbers of people, mainly men, but some women as well, to make themselves royal by seizing or aiming to seize someone else's throne. This was despite the manifest dangers of the job, and the various forms of violent death which were visited upon kings in office, and their relations. But there was also danger, not just to the individual kings, but to their very kingdoms: every Hellenistic kingdom was eventually extinguished, with the exception of some which were invented in the last century BC – and these scarcely lasted for very long. So having in one chapter considered the deaths of kings, here the subject will be those who stole a kingship (usurpers), and the end of the kingdoms they contended for (extinctions).

It is often difficult to distinguish usurpers from 'legitimate' kings. Was Demetrios I usurping the Seleukid kingship in 162 when he killed the boy Antiochos V and made himself king? Antiochos had certainly been the reigning king for the previous two years, but this was only because his father had seized the kingship in 175, when, if primogeniture was the means of succession, the king following Seleukos IV should have been Demetrios. Thus Demetrios no doubt felt that he was reclaiming a position of which he had been unjustly deprived.

The succession to every kingship was repeatedly disputed, but normally not in quite such an extreme way as by Demetrios. There is no doubt that Antiochos IV usurped Demetrios' claim, though he could justify his action by claiming to have saved the kingship from a worse usurpation by the minister Heliodoros, who is thought to have aimed to marry Seleukos IV's widow and so make himself king. Equally, Antiochos made himself the guardian, and then the killer, of Demetrios' younger brother, the child king Antiochos, so he was a double usurper, if there can be such a person. And yet the mother of Demetrios, and of the child Antiochos, had married Antiochos IV, so indicating that she accepted him as king, a factor of some importance in the succession; and there seems no indication that Antiochos faced any serious internal opposition to his rule (apart from the Jews of Judaea, who were not disputing his right to the kingship).[1] On the contrary, he appears to have inspired a strong loyalty, judging by the opposition his former ministers and governors mounted against Demetrios I. These men clearly considered Demetrios the usurper, not Antiochos IV.[2]

The Ptolemaic succession was similarly vulnerable. The successor to Ptolemy I, if primogeniture was to be used, should have been Ptolemy Keraunos, but the old king, after decades of indecision – or perhaps a refusal to decide – finally installed Keraunos' half-brother Philadelphos as his heir, and made him joint king with him for the final two years of his reign. Keraunos and his mother and siblings were justifiably angered and decamped for refuge elsewhere.[3] Was then Philadelphos a usurper? The right to choose a successor lay, if it lay anywhere, with the reigning king, who usually adhered to the primogeniture 'rule', but it was the reigning king's choice which was paramount, and since the choice fell on Philadelphos this meant that he was presumably the legitimate king. Just as crucial in the decision was the fact that Keraunos was a long way from Egypt by the time Ptolemy I died, and Philadelphos was present at the deathbed in Alexandria, and so at once able to assume control. Keraunos is said to have written a letter renouncing any rights to the kingship;[4] on the other hand, had Keraunos been able to seize the Ptolemaic kingship he would no doubt have argued that he was, like Demetrios I much later, simply reclaiming what was rightfully his.

So, discovering just who was a usurper is by no means easy. Adapting Sir John Harrington's point about treason, one may say that 'usurpation never can prosper, for if it prospers, none will call it usurpation' – though later historians' judgement, made at leisure in a study, may be different. And the reverse of the question is how is one to discover who is a legitimate king? The obvious test is nomination by the previous king, as Seleukos clearly nominated Antiochos I and Ptolemy nominated Ptolemy II, in each case by installing them as joint kings for some time before the elder men died. But this will not do for some others who were apparent usurpers. Antiochos IV must be counted as a legitimate king simply because he was accepted by his subjects and exercised power without opposition until he died.

There are a few clear cases of obvious usurpers seizing a kingship, either by removing a ruling king or by intervening in a succession process, though their success was usually no more than temporary. Among the Ptolemies it is difficult to find a clear case, for the many disputes within the royal family were usually between men and women who were actually kings already, and the disputes were about who should hold the power, if that can be separated from the office of king. This was the case with Ptolemy VI and VIII, who had been made kings as infants; similarly with the disputes and wars between Ptolemy VIII and his wives, Kleopatra II and III, both of whom could claim to be as legitimate kings as Ptolemy himself. These therefore were not usurpations. In the dynasty's last half-century, on the other hand, after the failure of the legitimate line in 80, the disputes look much more like usurpations.

In 80 Ptolemy XII was made king by a decision of the 'Alexandrians', which probably means the men of the court and the city aristocracy, though they had been reduced to Ptolemy and his brother as candidates. They were the sons of Ptolemy IX by a marriage (or perhaps a concubine) which was not regarded as a legal union in terms of Greek law; Ptolemy XII's succession made it clear that such a legal quibble could be disregarded.[5] In 58, annoyed at his lack of reaction to the Roman annexation of Cyprus (after which his brother, who had been king there since 80, had committed suicide), and of his policy of bribing Roman politicians, these 'Alexandrians' forced the king to leave Egypt. They put in his place his eldest daughter Berenike IV.[6] Three years later Ptolemy XII returned with a Roman army and reclaimed his throne, immediately killing Berenike.[7] Were these usurpations? If the courtiers and the others had the right to install Ptolemy as king in the first place, it may be said that they also had the right to remove him; so in 80 and 58 the events perhaps do not rank as usurpations; instead the participants were installing a ruler in the empty kingship – a form of election, perhaps. But in 55 Ptolemy's return certainly usurped his daughter's legitimate authority, putting him in place as king against the wishes of those who had installed her.

The final Ptolemaic ruler, Kleopatra VII, must be considered not just a usurper but a serial usurper. She inherited the throne from Ptolemy XII along with her brother, Ptolemy XIII, who was ten years her junior. They were to rule jointly, according to their father's will. This arrangement lasted for a very short time; within less than six months after their father had died in 51 Kleopatra had dethroned her brother and was ruling alone. In turn Ptolemy XIII gathered support and removed Kleopatra – these may thus be termed mutual successive usurpations.[8] The lesson here surely was that if one is going to remove a king he must also be killed, as Ptolemy XII had killed their stepsister Berenike IV, but neither sibling went this far at the beginning. Caesar's intervention in Alexandrian affairs in 48–47 resulted in the boy Ptolemy XIII's death during the fighting, and in his place an even younger brother, Ptolemy XIV, became Kleopatra's joint king.[9] He lasted for three years, and was eventually killed at her orders; given that male kings took precedence over their wives, this was another usurpation. She now had a son by Caesar, Ptolemy XV Caesarion, who eventually became another joint king. (This was another liaison which could not count as a legal union – in either Greek or Roman eyes).

This career of murders by Kleopatra VII is in fact a sequence of usurpations, if it be accepted that the father of these people had the power to decide the succession. Kleopatra had first usurped Ptolemy XIII's position, then was usurped by him; after his death she was partnered with Ptolemy XIV, then had him killed, another usurpation.[10] (She also had her younger sister Arsinoe (IV) murdered, in the sanctuary of the temple at Ephesos, getting Mark Antony to order it.[11])

This series of murders and usurpations shows just how difficult it can be to decide on the exact legitimacy status of some kings. The fact that Kleopatra retained her position as ruler for twenty years is surely significant, and must provide her with a cloak of legitimacy. At the same time, the fact that she is regarded with some admiration, particularly among modern feminists, should not influence us in characterising her behaviour. She was able to keep control of her court (using multiple murders to do so, of course), which is another sign of legitimacy in a ruler; the general Egyptian population had no say in the matter, though it is clear that Ptolemy XIII had been able to call on considerable popular support in Alexandria; this, however, may well have been based on general detestation for the Roman intervention, which Alexandrians knew well was aimed at securing Egyptian wealth, not the well-being of either rulers or ruled. Kleopatra scarcely discouraged such intervention in Egyptian affairs. She must be accepted as a legitimate ruler in the same way as Antiochos IV and Demetrios I, despite the methods she had used to reach and retain power.

The other dynasties of which we have some detailed information as to legitimacy and otherwise also demonstrate some of the problems of usurpation. Among the Antigonids there were no obvious cases of usurpation, but there was a case which hostile propaganda claimed to be one, and among the Attalids there was one ambiguous case and one which was certain. Two of these three were in defiance of decisions which involved Rome; their failure was thus almost guaranteed. King Perseus of Macedon was accused, at least in Roman historical writing, of usurping the position of his brother Demetrios, but Livy's account of Perseus' reign is a continuous denigration of the man, so it is worth considering the case from a more neutral standpoint. The implication of Livy's account is that Perseus pushed Demetrios aside and traduced him to their father Philip V. Demetrios was then supposed to have been killed. In fact it seems that Perseus was the elder brother, and so the obvious heir; if anyone was agitating to change Philip V's intentions it was Demetrios, and he failed. Demetrios certainly vanished soon after Perseus succeeded as king, and the assumption must be that he was murdered by Perseus, or on his orders; this was hardly surprising if Demetrios was so clearly his enemy. That is, the usurpation which Livy implies did not take place.[12]

The latter years of the Attalid dynasty saw one certain and one near usurpation. The death of Eumenes II in a landslide at Delphi was reported to his brother, Attalos, who immediately married Eumenes' widow; when it emerged that Eumenes was still alive, the lady was transferred back to her first husband.[13] The episode occasioned much amusement, of course, but it is worth noting that the practice of marrying a dead king's widow was so common as to count as normal – Antiochos IV married his brother's widow, Antigonos III married the widow of his brother Demetrios II, and there are cases in the latter Seleukid years, and among the Maccabees, and eventually, after Eumenes II really had died, Attalos II remarried the widow; the occasions in the Ptolemaic dynasty are perhaps too numerous to list. It was therefore not the royal marriage which caused the amusement, but its reversal. It is worth noting that once again Rome was tangentially involved, for when Attalos visited the city he was urged, almost openly, by several senators to unseat Eumenes and take his place. Attalos refused to do so, evoking admiration for his loyalty from the senators – those who had not been involved, no doubt.[14] But it is a sign, and a matter to be returned to later in this chapter, of the attitude of the Senate later over similar cases.

Then there was the Attalid actual usurpation. The end of the dynasty was marked by a serious attempt to overthrow the terms of Attalos III's will, in which he left his personal possessions, the royal treasure, and his kingdom to Rome. A bastard son of Attalos II, Aristonikos, seized power after his father's death and defied Rome. In fact, he had a reasonable case to make as a likely successor – Attalos III had been a bastard son himself – and the terms of the will could be interpreted to make his kingship possible, but Rome had its eye on the wealth which the city would acquire by the inheritance and so Aristonikos was unlucky. Defying Rome was also, of course, a dangerous thing to attempt, and Aristonikos paid for it with his life, as did large numbers of his supporters and potential subjects. This attempt may be counted as a usurpation, though Rome regarded it as a rebellion.[15]

Fifty years later a similar situation arose where a possible challenge to the bequest of Nikomedes IV of Bithynia was made by another bastard son, but not one related to the dead king. Rome this time was keen to shift its bounds close to the heartland of the kingdom of Mithradates of Pontos, one of its more inveterate enemies, and the child's claim was dismissed. This time, though war eventually resulted, it was not one raised by the potential usurper, but by Mithradates, who had supported the child's claim – he was the son of Nikomedes' wife by another man – largely to maintain the separation from Roman territory which an independent, royal Bithynia had hitherto provided.[16]

The usurpations so far noted were all, except one, unsuccessful. Only those by Kleopatra VII may be said to have led to the usurper retaining power – and in her case the usurper began with the advantage of a joint inheritance of that which she seized. In the Seleukid kingdom, however, a sequence of usurpers in the space of thirty years followed on from the earlier cases of Antiochos IV and Demetrios I. Demetrios was overthrown by Alexander Balas, whose cause was pushed by Ptolemy VI, Eumenes II, and Attalos II, and by a conspiring group of the former ministers of Antiochos IV, who were all generally, if distantly and ineffectually, encouraged by Rome. He was, in all probability, a bastard son of Antiochos', which gave him a colourable claim to the kingship.[17] But once he had seized it, he was at once opposed by Demetrios I's son, Demetrios II, who succeeded in removing his father's nemesis, first by defeating him, and then by persuading his host to kill him. (Balas had captured and killed Demetrios I's eldest son Antigonos, and his widow.) But Balas was accepted as king for several years, so Demetrios II's success amounted to a new usurpation. Then Demetrios II, when he succeeded in removing Balas, was subjected to an uprising in the name of Alexander's son, Antiochos VI; when the boy died, his minister Diodotos took over the uprising in his own name, taking the throne name Tryphon.

This was a sequence of usurpations such that it must have been very difficult for some of the subjects of these several kings and claimants to decide which man was the rightful king. But it was not yet finished. Demetrios II went off to fight in the east, and his wife called in his brother Antiochos VII and married him – while Demetrios was still actively fighting in Babylonia. Antiochos was thereby made king because he had married the preceding king's wife (as with Attalos II and Eumenes II), then he was able to gather the loyalty of the Syrian part of the kingdom to himself against Diodotos/Tryphon, and against his unpopular brother (who was soon captured by the Parthians, to be held a prisoner as a constant threat to Antiochos). There can be no doubt that Antiochos was a usurper, given that his brother was still king when he was made king, and while Tryphon still had a fair deal of support within Syria.

It was still not finished, for when Antiochos VII died in battle in 129, Demetrios II returned, and was then undermined by yet another pretender, Alexander II Zabeinas, who was thrown into the kingdom by Ptolemy VIII and maintained himself as king with minimal Ptolemaic support for a few years. The death by murder of Demetrios II left the way clear for his son Antiochos VIII to sweep the field by removing Alexander; he then eliminated his mother, the interfering Kleopatra Thea, who had killed her eldest surviving son Seleukos V, and had made herself joint king with her next son. With her death Antiochos VIII became, for the first time in thirty years, the only ruling Seleukid king; the knowledge must have been a considerable relief to his subjects.

These usurpations – every Seleukid king between 175 and 120 was a usurper – provide a perfect sequence of proliferating trouble originating from the murder of Seleukos IV by his minister Heliodoros. Every later royal revolution was a consequence of that act, and the result was the slow destruction of the kingdom, a process which lasted for a century. Within that sequence the irony is that the one person who held the dynasty together was the Ptolemaic princess Kleopatra Thea, whose successive husbands – Alexander Balas, Demetrios II, Antiochos VII – successively failed as kings – and whose sons she attempted to exclude from power, having acquired a strong taste for it herself. Her fecundity also meant that two of her sons, from separate fathers, revived the contest in 113 when Antiochos IX Kyzikenos challenged his half-brother; they then fought each other to the death over a period of twenty years. The kings caught in this never-ending and impossible situation were on the whole able men, particularly Antiochos VII – even if they failed in facing difficulties which even their abilities could not overcome – but had the rule of primogeniture been followed, none of them, except Demetrios I, would ever have become kings at all.

It is noticeable that usurpations usually took place in the latter part of a dynasty's life. Among the Ptolemies none took place until the last thirty years (if the exclusion of Ptolemy Keraunos from the succession is discounted), though the murder of Ptolemy V might be counted as such; among the Seleukids the dynasty had lasted almost a century and a half before Antiochos IV's usurpations which had such continuing and disastrous effects. It is worth noting also that Rome was involved in most of these matters. Its involvement is typified by the reply the Senate gave to the attempted usurper Timarchos who was trying to unseat Demetrios I – who in turn had annoyed the Senate by escaping from Italy and away from his status as a hostage. When Timarchos asked the Senate to accept him as king, the Senate obliged, but actually did nothing to help him.[18]

The refusal of the Senate twice to allow Demetrios I to return to Syria to claim the kingship was a direct interference in the situation in the Seleukid kingdom.[19] However, once Demetrios had made his escape, it was no longer necessary for Rome to interfere. The disputes within the kingdom were quite sufficient for Roman purposes, which were essentially to ensure that the Seleukid state was weakened. Timarchos and Alexander Balas were given tacit encouragement by the Senate, and senatorial delegations went to see what was going on at intervals.[20] However, the continuing dynastic and external wars were doing all that Rome wished in weakening its rival; whether Rome understood it or not, the preoccupation of Alexander Balas with the threat of Demetrios II from the west was what permitted the Parthians to invade and conquer first Iran and then Babylonia. If Rome did not get the point at first, the visit of Scipio Aemilianus in 144 will have brought the situation to the Senate's attention – and Polybios, one of Scipio's circle, certainly knew. The reduction in Seleukid power which came with the loss of these eastern territories was decisive. Rome, in the short term, was interested only in undermining Demetrios and any other king showing any ability, just in case the Seleukids were aiming for a return match to recover the territories lost in 188 – there is no sign that any Seleukid king did so – and more widely in reducing any power, Attalid, Ptolemaic, Macedonian, Seleukid, which looked powerful; a dynastic civil war was the exactly the sort of problem Rome liked to exacerbate.

The question of the legitimacy of a king's power was therefore central to the issue of the kingdoms' continuation, and indeed of their very existence. The Hellenistic kingdoms were personal to the king, indeed they only existed because there was a king, and none of them, perhaps with the exception of Macedon and some of the smaller national-type kingdoms, had any 'natural' existence. The kings had instituted heredity as the means of succession, and, while this was fully in keeping with the social milieu in which they existed, it was a poor foundation upon which to build a whole kingdom; any king could be removed, any dynasty could die out. In 223–220 both the Seleukid and Ptolemaic dynasties were reduced to a single male representative and, while the Seleukids recovered, the succession among the Ptolemies was always precarious from then on, thanks to their habit of fighting and killing each other. Without a king there would be no kingdom; its territories would separate out, as in fact happened to the Seleukid kingdom in the first century BC. Dynastic disputes therefore brought about the decisive weakening in such states, and any state which feared the enmity of another could always exacerbate these disputes with little difficulty, even, as Ptolemy VIII did, by inventing a pretender such as Alexander Zabeinas; with sufficient internal enmities, it was not difficult to promote a civil war. Such disputes therefore were always liable to lead to the elimination of a kingdom. And it was Rome that benefited most from such collapses.

It was Rome also, of course, which was the prime agent in causing the extinction of the numerous kingdoms. This process fuels the perception of Rome as basically anti-monarchical, but at the time of the republic it got along well enough with many monarchic powers, and for a time Rome was only one power among several which extinguished rival kingships. It was not being against the idea of monarchy which led to the kingdoms being suppressed by Rome, rather it was the process of conquest which reduced the kingdoms to the status of Roman provinces, replacing the kings with governors, who usually inherited the royal powers. That is, Rome's takeover of these king-doms was accomplished merely by the elimination of the ruling dynasties; the kingdoms were so fragile, even in many cases, artificial, that it was only the existence of the dynasties which allowed them to continue. On the other hand, the fact that Rome insisted on removing the kings suggests strongly that the kings had become strong foci of loyalty, and that the prospect of being part of the Roman Empire was not something the subjects of those as well as kings contemplated with any pleasure.

Rome's method was in fact not too dissimilar from the practice of the greater Hellenistic kings in reducing their weaker neighbours to a subordi-nate status, which in some cases might result in the extinction of a monarchy, and it was the Hellenistic kingdoms which began the process of simplifying the political map by suppressing kingships which might provide a basis of loyalty to rival the greater imperial powers. In Ptolemy I's empire there were kingships in the Phoenician cities and in Cyprus. By the end of Ptolemy I's reign only one king remained. The Cypriot kings had rebelled at one point and most had been eliminated; the last, Nikokles of Salamis, committed suicide in a spectacular fashion in about 310.[21] Of the Phoenician cities Tyre had been besieged to destruction twice, by Alexander in 332 and then by Antigonos I in 315–314, and any kingship had clearly vanished in the process, probably even before Alexander. Sidon had surrendered quickly to Alexander and retained its monarchy, and still had a king, Philokles, into the reign of Ptolemy II. He was employed as a Ptolemaic naval viceroy in the Aegean for a time. He appears to have been the last Sidonian king; it is not even certain that he ruled at the city.[22]

The one Phoenician kingdom which remained for a time was Arados, which was in that part of Syria which fell to Seleukos. It seems that the kings of the city survived until about 259. King Gerostratos had commanded part of the Persian fleet in the Aegean and when Alexander threatened his city he opportunely changed sides; he and his successors appear to have accepted Seleukid suzerainty for another seventy years, so allowing the monarchy to survive. How the kingship ended is not known, but as the only monarchy left among the Phoenician cities it is probable that it was abolished in an internal decision. Arados was always the most independently minded of the Phoeni-cian cities and repeatedly attempted to detach itself from whoever controlled the mainland, from the time of Seleukos I onwards, finally succeeding in 129. It may be that holding on to its local monarchy was part of that ambition for full independence, or alternatively that the monarchy bequeathed a sentiment for independence to the republican city which succeeded it.[23] At all events between them the first Seleukid and Ptolemaic kings eliminated all the local monarchies in the eastern Mediterranean.

The attitude of both these imperial powers was hardly anti-monarchic, and the same may be said of Rome, despite the myth. There are several examples to illustrate this. In 263 Rome was content that Hiero should continue as king in Syracuse. He was, of course, in a strong position, with an intact army, a most powerfully fortified city, and in a situation where he was holding the balance of power between Rome and Carthage in Sicily. Even when Hiero died in 215 the kingship continued in the person of his grandson, until it was suppressed by an internal republican revolution. The Romans then conquered the city and so annexed a state which had a republican government; all the signs are that so far as Rome was concerned the monarchy could have continued, provided it remained Rome's ally.

Across the Adriatic Sea Rome collided several times with a monarchy which had developed in Illyria north of Epeiros. Two Romano-Illyrian Wars were fought, in 229 and 219, but the monarchy, though damaged by the defeats, continued for another half-century. Eventually another king, Genthius, was in power in the same area at the time of the Third Romano-Macedonian War. He attempted to negotiate with both sides, being trapped between them, and both sides betrayed him (he thus attempted to emulate Hiero in balancing between the two antagonists, but clearly over-estimated his own strength). He ended by gracing a triumph in Rome followed by a death in prison.[24] The monarchy then disappeared, but it does not seem that it was deliberately targeted by Rome; after all, the Illyrians suffered defeats in 229 and 219 without the monarchy being suppressed. Instead the kingdom was annexed and organised as a set of cities dependent on Rome, and so the monarchy disappeared. This probably happened because the Macedonian kingship was also suppressed and the country divided up at the same time.

The kingdom of Magas in Cyrenaica broke down after his death, like that of Hiero. It was taken over by Ptolemy III after the death of King Demetrios the Fair, which like at Syracuse was succeeded by a brief republican interlude. The exact condition of the kingdom at the moment of its annexation – re-annexation – by Ptolemaic Egypt is not clear, but it had certainly ceased, like Syracuse later, to be a peaceful place. The marriage of Magas' daughter Berenike to Ptolemy III united the two kingdoms, and yet Cyrenaica remained a separate political entity, emerging twice more as a state separate from Egypt before being annexed as a set of quarrelling cities, by Rome twenty years after the end of its monarchy.[25]

The removal of a monarchy was thus essentially a by-product of either an internal revolution – Syracuse, Cyrenaica, Arados – or of the kingdom's annexation by a greater power – Cyprus, Sidon, Illyria, Macedon. The practices of Rome in its slow and erratic expansion were thus broadly similar to those of the Hellenistic kingdoms.

Antiochos III's campaigns to restore the old bounds of his ancestral kingdom repeatedly brought secessionist kingdoms under his suzerainty. His methods varied: he dispossessed Parthia of the territory its first king had seized from Antiochos' ancestors but did not annex Parthian territory beyond his original boundary; he deprived both Euthydemos of Baktria and Sopha-gasenos of the Paropamisadai of their elephants and treasure, but not their territories; by this process he therefore accepted the continued existence of these kingdoms, which he could well have annexed by the argument that he was suppressing a rebellion. It seems likely that it was the sheer distance of these places from the centre of Seleukid government, which of necessity lay in the west, where the major existential threats were, which restrained Antiochos from assuming the responsibility of governing such difficult places as Baktria. The history of his dynasty's involvement in the 'Hellenistic Far East' showed that only a constant royal presence and full attention on the spot would hold the place together and as part of the imperial territory; political difficulties in the west of the Seleukid kingdom precluded the king staying for very long in the east; the organisation of the east as a viceroyalty was always a temp-tation for any governor to rebel with the intention of seizing the kingdom. It was more practical, and safer, to establish friendly relations with the local kings and let them do the work. In the end, of course, the Parthian kings seized the moment of another dynastic war in the west to emulate rebellious Seleukid governors and conquer the Iranian and Babylonian territories.

In the case of Xerxes of Armenia, Antiochos took Xerxes' treasure, imposed an annual tribute of horses on him – a similar process to that inflicted on the easterners – and in addition gave him his sister Antiochis as his wife. She soon murdered him, possibly because he was pursuing some sort of independence agenda, and the Armenian kingship was then replaced by two governors – that is, the kingdom was annexed and divided.[26] This took place at the same time, 212–211, as the Roman annexation of the kingdom of Syracuse. In both cases the abolition of the monarchy could be said to have been the result of internal developments, and in both cases the ruling kings' deaths brought the end of the monarchies. (The two governors later made themselves independent kings when Antiochos died.) Antiochos had already recovered a large extent of territory from Attalos I and Akhaios in Asia Minor; as in Baktria and Parthia (and at first in Armenia), he left Attalos in control of his ancestral city.

In the same period, only ten years after the suppression of the Cyrenaican kingdom, the Epeirote kingship had been abolished by an internal collapse, the several cities and tribes which had joined to form the kingdom now replaced the monarchy with a federal republic. The extinction of kingdoms was thus, in the third century, more likely to be the result of internal revolu-tion than external conquest. The defeat of a kingdom in war usually resulted in the loss of territory, but not necessarily in the suppression of the kingship. (For a list of eliminated monarchies of the Hellenistic period see Appendix II.)

The Roman wars against Macedon were of the same pattern, until the Third War between them (172–167). There was no obvious war aim in Rome to remove the kings, either Philip V or Perseus, so far as can be seen, and King Perseus had sons who could have inherited the state had Rome not decided to destroy it. It seems likely that it was the long and tough resistance made by the Macedonians against the Roman attacks which drove home to Rome exactly how strong and cohesive the kingdom was and how loyal the population was to the dynasty. Its destruction, once it had been defeated – with very large military casualties – was the result.[27] The kingship was then abolished, and the kingdom broken up, but twenty years later it was reconstituted instantly by the arrival of a usurper – transparently a usurper – Andriskos, who claimed to be a son of Perseus. Though he was very obviously a fake, Andriskos ('Philip VI') roused the Macedonians and led them to defeat a Roman army before a bigger army and a better commander defeated and killed him. Thus a mere and obvious usurper destroyed the rickety Roman settlement of 167 with revealing ease.[28] The lesson was clear. The danger of a repeat was averted by the annexation of the kingdom and its conversion into a Roman province, with a Roman-appointed governor taking the place of the king (though rebellions occurred for years afterwards); the Macedonians therefore achieved one of their aims, which was to reunite their divided land. The end of Andriskos was thus the second abolition of the Macedonian monarchy. It is noticeable that neither the forced division of Armenia nor that of Macedon were successes in the sense of their replacements by the victors continuing afterwards.

The suppression of the Macedonian kingship was actually only one of several such abolitions which took place in Greece at much the same time. Between them the Roman armies and Philip V suppressed the kingship among the Athamanians, an easy target whose kings, like the Illyrians, had tried to manoeuvre between the greater neighbours until eventually exasperating both.[29] The constituent cities were set up as pseudo-independent states, as in Illyria. Between them the Romans and the Achaian League finally removed the kingship of the Spartans. Again this came about in part as a result of internal changes, which had seen repeated attempts to return to what was conceived of as the ancient Spartan way, but whose effects in increasing Spartan military power always frightened the neighbours. Internally the ancestral dual monarchy had already been replaced by a single king, partly because during the wars the last representatives of the two families of kings had been killed off. With only one king, Nabis, who had only the most tenuous claim to the royal inheritance, and who was both oppressive internally and aggressive to his neighbours, the monarchy's abolition proved to be relatively easy.[30] At the same time, the abolition of the kingship in Sparta did not reduce the aspirations of the Spartans to independence, and it was their agitation against Achaian domination which eventually provoked Rome into destroying the Achaian League. In the case of both Sparta and Athamania the impetus for destroying the kingships came mainly from their Greek neighbours; Rome was involved mainly as the military instrument.

Between the emergence of the new kingships after Alexander, therefore, and the defeat of Antiochos the Great at Magnesia in 188, the likelihood was that a vulnerable kingdom and its kingship would most likely be suppressed by one of the greater kingdoms than by Rome, but from 167 onwards Rome became the main instrument of this suppression. Meanwhile the greater kingdoms were beginning to shed provinces which made themselves into new kingdoms. These were generally small, and as the Roman revolution spread throughout the Mediterranean region, many of these small kingdoms were taken over, but only occasionally abolished and annexed. The usual form was to adopt the Hellenistic method by imposing Roman suzerainty on the continuing kingdom. Kappadokia, numerous Syrian kingdoms, the Bosporan kingdom, Armenia, Kommagene, all survived, many of them until well into the imperial period. Once again it was easier for Rome to take over a kingdom as a going concern, as it had been with Syracuse back in 212–211, than to exert itself to reorder the region and impose a new administration – Macedon was a useful lesson. Only serious and powerful enemies – Pontos, Ptolemaic Egypt – were suppressed, or those with seriously lengthy histories which might inspire widespread loyalty, such as the Seleukids. The Seleukids had been suppressed once by Tigranes of Armenia between 83 and 70, but had quickly returned with his disappearance to aspire once more to the north Syrian kingship; they were then suppressed again by Pompey, no doubt in part because of their persistence.[31]

For three centuries Rome dealt with kings and their kingdoms on a more or less equal basis, and most of the territories which were annexed had been kingdoms originally. Their administrative systems were taken over generally intact, and then operated by Roman governors. These men were thus near-kings in their authority and powers. The later practice of incorporating kingdoms into the empire, intact and with kings still in office, meant that those kings provided another link between the preceding Hellenistic period, from which they inherited their positions and powers, and the succeeding Roman Empire, a link moderated through those terrible Roman warlords, from Sulla to Octavian, who largely owed their powers to their military and administrative operations in the east as well as to their political machinations in Rome and Italy.

But one of the strangest, most important effects of the continuing contacts between Rome and the kings of the east came about in the final years of the kings. The great Roman warlords who dominated and destroyed the Roman Republic were frequently affected by the eastern kings in many ways. Mark Antony, of course, is the best known and the most extravagant in behaviour, but Caesar was seduced by Kleopatra as well, and his campaigns in the east funded his power at Rome, as had those of Pompeius before him – and those of Sulla still earlier. When Octavian arrived to supervise the deaths of both Antony and Kleopatra in Alexandria the most impressive kings left were only minor players such as Herod and his family, much less compelling in terms of power, if considerably so in terms of family drama and profligate lifestlye.

And yet the emperors who followed were essentially Hellenistic kings in a light Roman disguise. Between the Octavian of 30 BC and the Augustus of AD 14 the transformation is clear, from a republican warlord operating in the same way as Caesar or Antony to an emperor who set the tone for the next four or five centuries. Augustus might claim to be the inheritor and reviver of Roman Republican traditions and practices, but in Alexandria he had quite deliberately taken upon himself to open up Alexander's sarcophagus. At that time he was the same age as Alexander when the latter died. It was the fact that he lived on for another 44 years which allowed him to bring the Roman Empire to a stable institutional condition. In this he resembled Seleukos I and Ptolemy I much more than Alexander.

Augustus might theoretically, and Tiberius perhaps instinctively, resist the influence of the Hellenistic style of kingship, but from Caligula onwards the emperors had the same attributes and powers as any of the former kings; it is no accident Caligula was friends with one of the last of the Hellenistic kings Agrippa II. The emperors had a royal council of advisers, meeting in confidence and taking decisions to affect the whole empire, elections were for minor offices only, governors were appointed not elected, the Senate was no more than a law court – all these were exactly the same as in the preceding Hellenistic kingdoms. The emperors all felt that they needed to win a military victory against some hapless enemy to justify their position, even such unmilitary men as Claudius and Nero. This practice, of course, certainly had Roman antecedents, but, just like the Hellenistic kings from Alexander and Philip onwards, the Roman emperors owed their power to their command and control of the army, and 'Emperor' is, of course, an adaptation of 'imperator'. At their deaths the emperors became divine, as Vespasian, perhaps the most down-to-earth of emperors, noted when he remarked as he was dying, 'I think I am about to become a god.' For some emperors divinity of a sort was even adopted while they were still alive – another Hellenistic precedent being followed. The emperors may have felt that they were Roman, and called themselves by their citizen names, but by the time the republic had expired the ruling class of Rome was clearly Hellenised, and by the Flavian period was increasingly Hellenic. The Roman Empire was a Hellenistic state, the emperors were Hellenistic kings.

Chapter 13

Kings and Rome

The Roman Republic occasionally remembered that it had originated in a *coup d'état* in which its early monarchy was abolished. This legend was at times rolled out to justify some momentary policy in foreign affairs, in which Rome was supposed to be eternally anti-monarchic. There is, however, no clear unifying anti-monarchic principle detectable in that policy. And, of course, the supreme irony is that the republic became so dysfunctional by the end that it had to be rescued by its first emperor, after several dictators had failed to do the job for one reason or another.

Rome had relations of various sorts with Hellenistic kings from the second half of the fourth century BC onwards, colliding with several even as the city brought a precarious unity to peninsular Italy. In most of these early cases – Alexander and Pyrrhos of Epeiros, Kleonymos of Sparta, Agathokles of Syracuse – the blows the city suffered were no more than glancing, at least in the result, though individual battles could be bruising, and when the next king was encountered – Hiero of Syracuse – he, after an initial fight, took advantage of Roman power to retreat into its protection.

With one obvious exception, every encounter between a Hellenistic kingdom and Rome was a hostile collision. Some of these were unpleasant in the extreme. The war with King Pyrrhos produced repeated military defeats for Rome, which eventually resorted to an alliance with Carthage to contain him – an alliance in which both allowed their partners to fight alone – and it was not until well after the king had left Italy that Rome made any advance into his Italian territories.[1] The initial collision with Hiero of Syracuse was a battle in which Hiero was only just defeated and from which he withdrew with his forces scarcely damaged.[2] Had the king then resumed his former alliance with Carthage a Roman defeat and expulsion from Sicily would have been very likely.

Hiero chose to adhere to Rome, no doubt assuming from earlier similar experiences that Carthage was greedy to take over all Sicily. The initial peace treaty with him expired in 248, but both sides found it convenient to renew.[3] This policy ensured a long period of peace for Hiero's people, wealth for Syracuse, and regular supplies for the Roman forces in Sicily. Under his successor, who succeeded in the midst of the second Romano-Carthaginian

War, the arrangement broke down, and the city was besieged and sacked.[4] But it was then set up on its feet again, and continued in a modest prosperity as a part of the Roman province.

The island became Rome's first overseas possession, at first administered by a praetor from the western town of Lilybaion, who also commanded the Roman fleet stationed there.[5] That administration was little more than a military domination which enforced the payment of tribute, but when the Syracusan kingdom was taken over, after the capture of the city in 211, the royal administration of the eastern part of the island was also taken over as a going concern. In this way Rome, like all predator states, made no attempt to improve or change matters of administration which were working perfectly adequately, but simply acquired that set of practices and continued them. Whatever actual differences there were between the Roman republican confederation in Italy and those Hellenistic kingdoms it went on to fight and conquer, therefore, these progressively disappeared as the empire grew.

In other words, from 212 onwards, Rome became, in its conquests, increasingly pervaded by Hellenistic practices and methods. This, of course, also happened in cultural terms, with the increasing appreciation of Hellenistic drama, philosophy, sculpture, and so on. The cultural influence of third century Syracuse had spread widely, and now it reached Rome in full force with the loot transferred there after the conquest.[6] This was a process which happened repeatedly over the next two centuries, notably in the loot from Macedonia sent to Rome by Aemilius Paullus in 167, and twenty years later by the plunder from southern Greece collected by Mummius. The kings themselves, however, the Romans had no use for. It took half a century for them to resume the practice of destroying their kingdoms after dealing with Syracuse.

The greater Hellenistic kingdoms were well aware of what was happening in the west, just as Rome was fully alert to developments in the east. After all, Pyrrhos was a king who had relations with every power from the Seleukids to Carthage in one way or another. The elephants he brought to Italy had been donated by Antiochos I. The Ptolemies had relations with Agathokles of Syracuse, who married one of Ptolemy I's daughters, and Pyrrhos had married another; and Ptolemy's province of Cyrenaica bordered on Carthage. Archimedes of Syracuse designed and built a great ship, the *Syrakusia*, which King Hiero presented to Ptolemy. And, more to the point here, in 273 Ptolemy II made official contact with Rome and the two powers exchanged envoys.[7] This was clearly precautionary on Ptolemy's part, since he was officially friendly with all the contestants in the western area except Rome. As a result he and his successors were able to remain neutral in the wars in the west in the third century.

Not so Ptolemy's competitors. Philip V muscled in to join the Second Romano-Carthaginian War when he thought Carthage would win, only to be eventually attacked and punished by Rome in the 190s;[8] Antiochos III became involved in a long, slow dispute with the Senate between 198 and the outbreak of war with Rome in 192; the dispute was conducted by using envoys. (This means of negotiation had been largely eschewed by Rome in its relations with Macedon, where it preferred indirection and threats.) Repeatedly senatorial delegations and Seleukid envoys, usually in twos and threes, travelled back and forth between Rome and the king every few months; and the king was usually in western Asia Minor all this time. But despite much time taken and much talk in negotiation it is clear from the difficulties involved that neither side understood the other. In the end Antiochos III sent a small army into Greece, at least in part because he thought he had a responsibility to bring order and peace to the country after the Romans had left. The earlier responsibility had been Macedon's, but the defeat of Philip V in 197 had expelled Macedonian influence from Greece. As a result the country seemed to be sliding into disorder. Antiochos was, of course, disastrously mistaken in his assumption that Rome was no longer concerned.[9]

One result of Antiochos' defeat in that war was that one of his sons, who later became king as Antiochos IV, was sent to Italy as a 'hostage'.[10] Exactly what was the purpose of this is not clear. One would assume it to be a way of enforcing the terms of peace which had been dictated by the Romans at Apameia in 188, but this makes little sense. Antiochos was a younger son, and so not particularly valuable in a dynastic sense, and no Hellenistic king would hesitate to sacrifice a son if he could see advantage in it for the kingdom. And what could the Romans do? Killing Antiochos the hostage, which would be the obvious measure with which to threaten his father, would be thoroughly counter-productive: Antiochos the prince dead would end his hostage-value, and if the threat was made and then not carried out, that value would also end. And if he was killed, the king would have a justifiable grievance he could publicly exploit.

In fact, Antiochos the hostage clearly thoroughly enjoyed his stay at Rome, making a wide range of acquaintances, and being thoroughly alert to Roman political and military affairs.[11] From the king's point of view this might have been valuable experience, but the longer the hostage stayed in Rome the less useful that experience was, since he clearly became out of date with matters in his homeland. And anyway, the death of Antiochos III in 187, the year after the hostage was dispatched, rendered the terms of the peace null, and any value he had in terms of enforcing the peace vanished. The only peace term still unimplemented was the delivery of the indemnity money to Rome, and this stopped when Antiochos III died. (Other terms were also not enforced, such as the destruction of the Seleukid ships, the delivery of Greek politicians to Rome, and the killing of the Seleukid war elephants.) The pointlessness of the hostage notion is evident. Antiochos had also been by-passed in the succession, as he will have expected, since his elder brother Seleukos had already been installed as joint king before he left, and Seleukos had children to succeed him.

The general uselessness of Antiochos as a hostage makes it all the more strange that Rome should insist on exchanging him for his nephew Demetrios in 178 or 177.[12] Demetrios seemed a much more valuable hostage, in that he was the eldest son of Seleukos IV and so the presumptive heir. And yet primogeniture, though normally the Seleukid practice, was not an immutable rule, and when Seleukos was murdered in 175 his younger son was successfully installed as the next king, until Antiochos IV returned and took up the guardianship of the child – as it seemed.[13] And yet at that point Demetrios' function at Rome changed. He was now no longer a hostage for his father's behaviour, if he ever was, but had now become a threat to Antiochos, for he had a better claim to the kingship than either him or his stepson, so that Rome could now brandish the possibility of releasing the hostage as a threat. Antiochos himself clearly understood this, for when he himself had been released he had carefully avoided going to Syria and had stayed in Athens.[14] But once again this hostage proved useless, since if Demetrios was held in Italy, he ceased to be a threat, and if he was released, he ceased to be of any use to Rome. Demetrios was denied permission to return home by the Senate more than once,[15] and the details of this, and so of Demetrios' continuing threat, were no doubt carefully reported to Antiochos.

One result, however, was that there were now two Seleukid princes who were familiar with Rome and its ways. They lived in or near the city between 188 and 162, and in that period several other kings and princes turned up as well. It was a sign of Rome's predominant power after 188 that international diplomacy was largely concentrated at Rome, with envoys being sent from the city to deal with the problems raised. The period following the defeats of Philip V of Macedon and the Seleukid Antiochos III (197–189) was a time when several Hellenistic kings attempted to use the Roman Republic for their own advantage. Rome, more or less securely established as the most powerful state in the Mediterranean region, certainly understood what was involved, and was generally disdainful, if fairly patient, at least for a time.

Several kings or heirs of kings actually visited Rome in that period. It may have been Rome itself which encouraged this process by hosting the Seleukids Antiochos and Demetrios between 188 and 162. In the 170s and 160s half a dozen other kings or their heirs arrived in person to petition or warn or entreat the Senate. And in many cases the visits were theatrical in their performance to the mingled disdain and disgust and amusement of the Roman senators.

Eumenes II of Pergamon had long sensed the enmity of Philip V, but he felt he was actually threatened by Philip's successor Perseus, who succeeded his father in 179. He understood that the Roman Senate was nervous about Perseus, and set about exploiting that nervousness to build it into active enmity. He employed, in the best demagogic and diplomatic – 'duplicitous' – fashion, lies, exaggerations, and innuendo.[16] This was so successful that when he went to Rome personally in 173 he was able to persuade the Senate that it was time to deal with Perseus, and the war began the next year.[17]

At the end of that war, the Third Romano-Macedonian, King Perseus made an involuntary visit to Rome as the prisoner of the victor of the war, M. Aemilius Paullus, being exhibited in his triumph. He and his family were paraded through the streets as visible evidence of Paullus' victory, and Perseus himself soon died as a result of the ill-treatment he suffered, and despair.[18] (He could not be allowed to live long.) On the other hand, his wife, Laodike, who was the daughter of Seleukos IV (and therefore the sister of the later hostage Demetrios) was carefully returned to Syria without being subjected to the indignity of being paraded in the triumph. The crassness of Paullus' behaviour towards the king was clearly tempered by an alert diplomatic awareness of the value of the royal personages. Leaving any of them at large in the former kingdom would be dangerous. The contrast between the conduct towards the king and his children on the one hand and Laodike on the other makes it quite clear that the unpleasant treatment suffered by the former was quite deliberate. (When Demetrios returned to Syria he married Laodike.[19])

No other king could claim such a diplomatic success as Eumenes had achieved – he in effect recruited Rome to fight his war for him – though this was not, of course, wholly Eumenes' doing, and Rome was fully willing to undertake that war, and in fact Rome had been preparing diplomatically to attack Perseus even before Eumenes' visit to the city. Indeed, during the course of the war, Eumenes left virtually all the fighting to Rome, meanwhile pursuing his own ambitions in Asia Minor. The Senate was less than pleased, and after the war Eumenes was unable to gain any more favours. When he sent his brother Attalos to Rome to request help in fending off Galatian raids, Attalos was almost overtly encouraged by several senators to make a bid for his brother's kingship, though he failed to respond to their temptations.[20] Eumenes himself then set out for Italy to make a personal appeal, but was confronted by an invented law, which was supposed to deny any king entry to the Senate, and which therefore prevented the Senate from receiving him.[21] He had to deal with the Galatians himself.

This insulting episode happened just after the Senate had met another of Eumenes' enemies, King Prusias II of Bithynia, who had been entertained by the Senate and sent home with rich presents – the invented law did not apply, it seems, to anyone but Eumenes.[22] Nor did it apply when two of the contending Ptolemies arrived.

We are here at the mercy of Polybios, a much-admired historian and politician who was a contemporary with the events in Rome at the time. When Prusias visited, he had been excessively obsequious to the senators. He dressed in the clothes of a freedman, showing that he regarded himself as the Senate's client and creature, to do with as it wished. Polybios, always liable to insert his own personal opinions into his history, was disgusted at this exhibition of fawning and grovelling.[23] Prusias was at odds with Eumenes, and this display was clearly intended to show that he expected his collective patron, the Senate, to support him in the dispute, and shows that he was alert to the now frosty relations between the two. Prusias succeeded to the extent that he was listened to and rewarded with gifts, though practical results in Asia Minor did not result. Prusias' exhibition had been met by a complementary exhibition by the senators, but those who made the decisions in Rome were not those who were impressed by the theatricality.

This act was sufficiently successful, though, that Ptolemy VI put on his own more restrained version a little later. He also was in search of senatorial support, this time in his dispute with his brother, Ptolemy VIII. Ptolemy VI had been defeated in the internal disputes over control of Egypt. He went to Italy, travelling with an apparent lack of ostentation, and with a minimal suite of followers, consisting of one eunuch and three slaves. He lived at Rome with a Greek acquaintance, and exhibited no royal style whatsoever, deferring perhaps to the republican sentiments around him. The Seleukid prince Demetrios was shocked by what he thought to be Ptolemy's poverty-stricken condition, and offered him rich clothing and financial help, so that he should appear before the Senate, and in the city, in a condition Demetrios obviously thought more appropriate. Ptolemy demurred, reckoning rightly that the Senate would be more impressed and more sympathetic if he approached it in his humble guise; he had clearly understood the effect Prusias' ruse had had, and the bad taste it had left, and his own display was thereby much restrained, and yet dignified. It worked, and the Senate, which had not known that he was coming nor that he had arrived, excused itself for not greeting him properly when they discovered his presence, thereby ceding the diplomatic initiative to Ptolemy. (Again, note, the law debarring kings meeting the Senate had apparently vanished.)[24] Ptolemy had made his point and improved on it by not actually requesting any direct assistance. He did ask for verbal and diplomatic support in restoring himself to Egypt, and this he received.

His brother had meanwhile reminded the Alexandrians of how much they disliked him; he had been driven out of the city, and now adopted the same tactic of a visit to Rome, though he could hardly use the same faux-humble method of approach to the Senate as his brother.[25] He got much the same reply in the end, but in his absence Ptolemy VI had re-established himself firmly and immovably in Alexandria, and rejected the new partition of territories the Senate proposed. There is no evidence that Rome's support for either king had any effect whatever in Egypt; both kings had been attempting to use the city for their own ends, and by this time the Senate was no doubt fully aware of this tactic, just as the two rivals understood clearly enough that the Senate's main aim was to perpetuate their rivalry. This could be done by words alone.

The direct contacts between ruling kings and the Senate in Rome were thus rarely satisfactory for either party: the kings gained little or no help, other than words; the Senate may have been pleased to be fawned upon, but its actions and words had little influence in the eastern kingdoms and no obvious effect on the political situation there – unless they were to embark on a war. The kings discerned this quickly enough, but the example of Ptolemy VI is perhaps the most instructive. He had recovered Egypt and his brother had received Cyrenaica, but by a decision made by Ptolemy VI, even if it had been recommended by the Senate. Ptolemy VIII was not satisfied and in 154 he went to ask the Senate to increase his kingdom. The Senate eventually sent five of its members, each in a quinquereme, to insist that Ptolemy VI accommodate Ptolemy VIII by delivering Cyprus to him. The ships, the major warships of the time, were presumably intended to be a clear menace, even if a threat was not yet fully delivered. Ptolemy VIII eagerly gathered an army of mercenaries in preparation for his anticipated triumph. But Ptolemy VI simply took note of the senators' presence and did nothing to comply with their or his brother's demands, and failed to hand over Cyprus. The senators in the end simply went home, taking their ships with them.[26] Ptolemy VIII had to wait another ten years, until Ptolemy VI was dead, before acquiring both Cyprus and Egypt.

The Senate made it an intermittent practice to dispatch small groups of its members, usually three in number, to investigate what was going on in the east. Sometimes these men chose to exercise their supposed powers, but most of these embassies were merely investigative, and were probably intended only to be such; their timing was usually just after some major political re-arrangement in the east, and their purpose was thus clearly to probe the new situation and report back. These delegations were usually headed by a particularly distinguished senator, who was thus able to meet the kings on more or less even terms. Ti. Sempronius Gracchus went on at least two of these missions, and P. Cornelius Scipio Aemilianus also headed one.

Gracchus visited Syria at the time of Antiochos IV's great celebration at Daphne in 166, and in the aftermath of the destruction of Macedon by Rome and of Antiochos' war with Egypt. He was there reassured that the great military display he was watching was to be directed eastwards, and not to the west.[27] Scipio Aemilianus' visit took place in the midst of the Seleukid civil wars of the 140s, and just after the deaths of Ptolemy VI and Alexander Balas, and Ptolemy VIII's accession to power in Alexandria (and in the aftermath of his own capture and destruction of Carthage, and the conquest and destruction of Corinth). Such a visit by such a man could only be seen as threatening, but he did little more than investigate the political situation in the east. He could report the unlikelihood of the Syrian Wars ending soon, and that Ptolemy VIII was unpopular at home, and had withdrawn all Ptolemaic forces back to Egypt from both Syria and from the Aegean.[28] These missions, in other words, were sent to evaluate the level of threat to Rome which the eastern kingdoms might pose, and in that they were essentially precautionary. On occasion one of the members might take action if such a threat seemed to have appeared. Cn. Octavius in Syria in 163 decided that he should contribute to the continuing weakness of the Seleukid kingdom by undermining the authority of the regent Lysias, demanding that the destruction of ships and the killing of war elephants should be undertaken in accordance with the (expired) provisions of the Treaty of Apameia a quarter of a century before. Lysias was in such a weak position that he began to comply, which so angered the general population that one man murdered Octavius. The Senate, no doubt appreciating the reason for the murder as well as its own inability to interfere so far from Italy, did nothing to avenge him.[29]

The kings continually attempted to use Roman power and influence to their advantage, even when they did not actually visit Rome personally. The Ptolemaic regency government repeatedly appealed to Rome when they found that their attack on the Seleukid kingdom in 170 was a disaster and had provoked a retaliatory invasion of Egypt. By doing so while Rome was in the midst of a difficult war against Perseus of Macedon they found that the appeal was generally ignored, but once Perseus had been defeated, a delegation interviewed Antiochos IV outside Alexandria. In a notorious scene, M. Popillius Laenas drew a circle round the king in the sand and demanded instant acceptance of an ultimatum that he make peace with the Ptolemies.[30]

There is much about this incident which is unclear, but it is certainly a fact that Antiochos agreed to withdraw his forces, though he did so only slowly, in his own time, and carrying large quantities of loot with him, leaving the Ptolemaic kingdom considerably weakened and politically disturbed.[31] It is also clear, when his policy is examined, that the king had in fact been rescued by Laenas from a situation in which he had been trapped by the intransigence of the Ptolemaic regency government, which in turn was fuelled by rivalry between the two Ptolemaic kings and the difficulty the Ptolemaic regents had in agreeing to any sort of terms short of complete victory, dependent as they were on support from the Alexandrian population. Further, by involving Rome in the peace agreement, Laenas had put his city in the position of a guarantor of that agreement, thereby freeing Antiochos to go ahead with his plans to conduct a war in the east, since Egypt, once peace was made, was no longer a threat to him. It is no wonder that the great parade at Daphne in 166 was a celebration of victory. The whole affair is a classic example of a king using Rome for his own purposes, thwarting those who attempted to do the same.

Rome, of course, was mainly concerned with its own affairs and priorities, one of which was to keep its enemies divided one from another. It therefore suited the Senate to see the two most powerful kingdoms in the east remaining separate, for it had appeared from a distance that Antiochos might well be on a route which would result in the unification of the two. He was also friendly with the Attalid kingdom (the first and last Seleukid king to be so) while until 167 his niece was married to Perseus, though this had no effect on the Roman war with Macedon. This collection of associations looked very ominous from Rome's viewpoint, and its response was first to eliminate both Perseus and his kingdom, then to ensure the continued separation of the Seleukid and Ptolemaic kingdoms by means of Laenas' diplomacy. The intensity of the Senate's fears was demonstrated by their destruction of the Macedonian kingdom, and its division into four weak and unthreatening republics. This was disastrous for Macedon, but from the Roman point of view that was not the essence: it was advantageous for Rome, which was dictating the terms of peace.

The elimination of kings and the destruction of kingdoms were not the same. The Syracusan kingdom had been absorbed into the pre-existing Sicilian province, but by then the kingship had already been destroyed by internal revolution – though it is noticeable that Rome made no attempt to reinstate the kingship after conquering the city. In the Balkans the fact that Macedon had fought as hard in its Third Roman War as in its first and second was probably one of the main elements which decided Rome on the destruction of both monarchy and state. But it was not the only such monarchic casualty in the region. Almost casually, the minor kingdom of the Athamanes, between Macedon, Aitolia, and Epeiros, had been snuffed out and its towns sacked during this last Macedonian War. A dozen years earlier Roman power and Achaian enmity had destroyed the ancient Spartan monarchy. These two were removed for the same reason that the Antigonid kingship had been removed, because of their persistence in enmity to Rome, or rather, what amounted to the same thing, their persistence in maintaining a stubborn attitude of independence.

This was not a Roman anti-monarchic policy, in the sense that kings were Rome's targets because they were kings. In fact, when taking over a kingdom, Rome, as was pointed out earlier in the case of Sicily, also took over the kingdom's administration, just as it did when annexing a republican city. This meant that the praetors who were posted to the former kingdoms as governors had the local authority of the former kings.

The attempts by kings who faced difficulties to enlist Rome in their support had largely been unsuccessful, but Ptolemy VIII hit upon a new expedient. He felt, against all the evidence, that he was under threat from his brother even after he had been installed as king in Cyrenaica. In 155 he claimed to have escaped an attempted assassination, for which he blamed his brother. His response was to write a will in which it purported to leave 'the kingdom which belongs to me' to the Roman people. And he publicised an inscribed and edited version of the will in an inscription set up in Cyrene; copies of the full document had been sent, he said, to Rome, and another lay in the temple of Apollo in Cyrene.[32]

It is doubtful that Ptolemy really wanted any kingdom he ruled to go into Roman control. What he wanted was protection against another assassination attempt, or indeed against an attack of any sort, and he thought that a document like this might compel the Romans to protect him. (The fact that he set up the inscription in Cyrene rather suggests he might have felt that the danger of assassination came more from his Cyrenaican subjects than from his brother; the will was a weapon wielded in the face of his own subjects as much as his brother.) He visited Rome next year, and complained again about the alleged attempted murder, and displayed his scars to the assembled senators in yet another theatrical and distasteful exhibition. This, of course, was well in tune with, and in equally bad taste, the other theatrical displays by minor kings in the recent past, including by himself.

Rome paid no attention, at least so far as our sources are concerned, who universally ignore both the supposed will and the display of scars. It was, after all, only Ptolemy's word which accused his brother of the offence, and the everlasting disputes between the two had rendered any accusation by either against the other as highly suspicious. The first condition of the will was that if he had a child the will would become inoperative, so when his son by Kleopatra II was born in 144 it ceased to have any effect.

How far this policy of using Rome as proxy protection was publicised to the rest of the Hellenistic world is not known, but it was a ploy also adopted by three other kings later, which suggests that they thought it was a good idea. The most important of these was Attalos III, another king with no children at the time he made the will.[33] A wide variety of reasons for this have been suggested, most with little plausibility or less foundation in the ancient sources. But one result when Attalos died was a serious and extended attempt by Andronikos, a bastard son of Attalos II, and so Attalos' half-brother, who established himself as king as Eumenes III for three years before being suppressed by a Roman expeditionary force.

It is just such a situation which any Hellenistic king detested and feared. This is why Antiochos IV and Demetrios I killed their rivals, despite the opprobrium they must have anticipated receiving at having killed children – Ptolemy VIII acted in much the same way when he gained control of Egypt, by marrying his brother's widow and simultaneously killing her son. The dynastic challenge was always the most potent threat to a king, since (as argued in the previous chapter) a successful attempt automatically rendered the challenger the legitimate king, insofar as such a concept existed. It was also the most personal of challenges, since for the challenger to succeed the man in occupation had to die. Attalos III may have been, as the ancient sources claim, paranoid, secretive, and introspective, but as king he was surely aware of his half-brother's potential for causing him trouble. The fact that he left the kingdom to Rome was surely in part accidental; just like Ptolemy VIII, he was protecting himself against the current challenge, not willing away his kingdom. Attalos was about 30 years old and unmarried when he made the will, but the family was long-lived, and he surely had hope still of progeny; meanwhile perhaps the will would fend off Andronikos.

In the event Attalos died only five years into his reign. When the will was disclosed to the Senate the bequest was not immediately taken up. Andronikos put in a claim to the succession, and this was taken seriously, a factor which only encouraged him, so that when the decision was taken by the Senate to set his claim aside, he had already gained sufficient support to make a serious military attempt to deny the imposition of Roman authority. Roman hesitation, that is, resulted in a four-year war.

There were two more cases. Ptolemy Apion, son of Ptolemy VIII, was made king in Cyrenaica. This was another bequest, by his father (Ptolemy VIII), though it took Apion some years to secure access to, and gain control of, his kingdom; this in fact appears to have been achieved as a result of action by one of the kings or queens in Egypt. This difficult accession seems to have persuaded Apion to attempt to protect himself by his own will, leaving the kingdom to Rome (as his father had – the inscription Ptolemy VIII had put up was still no doubt visible in the city, and perhaps a copy of his will still sat in Apollo's temple there). But, like the case of Attalos III, death caught him first, in 96 BC.[34] But where Attalos' bequest was seized by Rome as a means of financing the reform programme of Tiberius Gracchus – and would, given the region's wealth, probably have been taken up fairly quickly anyway – Cyrenaica was not rich, and the Senate could not be bothered to make provision for its administration for the next quarter of a century.[35]

This did not mean that Rome was willing to let someone else take the land over. Cyrenaica had been a Ptolemaic province in one way or another for over two centuries, and since it is probable that Apion had been put in place there by one of the disputing Ptolemaic rulers, they might well have aimed to recover it as soon as the news of Apion's death arrived; their status as legitimate rulers could hardly be contested. Rome therefore had no wish to rule the area itself, but neither did it want to let anyone else do so. The ploy adopted was to declare the land 'free', a good Hellenistic concept dating back to Antigonos Monophthalamos' declaration at Tyre in 314. In this case it was effective in warding off any other power which might have designs on the land, specifically any of the Ptolemies, and at the same time avoided the nuisance to Rome of making any effort to govern it.

The last example was Nikomedes IV of Bithynia. He and his kingdom had been caught in wars between Rome and Mithradates VI of Pontos, with the result that he had been driven from his throne by Mithradates at least twice, and returned to his kingdom by Rome twice. This would be bad enough for any king, but such an experience was even worse for his people. He was restored each time by Roman arms, but effectively gave up the struggle before he died. His father is said to have commented to C. Marius, who asked him to supply troops, that his people had all been kidnapped or bought as slaves by Roman slave traders.[36] It was only partly true, and the selling was probably done mainly by Mithradates and his men, but Romans were also involved; since then the condition of the kingdom could only have become worse. Perhaps Nikomedes thought that if they owned the land themselves, the Romans might be more considerate of its people. After Nikomedes' death in 74 Mithradates made a half-hearted attempt to promote a bastard son of Nikomedes' wife as the next king; the Romans would have none of it, and executed the will, so that the land became a Roman province.[37]

This happened in the same year as the decision to finally take control of Cyrenaica, which had become unruly in its freedom, an almost casual judgement; it also provoked Mithradates of Pontos to a new pre-emptive war. In both cases the annexations pushed Roman territory much closer to the two remaining united and powerful kingdoms left in the Hellenistic east, Pontos and Ptolemaic Egypt. This was clearly not coincidental, and will have marked a new determination in Rome to sort out the remnants of the old kingdoms.

Within ten years the Roman frontier was in the Arabian Desert and the Caucasus Mountains.

In the cases of these curious wills the legacy did not reach Rome for some time, and whatever publicity Ptolemy VIII or Ptolemy Apion gave their decisions – and there was no point in their wills unless at least some of their enemies heard about them – that of Attalos III certainly came as a surprise to Rome, and perhaps that of Nikomedes of Bithynia also. So these legacies reached Rome irregularly and unexpectedly, and without Rome's initial involvement. It is worth noting, however, that that the practice of using Rome in this way was one of the more powerful means by which Rome advanced eastwards at the expense of the last Hellenistic kingdoms. In effect these kings who played with Rome brought the ravenous republic down on their subjects' heads. It is doubtful if they were grateful.

For two centuries and more the kings of the east had had intermittent relations with Rome. Beginning with the Spartans and Epeirotes and Sicilians active in southern Italy in the late fourth and early third centuries, these contacts continued through to the death of the self-dramatising Kleopatra VII in 30 BC, and even then the tale was not finished. The piecemeal Roman takeover of the eastern Mediterranean lands left the east deplorably confused, with Roman provincial territories and local kingdoms intermixed. The elder Pliny in his *Natural History* tried to list the kingdoms and principalities of Syria, but after naming perhaps twenty of them he finally gave up, ending by noting that there were 'seventeen tetrarchies with barbarian names'.[38] And that was just Syria; there were more in Asia Minor. But all of these kingdoms and tetrarchies and so on were within and part of the Roman Empire. Beyond both of these areas was the Parthian kingdom.

All these kingdoms, tetrarchies, ethnarchies, principalities, and so on, had their roots deep in the Hellenistic period – the Parthian kingdom was almost two centuries old when the first Roman official – Sulla – encountered it in about 95 BC.[39] Its kings bore proudly the same sort of self-congratulatory epithets as the Seleukid and Ptolemaic kings, with the addition of 'Phil-Hellene', which they had hardly needed. Their kingdom was a mirror image in many ways of Rome's empire, having taken over the Seleukid administration of the territories it had conquered as a going concern, its cities and its provinces and its client kingdoms, just as Rome ruled a collection of provinces which largely derived their administrative system and boundaries – and population – from the preceding kingdoms.

This legacy pervaded the whole empire, for it was essentially Hellenistic administrative practices which Rome extended to its western and northern provinces. But most of all it was Hellenistic royal practices which were adopted by the emperors. Even in the late Republic it was from the east that the great dictators arrived to clamp their power on Rome – Sulla from Greece, Pompey from Syria and Asia Minor, even Caesar in part from Egypt and the east, if less obviously. Mark Antony spent a decade ruling the east in a parody of Antiochos IV, encouraged in it all by the last Ptolemy, Kleopatra VII. And Octavian spent long years in the east governing, administering, settling affairs, and when he was not present his co-emperor Agrippa was usually there. All this meant that the practices of Hellenistic kingship were involuntarily and inevitably absorbed into the practices of Roman dictators and emperors. The final effect of the contact between Rome and the Hellenistic kings was to install replica Hellenistic kings in Rome, under the guise of Imperators.

Dynasties

Something over 250 individual kings and queens are known by name from the Hellenistic period (several more existed but their names are not known). In this appendix they are listed in their dynastic groups for relative ease of reference. Included are the dates of the kings, and regents, who are named in brackets. Omitted are members of a dynasty ruling before Alexander the Great or in the Roman period.

Where a king died violently, this is indicated by B (died in battle), or M (murdered), or S (suicide); where a king was removed without being killed, he is marked as D (deposed); returnees after deposition are marked R.

The dates of many of the kings, especially from about 150 BC onwards, are uncertain. Names in parentheses are rulers who were not formally kings; some others are identified as governors or satraps.

1. Antigonids

Antigonos I Monophthalamos (307–301). B
Demetrios I Poliorketes (301–285, died 283). D
Antigonos II Gonatas (276–274 (D), 272–239).
Demetrios II (239–229). B
Antigonos III Doson (regent 229–228; King 228–221).
Philip V (minority 229–221; King 221–179).
Perseus (179–167). D
Andriskos = 'Philip VI', pretender 149–148. B
[Roman conquest; extinction of dynasty]

2. Antipatrids

(Antipater, regent 336–319).
Kassandros (satrap 319–310; King 310–297).
Philip IV (297).
Antipater (297–294). M
Alexander V (297–294). M
[Extinction of dynasty]

3. Armenia

(a) Orontids
(Orontes II, Akhaimenid satrap, 344–331). B
(Mithrines, satrap, 331–317)
Orontes III (from 317). M
Samos (–260).
Arsames (260–228).
Xerxes (228–212). M
Orontes IV (212–200). M
[Seleukid conquest]

(b) Artaxiads
Artaxias I (governor from *c.*200; King 188–159).
Tigranes I (159–123).
Artavasdes I (123–95).
Tigranes II the Great (95–55).
[Dynasty lasted to *c.*AD 3, then replaced by an Arsakid dynasty]

4. Arsakids (Parthia)

Arsakes I (247–211).
Arsakes II (211–185).
Phriapatios (185–170).
Arsakes IV (170–168).
Phraates I (168–165).
Mithradates I (165–132).
Phraates II (132–126). B
Bagasis (126–125).
Artabanus II (126–122). B
Arsakes IX (122–121).
Mithradates II (121–91).
Sinatrukes I) (93/92–88/87). D
Gotarzes I (91–87). D
Mithradates III (87–67).
Orodes I (80–75).
Sinatrukes I (77–70). R
Phraates III (70–57). M
[Dynasty continued to AD 228, then supplanted by Sassanids]

5. Asia Minor and Thrace

Lysimachos (305–281). B
Antiochos Hierax (245–227). M

Akhaios (222–212). M
[See also Attalids]
[Numerous Thracian dynasties, controlling small territories, not here detailed]

6. Athamania

Theodoros (*c.250–c.220*).
Amynander (*c.220–178*).
Selipios (178–?167).
[Dynasty extingished]

7. Attalids

Philetairos (Lord of Pergamon 281–263).
Eumenes I (not king) (260–241).
Attalos I Soter (241–197).
Eumenes II Soter (197–160).
Attalos II (160–139).
Attalos III (139–133).
Aristonikos = 'Eumenes III' (pretender 133–129). B
[Roman conquest]

8. Baktria

(a) Diodotids
Diodotos I (governor 255–235).
Diodotos II (King 235–225). M?

(b) Euthydemids (Partly conjectural)
Euthydemos I (235–200).
Demetrios I (200–185).
Euthydemos II (200–190).
Antimachos I (190–180).
Pantaleon (185–175).
Agathokles (180–165).
Demetrios II (180–165).

(c) Eukratidids (Partly conjectural)
Eukratides I (171–155).
Heliokles I (155–140).
Plato (155–).
Menander (155–130).
Eukratides II (150–).

(d) Others (Dates largely unknown)

The dates and families of these later kings are even more uncertain than for the earlier rulers. They constituted at least four rival dynasties, possibly more, between *c.*150 and *c.*55 BC, during which time the kingdom disintegrated.

Zoilos I

Polyxenos

Epander

Antimachos II

Strato I

Archebios

Philoxenos

Lysias

Heliokles II

Antialkidas

Apollodotos

Peucolaos

Diomedes

Telephos

Ziolos II

Dionysios

Apollophanes

Hippostratos

Amyntas

Strato II

Hermaios

[Nomad conquest, *c.*55 BC]

9. Bithynia

Zipoetes (local chief, then King from 297–279).

Nikomedes I (279–255).

Elazeta (255–254). D

Ziaelas (250–230). B

Prousias I (230–182).

Prousias II (182–149). M

Nikomedes II (149–127).

Nikomedes III 127–94).

Nikomedes IV (94–90 D; 89–88 R).

Sokrates (90–89). D

Nikomedes IV (R 84–74).

Mithradates VI of Pontos (88–84).

[Kingdom bequeathed to Rome]

10. Charakene

Hyspaosines (governor from *c.*163; King from *c.*140).

Apadokos (ruling 109–105).

Tiraios I (ruling 90–88).

Tiraios II (ruling 78–48).

[Dynasty continued to *c.*225, then suppressed by Sassanids]

11. Cyrenaica

Magas (governor from 305; King 275–250).

Apama (250–248). D

Demetrios the Fair (248). M
Berenike (?246–222). M
[Kingdom absorbed by Ptolemies]
Ptolemy VIII (163–116).
Ptolemy Apion (?116) –96).
[Kingdom bequeathed to Rome]

12. Elymais

Kamniskires I Nikephoros (local chief from *c*.189; King 140).
Kamniskires II (140–138).
Okkonapses (139/8).
Tigraios (138/7–133/2).
Kamniskires III (satrap for Arsakids) (133–).
[Dynasty continued to after AD 200, then annexed by Sassanids]

13. Emesa

Samsigeramos (*c*.90–47).
[Dynasty continued to AD 72, then annexed by Rome].

14. Epeiros

Alexander I (342–331). M
Neoptolemus II (331–313 D; 302–295 R). M
Arrybas (323–322).
Aiakides (322–317 D; 313). B
Alketas II (313–307). M
Pyrrhos I (307–302 D; 295–272). B
Alexander II (270–*c*.240).
Pyrrhos II (*c*.240–?).
Ptolemy (?–235).
Deidameia (235–233) (Ruling status uncertain). M
[Extinction of dynasty]

15. Illyria (Ardiaian monarchy)

Pleuratos I (*c*.260–*c*.250).
Agron (*c*.250–*c*.230).
Pinnes (230–217).
(Teuta, regent 230–222).
(Demetrios of Pharos, regent 222–218). D
Skerdilaidas (regent 218–217; King 217–206).
Pleuratos II (205–181).
Genthius (181–168). D
[Roman conquest]

16. Judaea: Maccabees

(Judah Maccabee, war leader 166–161). B
Jonathan Maccabee (High Priest 152–142). M
Simon (High Priest 142–134). M
John Hyrkanos (High Priest 134–104).
Aristoboulos I (King 104–103). M
Alexander Yannai (103–76).
Salome Alexandra (76–67).
Hyrkanos II (67–40). D
Aristoboulos II (67–63). B
[Dynasty continued to 37 BC, then replaced by Herodians]

17. Kappadokia

Ariarathes I and II (local chieftains, dating unknown).
Ariarathes III (255–220).
Ariarathes IV Eusebes (220–163).
Ariarathes V Philopator (163–130).
Ariarathes VI Epiphanes (130–*c*.116). M
Laodike (116).
Ariarathes VII Philometor (*c*.116–*c*.101). M
Ariarathes VIII (*c*.101–96 D; 95 D).
Ariarathes IX (96–*c*.95). D
Ariobarzanes I Philorhomaios (*c*.95–62). Abdicated
[Dynasty continued to AD 17, then annexed by Rome]

18. Kommagene

(Ptolemaios, governor 163–130).
Samos (130–100; became King within that period).
Mithradates I Kallinikos (100–69).
Antiochos I Theos (69–40).
[Dynasty continued to AD 73, then Roman conquest]

19. Macedon

Ptolemy Keraunos (281–179). B
(Meleagros). B ⎫
Antipatros. B ⎪
(Sosthenes). ⎬ Period of anarchy, 279–277.
(Ptolemaios). B ⎪
(Arrhidaios). B ⎭
[See also Argeads, Antipatrids and Antigonids]

20. Media Atropatene

Atropates (satrap *c.*330–).
Artavazdes (King in 221).
Dareios (King in 65).
[Dynasty continued to *c.*AD 8, then annexed by Parthia]

21. Nabataea

Harithath I (ruling 169).
Maliku I (144–110).
Harithath II (110–95).
Obidath I (95–87).
Rabbil I (87).
Harithath III (87–62).
[Dynasty continued to AD 106, then Roman conquest]

22. Numidia

Syphax (–204). D
Massinissa (204–148).
Micipsa (148–118).
Gulussa (148–).
Mastanabal (148–).
Adherbal (118–112). D
Hiempsal I (118–117). M
Jugurtha (118–105). D
Gauda (105–).
Hiempsal II (88–62).
Hierbas (88–81). M
Juba I (62–46). M
[Roman conquest]

23. Osrhoene (Edessa)

Aryu (132–127).
Abdu bar Mazur (127–120).
Fradhasht bar Gebaru (120–115).
Bakru bar Fradhasht (115–112).
Bakru bar Bakru (112–92).
Manu I (94).
Abgar I Piqa (94–68).
Abgar II bar Abgar (68–52).
[Dynasty continued to AD 242, then Roman annexation]

24. Pontos

(Mithradates I, Akhaimenid satrap).
Mithradates II (302–266).
Ariobarzanes (266–250).
Mithradates III (250–185).
Pharnakes I (185–170).
Mithradates IV Philopator (170–150).
Mithradates V Euergetes (150–121). M
Mithradates VI Eupator (121–63). S
[Roman conquest]

25. Ptolemies

Ptolemy I Soter (satrap 323–305; King 305–283).
Ptolemy II Philadelphos (283–246).
Ptolemy III Euergetes (246–222).
Ptolemy IV Philopator (222–204).
(Sosibios and Agathokles, regents 204–203).
(Tlepolomos, regent 203–202).
Ptolemy V Epiphanes (204–181). M
(Kleopatra Syra, regent 181–176).
(Lenaios and Eulaios, regents 176–170).
Ptolemy VI Philometor (181–145). B
(Ptolemy 'VII' – never reigned.) M
Ptolemy VIII Euergetes (181–116; in Egypt 181–164 D; 145–116; in Cyrene
    163–116).
Kleopatra II (132–127, 116).
Kleopatra III (116–101). M
Ptolemy IX Soter II (in Egypt 116–108 D; 88–80; in Cyprus 108–88).
Ptolemy X Alexander I (in Cyprus 116–108; in Egypt 108–88). B
Berenike III (81–80). M
Ptolemy XI Alexander II (80). M
Ptolemy XII Auletes (80–58 D; 55–51 R).
Berenike IV (58–55). M
Ptolemy XIII (51–47). B
Kleopatra VII (51–30). S
Ptolemy XIV (47–44). M
Ptolemy XV Caesarion (44–30). M
[Roman annexation]

26. Seleukids

Seleukos I Nikator (satrap 323–315, 312–305; King 305–281). M
Antiochos I Soter (281–261).
Antiochos II Theos (261–246). ?M
Seleukos II Kalinikos (246–226). B
Seleukos III Soter (226–223). M
Antiochos III Megas (223–187). B
Seleukos IV Philopator (187–175). M
(Antiochos (175–170 – did not reign). M
Antiochos IV Epiphanes (175–164). B
Antiochos V Eupator (164–162). M
(Lysias, regent 165–162). M
Demetrios I Soter (162–150). B
Alexander I Balas (150–145). M
Antiochos VI Epiphanes (145–142).
(Diodotos, regent 145–142; King as Tryphon, 142–138). B
Demetrios II Nikator (145–139, 129–126). M
Antiochos VII Sidetes (139–129). B
Alexander II Zabeinas (128–123). M
(Kleopatra Thea, regent 126–121). M
Seleukos V (126). M
Antiochos VIII Grypos (126–96). M
Antiochos IX Kyzikenos (115–95). M
Seleukos VI Epiphanes Nikator (96–95). M
Antiochos X Eusebes Philopator (95–83). M or D
Antiochos XI Philadelphos (92). B
Philip I Philadelphos (95–83). M or D
Demetrios III Eukairos Soter (95–88). D
Antiochos XII Dionysos (87–84). B
Antiochos XIII Asiatikos (69–64). D
Philip II (65–64). D
[Roman annexation]

27. Sparta

(a) Agiad Dynasty / (b) Eurypontid Dynasty Kleomenes II (369–309)

(a) Agiad Dynasty	(b) Eurypontid Dynasty Kleomenes II (369–309)
Archidamos III (361–338). B	
	Agis III (338–331).
	Eudamidas I (331–300).
Areus I (309–264). B	Archidamos IV (300–).
	Eudamidas II (–244).
Akrotatos (264–255). B	

Areus II (255–251).
Leonidas II (254–242 D; 241–235 R).
Kleombrotos II (242–241).   Agis IV (244–241). M
Kleomenes III (235–222). D; M 219   Archidamos V (228–227). M
Eukleidas (227–221). B
Agesipolis III (219). M

(c) Later kings
Lykourgos (219–210).
Pelops (210–206). M
Nabis (206–192). M
[Achaian annexation]

28. Spartokids

Spartokos III (349–344).
Paerisades I (349–310).
Satyros II (310–309).
Prytanis (310–309).
Eumelos (310–304).
Spartokos IV (304–284).
Paerisades II (284–245).
Spartokos V (245–240).
Leukon II (240–220).
Hygiaemon (220–200).
Spartokos VI (200–180).
Paerisades III (150–125).
Paerisades IV (125–109).
[Annexation by Mithradates VI of Pontos]

29. Syracuse

Agathokles (strategos from 316; King 304–289).
(Pyrrhos of Epeiros 276–275). B
Hiero II (270–215).
Hieronymos (215–214). M
[Roman conquest]

Appendix II

Suppression of Monarchies

Date	Monarchy	Agent of Suppression
*c.*310	Salamis and Cyprus	Ptolemy I
*c.*270	Sidon	Ptolemy II
259	Arados	Antiochos II
246	Cyrenaica	Ptolemy III
233	Epeiros	Internal collapse
215	Syracuse	Internal revolution
212	(Akhaios/Asia Minor)	Antiochos III
212–211	Armenia	Antiochos III
192	Sparta	Rome/Achaian League
*c.*178	Athamania	Rome/Philip V
168	Illyria	Rome
167	Macedon	Rome
148	Revived Macedon	Rome
133–129	Attalid kingdom	Bequest to Rome
96	Cyrenaica	Bequest to Rome
83–70	Seleukid kingdom	Tigranes of Armenia
74	Bithynia	Bequest to Rome
64	Revived Seleukids	Rome
30	Ptolemaic kingdom	Rome

Notes

Chapter 1: Becoming a King

1. This is an obscure episode, though it is fairly clear that the 'Son' was a son of Ptolemy II acting as his viceroy in Asia Minor: see E. Will, *Histoire Politique du Monde Hellenistique*, 2 vols, Nancy, 1978–82, 1. 236; Welles, *Royal Correspondence*, no. 14.
2. Diodoros 19.105.1–4, naming the killer as Glaukias, one of Kassander's men; the matter was kept secret, and Alexander IV's years continued to be used for dating until 305, at least in Egypt.
3. Justin 16.1; Plutarch, *Demetrios*, 26–37; Diodoros 21.7; Pausanias 9.7.3.
4. Diodoros 21.16.4–7; Justin 2.7–9; H.J.W. Tillyard, *Agathocles*, Cambridge, 1908, 217–20; Theoxene's children formed a prominent dynasty of courtiers at the Ptolemaic court, emerging as the notorious regent Agathokles and his sister Agathokleia in the reign of Ptolemy IV.
5. Helen S. Lund, *Lysimachos, a Study in Hellenistic Kingship*, London, 1992.
6. Justin 17.1; Appian, *Syrian Wars*, 62; Memnon, *FGrH*, 434 F 5.6; Pausanias 1.10.3–5.
7. Trogus, *Prologue*, 26; E.R. Bevan, *The House of Seleucus*, 2 vols, London, 1902, 1.150.
8. J.D. Grainger, *The Syrian Wars*, Leiden, 2010, chs 7 and 8.
9. Ibid., 183–94; E. Will, 'Les premiers annees du regne d'Antiochos III', *Revue des Etudes Greques*, 75, 1962, 72–129 for more detail.
10. O. Morkholm, *Antiochos IV of Syria*, Copenhagen, 1966.
11. Plutarch, *Demetrios*, 17–18.
12. Ibid., 37–52, for this last stage in his career – 'careering' might be a better term.
13. Pausanias 1.7.2; celebrated in Kallimachos' *Hymn to Delos*, 185–7.
14. Strabo 13.4.1.
15. Ibid., 13.4.2; *I. Pergamon*, 13.
16. *OGIS*, 273–9; Strabo 13.4.2.
17. Memnon, *FGrH*, 454 F 12, 4–5; Diodoros 20.111; Livy 38.16.
18. Frank L. Holt, *Thundering Zeus, the Making of Hellenistic Bactria*, Berkeley CA, 1999.
19. See the chart of suggested families of kings in Narain's article in *CAH*, VIII, 420– 1; Peter Green, *Alexander to Actium*, London 1990, table p. 739, provides a suggested genealogy which is extremely fanciful.
20. Justin 41.4.7; see Musti in *CAH*, VII, 214; it must be regarded as possible that the invaders had been induced to attack Andragoras by one of the Seleukid contenders: they certainly did not retire from their conquest until forced to do so much later.
21. Polybios 40.48.11, and 5.57.5–7.
22. Arrian, *Anabasis*, 7.4.1 and 13.2; Polybius 5.55.1–3 and 7–10.
23. Strabo 11.14.5–6.
24. Summarised in J.D. Grainger, *Seleukos Nikator*, London, 1990, Ch. 11.
25. Diodoros 31.19.6; Strabo 13.534.

26. A. Laronde, *Cyrene et la Libye hellenistique*, Paris, 1987; Dee L. Clayman, *Berenice II and the Golden Age of Ptolemaic Egypt*, Oxford, 2014.

27. For a recent survey of the situation in Persis, see Josef Wiesehofer, 'Frataraka rule in Early Seleucid Persis; a Reappraisal', in Andrew Erskine and Lloyd Llewellyn-Jones (eds), *Creating a Hellenistic World*, Swansea, 2011, 107–22.

28. E. Schurer, *The History of the Jewish People in the Age of Jesus Christ*, 3 vols, rev. and ed. by G. Vermes *et al.*, Edinburgh, 1973–87, Vol. I; V. Tcherikover, *Hellenistic Civilisation and the Jews*, Philadelphia PA, 1959; J.D. Grainger, *The Wars of the Maccabees*, Barnsley, 2000; the (tendentious) main sources are in the books of Maccabees and those of the historian Josephus.

29. J.D. Grainger, *Syria, An Outline History*, Barnsley, 2016.

30. Holbl, *Ptolemaic Empire*, Ch. 5.

Chapter 2: Kings and the Gods

1. Austin 175.

2. A. Houghton and C. Corber, *Seleukid Coins: a Comprehensive Catalogue*, Lancaster PA, 2002, Vol. 1.

3. Strabo 16.2.6.

4. See the marble head of Ptolemy II reproduced in Holbl, *Ptolemaic Empire*, 97; for the great procession: Athenaios 5.201b–f, 202f–203e (Austin, 258), and E.E. Rice, *The Grand Procession of Ptolemy Philadelphus*, Oxford, 1983.

5. E.g., Austin 228; Polybios 18.41.

6. Plutarch, *Pyrrhos*, 6.

7. For a recent consideration see Stephan Pfeiffer, 'The God Serapis, his Cult, and the Beginnings of the Ruler Cult in Ptolemaic Egypt', in Paul McKechnie and Philip Guillaume (eds), *Ptolemy II Philadelphus and his World*, Leiden, 2008, 387–406.

8. Holbl, *Ptolemaic Empire*, 77–80.

9. Dorothy J. Thomson, *Memphis under the Ptolemies*, 2nd edn, Princeton NJ, 2012, Ch. 1.

10. Pausanias 1.6.3; Andrew Erskine, 'Life after Death: Alexandria and the body of Alexander', *Greece and Rome*, 49, 2002, 163–79.

11. Dorothy J. Thompson, 'Economic Reform in the mid-reign of Ptolemy Philadelphus', in Paul McKechnie and Philip Guillaume (eds), *Ptolemy II Philadelphus and his World*, Leiden, 2008, 27–38; 'reform' here has to be understood as inventing new taxes and increasing old ones.

12. Holbl, *Ptolemaic Empire*, 98–101.

13. As has been revealed by the recent underwater excavations of the sunken section of the ancient city: see the catalogue of the 2016 exhibition at the British Museum, Franck Goddio and Aurelia Masson-Berghoff (eds), *Sunken Cities, Egypt's lost worlds*, London, 2016.

14. Holbl, *Ptolemaic Empire*, 101–3.

15. This is the burden of the decree recorded on the Rosetta stone (*OGIS*, 90 = Austin 283) which should be compared with the earlier decrees on stones from Canopos and Memphis (*OGIS*, 56 = Austin 271, and Austin 276) which are much less accommodating of Egyptian and priestly feelings.

16. *OGIS*, 315; Welles, *Royal Correspondence*, 55–61; Austin 244.

17. Appian, *Syrian Wars*, 58; J.D. Grainger, *The Rise of the Seleukid Empire, 323–223 BC*, Barnsley, 2014, 36–40, 57–9.

18. The evidence is some coins: H. Seyrig, 'Le moneyage d'Hierapolis de Syrie a l'epoque d'Alexandre le Grand', *Revue Numismatique*, 11, 1971, 3–11.

19. Lukian of Samosata, *De Dea Syria.*
20. Susan M. Sherwin-White and Amelie Kuhrt, *From Samarkhand to Sardis, a New Approach to the Seleucid Empire*, London, 1993, 25.
21. For a more humble, but telling, case see E.A. Myers, *The Ituraeans and the Roman Near East, Reassessing the Sources*, Cambridge, 2010, Ch. 3.
22. A.E. Viesse, *Les 'revoltes Egyptiennes', Recherches sur les Troubles interieures en Egypt du Regne de Ptolemee III a la conquete romain*, Studia Hellenistica, 41, Louvain, 2004; also B. McGing, 'Revolt Egyptian style: Internal Opposition to Ptolemaic Rule', *AfP*, 43, 1997, 273–314.
23. R. van der Spek, 'The Babylonian City', in Amelie Kuhrt and Susan M. Sherwin-White, *Hellenism in the East*, London, 1987, 57–74.
24. *OGIS*, 744, 745 and 215; J.D. Grainger, *Seleukos Nikator*, London, 1990, 163–4.
25. The clerks of Apollo at Delos, for example, kept detailed lists of gifts, and can be seen as having accumulated a great deal of wealth; see Gary Reger, *Regionalism and Change in the Economy of Independent Delos*, Berkeley CA, 1994; an extract of the Delos accounts is at Austin 122.
26. The release of this wealth, by gifts and by general expenditure, above all in warfare, was a primary cause of the increasing prosperity of the Hellenistic world, and of the inflation this involved. For a discussion of Alexander's wealth see Frank L. Holt, *The Treasure of Alexander the Great*, Oxford, 2016, who denies that the value of the hoards can be used for such a purpose, but the hoards are only a fraction of the looted treasure – the rest went into circulation.
27. Arrian, *Anabasis*, 2.15.7–18; Curtius Rufus, *History of Alexander*, 4.2.1; Alexander justified the siege to his staff on strategic grounds; it was also in fact a matter of pique on his part.
28. Polybios 10.27.
29. Diodoros 28.3 and 29.15; Strabo 16.744; Justin 32.2.1; Aurelius Victor, *De viri illustri*, 54; Daniel 11.19
30. Polybios 5.9, 9.30, 11.7.2–3.
31. Ibid., 5.11.4–6.
32. Holbl, *Ptolemaic Empire*, 154–5.
33. Daniel 11.20; II Maccabees 3.
34. Austin 163; Sachs and Hunger, *Astronomical Diaries* , Vol. 1, '–273'.
35. Helodoros, who later contrived the murder of Seleukos IV, was a likely target to whom reprehesensible actions could be attributed.
36. Josephus, *AJ*, 12.246–7.
37. See J.D. Grainger, *The Wars of the Maccabees*, Barnsley, 2012, Ch. 2.
38. Holt, *Treasure of Alexander the Great.*
39. See the discussion by Angelos Chaniotis, 'The Divinity of Hellenistic Kings', in Andrew Erskine (ed.), *A Companion to the Hellenistic World*, Oxford, 2003, 431–46.
40. Austin 43.
41. Ibid., 42.
42. Athenaios 6.253b–f; Austin 43; see Chaniotis, 'Divinity', 431–2.
43. Douris, *FGrH*, 76 F 71.
44. Tacitus, *Histories*, 4.56.
45. Austin 206.
46. Ibid., 190; the man who composed the decree made a mistake in implying that Seleukos III was still alive by referring to him as 'king'.
47. *SEG*, 39, 1284; John Ma, *Antiochos III and the Cities of Western Asia Minor*, Oxford 1999, Appendix of documents, no. 2.

48. Ph. Gauthier, *Nouvelles Inscriptions de Sardes*, Vol. II, Paris, 1898; see also Ma, *Antiochos III*, 284–88.
49. Austin 200.
50. Ibid., 198.

Chapter 3: Kings and Kings

1. Diodoros 21.1.
2. Plutarch, *Demetrios*, 20.
3. Diodoros 31.18.
4. J.D. Grainger, *The Syrian Wars*, Leiden, 2010, Ch. 15.
5. Justin 26.3.2–6; Athenaios 12.550b–c; A. Laronde, *Cyrene et la Libye hellenistique*, Paris, 1987, 381–4; Dee L. Clayman, *Berenice II and the Golden Age of Ptolemaic Egypt*, Oxford, 2014, Ch. 1; Holbl, *Ptolemaic Empire*, 45–6.
6. Grainger, *Syrian Wars*, 153–7.
7. Particularly well-described examples are in 218 and 217, in and at the end of the Fourth Syrian War: Polybios 5.63.5–7, 67.4–13, and 87.5–6.
8. Polybios 15.25.4 and 13.
9. *I. Crete*, 1, Lyttos 8; S. Spyridakis, *Ptolemaic Itanos and Hellenistic Crete*, Berkeley CA, 1970; H. van Effentere, *Crete et le Monde grec*, Paris, 1948; Grainger, *Syrian Wars*, 139–40.
10. This may also be pure invention, either by Antiochos' propagandists, or by imaginative historians who felt that this was how kings should behave in negotiations.
11. Polybios 8.23.1–5.
12. Clayman, *Berenice II*, 49–51.
13. Polybios 5.55.1 and 10; no names of kings are known between Atropates and Artabarzanes. The fact that Seleukid kings who marched east – Seleukos I and Seleukos II – ignored Atropatene, and were able to leave it unattacked in their rear strongly implies the existence of suzerainty agreements to which the Atropatenians succumbed.
14. Ibid., 10.27–31; the sequence and dating of the Parthian kings has been sorted out by G.E. Assar, 'Genealogies and kings of the early Parthian rulers, I and II', *Parthica*, 6 and 7, 2006 and 2007.
15. Plutarch, *Demetrios*, 31–2.
16. Ibid., 35.
17. Ibid., 38; Appian, *Syrian Wars*, 59–61.
18. Plutarch, *Demetrios*, 50–2; Diodoros 21.20.
19. *Vita Aratoi*; Diogenes Laertes 7.1.8.
20. Justin 25.1.
21. The only time this may have happened was in the Khremonidean War, but actual co-ordination is never even hinted at in the (poor) sources.
22. Justin 28.2.2; the marriage did not last: Stratonike left her husband (who had married a second wife) and returned to Syria, where she attempted a coup against Seleukos II, who refused to marry her; she was chased down and executed.
23. Polybios 25.4.9; Livy 42.12.3–4.
24. Polybios 3.2.8, 16.1.9, 10.1 and 15.20; Livy 31.14.5; Appian, *Macedonian Wars*, 41; Justin 30.2.8; R.M. Errington, 'The Alleged Syro-Macedonian Pact and the Origin of the Second Macedonian War', *Athenaeum*, 49, 1971, 336–54; E.S. Gruen, *The Hellenistic World and the Coming of Rome*, Berkeley CA, 1984, 387–8; John Ma, *Antiochos III and the Cities of Western*

Asia Minor, Oxford, 1999, 74–92; Errington's extreme scepticism about the agreement has been replaced by a more general acceptance, though details are still much in dispute.
25. Livy 35.13.4.
26. Austin 38; Diodoros 19.105.1.
27. Diodoros 19.64.8.
28. Polybios 11.39.1–10; it is often assumed that the marriage did happen, and that therefore there was an alliance between the two states, but there is no actual record of the marriage, and no cooperation between the dynasty is known of, despite the conjectures of W.W. Tarn, *The Greeks in Baktria and India*, 2nd edn, Cambridge, 1951, Ch. 5; Peter Green, *Alexander to Actium*, London, 1990, calls the marriage 'possible' on p. 335, and marks it as certain in the genealogical table on p. 739.
29. Holbl, *Ptolemaic Empire*, displays these linkages in a table, pp. 358–9.
30. Strabo 17.1.11.
31. Alexander's relationship to Antiochos IV was disputed in the ancient world, presumably by his political enemies; it has been asserted by D. Ogden, *Polygamy, Prostitutes, and Death*, London, 1999.
32. I Maccabees 10.54–8; Josephos, *AJ*, 13.80–2.
33. I Maccabees 11.9–10; Josephus, *AJ*, 13.113–14.
34. Livy, *Perioche*, 52; Josephus, *AJ*, 13.116–17.
35. I Maccabees 11.86; Josephus, *AJ*, 13.120.
36. Appian, *Syrian Wars*, 38; Josephus, *AJ*, 13.222–7.
37. Justin 36.1.5.
38. Josephus, *AJ*, 13.249–53; Justin 38.10; Athenaios 210d–f, 540b–c.
39. Justin 39.1.4; Josephus, *AJ*, 13.268.
40. Appian, *Syrian Wars*, 69; Justin 39.1.9.
41. Appian, *Syrian Wars*, 68.
42. Athenaios 153a.

Chapter 4: Kings, Wives, and Children

1. Diodoros 17.16.2; Elizabeth Baynham, 'Why didn't Alexander marry a nice Macedonian girl before leaving home? Observations on factional politics at Alexander's court, 336–334 BC', in T.W. Hillard *et al.* (eds), *Ancient History in a Modern University*, Macquarie University NSW, 1998, Vol. 1, 148–55.
2. Arrian, *Anabasis*, 7.4.4, though probably meaning Stateira.
3. Curtius Rufus, *History of Alexander*, 7.4.27.
4. Arrian, *Anabasis*, 7.4.4.
5. Ibid.
6. Athenaios 13.557b–e (Satyros).
7. Ibid.
8. B.F. von Oppen de Reiter, 'Argaios, an Illegitimate son of Alexander the Great?', *ZPE*, 287, 2013, 206–10.
9. His wife, Stratonike, was the widow of Antigonos' elder brother; such remarriages kept dowries within the family.
10. Arrian, *Anabasis*, 7.4.6.
11. Curtius Rufus, *History of Alexander*, 7.1.7; Alexander was detained and then executed by Alexander, with no noticeable effect on Antipater's position: Diodoros 17.80.2.
12. Diodoros 18.18.7 and 30.1–5.
13. Diodoros 18.16.1–3; Arrian, *Successors*, 1. 26.

14. Pausanias 1.6.8.

15. Diodoros 19.59.3–6; Plutarch, *Demetrios*, 14.

16. Diodoros 18.23.3; Justin 13.6;

17. Plutarch, *Demetrios*, 46.3.

18. Diodoros 20.109.6–7.

19. It is probably also the case that none of the other competitors had any children who could be married off yet; Antipater's daughters were the only ones available.

20. Pausanias 1.16.2; Memnon, *FGrH*, 226, F 8.2; Appian, *Syrian Wars*, 62.

21. Plutarch, *Pyrrhos*, 4.6.

22. Grace McCurdy, *Hellenistic Queens*, Baltimore MD, 1932; this is the burden of this whole book; see also Elizabeth D. Carney, *Women and Monarchy in Macedon*, Norman OK, 2000.

23. Plutarch, *Alexander*, 9; McCurdy, *Hellenistic Queens*, 22–48 for Olympias.

24. Elizabeth D. Carney, 'Being Royal and Female in early Macedonian History', in Andrew Erskine and Lloyd Llewellyn-Jones (eds), *Creating a Hellenistic World*, Swansea, 2011, 195 220.

25. His sexual career was the subject of a book by his descendant Ptolemy VIII, *Hypemnemata* (*FGrH*, 234 F4).

26. Justin 17.1; Pausanias 1.10.3–4; Memnon, *FGrH*, 225n 6–14; Strabo 13.4.1; Helen S. Lund, *Lysimachos, a Study in Early Hellenistic Kingship*, London, 1992, 184–206.

27. Elizabeth D. Carney, *Arsinoe of Egypt and Macedon, a Royal Life*, Oxford, 2013, Ch. 3.

28. McCurdy, *Hellenistic Queens*, 111–30.

29. S.M. Burstein, 'Arsinoe II: a Revisionist View', in W.L. Adams and E.N. Borza (eds), *Philip II, Alexander the Great, and the Macedonian Heritage*, Washington DC, 1982, 197–212.

30. Aidan Dodson and Diane Hylton, *The Complete Royal Families of Ancient Egypt*, London, 2004, 241–57; D. Ogden, *Polygamy, Prostitutes, and Death*, London, 1999, 73–80, who asserts that pharaonic practice was one of the influences on the marriage, but his references are all either Hellenisitc or modern, none of them pharaonic; see also C.J. Bennett, 'Royal genealogies: Ptolemaic dynasty' (http/www/geocities.com/christopherjbennett/Ptolemies/Ptolemies.htm).

31. As is being increasingly revealed by the underwater excavations there: see Frank Goddio and Aurelia Masson-Berghoff (eds), *Sunken Cities, Egypt's Lost Worlds*, London, 2016, the catalogue of the British Museum exhibition 2016.

32. W.G. Waddell (ed. and trans.), *Manetho*, London, 1940; Gerald P. Verbrugghe and John M. Wickersham, *Berossos and Manetho, Native Traditions in Ancient Mesopotamia and Egypt*, Ann Arbor MI, 1996.

33. Plutarch, *Moralia*, 11A; Athenaios 14.620–1a.

34. By Burstein (see n. 29 above).

35. Plutarch, *Demetrios*, 31–2.

36. McCurdy, *Hellenistic Queens*, 80–1, points out that Stratonike in her religious dedications at Delos never identified herself as other than daughter of Demetrios, or of Phila and Demetrios, though this may not in fact be very significant.

37. Austin 173; *OGIS*, 225.

38. Porphyry, *FGrH*, 260 F 43.

39. *P. Zenon*, II, 59242 and 59251.

40. Austin 267.

41. Ibid., 266.

42. J.D. Grainger, *Syrian Wars*, Leiden, 2010, 117–36.

43. Trogus, *Prologue*, 26; Austin 168.

44. Plutarch, *Demetrios*, 38; Appian, *Syrian Wars* 59–60.
45. Lucian of Samosata, *De dea Syra*.
46. Susan M. Sherwin-White and Amelie Kuhrt, *From Samarkhand to Sardis, a New Approach to the Seleucid Empire*, London, 1993, 26.
47. At the very least she brought in Demetrios the Fair as a new suitor for her daughter, at the most she married him herself and made him king.
48. Josephus, *Against Apion*, 1.22 (from Agatharkides); McCurdy, *Hellenistic Queens*, 70–1.
49. McCurdy, *Hellenistic Queens*, 69–70; for Aratos, see W.W. Tarn, *Antigonos Gonatas*, Oxford, 1913, 226–7.
50. Holbl, *Ptolemaic Empire*, 143.
51. I Maccabees 11.8; Josephus, *AJ*, 12.106; Diodoros 33.9.
52. I Maccabees 15.10; Josephus, *AJ*, 13.222.
53. Eusebius, *Chronographia*, 1.259; Justin 38.10.10.
54. Appian, *Syrian Wars*, 69; Justin 39.1.9; Livy, *Epitome*, 60.
55. Appian, *Syrian Wars*, 69; Justin 39.1.7; for Kleopatra Thea see McCurdy, *Hellenistic Queens*, 93–100, and John Whitehorne, *Cleopatras*, London, 1994.
56. Porphyry, *FGrH*, 260 F 32.24; Josephus, *AJ*, 13.274 and 325.
57. Dee L. Clayman, *Berenice II and the Golden Age of Ptolemaic Egypt*, Oxford, 2014.
58. Polybios 5.34.1, 36.1, 15.25.1–2; Clayman, *Berenice II*, 171–3.
59. Polybios 5.83–84.1; 87.6–7.
60. Polybios 15.25.3.
61. Polybios 26.6; Diodoros 29.29; Porphyry, *FGrH*, 260 F 48.
62. Holbl, *Ptolemaic Empire*, 143, 194–204.
63. Appian, *Syrian Wars*, 4.
64. Ogden, *Polygamy, Prostitutes, and Death*, 135–6.
65. Ibid., 146–7; she was murdered after her husband's death in battle in 150 (Livy, *Epitome*, 50).
66. R.E. Allen, *The Attalid Kingdom, a Constitutional History*, Oxford, 1983, 200–6.
67. Polybios 5.43.
68. McCurdy, *Hellenistic Queens*, is very selective in her coverage and there are no athletes discussed, for example.
69. Polybios 22.3.8–9.
70. Diogenes Laertius 5.4.
71. Livy 42.16.9; they were married when Eumenes did die.
72. Polybios 20.5.7; Plutarch, *Aemilius*, 8.
73. Diodoros 30.7.2; John of Antioch, frag. 58.
74. Josephus, *AJ*, 12.384–319; I Maccabees 7.1–4; Appian, *Syrian Wars*, 47.
75. Even today, in the full glare of publicity, a change of regime in democratic societies is overseen by the armed forces and police on full alert; in dictatorships it is frequently the occasion for a coup.

Chapter 5: Kings and Palaces

1. There were also buildings which have been called 'governors palaces' of the Akhaimenid Empire, some of which were almost as capacious as those of the kings; however, these will be normally ignored in this study of kings' residences. There are two specific studies which will be referred to here: Inge Nielsen, *Hellenistic Palaces, Tradition and Renewal*, Aarhus, 1999, and chs 2 and 3 of Rolf Strootman, *Courts and Elites in the Hellenistic Empires*, Edinburgh, 2014.
2. Nielsen, *Hellenistic palaces*, 18–25.

3. Diodoros 15.3.5; Justin 7.1; Aelian, *Varia Historia*, 14.17.

4. Diodoros 17.7.1–5; Athenaios 12.541c (from Satyros); Plato, *Epistles*, 2.313a, 3.319a, 7.347a, and 348a.

5. Plutarch, *Timoleon*, 22; Diodoros 16.83; Richard J. Evans, *Syracuse in Antiquity, History and Topography*, Pretoria, 2009, fig. 9.

6. Cicero, *Verres*, 2.5.84–98.

7. Nielsen, *Hellenistic Palaces*, 65.

8. Vitruvius 2.8.10 and 13; S. Hornblower, *Mausollus*, Oxford, 1982, 302–4.

9. Nielsen, *Hellenistic Palaces*, 54–61; there were kings in Cyprus, of course, but also Persian governors; there will have been a palace at Cyrene under the Cyrenaican monarchy, but whether it had survived a century of republican rule is not clear.

10. Strabo 17.1.8; the palace is referred to by most historians discussing Hellenistic Egypt or Alexandria, but without description. The underwater exploration of the sunken part of Alexandria has not discovered anything about the building. Nielsen, *Hellenistic Palaces*, 130–8 says little, though has some conjectural details in her catalogue, 282–4.

11. Examples of such sources are Polybios on events in 205–200 (book 15); Diodoros 1.50 and 17.52; Caesar, *Civil Wars*, 3.112.3; Lucan, *Civil War*, 10.1; Athenaios 5.196–7, 203c, 14.654c; Plutarch, *Antony*, 54.3–4, and 72–4.

12. See the plan in Nielsen, *Hellenistic Palaces*, 132.

13. That the city plan was made by Alexander is stated by Arrian (*Anabasis*, 3.1.5–11) and Plutarch (*Alexander*, 26.4); more plausibly Quintus Curtius (4.8.2) gives him the responsibility for the outline of the city walls but no more. The site of the palace, on its peninsula, is not the obvious one, unless one was familiar with the Halikarnassos palace site, which Alexander had needed to fight hard to take, a powerful incentive.

14. The Satrap Stele: Holbl, *Ptolemaic Empire*, 80, 83–4.

15. Claude Mosse, 'Demetrios of Phaleron, a philosopher in power?', in Christian Jacob and François de Polignac (eds), *Alexandria, third century BC*, trans. Colin Clement, Alexandria, 2000, 74–82.

16. Strabo 16.1.5.

17. Plutarch, *Demetrios*, 17.

18. It had been Antigonos' satrapal centre while Alexander ruled, and it was regularly his residence later; it had been a Persian satrapal centre before Alexander (Xenophon, *Anabasis*, 1.2.7–9), and it is therefore certain that there was a palace in the city; Richard A. Billows, *Antigonos the One-Eyed and the Creation of the Hellenistic State*, Berkeley CA, 1992, 241–2, especially; the city was later renamed Apameia by (probably) Antiochos I.

19. Kassandreia was the brief refuge for Arsinoe II in 280, though reference is only to her being in the acropolis: the city is reputed generally hostile to the Antigonids (W.W. Tarn, *Antigonos Gonatas*, Oxford, 1913, 186, note 82); Thessalonike was the scene of conferences with Roman envoys in 185, and was Philip V's residence more than once in the 180s (F.W. Walbank, *Philip V of Macedon*, Cambridge, 1940, 232–4, 251, etc.).

20. Athenaios 5.203e–204d; Strabo 17.1.16; Dorothy J. Thompson, 'Hellenistic Royal Barges', in Kostas Buraselis *et al.*, *The Ptolemies, the Sea and the Nile, Studies in Waterborne Power*, Cambridge, 2013, 185–96.

21. Willy Clarysse, 'The Ptolemies visiting the Egyptian Chora', in Leon Mooren (ed.), *Politics, Administration, and Society in the Hellenistic and Roman Worlds*, Studia Hellenistica, 36, 2000, 29–54; at least fifty of such visits have been counted.

22. Nielsen, *Hellenistic Palaces*, 246–8; the palace ('Sudburg') is said to have been built by Nebuchadnezzar (reigned 605–562), but Babylon had been a royal city for a millennium by

that time; it was excavated by the German expedition active on the site before the First World War: R. Koldewey, *Die Konigsburgen von Babylon, I Die Sudburg*, Leipzig, 1931.

23. Nielsen, *Hellenistic Palaces*, 252–6.
24. Ibid., 266, for Pella; I take these figures from Neilsen's catalogue.
25. Ibid., 86–93 and 266–8.
26. V. Milojcic and D. Theochares, *Demetrias I*, Bonn, 1976; Nielsen, *Hellenistic Palaces*, 93–4, 268–79.
27. Strootman, *Courts*, 55, gives a list, somewhat longer than this.
28. J.D. Grainger, *Seleukos Nikator*, London, 1990, 127.
29. This was the second such city to be founded as a major government centre by Seleukos; he had founded Seleukeia-on-the-Tigris in Babylonia some years earlier. The city was of a size which deliberately rivalled that of Alexandria-by-Egypt, and probably was considerably larger than Antigoneia-in-Syria. And Seleukeia-on-the-Tigris contained a royal palace (largely ignored by Nielsen, *Hellenistic Palaces*).
30. Athenaios 4.155b (from Demetrios of Skepsis).
31. Polybios 26.1.1a and 1–14.
32. Nielsen, *Hellenistic Palaces*, 102–11, 270–2; site was excavated between 1878 and 1886, with major elements taken to Berlin; the report by G. Kawerau and Th. Wiegand, *Die Palaste von Hochburg (Altertumer von Pergamon V.1)*, Berlin, 1930.
33. Nielsen, *Hellenistic Palaces*, figs 54 and 55; it has to be said that the plans do not necessarily lend themselves obviously to such an interpretation.
34. Strabo 13.4.2 (founding); 13.1.54 (later sale); Plutarch, *Anthony*, 59.5 (Anthony's gift).
35. Located only at the palace at Pella; such a shrine is assumed by Nielsen to be normal at other palaces.
36. Evans, *Syracuse in Antiquity*.
37. Theokritos, *Idyll*, XVII.
38. G. Downey, *A History of Antioch in Syria*, Princeton NJ, 1961, fig. 3.
39. Justin 35.2.2.
40. The palace at Cyrene has not been located; the Italian army planted its own military post on where the palace must be within the acropolis; Philip Kenrick, *Libya Archaeological Guides: Cyrenaica*, London, 2013, 182.
41. Sachs and Hunger, *Astronomical Diaries*, Vol. I, –237, –234.
42. Employed by Strootman, *Courts*, Ch. 2; it also underlies much of his treatment, especially in Part III.
43. Diodoros 16.91.4–5.
44. Plutarch, *Demetrios*, 34.
45. Polybios 15.25.3–18 (= Austin 282).
46. Diodoros 31.16.2–3.
47. Plutarch, *Demetrios*, 17.2–5.
48. Strootman, *Courts*, lays great stress on this in his chapters 2 and 3; one cannot help feeling, however, that this idea of monarchy as theatrical performance owes more to modern disdain for monarchy as an institution than for the strength of the ancient evidence.
49. Sachs and Hunger, *Astronomical Diaries*, –210.
50. Nielsen, *Hellenistic Palaces*, 99–100; D.P. Dimitrov and M. Cirikova, *The Thracian City of Seuthopolis*, BAR S38, Oxford, 1978.
51. Nielsen, *Hellenistic Palaces*, 100–1.
52. Nielsen, *Hellenistic Palaces*, 146–51 and 286–8; G. Pesce, *Il 'Palazzo delle Colonne' a Tolemaide de Cirenaica*, Rome, 1950.

53. I Maccabees 16.11–17; Josephus, *AJ*, 13.228–30.
54. Nielsen, *Hellenistic Palaces*, 155–63 and 288–90, 295–307.
55. Rachel Mairs, *The Hellenistic Far East*, Berkeley CA, 2014.
56. J.-C. Gardin and P. Gentelle, 'Irrigation et peuplement dans la plaine d'Ai Khanoum de leepoque Achemenide a l'epoque musulman', *Bulletin de l'Ecole francais de l'Extreme Orient*, 61, 1976, 56–99, shows clearly that the surrounding land was fully occupied and well cultivated at the time the city existed, and had been for millennia.
57. Mairs, *Hellenistic Far East*, 29.

Chapter 6: Kings and Governing

1. As happened with the acclamation of Philip II (Diodoros 17.117; Justin 7.5.9–10).
2. Polybios 15.25.3–11.
3. Josephus, *AJ*, 13.135–41.
4. Inge Nielsen, *Hellenistic Palaces, Tradition and Renewal*, Aarhus, 1999, 84–8.
5. Leon Mooren, *La hierarchie du cour Ptolemaique*, Studia Hellenistica, 23, Louvain, 1977.
6. Polybios 5.40.
7. Polybios 5.43.1–4, 59.1, 62.4; he is therefore sometimes described as an 'admiral', which is both anachronistic and inaccurate.
8. Polybios 18.49.4; Livy 34.57.6; Appian, *Syrian Wars*, 6.
9. Appian, *Syrian Wars*, 6; Livy 34.57.6, 35.50.7 and 36.10.5; Diodoros 28.15.2–4.
10. *OGIS*, 239 and 240; Athenaios 4.155 a–b (from Demetrios of Skepsis).
11. Polybios 5.79.17, 82.9, 87.1 and 4; 21.14.4–17.10, 21.24.1–15; Livy 37.45.5.
12. For example, under Hermeias' influence, at Apameia (Polybios 5.43.7) and before the battle against Molon (Polybios 5.51.2–52.1; there are numerous other examples all through the reign.
13. Polybios 5.56.1–15.
14. Polybios 15.26–39.
15. Dee L. Clayman, *Berenice II and the Golden Age of Ptolemaic Egypt*, Oxford, 2014, 173; Polybios 5.35.7, and 15.25.16; Josephus, *AJ*, 12.2.2.
16. Austin 267; Polybios 15.25–7, 16.21.2.
17. C.P. Jones and C. Habicht, 'A Hellenistic Inscription from Arsinoe in Cilicia', *Phoenix*, 63, 1989, 317–46.
18. Tables in Rolf Strootman, *Courts and Elites in the Hellenistic Empires*, Edinburgh, 2014, 128–30, based in part on I. Savalli-Lestrange, *Les philoi royaux dans l'Asie Hellenistique*, Geneva, 1998, and Leon Mooren, *The Aulic Titulature in Ptolemaic Egypt: Introduction and Prosopography*, Brussels, 1975; see also E. Olshausen, *Prosopographie der Hellenistischen Konigsgesandten I, von Triparadisos bis Pydna*, Leuven, 1978.
19. W.S. Ferguson, *Hellenistic Athens*, London, 1911, Ch. 5; Christian Habicht, *Athens from Alexander to Antony*, trans. Deborah Lucas Schneider, Cambridge MA, 1997, Ch. 6.
20. Plutarch, *Aratos*, 33–4; Habicht, *Athens*, 162–6.
21. Trogus, *Prologue*, 26.
22. Frank L. Holt, *Thundering Zeus, The Making of Hellenistic Bactria*, Berkeley CA, 1999.
23. Molon: Polybios 5.41–8; Timarchos: Appian, *Syrian Wars*, 47, Trogus, *Prologue*, 34.
24. Josephus, *AJ*, 12.366, 379–80, 386.
25. Richard A. Billows, *Kings and Colonists, Aspects of Macedonian Imperialism*, Leiden, 1994, chs 4, 5, and 6.
26. Polybius 27.13.

27. Theodotos in 219: Polybios 5.61.3–4; Porphyry, *FGrH*, 260 F 44; Ptolemy son of Thraseas in 202: Jones and Habicht, n. 17 above.

28. *OGIS*, 226; Trogus, *Prologue*, 26; Appian, *Syrian Wars*, 56; Athenaios 13.593b; Frontinus, *Stratagems*, 3.9.10.

29. Holt, *Thundering Zeus*.

30. See Narain's list in *CAH*, VIII, 420–1.

31. The prominence of Seleukid royal names in the family suggests this, as does its intermarriage with the royal family – Akhaios' aunt Laodike married Antiochos II.

32. Austin 168.

33. Diodoros 19.61.1–3.

34. For Ptolemaic power abroad see Roger Bagnall, *The Administration of the Ptolemaic Empire outside Egypt*, Leiden, 1976; for the policy of Antiochos III extending his authority in Asia Minor, see John Ma, *Antiochos III and the Cities of Western Asia Minor*, Oxford, 1999. The Phoenician cities were caught between the two monarchies as well, for which see J.D. Grainger, *Hellenistic Phoenicia*, Oxford, 1991.

35. P.M. Fraser, *Cities of Alexander the Great*, Oxford, 1996; many cities claimed Alexander as their founder, but investigation suggests their origin was as garrisons during his conquest, or that the claim was simply invented.

36. Appian, *Syrian Wars*, 58; Cohen, *Hellenistic Settlements in the East*, 157–73.

37. Aelian, *Animalia*, 12.2; G. Goossens, *Hierapolis de Syrie*, Louvain, 1943; Getzel M. Cohen, *The Hellenistic Settlements in Syria, the Red Sea Basin and North Africa*, Berkeley CA, 2006, 172–8.

38. J. Sauvaget, *Alep*, Paris, 1941; Cohen, *Hellenistic Cities in Syria*, 153–5.

39. J.D. Grainger, *The Cities of Seleukid Syria*, Oxford, 1990, 35.

40. There was some undefined trouble in Syria on the death of Seleukos I in 281, but it quickly subsided; in the 140s there were riots and confusion in Antioch and perhaps in other cities, but this happened when the kingship was in dispute, and loyalties uncertain – and one king's rebellion would be his rival's display of loyalty.

41. Austin 173.

42. Based on the statement in Appian, *Syrian Wars*, 62 that there were '72' satrapies, which it is assumed is a mistake for hyparchies. There were probably no more than twenty satrapies (a number which varies with the extent of the empire); Susan M. Sherwin-White and Amelie Kuhrt and, *From Samarkhand to Sardis, a New Approach to the Seleucid Empire*, London, 1993, 44–8.

43. Austin 193.

44. *Oeconomica* (traditionally by Aristotle), 2.2.303a–c; Arrian, *Anabasis*, 7.25.6–8; Diodoros 18.14.1; Pausanias 1.6.3.

45. A.E. Viesse, *Les 'revoltes Egyptiennes', Recherches sur les Troubles interieures en Egypt du Regne de Ptolemee III a la conquete romain*, Studia Hellenistica, 41, Louvain, 2004, for a detailed account.

46. Descriptions of the system include, Claude Preaux, *La Monde Hellenistique*, 2 vols, Paris, 1936; M.I. Roztovtzeff, *Social and Economic History of the Hellenistic World*, 3 vols, Oxford, 1941; Holbl, *Ptolemaic Empire*, 25–7, 58–63.

Chapter 7: Kings and People

1. Plutarch, *Demetrios*, 42.2.

2. Ibid., 42.3–4.

3. Justin 7.5.9.

4. Diodoros 16.3.1.

5. Quintus Curtius 10.7.1–15; Arrian, *Successors*, *FGrH*, 156 F 1.1.

6. Plutarch, *Demetrios*, 17–18.

7. Kassandros was addressed by others as king, but may not have taken the title for some years; Antigonos Gonatas had been awarded the title of king by his father Demetrios, but it was not until he was accepted by the Macedonians after clearing the country of Galatian raiders that he was actually king in Macedon; Pyrrhos: Plutarch, *Demetrios*, 44 and *Pyrrhos*, 11.

8. Polybios 15.25.3.

9. Plutarch, *Aemilius Paullus*, 8; R.M. Errington, *A History of Macedon*, Berkeley CA, 1990, 176–7; S. Dow and C.F. Edson Jr, 'Chriseis', *Harvard Studies in Classical Philosophy*, 28, 1937, 127–35; W.W. Tarn, 'Philip V and Phthia', *Classical Quarterly*, 18, 1924, 17–30.

10. Polybios 2.71.4; Porphyry, *FGrH*, 260 F 45.

11. R.E. Allen, *The Attalid Kingdom, a Constitutional History*, Oxford, 1983, scarcely pays any attention to the successor mechanism, despite its clear relevance to his subject.

12. Polybios 4.48.1–12; 5.57.1–8 and 72.1–77.1.

13. E.T. Newell, *The Coinage of the Eastern Seleucid Mints*, New York, 1938, 35–6 and 204–5.

14. Diodoros 31.27a; Trogus, *Prologue*, 4; Arthur Houghton, 'Timarchos as king in Babylonia', *Revue Numismatique*, 21, 1976, 212–17.

15. Diodoros 19.61.1–5.

16. A Byzantine compilation, the *Suda*, explains that it was 'neither descent nor legitimacy' but command of an army and expertise in administration which was necessary to make a new king (*Suda*, *s.v. Basileus* = Austin 45), but after the chaos which succeeded Alexander, it was exactly descent and legitimacy which was vital. Control of armed force was, however, also required to rule.

17. Polybios 5.10 7.1–3.

18. A.E. Viesse, *Les 'revoltes Egyptiennes', Recherches sur les Troubles interieures en Egypt du Regne de Ptolemee III a la conquete romain*, Studia Hellenistica, 41, Louvain, 2004.

19. It was his large Median cavalry force as well as his Indian elephants that Seleukos used to promote the victory at Ipsos; he commanded between 10,000 and 15,000 cavalry, which can only have been recruited from the Medes (Plutarch, *Demetrios*, 28–9). Polybios 5.79.6; Livy 37.40.5.

20. See the description of the armies at Raphia and Magnesia (previous note).

21. Polybios 31.12 and 19; Josephos, *AJ*, 13.36; Justin 35.1.5.

22. Diodoros 31.40a.

23. Richard A. Billows, *Antigonos the One-Eyed and the Creation of the Hellenistic State*, Berkeley CA, 1992, 279–81.

24. See the disputes quoted in the Loeb volumes of *Select Papyri*, vols 3 and 4. There is a chapter on 'Order and Law' in the Ptolemaic kingdom – that is, Egypt – in J.G. Manning, *The Last Pharaohs, Egypt the Ptolemies, 305–30 BC*, Princeton NJ, 2010, 165–201, and 'trial record' of a case in the appendix, 207–16.

25. Ph. Gauthier, *Nouvelles Inscriptions de Sardeis*, Vol. II, Paris, 1989; the relevant inscriptions are repented in John Ma, *Antiochos III and the Cities of Western Asia Minor*, Oxford, 1999, 284–8.

26. Justin 37.1.9; Porphyry, *FGrH*, 260 F 43: *OGIS*, 54.

27. Diodoros 29.29; Porphyry, *FGrH*, 260 F 48.

28. Polybios 5.26.7– 27.6, 28.5–7. J.M. Helliesen, 'Andriscus and the Revolt of the Macedonias, 149–148 BC', *Ancient Macedon*, IV, Thessalonica 1986.

29. A recent reconsideration of the origins of Ptolemaic cleruchs is by Mary Stefanou, 'Waterborne Recruits: the Military Settlers of Ptolemaic Egypt', in Kostas Buraselis *et al.*, *The Ptolemies, the Sea and the Nile, Studies in Waterborne Power*, Cambridge 2013, 108–31.

30. For Memphis alone, Dorothy J. Thompson, *Memphis under the Ptolemies*, 2nd edn, Princeton NJ, 2012, notes Arabs, Carians, Idumaeans, Jews, Phoenicians, and unspecified immigrants, not to mention Greeks and Macedonians.

31. For the extent of migration to Syria see J.D. Grainger, *The Cities of Seleukid Syria*, Oxford, 1990.

32. *OGIS*, 219; Austin 267.

33. Appian, *Syrian Wars*, 65; Polyainos, *Stratagems*, 8.50.

34. *P. Gurob* (= *FGrH*, 160 = Austin 266.)

35. Polybios 5.50.7–8.

36. This appears only on the coins of Antioch and Seleukeia-in-Pieria: W. Wroth, *Catalogue of the Greek Coins of Galatia, Cappadocia and Syria*, London, 1878, 151–2.

37. Diodoros 32.9c; Josephus, *AJ*, 13.108 and 113.

38. Josephus, *AJ*, 13.225.

39. Josephus, *AJ*, 13.125–42; Diodoros 33.4.2–4; Porphyry, *FGrH*, 260 F 32.15.

40. A much-studied episode, notably by E. Schurer, *The History of the Jewish People in the Age of Jesus Christ*, rev. and ed. by G. Vermes *et al.*, Edinburgh, 1973–87, Vol. I; see also J.D. Grainger, *The Wars of the Maccabees*, Barnsley, 2012.

41. J.D. Grainger, *Hellenistic Phoenicia*, Oxford, 1991.

42. Grainger, *Cities*, 179–88.

43. Sachs and Hunger, *Astronomical Diaries, passim*: R. van der Spek, 'The Babylonian City', in Amelie Kurht and Susan M. Sherwin-White (eds), *Hellenism in the East*, London, 1987, 57–74: Amelie Kurht, 'The Seleukid Kings and Babylonia: New Perspectives on the Seleukid Realm in the East', in Per Bilde *et al.* (eds), *Aspects of Hellenistic Kingship*, Aarhus, 1996, 41–54.

44. Welles, *Royal Correspondence*, 36 and 37.

45. M. Hengel, *Judaism and Hellenism*, London, 1974, and *Jews, Greeks, and Barbarians*, London, 1980.

46. Diodoros 19.80.4.

47. Athenaios 5.201b–f and 202f–203e; E.E. Rice, *The Grand Procession of Ptolemy Philadelphus*, Oxford, 1983; Austin 258 (which has further modern references). Polybios, 30.25; Diodoros, 31.16.1.

48. The volumes of the *Prosopographia Ptolemaica*, though not easy to use, contain a large number of names; I made an attempt in *A Seleukid Prosopography and Gazetteer*, Leiden, 1996, to list all the names of the Seleukid subjects, but the repetitive nature of many of the entries indicates clearly enough the exiguous nature of the information.

Chapter 8: Kings and Cities

1. Diodoros 16.8.6 (Philippi); 16.8.44 and 100.15; Pliny, *NH*, 4.41 (Philippopolis).

2. Demosthenes 4.48; see N.G.L. Hammond, *The Macedonian State, the Origins, Institutions and History*, Oxford, 1989, 154–65.

3. Theagenes, *FGrH*, 774, F 3.

4. J.R. Ellis, *Philip II and Macedonian Imperialism*, London, 1976, 93–100.

5. Plutarch, *Alexander*, 9.1.

6. Arrian, *Anabasis*, 1.7–9; Diodoros 17.8.3–14; Plutarch, *Alexander*, 11–12.

7. P.M. Fraser, *Cities of Alexander the Great*, Oxford, 1996 – for attributions see the table on pp. 239–43; Getzel M. Cohen, *The Hellenistic Settlements in Syria, the Red Sea Basin and North Africa*, Berkeley CA, 2006, 55–81.
8. Tacitus, *Histories*, 4.83.1. The Satrap Stele; Holbl, *Ptolemaic Empire*, 80; P.M. Fraser, *Ptolemaic Alexandria*, Oxford, 1972; Cohen, *Hellenistic Settlements in Syria*, 363.
9. M. Chauveau, *L'Egypte au temps de Cleopatre*, Paris, 1997, 77–8.
10. Pliny, *NH*, 6.46–7; Getzel M. Cohen, *The Hellenistic Settlements in the East from Armenia and Mesopotamia to Bactria and India*, Berkeley CA, 2013, 245–50.
11. R.F. Hoddinott, *The Thracians*, London, 1981.
12. It was also reportedly renamed, Alexandria, then Antioch (for Antiochos IV), then Spasinou Charax (for Hyspaosines): Cohen, *Hellenistic Settlements in the East*, 109–17.
13. Strabo 16.2.25; Pliny, *NH*, 5.75; the renaming was perhaps done by Ptolemy II, but the city is so strategically placed that Ptolemy I, who invaded the region four times, will have occupied it.
14. Strabo 17.1.42; Cohen, *Hellenistic Settlements in Syria*, 350–2.
15. Diodoros 19.52.1–3.
16. Diodoros 19.54.2; Plutarch, *Moralia*, 8.463; Pausanias 9.7.1.
17. Diodoros 20.29.1.
18. Polyainos 8.57; Getzel M. Cohen, *The Hellenistic Settlements in Europe, the islands, and Asia Minor*, Berkeley CA, 1995, 177–80; Elizabeth D. Carney, *Arsinoe of Egypt and Macedon, a Royal Life*, Oxford, 2013, 36 and 47–8.
19. Strabo 16.2.10; Cohen, *Hellenistic Settlements in Syria*, 94–101.
20. Strabo 13.593.
21. Strabo 12.566; Stephanos of Byzantion, 'Nikaia'.
22. Strabo 14.646.
23. J.D. Grainger, *Seleukos Nikator*, London, 1990, 97–100; Cohen, *Hellenistic Settlements in the East*, 70–7, 79–81.
24. Appian, *Syrian Wars*, 58; Strabo 16.1.5; Pausanias 1.16.3; for an interpretation of the foundation story see J.D. Grainger, *The Rise of the Seleukid Empire 323–223 BC*, Barnsley, 2014, 36–40, 57–8; Cohen, *Hellenistic Settlements in the East*, 157–73.
25. Appian, *Syrian Wars*, 57.
26. Strabo 11.13.6; Pliny, *NH*, 6.115; *I.Estremo Oriente*, 271–2; Cohen, *Hellenistic Settlements in the East*, 218–20.
27. For all this see J.D. Grainger, *The Cities of Seleukid Syria*, Oxford, 1990; Cohen, *Hellenistic Settlements in Syria*.
28. Richard A. Billows, *Kings and Colonists, Aspects of Macedonian Imperialism*, Leiden, 1994.
29. Pausanias 1.6.8–7.3; Polyainos 2.28; François Chamoux, 'Le roi Magas', *Revue Historique*, 1956, 18–34.
30. Diodoros 19.61.1–5; Richard A. Billows, *Antigonos the One-Eyed and the Creation of the Hellenistic State*, Berkeley CA, 1992, 113–14.
31. W.W. Tarn and G.T. Griffith, *Hellenistic Civilisation*, 3rd edn, Cambridge, 1952, 145–6.
32. Austin 186; Rachel Mairs, *The Hellenistic Far East*, Berkeley CA, 2014, Ch. 2, is the latest to discuss the foundation date, inconclusively; Cohen, *Hellenistic Settlements in the East*, 225–44; it is curious that the only other prominent man with the name Kineas was the diplomatic agent of Pyrrhos in Italy in the 270s; the two were contemporaries, and one would be very tempted to identify them.
33. *CIG*, 6856.5–6 = *I.Estremo Oriente*, 3.
34. Pliny, *NH*, 6.117.

35. Cohen, *Hellenistic Settlements in the East*, 62–7.
36. For the latest examination of Seleukid finances see G.G. Aperghis, *The Seleukid Royal Economy*, Cambridge, 2004.
37. Pliny, *NH*, 6.49; L. Robert, 'Demodamas de Milet et la reine Apame', *Bulletin de Correspondence Hellenique*, 108, 1954, 467–72.
38. The figure of 5,000/6,000 is based on to later references to citizen numbers at Seleukeia-in-Pieria and Kyrrhos; these are possibly initial projections, and take no account of families, slaves, non-citizen immigrants, and the later growth of population.
39. Grainger, *Cities*, 75–7, id., *Seleukos Nikator*, London, 1990, 128; Cohen, *Hellenistic Settlements in Syria*, 190–6 (Seleukeia), and *Hellenistic Settlements in the East*, 67–9 (Apameia); the two were originally a single city, and when the river became the frontier in the late second century BC, Apameia became a separate city.
40. Dorothy J. Thompson, *Memphis under the Ptolemies*, Princeton NJ, 2012, suggests a population for the city of between 50,000 and 200,000: Thebes was smaller, Alexandria larger.
41. R. van der Spek, 'The Babylonian City', in Amelie Kuhrt and Susan M. Sherwin-White, *Hellenism in the East*, London, 1987, 57–74.
42. Justin 41.1.8.
43. 'Seleukeia-on-the-Eulaios'; Cohen, *Hellenistic Settlements in the East*, 194–9.
44. Several are published in Austin, from several kingdoms.
45. Thompson, *Memphis*, 136–7.
46. Dorothy J. Crawford, *Kerkeosiris, an Egyptian Village of the Ptolemaic Period*, Cambridge, 1971, 44 and 124.
47. J.D. Grainger, *Hellenistic Phoenicia*, Oxford 1991, Ch. 5.
48. As in the 270s, when Antiochos I was fighting to hold Asia Minor against the Galatians: Austin 163.
49. *P. Gurob* (= Austin 266).
50. Ibid.
51. Polybios 5.68.8–71.12.
52. Polybios 7.15.1–18.12 and 8.21.4–11; P. Gauthier, *Nouvelles Inscriptions de Sardes*, Vol. II, Paris, 1989.
53. Polybios 5.86.7–11; J.D. Grainger, *The Syrian Wars*, Leiden, 2010, 217.
54. John Ma, *Antiochos III and the Cities of Western Asia Minor*, Oxford 1999.
55. O. Morkholm, *Studies in the Coinage of Antiochos IV of Syria*, Copenhagen, 1963, and *Antiochos IV of Syria*, Copenhagen, 1966.
56. Justin 40.1.
57. Polyainos 4.18 and 6.7.
58. Sachs and Hunger, *Astronomical Diaries*, '–140'.

Chapter 9: Kings and War

1. Plutarch, *Demetrios*, 32; Porphyry, *FGrH*, 260 F 32.2.
2. Plutarch, *Demetrios*, 47–52: Polyainos 4.9.2, 3 and 5; Diodoros 21.1.20.
3. See J.D. Grainger, *The Seleukid Empire of Antiochos III*, Barnsley, 2014.
4. M. Cary, *A History of the Greek World from 323 to 146 BC*, London, 1951; Susan M. Sherwin-White and Amelie Kuhrt, *From Samarkand to Sardis, A New Approach to the Seleucid Empire*, London, 1993, 190, approving of Cary's description of Antiochos' policy as '*restitutor orbis*'.
5. At Raphia in 217 (Polybios 5.84.8–9), and at the Arios River in 210, where he had several teeth knocked out (Polybios 10.49).

6. Pithom Stele, 15–16; Holbl, *Ptolemaic Empire*, 40., Ptolemaic Empire
7. *P. Gurob* (= Austin 266).
8. It was claimed that he went as far as Babylon, and that he received submissions from as far east as Baktria (*OGIS*, 54 = Austin 268; Polyainos 8.50); neither of these achievements is believable.
9. Polybios 5.82–5; an exaggerated version, emphasising Ptolemy's supposed personal contribution to the battle, and made for propagandising home consumption, is in a decree of Egyptian priests dated November 217 (Austin 276).
10. Memnon 226a.
11. Ibid.
12. Pausanias 1.7.2–3.
13. See also J.D. Grainger, *The Syrian Wars*, Leiden, 2010, and *Great Power Diplomacy in the Hellenistic World* (forthcoming).
14. Strabo 13.4.1–2; *OGIS*, 273–9; J.D. Grainger, *The Roman War of Antiochos the Great*, Leiden 2002, especially 257–65, for Eumenes' involvement; he had spent the previous years doing his best to acquire a Roman alliance while Antiochos had similarly striven to avoid colliding with him.
15. See on the Syrian Wars in n. 12 above.
16. Holbl, *Ptolemaic Empire*, 42–3; Hans Hauben, 'Callicrates of Samos and Patroclus of Macedon, champions of Ptolemaic Thalassocracy', in Kostas Buraselis *et al.* (eds), *The Ptolemies, the Sea and the Nile, Studies in Waterborne Power*, Cambridge, 2013, 39–65.
17. Theodotos of Aitolia – Polybios 5.45–6 and 61–2; Ptolemy son of Thraseas – Polybios 5.65.1; Polybios 16.39.1; Porphyry, *FGrH*, 260 F 45–6.
18. Justin 37.1.9; Porphyry, *FGrH*, 260 F 43.
19. Polybios 5.83.1–3 (the pre-fight parade), 85.7–8 (Ptolemy's sudden appearance in the midst of the fighting).
20. Holbl, *Ptolemaic Empire*, 183–9.
21. Polybios 27.6.1–6 and 10–11; Appian, *Syrian Wars*, 45; Livy 38.8.5 and 18.1–5.
22. Grainger, *Syrian Wars*, 293–4; O. Morkholm, *Antiochus IV of Syria*, Copenhagen, 1966, 66–74
23. Polybios 5.45.8–46.4.
24. Stephen Mitchell, *Anatolia, Land, Men, and Gods in Asia Minor*, Vol. I, *The Celts and the Impact of Roman Rule*, Oxford, 1993, 19–26.
25. J.D. Grainger, 'Antiochos III in Thrace', *Historia*, 45, 1996, 329–43.
26. This is the burden of the interpretation by Arthur M. Eckstein, *Mediterranean Anarchy, Interstate War, and the Rise of Rome*, Berkeley CA, 2006.
27. Angelos Chaniotis, *War in the Hellenistic World*, London, 2005, 46–51.
28. Porphyry, *FGrH*, 260 F 32.9; Appian, *Syrian Wars*, 60; Polybios 32.71.14 and 5.40.5.
29. Polybios 5.56.1–15; E. Will, 'Les premieres annees de la regne d'Antiochos III', *Revue des Etudes Grecques*, 75, 1976, 72–129.
30. Polybios 5.51.3–54.5.
31. Polybios 5.58.3–61.2.
32. Plutarch, *Demetrios*, 29.
33. Antiochos commanded part of the army at the battle of Panion in 200 (Polybios 16.18.6–19.1); for Seleukos see n. 23 above.
34. Note especially the fruitless campaign by Tryphon against Simon Maccabee, who simply blocked every passage into Judaea from the low lands, and left Tryphon and his army marching back and forth fruitlessly: Josephus, *AJ*, 13.187–92.

35. Josephus, *AJ*, 13.335–44.
36. Justin 36.1.2–6; Josephus, *AJ*, 13.184–6.
37. It is thus relatively easy to describe any Hellenistic army, just as it is a Roman.
38. Polybios 5.84.2–8.
39. Ibid., 5.85.8.
40. Livy, *Epitome*, 50; Zonaras/Dio Cassius 9.28.
41. Polybios 5.85.1–4.
42. It perhaps needs to be pointed out that, despite the different terms for the units, Roman warfare was essentially phalanx-war; the organisation of a legion may in diagram form look much looser than a Hellenistic phalanx, but in action that looseness rapidly disappeared as the maniples closed up; the final destruction of the legion/phalanx came at the battle of Adrianople in 378; after that the formation fell into disuse for 1,000 years.
43. Diodoros 19.81.5, and 83.1–4.
44. Seleukids: Polybios 11.39 and 30.37; Ptolemy II: S.M. Burstein, 'Elephants for Ptolemy II: Ptolemaic Policy in Libya in the Third Century BC, in Paul McKechnie and Philip Guillaume (eds), *Ptolemy II Philadelphus and his World*, Leiden, 2008, 135–47.
45. Livy 37.40.12 and 41.6–7; Livy 37.42.7–8; Justin 31.8.6; B. Bar-Kochva, *The Seleucid Army, Organisation and Tactics in the Great Campaigns*, Cambridge, 1976, 171–2.
46. Polybios 10.29.1–31.4 (Elburz) and 69.1–11 (Lebanon).
47. W.W. Tarn, *Hellenistic Naval and Military Developments*, Cambridge, 1930 (repr. 1975), is still a very useful summary.
48. S. Casson, *Ships and Seamanship in the Ancient World*, Baltimore MD, 1995; William M. Murray, *The Age of Titans, the Rise and Fall of the Great Hellenistic Navies*, Oxford, 2012; J.D. Grainger, *Hellenistic and Roman Naval Wars 336–31 BC*, Barnsley, 2011.
49. Plutarch, *Crassus*, 25–31.
50. Arrian, *Anabasis*, 1.6.1–4.
51. Diodoros 16.74.2–76.4; Plutarch, *Alexander*, 9.1.
52. Diodoros 29.15; Strabo 16.1.18.
53. For a summary of this episode, see Dee L. Clayman, *Berenice II and the Golden Age of Ptolemaic Egypt*, Oxford, 2014.
54. Trogus, *Prologue*, 17; Memnon 228a.
55. Polybios 18.51.8 and 21.6.1–6; Appian, *Syrian Wars*, 26 and 45; Livy 38.8.5.
56. Polybios 18.53.1–54.6.
57. Ibid., 16.21.1.
58. Trogus, *Prologue*, 26 (Seleukos); Holbl's formulation (*Ptolemaic Empire*, 44) is that Ptolemy the Son 'no longer figures in Egyptian dating formulae', an interesting euphemism for death.
59. Justin 41.6.5.
60. The murder of Simon by his son-in-law (Josephus, *AJ*, 13.228).
61. Appian, *Syrian Wars*, 68; Strabo 16.2.10; Diodoros 33.28–28a.
62. Diodoros 33.4.1.
63. Josephus, *AJ*, 13.365; Strabo 16.2.7.
64. Justin 41.6.3.
65. N.C. Debevoise, *A Political History of Parthia*, Chicago IL, 1938; J. Harmatta, 'Parthia and Elymais in the second century BC', *Acta Antiqua Academiae Scientiarum Hungaricae*, 29, 1981, 189–217.
66. B.C. McGing, *The Foreign Policy of Mithradates VI Eupator, King of Pontus*, Leiden, 1986.
67. Polybios 32.16.1–5, 33.12.1–13.10; Appian, *Mithradatic Wars*, 3.

Chapter 10: Kings and Death

1. Quintus Curtius 10.10.9–13.
2. Diodoros 18.26.2 and 28.2–4.
3. Arrian, *Successors*, *FGrH*, 156, F 24, 25.
4. It is curious that so many historians, generally sceptical of stories such as this, accept the intervention story without looking at a map, which is the datum which reveals that it was obviously a put-up job.
5. Strabo 17.1.8.
6. Suetonius, *Augustus*, 18; Dio Cassius 51.16; one does not have to accept that it really was Alexander's preserved body, of course.
7. In the dynastic lists in Appendix I those suffering violent deaths are indicated.
8. Athenaios 13.593c–d (from Phylarchos); also, Appian, *Syrian Wars*, 65.
9. Murdered by her son because she favoured his brother for the succession: Plutarch, *Demetrios*, 36 and *Pyrrhos*, 6; Justin 16.1.1–9; Diodoros 21.7; Pausanias 9.7.3.
10. On this see Suzanne Funke, 'Apeiros 317–272 BC: the Struggle of the Diadochi and the Political Structure of the Federation', in Leon Mooren (ed.), *Politics, Administration, and Society in the Hellenistic and Roman Worlds*, Studia Hellenistica, 36, 2000, 107–22.
11. Large numbers of coins from Afghanistan have been found (and usually sold) in the past fifty years, revealing the names of several 'new' kings: Frank L. Holt, *Lost World of the Golden King*, Berkeley CA, 2012.
12. Compare this record with the mediaeval kings of England from Alfred the Great to Richard III: eleven died by violence out of thirty-one kings, in a society which is probably even more violent and addicted to brutal warfare than the Hellenistic.
13. Appian, *Syrian Wars*, 69; Josephus, *AJ*, 13.367–8.
14. See n. 2 above.
15. He does not get a number in our lists, but he appears as king on coins, with his mother as regent, after his father's murder.
16. Diodoros 30.7.2.
17. Josephus, *AJ*, 12.390; Appian, *Syrian Wars*, 66; Trogus, *Prologue*, 34.
18. Appian, *Syrian Wars*, 68–9; Porphyry, *FGrH* 260 F 32.22.
19. Appian, *Syrian Wars*, 69; Josephus, *AJ*, 13.366; Plutarch, *Moralia*, 486E.
20. Memnon 226a–b; Pausanias 1.16.1; Appian, *Syrian Wars*, 62; Justin 7.2.1–5.
21. That is, he had a Macedonian name (Nikanor) but this did not necessarily mean he was from Macedon: Seleukid kings called themselves 'Macedonian', though none after Seleukos I set foot in that land.
22. Porphyry, *FGrH*, 260 F 44; Appian, *Syrian Wars*, 68; Polybios 5.40.5 and 32.71.4.
23. Appian, *Syrian Wars*, 45.
24. Justin 29.1.7–8; Josephus, *AJ*, 13.268: Appian, *Syrian Wars* 68; on Kleopatra Thea's responsibility see J.D. Grainger, *The Syrian Wars*, Leiden, 2010, 383.
25. Athenaios 153b (from Poseidonios); Josephus, *AJ*, 13.365.
26. Josephus, *AJ*, 13.117; Diodoros 32.9d.
27. Josephus, *AJ*, 13.187; Justin 36.1.7; Livy, *Epitome*, 55; I Maccabees 13.31; Appian, *Syrian Wars*, 68; Diodoros 33.28.
28. Diodoros 29.29; Porphyry, *FGrH*, 260 F 46.
29. Appian, *Syrian Wars*, 69; Justin 39.2.7.
30. Diodoros 34/35.14; Justin 38.8.13–15.
31. Plutarch, *Moralia*, 753e–f; Ptolemy VIII, *Hypomnemata*, *FGrH*, 234 F 4; Elizabeth D. Carney, *Arsinoe II of Egypt and Macedon, a Royal Life*, Oxford, 2013, 126–8.

32. Trogus, *Prologue*, 26.
33. Diodoros 30.7.2; G. Le Rider, 'L'Enfant-roi Antiochos et la reine Laodike', *Bulletin de Correspondence Hellenique*, 110, 1986, 409–17: O. Morkholm, *Antiochos IV of Syria*, Copenhagen, 1966, 41–50.
34. Morkholm, *Antiochos IV*.
35. John of Antioch, frag. 58.
36. Josephus, *AJ*, 13.319; Appian, *Syrian Wars*, 66; Trogus, *Prologue*, 34.
37. Livy 41.24.4–6; Polybios 23.1–2, 3.4–9; E.S. Gruen, 'The Last Years of Philip V', *Greek, Roman, and Byzantine Studies*, 16, 1974, 221–46.
38. Polybios 5.4.1, 5.36.1, 15.25.1–2.
39. Dee L. Clayman, *Berenice II and the Golden Age of Ptolemaic Egypt*, Oxford, 2014, 171–3.
40. Polybios 15.25.3; Arsinoe's death was concealed, but since it had taken place some time before it was announced it is normally assumed to have been a secret murder.
41. Justin 38.8.2–3; Diodoros 33.13.
42. Justin 17.2.
43. Peter Green, *Alexander to Actium*, London, 1990, 538.
44. P. Oxy 1241.
45. Holbl, *Ptolemaic Empire*, 195.
46. A.E. Viesse, *Les 'revoltes Egyptiennes', Recherches sur les Troubles interieures en Egypt du Regne de Ptolemee III a la conquete romain*, Studia Hellenistica, 41, Louvain, 2004; Holbl, *Ptolemaic Empire*, 198–9.
47. Grainger, *Syrian Wars*, 374–85.
48. Livy, *Epitome*, 50.
49. Appian, *Syrian Wars*, 68–9; Porphyry, *FGrH*, 260 F 32.20.
50. Justin 39.3–12.
51. Justin 39.4.2; Appian, *Syrian Wars*, 69.
52. Josephus, *AJ*, 13.419; Strabo 16.2.3.
53. Justin 39.4.4–5.
54. Plutarch, *Anthony*, 85.2–8; Strabo 17.1.10
55. Apart from the numerous sons, there were also many daughters, who were handed out to members of the surrounding dynasties as wives of kings. As a result every dynasty from Macedon to Parthia became descended from a Seleukid king, and it was still possible in the second century AD for a Roman governor of Syria, Avidius Cassius, to boast that he was a Seleukid descendant. This could never be said of the Ptolemies after the death of the last king of Numidia Juba II in 40AD.
56. Pausanias 1.9.3; Cicero, *Agr.*, 11.42; Holbl, *Ptolemaic Empire*, 222.
57. Dio Cassius 51.15.5; Plutarch, *Anthony*, 82.1; Suetonius, *Augustus*, 17.5
58. Appian, *Syrian Wars*, 63.
59. Clayman, *Berenice II*, 183–5.
60. P.M. Fraser, *Ptolemaic Alexandria*, Oxford, 1971, Vol. 1, 17–18.
61. M. Andronikos, 'Verghina, the Prehistoric Necropolis and the Hellenistic Palace', *Mediterranean Archaeology*, 13, 1964, and *Verghina*, Athens, 1984.
62. Diodoros 22.3.4; Pausanias 10.19.7; Justin 24.5.1–7.
63. Polybios 5.59.1.

Chapter 11: Kings and Intellectuals

1. Plutarch, *Alexander*, 7.2–5.
2. Pliny, *NH*, 8.16.44.

3. Plutarch, *Alexander*, 26.1–2.
4. Arrian, *Anabasis*, 4.14.3; Curtius Rufus, *History of Alexander*, 8.8.20–1; as Arrian points out, the stories of Kallisthenes' death are disturbingly varied.
5. Peter Green, *Alexander of Macedon*, London, 1970, 61.
6. Arrian, *Anabasis*, 1.1.
7. See the Loeb edition of Arrian, by P.A. Brunt, xviii–xxxiv, for a discussion of Alexander sources; also Lionel Pearson, *The Lost Histories of Alexander the Great*, New York, 1960.
8. Arrian, *Anabasis*, 7.27.1; Plutarch, *Alexander*, 7–8, 25.
9. Plutarch, *Moralia*, 182d–e; Aelian, *Varia Historia*, 9.36 (also told of Philip II).
10. Pliny, *NH*, 35.90, 96, and 106; Strabo 14.2.19; Richard A. Billows, *Antigonos the One-eyed and the Creation of the Hellenistic State*, Berkeley CA, 1992, 311–13.
11. Strabo 2.1.17; 11.11.6; Pliny, *NH*, 6.17.58, 6.11.31, and 2.67. P.J. Kosmin, *The Land of the Elephant Kings*, Cambridge MA, 2014, 167–8 persists in calling the voyage 'imaginary' or a 'fabrication', where it is better to assume Patrokles was merely mistaken, or that his readers misunderstood him. The description of his expedition includes only that he sailed along the southern coast of the sea.
12. Klaus Karttunen, *India and the Hellenistic World*, Helsinki, 1997, Ch. 3.
13. Strabo 2.1.4, 15.1.12, 20, 35–60, 68; Athenaios 153d (Megasthenes); Strabo 2.68, 70, 76 (Deimachos).
14. Charles Allen, *Ashoka, The Search for India's Lost Emperor*, London, 2012, 50–8.
15. So Diodoros 17.93.2; Plutarch, *Alexander*, 62.3 says 6,000; Curtius Rufus 3,000, quoting Phegeus – any of these numbers would frighten an army recently defeated, as Alexander's had been at the Jhelum in 326.
16. Pliny, *HN*, 6.49.
17. Athenaios 682d; L. Robert, 'Demodamas de Milet et la reine Apame', *Bulletin de Correspondence Hellenique*, 108, 1954, 467–72; Susan M. Sherwin-White and Amelie Kuhrt, *From Samarkhand to Sardis, a New Approach to the Seleukid Empire*, London, 1993, 103–27; Kosmin, *Land of the Elephant Kings*, Ch. 2.
18. Sherwin-White and Kuhrt, *Samarkhand to Sardis*, 19.
19. Athenaios 5.197–203; the visit was celebrated in Ptolemy II's 'great procession' in the 270s, and had thus presumably taken place sometime before that; in which case the Indian emperor he visited was Bindusara.
20. Steven E. Sidebotham, *Berenike and the Ancient Maritime Spice Route*, Berkeley CA, 2011, Ch. 3; Christian Habicht, 'Eudoxus of Cyzicus and Ptolemaic Exploration of the Sea Route to India', in Kostas Buraselis *et al.* (eds), *The Ptolemies, the Sea and the Nile, Studies in Waterborne Power*, Cambridge, 2013, 197–206; S.M. Burstein, 'Elephants for Ptolemy II: Ptolemaic Policy in Libya in the Third Century BC', in Paul McKechnie and Philip Guillaume (ed.), *Ptolemy II Philadelphus and his World*, Leiden, 2008, 135–47; Holbl, *Ptolemaic Empire*, 55–8.
21. Pliny, *HN*, 6.180, 183–94; Athenaios 9.319b; L.A. Thompson, 'Eastern Africa and the Greco-Roman World', in L. Thompson and J. Ferguson (eds), *Africa in Classical Antiquity*, Ibadan, Nigeria, 1969, 26–61; M. Cary and E.H. Warmington, *The Ancient Explorers*, rev. edn, Harmondsworth, 1963, 208–10; Derek A. Welsby, *The Kingdom of Kush*, London, 1996.
22. P.M. Fraser, *Ptolemaic Alexandria*, Oxford, 1972, Vol. 1, 152 and 522; Francesco Prontera, 'Timosthenes and Eratosthenes: Sea Routes in Hellenistic Geography', in Kostas Buraselis *et al.* (eds), *The Ptolemies, the Sea and the Nile, Studies in Waterborne Power*, Cambridge, 2013, 207–17.

23. L. Basch, 'The Isis of Ptolemy II Philadelphos', *The Mariner's Mirror*, 71, 1985, 142–51; William M. Murray, 'The Trireme named *Isis*, the Graffito from Nymphaeum', *International Journal of Naval Archaeology*, 30, 2000, 250–6.

24. A well-known chap; see for a summary, Christian Jacob, 'Eratosthenes: Intellectual Athlete', in Jacob and de Polignac, *Alexandria*, 101–14; George Sarton, *Hellenistic Science and Culture in the Last Three Centuries BC*, Cambridge MA, 1959, 99–114.

25. But note that it was only after the overthrow of Demetrios that Epikouros and Zeno settled – or perhaps could settle – in Athens.

26. Polyainos 4.7.6; Plutarch, *Demetrios*, 8.4–9.1; Diodoros 20.45.2–3; Billows, *Antigonos the One-Eyed*, 148–50.

27. Claude Mosse, 'Demetrios of Phaleron: a Philosopher in Power?', in Christian Jacob and François de Polignac (eds), *Alexandria, third century BC*, trans. Colin Clement, Alexandria, 2000, 74–82; he describes Demetrios, rather curiously, as 'the last great man in the history of Athens'.

28. A succinct summary is in Sarton, *Hellenistic Science*, 28–32.

29. Ibid., 33.

30. Elizabeth D. Carney, *Arsinoe II of Egypt and Macedon, a Royal Life*, Oxford, 2013, 16–17.

31. Diogenes Laertius 5.4.

32. Ibid., 5.78–9.

33. John Tzetzes, *Proemium II*, quoted by Robert Barnes, 'Cloistered Bookworms in the Chicken-coop of the Muses: the Ancient Library of Alexandria', in Roy McLeod (ed.), *The Library of Alexandria, Centre of Learning in the Ancient World*, London, 2004, 61–78.

34. Diodoros 1.46.8 (or perhaps Hekataios); Holbl, *Ptolemaic Empire*, 26–7.

35. Plutarch, *Moralia, De Iside et Osiride*, 28.

36. *Letter of Aristeas*.

37. Pliny, *HN*, 30.4.

38. Syncellus, *Chronographia*, 1.516.3–10; Tzetzes, *Proemium*, II.

39. Menander is the protagonist in the *Milindapanha*, a Pali text discussion of Buddhist beliefs; his death and funeral is the subject of Plutarch, *Moralia* 821d–e. Karttunen, *India and the Hellenistic World*, 296; A.K. Narain, *The Indo-Greeks*, Oxford, 1957, 118–20, plate VI.

40. Alain Le Boulluec, 'Alien Wisdom', in Christian Jacob and François de Polignac (eds), *Alexandria, third century BC*, trans. Colin Clement, Alexandria, 2000, 56–72.

41. Jean Callot, 'Zenodoros: the Editor of Homer', in Christian Jacob and François de Polignac (eds), *Alexandria, third century BC*, trans. Colin Clement, Alexandria, 2000, 83–8.

42. He was probably not the first to work on this, for several men are credited with attending to certain groups of texts, but he appears to have been the first to draw up a comprehensive list in *Pinakes* ('Tables'), listing the library's resources in 120 volumes.

43. Christian Jacob, 'Callimachus, a poet in the Labyrinth', in Christian Jacob and François de Polignac (eds), *Alexandria, third century BC*, trans. Colin Clement, Alexandria, 2000, 89–100.

44. Apollonius Rhodios, *The Argonautica*, ed. Peter Green, Berkeley CA, 1997.

45. Athenaios 1.3b.

46. Galen, *Commentary on Hippocrates' Epidemics III*, 17D, 606k, cited by Roy McLeod, 'Introduction', in Roy McLeod (ed.), *The Library of Alexandria*, London, 2004, 4–5.

47. Athenaios 14.621a–b.

48. Diogenes Laertius 5.78–9.

49. Athenaios 154c, 182e–f, 184a; *Suda*, sv Euphorion.

50. For both of these see Gerald P. Verbrugghe and John M. Wickersham, *Berossos and Manetho, Native Traditions in Ancient Mesopotamia and Egypt*, Ann Arbor MI, 1996.

51. Plutarch, *Antony*, 58–9; Sarton, *Hellenistic Science*, 231–2.
52. But only through a papyrus fragment (P. Oxy. 1241), recording a schoolboy's exercise where he had to list the librarians; this is scarcely reliable as an historical source.
53. Andrew Erskine, *The Hellenistic Stoa, Political Thought and Action*, London, 1990, 78–84.
54. 'Audience': Diogenes Laertius 7.15; 'Servitude': Aelian, *Varia Historia*, 2.20.
55. Sarton, *Hellenistic Science*, 132–4.
56. Ibid., 69–80; Plutarch, *Marcellus*, 19.4–6.
57. Sarton, *Hellenistic Science*, 3547.
58. Olga Palagia, 'Aspects of the Diffusion of Ptolemaic Portraiture Overseas', in Kostas Buraselis *et al.* (eds), *The Ptolemies, the Sea and the Nile, Studies in Waterborne Power*, Cambridge, 2013, 143–59.
59. J.J. Pollitt, *Art in the Hellenistic Age*, Cambridge, 1986, 3 and 55.
60. Plutarch, *Aemilius Paullus*, 20.
61. Discussed by McLeod (ed.), *Library*, 1, 8–10.
62. For his life as Egyptian ruler see Holbl, *Ptolemaic Empire*, 194–204.
63. *P. Oxy.* 1241; Holbl, *Ptolemaic Empire*, 194–5.
64. We do not know, however, how much of this was his own work; we are all too familiar with 'ghost writers' in our own day; there seems no reason to believe that kings in the Hellenistic period did not resort to such tactics.
65. Strabo 2.98–102; Poseidonios, *FGrH*, 87 F 28.4–5.
66. Raoul McLaughlin, *The Roman Empire and Indian Ocean*, Barnsley, 2014, 77–9; Steven E. Sidebotham, *Roman Economic Policy in the Erythra Thalassa*, Leiden, 1986.

Chapter 12: Usurpations, Legitimacy, and Extinctions

1. O. Morkholm, *Antiochos IV of Syria*, Copenhagen, 1966.
2. The rebel Timarchos and his brother Herakleides were the centre of this loyalty set; Demetrios had his own group working for him while he was in exile.
3. Holbl, *Ptolemaic Empire*, 24–5.
4. Justin 17.2.9–10.
5. Pausanias 1.6.3; Holbl, *Ptolemaic Empire*, 222.
6. Diodoros 39.12; Plutarch, *Pompey*, 49.7; Porphyry, *FGrH*, 260 F2.14.
7. Diodoros 39.5–58; Strabo 17.1.11; Josephus, *BJ*, 1.175 and *AJ*, 14.99; Plutarch, *Antony*, 3.4–7.
8. Diodoros 52.35; Holbl, *Ptolemaic Empire*, 230–1.
9. *Bellum Alexandrinum*, 26–32; Dio Cassius 42.43.
10. Porphyry, *FGrH*, 260 F 2.16–17; Josephus, *AJ*, 15.89.
11. Josephus, *AJ*, 15.89.
12. Peter Green, *Alexander to Actium*, Berkeley CA, 1990, 425–6, for a succinct account of the affair.
13. Livy 42.16.9.
14. Livy 45.19.1–3; Polybios 30.1–3.
15. Robert Kallet-Marx, *Hegemony to Empire, the Development of the Roman Imperium in the East from 148 to 62 BC*, Berkeley CA, 1995, 99–109.
16. Ibid., 299–300.
17. So argued by D. Ogden, *Polygamy, Prostitutes, and Death*, London, 1999, 141–6; Alexander's sister, Laodike, was married to Mithradates IV of Pontos, which argues that her royal birth was accepted.
18. Diodoros 31.27a.

19. Polybios 31.12 and 19.
20. Polybios 33.15.
21. Diodoros 19.62.5–6, 79.4.
22. J. Seibert, 'Philokles' Sohn de Apollodorus, Konig von Sidonier', *Historia*, 19, 1790, 337–51.
23. J.D. Grainger, *Hellenistic Phoenicia*, Oxford, 1991, 33–4, 55–6.
24. S.I. Oost, *Roman Policy in Epirus and Acarnarnia in the Age of the Roman Conquest of Greece*, Dallas TX, 1954; K.-E. Petzold, 'Rom und Illyrien', *Historia*, 20, 1971, 199–223.
25. A. Laronde, *Cyrene et la Libye hellenistique*, Paris, 1987.
26. Polybios 10.27–31; Justin 41.5.7.
27. For the new conditions in Illyria and Macedon see J.A.O. Larsen, *Greek Federal States*, Oxford, 1968, 295–300.
28. For Andriskos' career see J.D. Grainger, *Rome, Parthia, India, the Violent Emergence of a New World Order 150–140 BC*, Barnsley, 2013, Ch. 3.
29. S.I. Oost, 'Amynander, Athamania, and Rome', *Classical Philology*, 52, 1957, 1–15; 'Athamania', Wikipedia, accessed 24 August 2016.
30. Paul Cartledge and Anthony Spawforth, *Hellenistic and Roman Sparta, a Tale of two Cities*, London, 1989, 75–8.
31. For a summary of Tigranes' career see Strabo 11.14.15, Justin 38.3.1; A.N. Sherwin-White, *Roman Foreign Policy in the East*, Norman OK, 1983, 173–5; for Pompeius in Syria see Sherwin-White, 206–18.

Chapter 13: Kings and Rome

1. Taras/Tarentum was taken in 272: Livy, *Per.*, 14; Dio Cassius/Zonaras 8.6 and 8.8.
2. Livy, *Per.*, 16; Polybios 15.6–8; J.F. Lazenby, *The First Punic War*, London, 1996, 43–52.
3. Dio Cassius/Zonaras 8.16.
4. Livy 24–6; Plutarch, *Marcellus*; Polybios 8.3.1–7.12, 37.1–13.
5. M.I. Finley, *Ancient Sicily to the Arab Conquest*, London, 1968, 116–27, for a survey of the effects of the Roman acquisition.
6. J.J. Pollitt, *Art in the Hellenistic Age*, Cambridge, 1986, 281.
7. Livy, *Per.*, 14; Dionysios of Halikarnassos 20.14; Cassius Dio/Zonaras 8.6; Justin 18.2.9; see the extended discussion by Anssi Lampela, *Rome and the Ptolemies of Egypt, the Development of their Political Relations 273–80 BC*, Helsinki, 1998.
8. R.M. Errington, *A History of Macedon*, Berkeley CA, 1990, for a summary account.
9. J.D. Grainger, *The Roman War of Antiochos the Great*, Leiden 2002.
10. Appian, *Syrian Wars*, 39.
11. Livy 42.1.6–12.
12. Appian, *Syrian Wars*, 45; Justin 34.3.6–8.
13. O. Morkholm, *Antiochos IV of Syria*, Copenhagen, 1966.
14. *SEG*, XXXII, 137; S.V. Tracy, 'Greek Inscriptions from the Athenian Agora: third to first century BC', *Hesperia*, 51, 1982, 3.
15. Polybios 31.12 and 19.
16. He made several charges, notably in accusing Perseus of plotting to have him assassinated when he was caught in a landslide at Delphi: Livy 42.40.3–9; Appian, *Macedonian Wars*, 11.4–7; Polybios 22.18.2–5.
17. Livy 42.6.3.
18. Livy 45.35.1, 40.6–7, 42.4; Plutarch, *Aemilius Paullus*, 37.
19. D. Ogden, *Polygamy, Prostitutes, and Death*, London, 1999, 146–7.

20. Livy 45.19.1–20.3.
21. Livy, *Per.*, 46; Polybios 30.19.3–9.
22. Livy 45.44.5–46.2.1.
23. Polybios 30.18.1–7.
24. Diodoros 31.18.1–2; Valerius Maximus 5.1.1–2; E.S. Gruen, *The Hellenistic World and the Coming of Rome*, Berkeley CA, 1984, 694–5.
25. Polybios 31.10.1–3.
26. Polybios 33.11.1–7.
27. Polybios 30.27–31.3, *passim*; Diodoros 31.17.28 and 33.28 b; Justin 38.8.8; Strabo 14.5.2; Plutarch, *Moralia*, 200e–f and 777a; Athenaios 6.273 a.
28. A.E. Astin, *Scipio Aemilianus*, Oxford, 1967, 138–9; the date of the embassy is usually put at *c.*140, but is better dated to *c.*144; H.B. Mattingly, 'Scipio Aemilianus' Eastern Embassy', *Classical Review*, 36, 1986, 491–5; Lampela, *Rome and the Ptolemies*, 200.
29. Polybios 31.2.9–14, 11.1–3, 33.1–4; Diodoros 31.29; Appian, *Syrian Wars*, 46–7.
30. Polybios 29.27.1–13; Diodoros 31.2; Livy 45.12; Appian, *Syrian Wars*, 66; Justin 34.3.
31. Interpretations vary: Gruen, *Hellenistic World*, 657–60; Lampela, *Rome and the Ptolemies*, 124–38; J.D. Grainger, *The Syrian Wars*, Leiden, 2010, 305–8; W. Gwyn Morgan, 'The Perils of Schematism: Polybius, Antiochos Epiphanes and the "Day of Eleusis"', *Historia*, 39, 1990, 37–76; Holbl, *Ptolemaic Empire*, 145–8.
32. Austin 289; Polybios 33.11.2; Gruen, *Hellenistic World*, 702–5.
33. Livy, *Per.*, 58–9; Plutarch, *Tiberius Gracchus*, 13.1 and 14.1; Appian, *Civil Wars*, *1.14*; A.N. Sherwin-White, *Roman Foreign Policy in the East*, Norman OK, 1983, 80–4; Robert Kallet-Marx, *Hegemony to Empire, the Development of the Roman Imperium in the East from 148 to 62 BC*, Berkeley CA, 1995, 99.
34. Justin 39.5.2; Livy, *Per.*, 70.
35. Taken up in 74: Kallet-Marx, *Hegemony to Empire*, 364–7.
36. Diodoros 36.3.1.
37. Appian, *Mithridatic Wars*, 7.71; Appian, *Civil Wars*, 1.111; Livy, *Per.*, 93.
38. Pliny, *NH*, 5.81–2; discussed by A.H.M. Jones, *Cities of the Eastern Roman Provinces*, 2nd edn, Oxford, 1971, 260–3.
39. Plutarch, *Sulla*, 5.8–10; Livy, *Per.*, 70; N.C. Debevoise, *The Political History of Parthia*, Chicago IL, 1938, 47; E. Badian, 'Sulla's Cilician Command', in *Studies in Greek and Roman History*, Oxford, 1964, 157–78.

Bibliography

Abbreviations

Austin – M.M. Austin, *The Hellenistic World from Alexander to the Roman Conquest*, 2nd edn, Cambridge, 2006.

CAH – Cambridge Ancient History.

FGrH – Die Fragmente der griechischen Historiker, ed. F. Jacoby, Berlin, 1923–.

Holbl, *Ptolemaic Empire* – G. Holbl, *A History of the Ptolemaic Empire*, London, 2001.

I. Crete – Inscriptiones Creticae, ed. M. Guarducci, Rome, 1935–50.

I. Estremo Oriente – Iscrizioni dello Estremo Oriente greco, ed. P. Canali di rossi, Bonn, 2004.

I. Pergamon – Inschriften von Pergamon.

Josephus, *AJ* – Josephus, *Jewish Antiquities*.

OGIS – *Orientis Graeci Inscriptiones Selectae*, ed. W. Dittenberger, Leipzig, 1903–5.

P. Zenon – Catalogue general des Antiquites egyptiennes du Musee du Caire: Zenon Papyri, ed. C.C. Edgar, Cairo, 1925–40

Sachs and Hunger, *Astronomical Diaries* – A.J. Sachs and H. Hunger, *Astronomical Diaries and Related Texts from Babylonia*, 3 vols, Vienna, 1988–2005.

SEG – Supplementum Epigraphicum Graecum.

Welles, *Royal Correspondence* – R.C. Welles, *The Royal Correspondence of the Hellenistic Period*, New Haven RI, 1934.

Books and Articles

Allen, Charles, *Ashoka, The Search for India's Lost Emperor*, London, 2012.

Allen, R.E., *The Attalid Kingdom, a Constitutional History*, Oxford, 1983.

Andronikos, M., 'Verghina, the Prehistoric Necropolis and the Hellenistic Palace', *Mediterranean Archaeology*, 13, 1964.

Andronikos, M., *Verghina*, Athens, 1984.

Aperghis, G.G., *The Seleukid Royal Economy*, Cambridge, 2004.

Assar, G.E., 'Genealogies and kings of the early Parthian rulers, I and II', *Parthica*, 6 and 7, 2006 and 2007.

Astin, A.E., *Scipio Aemilianus*, Oxford, 1967.

Badian, E., 'Sulla's Cilician Command', *Studies in Greek and Roman History*, Oxford, 1964, 157–78.

Bagnall, R.S., *The Administration of the Ptolemaic Empire outside Egypt*, Leiden, 1976.

Bar-Kochva, B., *The Seleucid Army, Organisation and Tactics in the Great Campaigns*, Cambridge, 1976.

Barnes, Robert, 'Cloistered Bookworms in the Chicken-coop of the Muses: the Ancient Library of Alexandria', in Roy McLeod (ed.), *The Library of Alexandria, Centre of Learning in the Ancient World*, London, 2004, 61–78.

Basch, L., 'The Isis of Ptolemy II Philadelphos', *The Mariner's Mirror*, 71, 1985, 142–51.

Baynham, Elizabeth, 'Why didn't Alexander marry a nice Macedonian girl before leaving home? Observations on factional politics at Alexander's court, 336–334 BC', in T.W. Hillard and E.A. Judge (eds), *Ancient History in a Modern University*, 2 vols, Macquarie University NSW, 1998, Vol. 1, 148–55.

Bennett, C.J., 'Royal genealogies: Ptolemaic dynasty', available at http/www/geocities.com/christopherjbennett/Ptolemies/Ptolemies.htm (accessed 25 November 2016).

Bevan, E.R., *The House of Seleucus*, 2 vols, London, 1902.

Billows, Richard A., *Antigonos the One-Eyed and the Creation of the Hellenistic State*, Berkeley CA, 1992.

Billows, Richard A., *Kings and Colonists, Aspects of Macedonian Imperialism*, Leiden, 1994.

Buraselis, Kostas, Mary Stephanou and Dorothy J. Thompson (eds), *The Ptolemies, the Sea and the Nile, Studies in Waterborne Power*, Cambridge, 2013, 39–65.

Burstein, S.M., 'Arsinoe II: a Revisionist View', in W.L. Adams and E.N. Borza (eds), *Philip II, Alexander the Great, and the Macedonian Heritage*, Washington DC, 1982, 197–212.

Burstein, S.M., 'Elephants for Ptolemy II: Ptolemaic Policy in Libya in the Third Century BC', in Paul McKechnie and Philip Guillaume (eds), *Ptolemy II Philadelphus and his World*, Leiden, 2008, 135–47.

Callot, Jean, 'Zenodoros: the Editor of Homer', in Christian Jacob and François de Polignac (eds), *Alexandria, third century BC*, trans. Colin Clement, Alexandria, 2000, 83–8.

Carney, Elizabeth D., *Women and Monarchy in Macedon*, Norman OK, 2000.

Carney, Elizabeth D., 'Being Royal and Female in early Macedonian History', in Andrew Erskine and Lloyd Llewellyn-Jones (eds), *Creating a Hellenistic World*, Swansea, 2011, 195–220.

Carney, Elizabeth D., *Arsinoe II of Egypt and Macedon, a Royal Life*, Oxford, 2013.

Cartledge, Paul, and Anthony Spawforth, *Hellenistic and Roman Sparta, a Tale of two Cities*, London, 1989, 75–8.

Cary, M., *A History of the Greek World from 323 to 146 BC*, London, 1951.

Cary, M., and E.H. Warmington, *The Ancient Explorers*, rev. edn, Harmondsworth, 1963.

Casson, S., *Ships and Seamanship in the Ancient World*, Baltimore MD, 1995.

Chamoux, François, 'Le roi Magas', *Revue Historique*, 1956, 18–34.

Chaniotis, Angelos, 'The Divinity of Hellenistic Kings', in Andrew Erskine (ed.), *A Companion to the Hellenistic World*, Oxford, 2003, 431–46.

Chaniotis, Angelos, *War in the Hellenistic World*, London, 2005.

Chauveau, M., *L'Egypte au temps de Cleopatre*, Paris, 1997.

Clarysse, Willy, 'The Ptolemies visiting the Egyptian Chora', in Leon Mooren (ed.), *Politics, Administration, and Society in the Hellenistic and Roman Worlds*, Studia Hellenistica, 36, 2000, 29–54

Clayman, Dee L., *Berenice II and the Golden Age of Ptolemaic Egypt*, Oxford 2014.

Cohen, Getzel M., *The Hellenistic Settlements in Europe, the islands, and Asia Minor*, Berkeley CA, 1995.

Cohen, Getzel M., *The Hellenistic Settlements in Syria, the Red Sea Basin, and North Africa*, Berkeley CA, 2006,

Cohen, Getzel M., *The Hellenistic Settlements in the East from Armenia and Mesopotamia to Bactria and India*, Berkeley, CA, 2013.

Crawford, Dorothy J., *Kerkeosiris, an Egyptian Village of the Ptolemaic Period*, Cambridge, 1971.

Debevoise, N.C., *A Political History of Parthia*, Chicago IL, 1938.

Dimitrov, D.P., and M. Cirikova, *The Thracian City of Seuthopolis*, BAR S38, Oxford, 1978.

Dodson, Aidan, and Diane Hylton, *The Complete Royal Families of Ancient Egypt*, London, 2004.

Dow, S. and C.F. Edson Jr, 'Chriseis', *Harvard Studies in Classical Philosophy*, 28, 1937, 127–35.

Downey, G., *A History of Antioch in Syria*, Princeton NJ, 1961.

Eckstein, Arthur M., *Mediterranean Anarchy, Interstate War, and the Rise of Rome*, Berkeley CA, 2006.

Ellis, J.R., *Philip II and Macedonian Imperialism*, London 1976.

Errington, R.M., 'The Alleged Syro-Macedonian Pact and the Origin of the Second Macedonian War', *Athenaeum*, 49, 1971, 336–54.

Errington, R.M., *A History of Macedon*, Berkeley CA, 1990.

Erskine, Andrew, *The Hellenistic Stoa, Political Thought and Action*, London, 1990.

Erskine, Andrew, 'Life after Death: Alexandria and the body of Alexander', *Greece and Rome*, 49, 2002, 163–79.

Evans, Richard J., *Syracuse in Antiquity, History and Topography*, Pretoria, 2009.

Ferguson, W.S., *Hellenistic Athens*, London, 1911.

Finley, M.I., *Ancient Sicily to the Arab Conquest*, London, 1968.

Fraser, P.M., *Ptolemaic Alexandria*, Oxford, 1972.

Fraser, P.M., *Cities of Alexander the Great*, Oxford, 1996.

Funke, Suzanne, 'Apeiros 317–272 BC: the Struggle of the Diadochi and the Political Structure of the Federation', in Leon Mooren (ed.), *Politics, Administration, and Society in the Hellenistic and Roman Worlds*, Studia Hellenistica, 36, 2000, 107–22.

Gardin, J.-C., and P. Gentelle, 'Irrigation et peuplement dans la plaine d'Ai Khanoum de leepoque Achemenide a l'epoque musulman', *Bulletin de l'Ecole francais de l'Extreme Orient*, 61, 1976, 56–99.

Gauthier, Ph., *Nouvelles Inscriptions de Sardes*, Vol. II, Paris 1998.

Goddio, Franck, and Aurelia Masson-Berghoff (eds), *Sunken Cities, Egypt's Lost Worlds*, London, 2016.

Goossens, G., *Hierapolis de Syrie*, Louvain, 1943.

Grainger, J.D., *The Cities of Seleukid Syria*, Oxford, 1990.

Grainger, J.D., *Seleukos Nikator*, London, 1990.

Grainger, J.D., *Hellenistic Phoenicia*, Oxford, 1991.

Grainger, J.D., 'Antiochos III in Thrace', *Historia*, 45, 1996, 329–43.

Grainger, J.D., *A Seleukid Prosopography and Gazetteer*, Leiden, 1996.

Grainger, J.D., *The Wars of the Maccabees*, Barnsley, 2000.

Grainger, J.D., *The Roman War of Antiochos the Great*, Leiden, 2002.

Grainger, J.D., *The Syrian Wars*, Leiden, 2010.

Grainger, J.D., *Hellenistic and Roman Naval Wars 336–31 BC*, Barnsley, 2011.

Grainger, J.D., *The Wars of the Maccabees*, Barnsley, 2012.

Grainger, J.D., *Rome, Parthia, India, the Violent Emergence of a New World Order 150–140 BC*, Barnsley, 2013.

Grainger, J.D., *The Rise of the Seleukid Empire, 323–223 BC*, Barnsley, 2014.

Grainger, J.D., *The Seleukid Empire of Antiochos III*, Barnsley, 2014.

Grainger, J.D., *Great Power Diplomacy in the Hellenistic World*, London, 2016.

Grainger, J.D., *Syria, An Outline History*, Barnsley, 2016.

Green, Peter, *Alexander of Macedon*, London, 1970.

Green, Peter, *Alexander to Actium*, London, 1990.

Gruen, E.S., 'The Last Years of Philip V', *Greek, Roman, and Byzantine Studies*, 16, 1974, 221–46.

Gruen, E.S., *The Hellenistic World and the Coming of Rome*, Berkeley CA, 1984.

Habicht, Christian, *Athens from Alexander to Antony*, trans. Deborah Lucas Schneider, Cambridge MA, 1997.

Habicht, Christian, 'Eudoxus of Cyzicus and Ptolemaic Exploration of the Sea Route to India', in Kostas Buraselis *et al.* (eds), *The Ptolemies, the Sea and the Nile, Studies in Waterborne Power*, Cambridge, 2013, 197–206.

Hammond, N.G.L., *The Macedonian State, the Origins, Institutions and History*, Oxford, 1989.

Harmatta, J., 'Parthia and Elymais in the second century BC', *Acta Antiqua Academiae Scientiarum Hungaricae*, 29, 1981, 189–217.

Hauben, Hans, 'Callicrates of Samos and Patroclus of Macedon, champions of Ptolemaic Thalassocracy', in Kostas Buraselis *et al.* (eds), *The Ptolemies, the Sea and the Nile, Studies in Waterborne Power*, Cambridge, 2013, 39–65.

Helliesen, J.M., 'Andriscus and the Revolt of the Macedonians, 149–148 BC', *Ancient Macedon*, IV, Thessalonica, 1986.

Hengel, M., *Judaism and Hellenism*, London, 1974.

Hengel, M., *Jews, Greeks, and Barbarians*, London, 1980

Hoddinott, R.F., *The Thracians*, London, 1981

Holt, Frank L., *Thundering Zeus, The Making of Hellenistic Bactria*, Berkeley CA, 1999.

Holt, Frank L., *Lost World of the Golden King*, Berkeley CA, 2012.

Holt, Frank L., *The Treasure of Alexander the Great*, Oxford, 2016.

Hornblower, S., *Mausollus*, Oxford, 1982.

Houghton, Arthur, 'Timarchos as king in Babylonia', *Revue Numismatique*, 21, 1976, 212–17.

Houghton, Arthur, and Catherine Corber, *Seleukid Coins: a Comprehensive Catalogue*, 2 vols, Lancaster PA, 2002.

Jacob, Christian, 'Callimachus, a poet in the Labyrinth', in Christian Jacob and François de Polignac (eds), *Alexandria, third century BC*, trans. Colin Clement, Alexandria, 2000, 89–100.

Jacob, Christian, 'Eratosthenes: Intellectual Athlete', in Christian Jacob and Francois de Polingac, *Alexandria, third century BC*, trans. Colin Clement, Alexandria, 2000, 101–14.

Jacob, Christian, and François de Polignac (eds), *Alexandria, third century BC*, trans. Colin Clement, Alexandria, 2000.

Jones, A.H.M., *Cities of the Eastern Roman Provinces*, 2nd edn, Oxford, 1971.

Jones, C.P. and C. Habicht, 'A Hellenistic Inscription from Arsinoe in Cilicia', *Phoenix*, 63, 1989, 317–46.

Kallet-Marx, Robert, *Hegemony to Empire, the Development of the Roman Imperium in the East from 148 to 62 BC*, Berkeley CA, 1995.

Karttunen, Klaus, *India and the Hellenistic World*, Helsinki, 1997.

Kawerau, G., and Th. Wiegand, *Die Palaste von Hochburg (Altertumer von Pergamon V.1)*, Berlin, 1930.

Kenrick, Philip, *Libya Archaeological Guides: Cyrenaica*, London, 2013.

Koldewey, R., *Die Konigsburgen von Babylon, I Die Sudburg*, Leipzig, 1931.

Kosmin, P.J., *The Land of the Elephant Kings*, Cambridge MA, 2014.

Kuhrt, Amelie, 'The Seleukid Kings and Babylonia: New Perspectives on the Seleukid Realm in the East', in Per Bilde, T. Engberg-Pedersen, I. Hannestad and J. Zahke (eds), *Aspects of Hellenistic Kingship*, Aarhus, 1996, 41–54.

Lampela, Anssi, *Rome and the Ptolemies of Egypt, the Development of their Political Relations 273–80 BC*, Helsinki, 1998.

Laronde, A., *Cyrene et la Libye hellenistique*, Paris, 1987.

Larsen, J.A.O., *Greek Federal States*, Oxford, 1968.

Lazenby, J.F., *The First Punic War*, London, 1996.

Le Boulluec, Alain, 'Alien Wisdom', in Christian Jacob and François de Polignac (eds), *Alexandria, third century BC*, trans. Colin Clement, Alexandria, 2000, 56–72.

Le Rider, G., 'L'Enfant-roi Antiochos et la reine Laodike", *Bulletin de Correspondence Hellenique*, 110, 1986, 409–17.

Lund, Helen S., *Lysimachos, a Study in Hellenistic Kingship*, London, 1992.

Ma, John, *Antiochos III and the Cities of Western Asia Minor*, Oxford, 1999.

McCurdy, Grace, *Hellenistic Queens*, Baltimore MD, 1932.

McGing, B.C., *The Foreign Policy of Mithradates VI Eupator, King of Pontus*, Leiden, 1986.

McGing, B.C., 'Revolt Egyptian style: Internal Opposition to Ptolemaic Rule', *AfP*, 43, 1997, 273–314.

McLaughlin, Raoul, *The Roman Empire and Indian Ocean*, Barnsley, 2014.

McLeod, Roy, 'Introduction', in Roy McLeod (ed.), *The Library of Alexandria*, London, 2004, 4–5.

Mairs, Rachel, *The Hellenistic Far East*, Berkeley CA, 2014.

Manning, J.G., *The Last Pharaohs, Egypt the Ptolemies, 305–30 BC*, Princeton NJ, 2010.

Mattingly, H.B., 'Scipio Aemilianus' Eastern Embassy', *Classical Review*, 36, 1986, 491–5.

Milojcic, V., and D. Theochares, *Demetrias I*, Bonn, 1976.

Mitchell, Stephen, *Anatolia, Land, Men, and Gods in Asia Minor*, Vol. I, *The Celts and the Impact of Roman Rule*, Oxford, 1993.

Mooren, Leon, *The Aulic Titulature in Ptolemaic Egypt: Introduction and Prosopography*, Brussels, 1975.

Mooren, Leon, *La hierarchie du cour Ptolemaique*, Studia Hellenistica 23, Louvain, 1977.

Morgan, W. Gwyn, 'The Perils of Schematism: Polybius, Antiochos Epiphanes and the "Day of Eleusis"', *Historia*, 39, 1990, 37–76.

Morkholm, O., *Studies in the Coinage of Antiochos IV of Syria*, Copenhagen, 1963.

Morkholm, O., *Antiochos IV of Syria*, Copenhagen 1966.

Mosse, Claude, 'Demetrios of Phaleron, a philosopher in power?', in Christian Jacob and François de Polignac (eds), *Alexandria, Third Century BC*, trans. Colin Clement, Alexandria, 2000, 74–82.

Murray, William M., 'The Trireme named *Isis*, the Graffito from Nymphaeum', *International Journal of Naval Archaeology*, 30, 2000, 250–6.

Murray, William M., *The Age of Titans, the Rise and Fall of the Great Hellenistic Navies*, Oxford, 2012.

Myers, E.A., *The Ituraeans and the Roman Near East, Reassessing the Sources*, Cambridge, 2010.

Narain, A.K., *The Indo-Greeks*, Oxford, 1957.

Newell, E.T., *The Coinage of the Eastern Seleucid Mints*, New York, 1938.

Nielsen, Inge, *Hellenistic Palaces, Tradition and Renewal*, Aarhus, 1999.

Ogden, D., *Polygamy, Prostitutes, and Death*, London, 1999.

Olshausen, E., *Prosopographie der Hellenistischen Konigsgesandten I, von Triparadisos bis Pydna*, Leuven, 1978.

Oost, S.I., *Roman Policy in Epirus and Acarnarnia in the Age of the Roman Conquest of Greece*, Dallas TX, 1954.

Oost, S.I., 'Amynander, Athamania, and Rome', *Classical Philology*, 52, 1957, 1–15.

Oppen de Reiter, B.F. von, 'Argaios, an Illegitimate son of Alexander the Great?', *ZPE*, 287, 2013, 206–10.

Palagia, Olga, 'Aspects of the Diffusion of Ptolemaic Portraiture Overseas', in Kostas Buraselis *et al.* (eds), *The Ptolemies, the Sea and the Nile, Studies in Waterborne Power*, Cambridge 2013, 143–59.

Pearson, Lionel, *The Lost Histories of Alexander the Great*, New York, 1960.

Pesce, G., *Il 'Palazzo delle Colonne' a Tolemaide de Cirenaica*, Rome, 1950.

Petzold, K.-E., 'Rom und Illyrien', *Historia*, 20, 1971, 199–223.

Pfeiffer, Stephan, 'The God Serapis, his Cult, and the Beginnings of the Ruler Cult in Ptolemaic Egypt', in Paul McKechnie and Philip Guillaume (eds), *Ptolemy II Philadelphus and His World*, Leiden, 2008, 387–406.

Pollitt, J.J., *Art in the Hellenistic Age*, Cambridge, 1986.

Preaux, Claude, *La Monde Hellenistique*, 2 vols, Paris, 1936.

Prontera, Francesco, 'Timosthenes and Eratosthenes: Sea Routes in Hellenistic Geography', in Kostas Buraselis *et al.* (eds), *The Ptolemies, the Sea and the Nile, Studies in Waterborne Power*, Cambridge, 2013, 207–17.

Reger, Gary, *Regionalism and Change in the Economy of Independent Delos*, Berkeley CA, 1994.

Rice, E.E., *The Grand Procession of Ptolemy Philadelphus*, Oxford, 1983.

Robert, L., 'Demodamas de Milet et la reine Apame', *Bulletin de Correspondence Hellenique*, 108, 1954, 467–72.

Roztovtzeff, M.I., *Social and Economic History of the Hellenistic World*, 3 vols, Oxford, 1941.

Sarton, George, *Hellenistic Science and Culture in the Last Three Centuries BC*, Cambridge MA, 1959.

Sauvaget, J., *Alep*, Paris, 1941.

Savalli-Lestrange, I., *Les philoi royaux dans l'Asie Hellenistique*, Geneva, 1998.

Schurer, E., *The History of the Jewish People in the Age of Jesus Christ*, 3 vols, rev. and ed. by G. Vermes, Fergus Millar and Matthew Black, Edinburgh, 1973–87.

Seibert, J., 'Philokles' Sohn de Apollodorus, Konig von Sidonier', *Historia*, 19, 1970, 337–51.

Seyrig, H., 'Le moneyage d'Hierapolis de Syrie a l'epoque d'Alexandre le Grand', *Revue Numismatique*, 11, 1971, 3–11.

Sherwin-White, A.N., *Roman Foreign Policy in the East*, Norman OK, 1983.

Sherwin-White, Susan M., and Amelie Kuhrt, *From Samarkhand to Sardis, a New Approach to the Seleucid Empire*, London, 1993.

Sidebotham, Steven E., *Roman Economic Policy in the Erythra Thalassa*, Leiden, 1986.

Sidebotham, Steven E., *Berenike and the Ancient Maritime Spice Route*, Berkeley CA, 2011.

Spyridakis, S., *Ptolemaic Itanos and Hellenistic Crete*, Berkeley CA, 1970.

Stefanou, Mary, 'Waterborne Recruits: the Military Settlers of Ptolemaic Egypt', in Kostas Buraselis *et al.* (eds), *The Ptolemies, the Sea and the Nile, Studies in Waterborne Power*, Cambridge, 2013, 108–31.

Strootman, Rolf, *Courts and Elites in the Hellenistic Empires*, Edinburgh, 2014.

Tarn, W.W., *Antigonos Gonatas*, Oxford, 1913.

Tarn, W.W., 'Philip V and Phthia', *Classical Quarterly*, 18, 1924, 17–30.

Tarn, W.W., *Hellenistic Naval and Military Developments*, Cambridge, 1930 (repr. 1975).

Tarn, W.W., *The Greeks in Baktria and India*, 2nd edn, Cambridge, 1951.

Tarn, W.W., and G.T. Griffith, *Hellenistic Civilisation*, 3rd edn, Cambridge, 1952.

Tcherikover, V., *Hellenistic Civilisation and the Jews*, Philadelphia PA, 1959.

Thompson, Dorothy J., 'Economic Reform in the mid-reign of Ptolemy Philadelphus', in Paul McKechnie and Philip Guillaume (eds), *Ptolemy II Philadelphus and his World*, Leiden, 2008, 27–38.

Thompson, Dorothy J., *Memphis under the Ptolemies*, 2nd edn, Princeton NJ, 2012.

Thompson, Dorothy J., 'Hellenistic Royal Barges', in Kostas Buraselis *et al.* (eds), *The Ptolemies, the Sea and the Nile, Studies in Waterborne Power*, Cambridge, 2013, 185–96.

Thompson, L.A., 'Eastern Africa and the Greco-Roman World', in L. Thompson and J. Ferguson (eds), *Africa in Classical Antiquity*, Ibadan, Nigeria, 1969, 26–61.

Tracy, S.V., 'Greek Inscriptions from the Athenian Agora: third to first century BC', *Hesperia* 51, 1982.

Tillyard, H.J.W., *Agathocles*, Cambridge, 1908.

van der Spek, R., 'The Babylonian City', in Amelie Kuhrt and Susan M. Sherwin-White, *Hellenism in the East*, London, 1987, 57–74.

van Effentere, H., *Crete et le Monde grec*, Paris, 1948.

Verbrugghe, Gerald P. and John M. Wickersham, *Berossos and Manetho, Native Traditions in Ancient Mesopotamia and Egypt*, Ann Arbor MI, 1996.

Viesse, A.E., *Les 'revoltes Egyptiennes', Recherches sur les Troubles interieures en Egypt du Regne de Ptolemee III a la conquete romain*, Studia Hellenistica, 41, Louvain, 2004.

Waddell, W.G. (ed. and trans.), *Manetho*, London, 1940.

Walbank, F.W., *Philip V of Macedon*, Cambridge, 1940.

Welsby, Derek A., *The Kingdom of Kush*, London, 1996.

Whitehorne, John, *Cleopatras*, London, 1994.

Wiesehofer, Josef, 'Frataraka rule in Early Seleucid Persis; a Reappraisal', in Andrew Erskine and Lloyd Llewellyn-Jones (eds), *Creating a Hellenistic World*, Swansea, 2011, 107–22.

Will, E., 'Les premiers annees du regne d'Antiochos III', *Revue des Etudes Grecques*, 75, 1976, 72–129.

Will, E., *Histoire Politique du Monde Hellenistique*, 2 vols, Nancy, 1978–82.

Wroth, W., *Catalogue of the Greek Coins of Galatia, Cappadocia and Syria*, London, 1878.

Index